Bad Elements

Bad Elements

Chinese Rebels from
Los Angeles to Beijing

Ian Buruma

RANDOM HOUSE

NEW YORK

Library of Congress Cataloging-in-Publication Data
Buruma, Ian.
Bad elements: Chinese rebels from Los Angeles to Beijing / Ian Buruma.—1st ed.
p. cm.
ISBN 0-679-45768-2 (alk.)
1. China—Politics and government—1976–   2. Dissenters—China.   3. Human rights—China.
I. Title.
DS779.26 .B864   2001   951.05'7—dc21   2001019365

Random House website address: www.atrandom.com
Printed in the United States of America on acid-free paper
2 4 6 8 9 7 5 3
First Edition

Book design by J. K. Lambert

For R. V. Schipper

. . . "Is there one single maxim that could ruin a country?"

Confucius replied: "Mere words could not achieve this. There is a saying, however: 'The only pleasure of being a prince is never having to suffer contradiction.' If you are right and no one contradicts you, that's fine; but if you are wrong and no one contradicts you—is this not a case of 'one single maxim that could ruin a country'?"

The Analects of Confucius
Translation by Simon Leys

Contents

PART III: THE MOTHERLAND

Introduction:
Chinese Whispers

Strange things happen when Chinese dynasties near their end. Dams break, earthquakes hit, clouds appear in the shape of weird beasts, rain falls in odd colors, and insects infest the countryside. These are the ill omens of moral turpitude and political collapse. While greed and cynicism poison the society from within, barbarians stir restlessly at the gates. Corrupt officials, whose authority can no longer rely on the assumption of superior virtue, exercise their power with anxious and arbitrary brutality. When people, even those who live far from the centers of power, begin to sense that the Mandate of Heaven is slipping away from their corrupted rulers, rebellious spirits press their claims as the saviors of China, with promises of moral restoration and national unity. Millenarian cults and secret societies proliferate and sometimes explode in massive violence.

At the end of the Han dynasty, in the second century, a faith-healing sect named the Yellow Turbans caused havoc. Their leader, a Taoist priest, promised to lead his followers to "the Way of Great Peace" (*Taiping Dao*), and although he was killed in 184 A.D., the rebellion of the Yellow Turbans took more than twenty years to put down.

The end of the Mongol Yuan dynasty, in the fourteenth century, came after a rash of local rebellions. One of them was staged by a secret society called the White Lotus, whose folk-Buddhist leaders issued dark warnings of an imminent apocalypse. The apocalyptic theme was later picked up by another peasant messiah, a martial arts master and herbal healer named Wang Lun, who rebelled against the Manchu rulers of the Qing dynasty at the end of the eighteenth century. In 1900, a martial arts sect known in the West as the Boxers rose, convinced that a sacred spirit made them impervious to foreign bullets. They were wrong and died in large numbers.

The Qing was finally brought down in 1911, about fifty years after a frustrated scholar called Hong Xiuquan unleashed his Taiping army to establish God's Heavenly Kingdom in China. He claimed to be a brother of Jesus Christ. He denounced the Manchus as agents of Satan. His crusade left 20 million dead.

Mao Zedong fitted quite neatly in this long line of peasant messiahs. Like his predecessors, he led a rural revolt to expel the barbarians, punish evildoers, and unite the empire. He abhorred superstition, but his version of "scientific socialism" would reach the same degree of religious frenzy as Hong's Heavenly Kingdom.

Many people in China felt that the Mandate of Heaven had slipped from the Communist Party in the summer of 1989. Once the terrified rulers had sent in tanks to crush unarmed citizens, they had lost their claim to superior virtue. Marxism-Leninism and Mao Zedong Thought, which had replaced Confucianism as the official dogma and system of ethics, could no longer captivate minds, even in the Party itself. The rigid puritanism of Mao's age had made way for the heady amorality and wild corruption of China's new capitalism. And at the end of the millennium, a new millenarian cult had arrived, led by yet another faith-healing messiah. Most followers of Falun Gong were harmless elderly folk trying to preserve their good health through breathing exercises. Yet the government behaved as if another revolution were at hand.

Strange flowers bloom in the People's Republic of China. They also bloom in Taiwan, the United States, Hong Kong, and Singapore. But in a dictatorial one-party state, religion fills the gaps left by the absence of secular politics. That is why meditators, tree huggers, heavy breathers, or

Evangelical Christians can suddenly find themselves blown up into dangerous counterrevolutionaries. In China, every believer in an unorthodox faith is a potential dissident, whether he knows it or not. When the right to rule is justified by dogma, a moral code, a controlling worldview, and the fatherly wisdom of leaders blessed with superhuman virtue, any alternative dogma existing outside the control of the great and virtuous leaders will be seen as a mortal threat.

I believe that Communist Party rule will end in China; sooner or later all dynasties do. But when or how, I cannot say. Will one authoritarian dynasty be replaced, once again, by another, in the name of national unity and superior virtue? Or will the Chinese finally be able to govern themselves in a freer and more open society? The example of Taiwan, whose citizens can now speak freely and elect their own government, shows that it is possible. The example of Singapore, which combines relative economic liberalism with political authoritarianism, points in another, equally plausible, direction.

It was with these questions in mind that I traveled through the Chinese-speaking world between 1996 and 2001—from the diaspora of exiles in the West, to Singapore, Taiwan, Hong Kong, and the People's Republic of China. During these years, I witnessed the "handover" of Hong Kong, the first free presidential election in Taiwan, and the beginning of the Falun Gong demonstrations in China. I saw a great deal of vitality—even optimism—on the way, especially in the economic sphere, in China no less than in Singapore or Hong Kong. But there were constant rumblings, too, a kind of background noise of angry people thrown out of work in newly privatized factories, of farmers being squeezed for money by corrupt officials, of religious believers being punished for exercising their faith in public. There was an unmistakable stink of political, social, and moral decay in the People's Republic, the smell of a dynasty at the end of its tether.

———

How to describe the problem of China, with its perpetual seesaws between enforced unity, order, and moral orthodoxy on the one hand and violent religious and political mutinies on the other? It had haunted me since that summer of 1989, when so many Europeans regained their liberties while Chinese failed in their attempt to gain theirs. Perhaps I should start with three stories about walls, metaphorical and real.

In the beginning there were many walls—often little more than small fortified humps in the northern plains—which separated settled Chinese states from the barbarian nomads. But legend has it that in the third century B.C., slaves of the wicked Qin emperor pulled the various walls together to form one Great Wall. The Qin emperor was the first monarch to turn several states into one. China really began with him. The Western term for China is named after his state. We don't actually know much about the Qin emperor. But he has gone down in history as the first great dictator, the pinnacle of a new cosmic order, who killed his critics and made bonfires of their books. Mao Zedong, a keen amateur historian, admired him greatly.

The Great Wall was never very effective in keeping out belligerent barbarians, and there are few remaining traces of the Qin. Much of the wall was built only in the sixteenth century, and even those parts are crumbling. It is more as an idea, or a symbol, that the Great Wall cast a lasting spell. First it was a symbol of China's isolation and its rulers' wish to control an enclosed, secretive, autarchic universe, a walled kingdom in the middle of the world. The Great Wall was seen as an expression of the Qin emperor's dream of controlling everything and everyone in his empire. He wished to rule not only over his subjects' bodies but also over their thoughts. The Great Wall, replicated in smaller city walls all over China— and within those city walls in even smaller walls, encircling private family compounds—stands for protection as well as oppression. One implies the other: You are controlled for your own protection; a giant prison is built for the safety of its inmates. An author from Hong Kong once wrote: "There are numerous walls within the Chinese world; the Great Wall itself merely protects the Chinese against Devils from without."

The notion of protecting China, or Chineseness, has a long history. Chinese rebels against the Mongol rulers of the Yuan dynasty (1279–1368) and against the Manchus of the Qing (1662–1911) claimed to be saving Chinese civilization from the barbarians. But the Manchu emperors, too, justified their rule by acting as the self-appointed protectors of Chinese civilization; after all, they claimed to have restored order and virtue and to have unified the empire after the chaos of the late Ming dynasty. The same symbols recur in Chinese history, but their meanings can shift with time. From having been for centuries a symbol of tyranny, the Great Wall after the late nineteenth century became a positive symbol of Chinese achievement, national unity, and cultural security. France had its Eiffel Tower, and the British had their houses of Parliament; China had its Great Wall.

The dream of Chinese unity behind the protective stones of the Great Wall has not faded. The "homecoming" of Hong Kong in 1997 was celebrated by a massive ballet performance in Beijing featuring, among other set pieces, a Great Wall constructed from an army of drilled Chinese bodies, glistening with the sweat of their exertions. Large drums were thumped. Massive choruses rejoiced: The compatriots of Hong Kong were safely back inside the gates, under the protection and control of the Qin emperor's political descendants. How the Hong Kong Chinese themselves felt about this blessing was not considered to be relevant.

In 1978 and 1979, however, another kind of wall had suddenly come into public view. It was made of gray brick, stood long and low in the center of Beijing, and was nothing much to look at, certainly not a tourist attraction. Mao Zedong had died two years earlier. After decades of total government control, a political thaw of sorts had set in, and the low wall in Beijing was quickly covered in poems, posters, letters, and proclamations, which often voiced complaints about abusive officials. In those giddy days of transition from Maoism to Deng Xiaoping's authoritarian semi-capitalism, or "socialism with Chinese characteristics," that unpretentious wall in Beijing was almost the only forum of free public debate in China. And it was there that a little-known electrician and underground magazine editor pinned up his poster about the "Fifth Modernization" and signed it with his name: Wei Jingsheng. Deng had announced four modernizations: in agriculture, science, technology, and national defense. Wei added democracy, without which, he wrote, "the four others are nothing more than a newfangled lie."

It was an extraordinary thing to have done. Wei said what many Chinese thought. But to do so in public was an act of extreme bravery, and to put his own name to it was foolhardy. He had gone against the orthodoxy of the state and openly criticized its supreme ruler. He lived under a dictatorship but behaved as if he were free. As most Chinese would have expected, the hand of authority came down hard, on Wei himself and on the so-called Democracy Wall movement. Wei would spend the next sixteen years in jail, much of the time in solitary confinement, tormented to the point of madness, but never broken. The Democracy Wall movement became part of a silent history, suppressed by the government but kept alive among Chinese in exile. The wall itself was torn down, to make way for a branch of the Bank of China and a glass-paneled display promoting China's economic progress under the benevolent guidance of Deng Xiaoping.

There is also a third wall, fictional, the wall of a prison cell. It was described by a brilliant novelist, Han Shaogong. Like many Chinese intellectuals, Han was forced to "go down" to a remote rural area after the Cultural Revolution. He spent the 1970s tilling the fields in a small Hunanese village. Out of this experience came an extraordinary novel, *Maqiao Dictionary,* which is a kind of spoof anthropological dissection of village life through the language of its people. Each chapter is inspired by a slang expression. One of these is "democracy cell."

The story is told by a local gambler, whom Han springs from jail by paying his fine. Dressed in rags, his hair matted with lice, the gambler stinks so badly that Han makes him take a bath before hearing his story. Refreshed, the man starts to whine. He had been really unlucky this time.

Unlucky?

Yes, this time he had experienced the worst: a democracy cell.

A democracy cell?

Well, says the man, it's like this: In most prisons, every cell has a boss and a hierarchy of henchmen. The boss gets to eat the best food and the best spot to sleep, and when he wishes to peep at the female prisoners through a tiny window in the wall, his cellmates must prop him up, sometimes for hours, until they buckle under the strain. But, hard though it may be, at least there is order. Every man gets his food. You have time to wash your face and to piss. You might even get some rest. Such an arrangement is better than a democracy cell. Democracy is what you get when there is no cell boss. The men fight one another like savages. They all want to be boss. Unity breaks down. Gangs go to war: Cantonese against Sichuanese, northeasterners against Shanghainese. There is no chance of getting sleep. You can't wash. You get lousy in no time, people are injured, and sometimes even killed.

This vignette of rural prison life is a perfect illustration of a common Chinese attitude toward democracy, or indeed political freedom. Many Chinese—and not just the rulers—associate democracy with violence and disorder. Only a big boss can make sure the common people get their food and rest. Only the equivalent of an emperor can keep the walled kingdom together. Without him, the Chinese empire will fall apart: region will fight region, and warlord will fight warlord. These assumptions rest on thousands of years of authoritarian rule, beginning with the first Qin emperor and his cursed Great Wall. And they are faithfully repeated by many in the West who presume to understand China.

This is what Deng Xiaoping is alleged to have feared in 1989, when he decided to take harsh measures to stop the student demonstrations. Meeting at his walled compound with the standing committee of the Politburo, Deng said: "Of course we want to build socialist democracy, but we can't possibly do it in a hurry, and still less do we want that Western-style stuff. If our one billion people jumped into multiparty elections, we'd get chaos like the 'all-out civil war' we saw during the Cultural Revolution."

"That Western-style stuff." It is a recurring theme in China, and other autocracies outside the Western world, the assumption that only Europeans and Americans should have the benefit of democratic institutions. It is of course a theme running through European colonial history, too. But if China has a history of despots ruling over the great Chinese empire, it also has a history of schisms and disorder and disunity, of rebellions, and of brave, mad, and foolhardy men and women who defied the orthodoxy of their given rulers. Of course rebels are not necessarily democrats. But dismissing democracy as "Western-style stuff" would consign 1 billion Chinese to political subservience forever. That is why I approach the Chinese-speaking world in this book through the rebels, the dissidents, the awkward squad that resists authoritarianism. What is their idea of freedom? Or of China? What does dissidence mean in a Chinese society? What makes people try, against all the odds, to defy their rulers?

What chance do they have of succeeding? Will those virtual walls that make China the largest remaining dictatorship on earth ever come down?

———

When I studied Chinese at university in the early 1970s, at the end of the Cultural Revolution, China was mostly an abstraction, as remote and physically inaccessible as the distant past. You could not go and see China with your own eyes unless you joined an organized tour of "Friends of the Chinese People" or a rigidly supervised scholarship program. For most of us, then, looking at China was an exercise in philology or semiology: You examined the official texts for subtle shifts of tone in Party propaganda, and for added information, you scrutinized photographs to observe who was sitting where at what state banquet. This kind of thing never appealed to me. I had no interest in trying to decipher the intrigues inside Mao's court by catching the tiny rays of light that sometimes penetrated the Chinese wall. I was never a China watcher.

Yet I remained preoccupied with China, for the same reasons that I have been interested in Germany and Japan. Chinese, like Japanese and Germans—and most other peoples in fact, though not always with similar dire consequences—carry a heavy load of national mythology. Yet while Chinese have no trouble identifying themselves with China, they are often hard-pressed to explain what they mean by that. Modern Chinese nationalism, like all forms of mystical nationalism, is based on a myth—the myth of "China" itself, which rests on a confusion of culture and race. Again and again, Chinese have sacrificed themselves and others for the sake of this myth, as abstract in its way as the China we studied in the early 1970s.

During the handover of Hong Kong to the People's Republic of China in 1997, a man named Lim Ken-han caused an astonishing fuss. Lim was the conductor of the Hong Kong China Philharmonic orchestra, which prided itself on being "100 percent Chinese," unlike the Hong Kong Philharmonic, which contained musicians of various nationalities. Lim was furious when the latter was invited to play at the patriotic handover festivities, instead of his own orchestra, which was, in his words, "racially more suited." What, apart from hurt professional pride, was the source of his fury? Lim was not a Communist. He was born in the Dutch East Indies, educated in Amsterdam, and went to live in China only in 1952, to help rebuild the motherland. Like so many other patriots from overseas, Lim became a victim of the Cultural Revolution. His sin was to have claimed that Western composers were worth hearing, even in China. Before he escaped to the relative freedom of Hong Kong, Lim's patriotism was rejected in a horrible manner. For five years he was forced to clean toilets. Yet here he was in a rage because he was unable to express his love for China, or "China," with his "100 percent Chinese" orchestra.

What, then, is the "China" that inspires such devotion? Going through some old magazine cuttings from the time I lived in Hong Kong in the 1980s, I found various expressions of "Chineseness," all vague, all, it seems, deeply felt. In 1984, an Indonesian-Chinese wrote in a Hong Kong paper: "Back in my Southern Hemisphere, I feel the wind of the night in my face and lean out of my window, looking longingly at the stars—I pray with all my heart for the glory and good fortune of my ancestral land." A Chinese-American expressed his sentiments in another Hong Kong magazine: " 'China' is a cultural entity which flows incessantly, like the Yellow River, from its source all the way to the present time, and from here to a boundless future. This is the basic and unshakable belief in the mind of every Chinese. It is also the strongest basis for Chinese nationalism. No matter which government is in power, people will not reject China, for there is always hope for a better future a hundred or more years from now." This same man described the Chinese people, wherever they may be, in Beijing, or Toronto, Hong Kong, or Amsterdam, as "an almost sacred and thus unassailable entity."

The language is overblown, but the Chinese-American patriot managed to convey the nature of Chinese nationalism, of the myth of "China." The religious phrases form part of the confusion. "China" is more than a nation-state, although both the nation and the state are parts of the myth; "China" is all that is "under heaven," a cosmic idea. Even though China has been broken up into various states throughout much of its history, the ideal state of affairs is the unity of all under heaven, protected by barbarian-resistant walls. Although Chinese is not one language but many languages that can be expressed in more or less the same literary form, the myth is that "Chinese" is one. Although many races live under heaven, the majority Han race is supposed to be one, and when Chinese speak of "Chinese," they really mean the Han; but in fact even the Han are made up of many different ethnic groups, whose origins may not even be in China. Although the cosmic state under heaven is supposed to represent harmony and order, the real state of China has been marked by thousands of years of conflict and disorder. Although Chinese civilization is a complex mixture of many cultures, both high and low, the myth has reduced it to one great tradition, roughly described as Confucianism.

"China," then, is an orthodoxy, a dogma, which disguises politics as culture and nation as race. Order under heaven is based on "correct thinking." Heterodoxy "confuses" people's minds and should therefore be stamped out. The Communist Party imposed its own dogma while claiming the Chinese myth, too. Marxism-Leninism, Mao Zedong Thought, and, latterly, socialism with Chinese characteristics may have replaced Confucianism as the reigning orthodoxy, but those who challenge the orthodoxy—the most precise definition of dissidents—are branded as "unpatriotic," "anti-Chinese," or even "un-Chinese," as well as "counter-revolutionary," as though all these amounted to the same thing.

———

My general preoccupation with the Chinese myth came into sharper focus one evening in the winter of 1996, when I was asked to introduce the activist Harry Wu to an audience in Amsterdam. Wu, who lived in California, was in Europe to promote his latest book on political prisoners in China's forced-labor camps. I met him for breakfast on the day of his talk. He struck me as a man who was driven by his cause to the point of obsession. After spending nineteen years in prison for being a "rightist" (he had criticized the Soviet crackdown on the Hungarian uprising in 1956), this was hardly surprising. While fiercely spearing his ham and scrambled eggs, he spoke about thousands of prisons and labor camps in China containing hundreds of thousands of prisoners. He spoke about the brutal struggle for survival in those terrible places. He spoke about the trade in organs plucked from the corpses of freshly executed prisoners. And he spoke about China, a "miserable country," with venom; the Chinese people were "fanatical in their selfishness," he said. He gobbled his breakfast up in big mouthfuls. The sound of his mouth working on his ham and eggs was all that broke, for a few seconds at a time, his tirade against his fellow Chinese.

That evening, he spoke to a large audience. Again the stories about the labor camps, the detention centers, and the prisons. Again the tales of his personal suffering and his sense of guilt at having survived, by stealing the last scraps of food from others who were starving. (Once he actually scraped something barely edible from a rat hole, thereby depriving the rat.) He finished by making an eloquent speech in favor of civil liberties and democracy.

Then it was time for questions. One man asked him about the approximate number of people who had been detained in labor camps. About 50 million, Wu thought. Someone else asked him about Mao, and yet another person about the reforms under Deng Xiaoping. Then a young woman raised her hand. She looked Chinese and I assumed she was until she opened her mouth and spoke English in a thick Dutch accent. "Mr. Wu," she said. "We are both Chinese, and it is not easy to talk about our culture in front of non-Chinese." Indeed, she found it painful to discuss the problems of "our Chinese culture." But, she continued, wouldn't Mr. Wu agree with her that democracy was an alien concept in Chinese culture? And that being so, how could we possibly expect such Western values to take root in "our Confucian tradition"?

Wu looked at her impatiently. I could see the muscles in his jaw stiffen. I can't remember his precise answer. But he was used to this kind of thing; he heard it from Chinese-Americans all the time. In her naïve way, the Dutch woman expressed the Chinese myth, the orthodoxy, seemingly as a critic but in fact as someone who took it at face value, as though "our Confucian tradition" were a stone monument, unchanged and unchanging, as though it were the only tradition in China.

Harry Wu comes from a highly educated Catholic family in Shanghai. This alone would have made him an outsider in Communist China. He is also a damaged survivor of terrible brutality, which makes him obsessive, difficult, impatient, and perhaps ruthless. But for whatever reason, he is a man who defied orthodoxy. There are other Chinese like him, who are neither Christian nor from a background of high education. It was while listening to Wu and his Dutch questioner that evening that I had the idea of writing about "China" from the point of view of the mavericks, the rebels, and the dissidents. Their personal stories would, I hoped, help us understand the mesmerizing force of the Chinese myth as well as the reasons why some people are brave or mad enough to challenge it.

These stories took me to all parts of the Chinese-speaking world, because I wanted to show how people who shared the same cultural traditions could choose very different ways to organize their societies. Politics is never a pure reflection of some monolithic culture. There are in fact several Chinas. Seen from Beijing, Taiwan is a renegade Chinese province. Seen from Taipei, Taiwan is the legitimate Republic of China to some and the independent republic of Taiwan to others, depending on their politics. Hong Kong is now part of the People's Republic of China (PRC) but still retains its own government. Although more than 70 percent of its citizens are ethnically Chinese, Singapore is not part of China at all. But its government likes to think of itself as a model Chinese government, based on so-called Asian values, which are really more like a pastiche of Confucian values, which serve very nicely as a justification for the conservative Chinese ideal of that moral authoritarian order in which every person knows his place under heaven.

Encounters with Chinese dissidents and protesters threw up new questions. Why were so many of them Christians? Some, like Harry Wu, had Christian parents; many more had converted. Is it perhaps true, as Christians often claim, that a faith which came of age in Europe can be the only basis for liberal institutions that also ripened there? Is there something about Christianity—its egalitarianism, perhaps—that lends itself to struggles for political freedom? Or will other faiths, more in tune with Chinese traditions, provide the spur for political change? What, if any, is the connection between spiritual and political change?

This book, the product of my journeys among the Chinese awkward squad, cannot offer a definite answer to these questions. The Chinese world is changing too fast for anyone to be definite about anything. My conclusions have to be tentative. Naturally, I have my sympathies and prejudices, which reflect to some degree my own background and upbringing. Testing them in places where different norms operate is part of the fascination of travel. But my aim is not to tell the reader what to think, or to predict the future; it is, rather, to make political questions less abstract by providing a context that is nothing if not human, personal, individual. Having studied China as an abstraction in the early 1970s, I have tried to bring it alive as a society of individuals, with peculiar personal histories. If this helps readers to understand the politics of Chinese-speaking nations, so much the better. If it makes them realize that Chinese (not "the Chinese," another abstraction) are not utterly unlike us, whoever we may be, and that freedom from torture, persecution, and spiritual or intellectual coercion is a common desire among all human beings and not merely a Western notion, it would be better still.

My Chinese journeys were not continuous. But if there is no strictly chronological logic to the journeys, there is a geographical one. I approached the center from the periphery: Beijing is the center, the last stop. From Los Angeles, then, to Taiwan, Singapore, Hong Kong, the Special Economic Zones (SEZs) on the fringes of China, to the final destination. This lends a certain coherence to my enterprise, but there is a political logic to it as well: As a rule, individual freedom diminishes the closer one gets to the center. The U.S. is freer than Taiwan, Taiwan is freer than Hong Kong, Hong Kong is freer than the SEZs, and the SEZs are freer than Beijing. If one imagines Chinese state orthodoxy to be a game of Chinese whispers, the greater the distance from the center, the more the message loses its power, even though faint echoes can still be heard as far away as Amsterdam.

Part I

The Exiles

Chapter 1

Exile from
Tiananmen Square

We will never know how many people were killed during that sticky night of June 3 and the early hours of June 4, 1989. A stink of burning vehicles, gunfire, and stale sweat hung heavily on Tiananmen Square; thousands of tired bodies huddled in fear around the Monument to the People's Heroes, with its carved images of earlier rebels: the Taiping, the Boxers, the Communists of course, and also the student demonstrators of May 4, 1919, who saw "Mr. Science" and "Mr. Democracy" as the twin solutions to China's political problems. The huge, rosy face of Chairman Mao stared from the wall of the Forbidden City across three or four dead bodies lying where his outsize shoes would have been had his portrait stretched that far. Tracer bullets and flaming cars lit up the sky in bursts of pale orange. Loudspeakers barked orders to leave the square immediately, or else. Spotlights were switched off and then on again. And over the din of machine-gun fire, breaking glass, stamping army boots, screaming people, wailing sirens, and rumbling APCs, young voices, hoarse from exhaustion, sang the "Internationale," followed by the patriotic hit song of the year, "Descendants of the Dragon":

In the ancient East there is a dragon;
China is its name.
In the ancient East there lives a people,
The dragon's heirs every one.
Under the claws of this mighty dragon I grew up
And its descendant I have become.
Like it or not—
Once and forever, a descendant of the dragon . . .

The words, which reduced the remaining students to tears, expressed pride in "Chineseness" as well as a sense of oppression that goes with it. The singer and composer of the song was Hou Dejian, a Taiwanese rock star who had moved to China from Taiwan in 1983, his way of coming "home," of feeling fully Chinese. But the oppression soon got to him. So he became a kind of rock-and-roll mentor of the Tiananmen Movement, his last great hope for a patriotic resolution to China's problems. When the shooting began, some students elected to die rather than retreat, but Hou talked them out of such pointless self-sacrifice, and negotiated with the army so the students could leave the Square alive. Afterward, he was forced to go back to Taiwan, where, disgusted with Chinese politics, he turned his attention to Chinese folk religions instead.

By 5 A.M. on June 4, the massacre in Beijing was more or less over, though some people were still shot in the head or chest by snipers from the 27th Army, which had last seen action during the Sino-Vietnamese war, more than ten years earlier. By daybreak the last students had retreated from the square in a single file. The Tiananmen demonstrations for free speech, independent student and workers' unions, and the recognition of the student demonstrators as "patriots" had ended in failure. The government had offered no concessions. Five days after the killings, the paramount leader of China, Deng Xiaoping, praised the army for crushing the plot of "a rebellious clique" bent on establishing "a bourgeois republic entirely dependent on the West."

Compared to the famines caused by Chairman Mao's Great Leap Forward between 1958 and 1962 (more than 30 million dead) or the regular purges of "rightists," "revisionists," and other "counterrevolutionary elements" during the 1950s and 1960s, the death toll in Beijing was modest. The figured offered by the Chinese government, as well as some foreign journalists, is around three hundred. Other estimates range from twenty-seven hundred to many more. But never before had the People's Liberation Army (PLA) publicly aimed its guns at unarmed Chinese citizens with the intention of murdering them, and not just in the capital but in more than three hundred cities all over China. Most of the victims—on the night itself and in the following months—shot in the neck with single bullets, for which their families were duly billed, were not students but ordinary citizens. The PLA had done to its own people what Soviet tanks had done decades before in Budapest and Prague.

Since the recent publication of *The Tiananmen Papers,* we probably know a little bit more about what went on behind the walls of Zhongnanhai, the government quarters next to the Forbidden City. There, the Communist leaders fought among themselves in an atmosphere of intrigue and panic as scattered student protests grew into a movement in early May. "Reformists," led by Party general-secretary Zhao Ziyang, advocated a peaceful solution, by negotiating with the students, but "hard-liners," led by Premier Li Peng, opposed any kind of compromise. In the end, the hard-liners, backed by a group of Party elders, some of them barely literate, prevailed. Deng Xiaoping, the paramount leader, made his decision. Zhao would have to step down. No concessions to the counterrevolutionaries. And on May 20, martial law was imposed on Beijing.

Fissures running through the student movement were as deep as those that split the government. Some student leaders wanted to declare victory in May and retreat from the Square. Others—prompted by new batches of students freshly arrived from the provinces, and egged on by radicalized Beijing intellectuals thirsting for action—favored a tougher line: hunger strikes, no retreat, no compromise with government officials no matter who they were. Tactical quarrels and mutual denunciations went on until the night of the killings. And they continue to this day, inside the government, but also among the dissidents and former student leaders living in exile.

Since none of this can be openly discussed in China, the fallout of Tiananmen rains down in peculiar ways. The internal Party documents published as *The Tiananmen Papers,* were probably compiled and smuggled out of China by people in the reformist camp, as a way to discredit Li Peng and his fellow hard-liners. And Chinese in exile still tear one another apart over the failures of 1989. Should the students have retreated before the tanks came in? Should they have given the government "face," and thus helped Zhao Ziyang retain his position? Did they have a choice? Is slow reform, beginning inside the Communist Party itself, the only way forward? Or will it take a revolution to break the Party's monopoly on power? These are all fascinating questions that are too often buried in a poisonous brew of hostile gossip and recrimination.

My own interest in these quarrels was not as a historian of Tiananmen. I wanted to know more about the rebels themselves and the nature of their dissent. The politics of the students, intellectuals, workers, journalists, and others who became involved in the rebellion were too confused, contradictory, and murky to invite easy conclusions. And what they say ten years after the fact about 1989 should not be taken at face value. What we have are interpretations, a *Rashomon* story. The interpretations, as always with such tales, tell us more about the people who offer them than about the story itself. To complicate things, the interpretations change over time, according to circumstances. As my first step into the world of Chinese rebellions, the *Rashomon* of Tiananmen seemed an obvious place to start.

———

Most of the prominent student leaders of Tiananmen Square are now living abroad, in the United States, France, and elsewhere. They have joined older dissidents from previous mutinies in one of the largest political diasporas in history, comparable to that of the French Huguenots in the seventeenth century, Russians after 1919, Germans after 1933, or Hungarians and Czechs in the 1950s and 1960s.

Wang Dan, bookish, bespectacled, the most reflective figure among his peers, led the Autonomous Federation of Students in 1989. He arrived in America in 1998, after several years in jail, to study history at Harvard. Chai Ling, the so-called chief commander on the Square, is the CEO of a computer software company in Cambridge, Massachusetts. Or at least she was when I last saw her in 1999. Feng Congde, Chai Ling's ex-husband, lived in Paris and was rumored to have gone through various religious phases: Taoism, Christianity, Buddhism. Li Lu, Chai's "deputy" on the Square, manages a hedge fund in Manhattan. Wang Chaohua, one of the oldest and more politically astute Federation of Students leaders in 1989, was studying Chinese literature at UCLA. Zhang Boli, founder, on the eve of the massacre, of the so-called Democracy University on the Square, was studying to be a Protestant minister in California. Wu'er Kaixi, the student leader with rock-star charisma, was a radio-talk-show host in Taiwan.

Chai Ling was seen on television all over the world every day for almost a month: a small, frail girl in a grubby white T-shirt and baggy jeans, admonishing, entertaining, and hectoring the crowds through a megaphone that seemed to hide her whole face. Her image—the megaphone in jeans—was as emblematic of that year of revolutions as the short film clip of the young man trying to defy a tank on Chang'an Avenue. She was on the cover of magazines. Her statements were distributed on audiotapes. There were Chai Ling T-shirts on sale in Hong Kong. Only twenty-three years old at the time, Chai, then a graduate student of psychology at Beijing Normal University, seemed to have appeared from nowhere. Feng Congde was the political one. She followed her husband. That, at any rate, is how she remembers it. But Chai displayed a remarkable capacity for making men follow her. It was one of the main reasons other student leaders set her up as a figure to rally around on the Square. Her oddly affecting physical presence—the ready smile, the quick tears, the appealing eyes—and her gift for oratory held together a disparate, fractious movement, especially when morale was flagging.

Chai's speech on May 12 moved hundreds of people to go on a hunger strike when the government ignored the students' demands for a public "dialogue," and she galvanized the support of many thousands of others. "We, the children," she said, her reedy voice breaking with emotion, "are ready to die. We, the children, are ready to use our lives to pursue the truth. We, the children, are willing to sacrifice ourselves." Who could resist such innocence, such purity? Chai's tearful rhetoric of blood sacrifice owed something to universal student romanticism, exploited by Mao during the Cultural Revolution, but there were echoes too of an older Chinese tradition shaped less by romance than by force of circumstance: It was not rare for critics of the emperor to sacrifice their lives as the ultimate price for telling the truth. Days after the crackdown, while Chai was on the run, a tape of her recalling the last hours on the Square was smuggled out of China. The students, she said, sang "Descendants of the Dragon" with tears in their eyes. And then: "We embraced each other and held hands, for we knew that the end had come. It was time to die for the nation."

This message was broadcast in Hong Kong. But she had made another statement a week before, not meant for public consumption. It was recorded in a Beijing hotel room by an American reporter named Philip Cunningham. The interview became the centerpiece of a 1995 documentary film about Tiananmen, *The Gate of Heavenly Peace.* In it, Chai is sitting on a bed, small, thin, and jittery with nervous exhaustion. Government troops have moved into Beijing. Factions within the student movement are quarreling about tactics, aims, pecking orders, and money. Chai is sobbing as she speaks: "My students keep asking me, 'What should we do next? What can we accomplish?' I feel so sad, because how can I tell them that what we are actually hoping for is bloodshed, the moment when the government is ready to butcher the people brazenly? Only when the Square is awash with blood will the people of China open their eyes. Only then will they really be united. But how can I explain any of this to my fellow students?"

I first met Chai in 1996, when we were both visiting Taiwan for the first free presidential elections in Chinese history. I was there to write a magazine article. She was a political celebrity making the rounds of talk shows and official dinners. It was hard to imagine the Chai I met in Taipei being the same person as that hysterical, sobbing girl in the Beijing hotel room in 1989. Her small body had thickened, her narrow eyes had widened, and she was dressed smartly in the style of an American businesswoman: white skirt, maroon blazer, gold buttons. Divorced from her Chinese husband, she now spoke softly in almost flawless American sentences. Only her sweet, dimpled smile reminded me of earlier images I had seen.

We were sitting around the breakfast table one morning in our hotel, and were joined by two Chinese-Americans, David and Gloria, from St. Petersburg, Florida. David, a dapper man in pale cream trousers, and Gloria, a small woman wearing thick white makeup, had strong opinions about Taiwanese politics. The Taiwanese people, they said, were clearly not ready for democracy. Just look at the corruption and the crime rate. And that President Lee Teng-hui, why, he spoke better Japanese than Chinese. Was he even Chinese at all? He was clearly being manipulated by Japan into provoking China with all his talk of Taiwan going its own way. Gloria then turned to me to explain why Chinese people everywhere needed to be united. I was only half listening, for I was watching Chai in fascination. She was speaking soothingly to David, in English, about "the dignity of free choice" and the need for "constitutional limits of power." David was clearly irritated. He said the most important thing was to stick to the goal of a united China. Then, while he was still in full flow, Chai glanced at her chunky gold watch, smoothed her blazer, and said with a smile: "Pardon me, but I've got to go. David, Gloria, I want you to know I really respect your opinions and thank you for a real fruitful communication. Have a nice day."

From blood sacrifice to constitutionalism and "Have a nice day": The shift in rhetoric and the slickness of its presentation were remarkable. Three years later, I saw Chai again. We met for a cappuccino in a nice outdoor café in Cambridge, Massachusetts, where she had been living since she enrolled at Harvard Business School in 1996. Once again, I was struck by her eagerness to charm, her coquettishness, and the steeliness within the cuddly frame. Occasionally, there would be a sudden hint of suspicion—"Who told you that?" "Why do you want to know that?"—but such outbursts were followed by a cocked head, the dimpled smile, and a disarming assurance that "of course, I trust you. You are my friend."

We talked about her Internet company, backed by executives from Reebok and Microsoft. The clichés of American political science had made way now for those of the corporate world. America, she said, was "a wonderful land of opportunity for anyone prepared to work his butt off." Her aim, by selling communication technology to American colleges, was to "create an environment where people can interact creatively." Her partner was the Republican former state treasurer of Massachusetts and her main adviser was her former boss in a "global strategy consultancy firm."

Chai handed me a folder with promotional material. It contained references to her career at the Harvard Business School and her "leadership skills" on Tiananmen Square. She spoke to me about her plans to liberate China via the Internet. She joked that she wanted to be rich enough to buy China, so she could "fix it." But although she was not shy to use her celebrity to promote her business, she was oddly reluctant to discuss the past. When I asked her to go over some of the events in 1989, she asked why I wanted to know "about all that old stuff, all that garbage." What was needed was to "find some space and build a beautiful new life." What was wanted was "closure" for Tiananmen. I felt the chilly presence of Henry Ford's ghost hovering over our cappuccinos in that nice outdoor café. From being an icon of history, Chai had moved into a world where all history is bunk.

Li Lu was Chai's most strident deputy in 1989. He had refused to leave the Square just days before the crackdown, after other student leaders, including Wang Dan, Wu'er Kaixi, and Chai, had decided by vote to urge the crowds to do so. Chai changed her mind, tearfully, because of Li Lu. When some well-known Beijing intellectuals advised the students to avoid a bloody confrontation, Li Lu denounced them as "government agents." Like Chai's, Li's appearance on the scene in 1989 was sudden. But within days of arriving in the capital, this provincial student from Nanjing had managed to meet all the main student leaders. A partnership with Chai suited them both: She would be his metropolitan patron, and he her trusted adviser.

Li Lu's office was on the twenty-sixth floor of a building on Madison Avenue. I waited outside his door while he concluded a phone call. I could hear a bluff voice calling out: "Hey, Bill, cancel my lunch with Dick on Tuesday." There was a slight burr, a tone more than an accent, that hinted at the speaker's non-American origin. I glanced at the books on the shelves: tax guides, Wei Jingsheng's prison letters, business journals. I flipped through some newspaper clippings I had brought with me. There was a profile in *The New York Times Magazine*. There were articles in *The Washington Post*. There was a piece quoting Li Lu's remark that the U.S. stock market boom was like a woman's multiple orgasm. I knew that he had received an M.B.A. as well as a law degree from Columbia University, and that he had been the honored guest of presidents, senators, and television-talk-show hosts only months after being smuggled out of

China by boat. Then, suddenly, there he was, emerging from his office with a smile and an outstretched hand, wearing horn-rimmed glasses and a dark flannel suit: "What'ya want: Coke, Evian, coffee . . . ?" Evian, I said. "Hot or cold? Hey, you're European. You guys always have it warm, right?" And this was a man who hardly spoke English in 1989.

The first thing you notice about Chai Ling, Li Lu, and many others of their generation, is their smooth way with words, a sign, perhaps, of their intelligence, or at least of an extraordinary talent to adapt. Maybe it has something to do with their background, too. They grew up in a society where jargon is the only currency of public political life. The wooden language of the Party has replaced the ancient Confucian clichés with disastrous results. Language is deprived of meaning. "Correct thinking" is learned by rote. People use words whether or not anyone believes them. But orthodoxy changes suddenly, depending on who is up or down in the political hierarchy. What was black yesterday could very well be white today, and you had better be sure which is which. This can result in a facility for rhetoric or a talent for lying to survive. It breeds a cynicism, so that no one is assumed to hold an opinion without ulterior—usually sinister—motives. And because politics, among government officials as well as their opponents, is often confused with morality, unorthodox views, or simply opinions other than one's own, are seen as a sign of bad character.

This may be one reason why Chai Ling and Li Lu are hated in the Chinese diaspora. Their transformation from idealistic young patriots to go-getting Americans looks too transparent, too self-serving. Foreign adulation also invites jealousy, which is another reason for hatred. A Chinese friend of mine, who is by no means sympathetic to the Communist regime, called Chai Ling and Li Lu "scum." A well-known Chinese writer referred to them as "extremists" and "Mao Zedong's best students," implying that they shared the violent attitudes of Red Guards. Several people told me the former student leaders had "built their careers on the blood of the Tiananmen victims."

Rhetoric was at the heart of the most bitter Tiananmen controversy after 1989. The filmmakers Carma Hinton and Richard Gordon made their 1995 documentary, *Gate of Heavenly Peace,* as a polemic against the "radical" student leaders, specifically Chai Ling. Through the deft use of archive material and narration, they argued that the most extreme students had hijacked the leadership of the demonstrations: It was the radical behavior of Chai Ling and her cohorts, behavior that reflected the extremism of the Communist Party itself, that had provoked the hardliners in the government to crack down with such brutality. The main evidence for this was the infamous interview with Chai in the Beijing hotel room a few days before the killings began. And the most contentious sentence was: ". . . what we are actually hoping for is bloodshed." Chai claims that the word for "hoping for" can also mean "to expect" in Chinese, depending on the context. Her defenders say she is right. Her critics said she was lying. Chai accused the filmmakers of "pleasing the [Chinese] government for their personal gain" and "hawking" their film "for crude commercial profit." To look for the truth, then, was no longer the point: Debate was stifled by mutual denunciation.

Denunciation is the common poison within any dictatorship based on dogma. And paranoia is not a uniquely Chinese vice. Political exiles fight among themselves wherever they come from: Cut off from a common enemy, they tear into each other. In the course of talking to Chinese exiles and activists, I found almost no one with anything good to say about anyone else. Mention a name, and I would be told that person was a liar, a government agent, a spy, an opportunist, a gangster, an extremist, or corrupted by sex or power—or both. I was often reminded of a Japanese ex-convict who said the most-used word inside Japanese jails was *liar*. In a climate of denunciation, nothing that anybody says can be trusted: "X is going to be released next week"—"Liar!" "An extra ration of meat on the emperor's birthday"—"Liar!" "The weather was fine today"—"Liar!"

Mutual suspicion is not just an exile's disease, however. It reveals a deeper wound in Chinese civilization. If cynicism is pervasive in a country where telling lies is a matter of daily survival, then slander is the main tool of oppression. Lying trickles down from the top to the rest of society. Survivors develop a facility for it. They know what subjects to avoid, how to affect ignorance, and how to say one thing in public and something quite different in private. Chinese themselves are the first to state how "double-faced" they are as a people. They often say this with an air of distress and embarrassment, but sometimes also with a perverse kind of pride, as though a habit of duplicity were a sign of superior sophistication. "We are such a complicated people," one is told over and over. "Our culture is so complicated, you foreigners can never understand us," as if "you foreigners" are a bit simpleminded in your earnest attempts to blurt out the truth.

The culture of duplicity, however, is older than Marxism-Leninism and Mao Zedong Thought. "Correct thinking" articulated by a class of highly educated scribes or scholar-officials and enforced by the state, has been a feature of all East Asian societies, where authority is justified by Confucianist dogmas. One of the dogmas is that "harmony" and "unity," at the expense of individual liberty, define Chinese culture and are indeed the essence of "Chineseness." The extreme orthodoxy of North Korean communism is a grotesque perversion of this kind of thinking. In Korea, China, and Vietnam, communism simply adapted itself to the worst features of the older tradition.

To blame Confucius for this would be to miss the point, for the sage often talked about the need for cultivated men to tell the truth, however unwelcome it might be to the ears of their rulers. As a warning against tyranny, he recalled the story of a despotic king who tested the loyalty of his subjects by pointing to a deer and calling it a horse. Naturally, the subjects were too terrified to contradict him. So Chinese were already aware more than two thousand years ago that lies corrupt politics. Only if the truth can be told, preached Confucius, and false names rectified, can good government follow.

And yet the Japanese, who have more freedom to speak their minds than most East Asians, still consider the tension between public truth (*tatemae*) and personal motive (*honne*) to be the key to their social behavior. Because words are always suspect and true motives rarely stated, Japanese and Chinese idealize the virtue of sincerity. A sincere person doesn't always need to speak the truth as long as his or her motives are pure. This, too, is perverted under Communist rule: It isn't enough for a political prisoner to repeat the official dogmas; he must do so "sincerely"—that is, his spirit must be purged of any vestige of individual critical thought. Like the Christians in seventeenth-century Japan, the heterodox must correct their errors by acts of apostasy: stamping on images of the Virgin Mary in the case of the Japanese Christians, denouncing "reactionaries"—even if they were your parents or best friends—if you were a prisoner under Mao. One of the reasons ordinary citizens in Beijing came out in such large numbers to support the students in 1989, especially after the hunger strikes in May, is that the students' professions of martyrdom and sacrifice for the nation were seen as the highest forms of sincerity.

—

In the winter of 1998, I flew to Taichung, a large, brash, ugly, businesslike city in the center of Taiwan. I wanted to meet Wu'er Kaixi, the most charming, most eloquent, most swaggering of the student leaders. Who can forget the sight of him in May 1989, after the first hunger strike, fresh from his hospital bed, still dressed in his pajamas, sucking his oxygen bottle like a big baby, wagging his finger at Premier Li Peng in the Great Hall of the People? It was like a farcical reenactment of "struggle sessions" during the Cultural Revolution, when students tormented their elders, often to death. Except this time the student held no power, and violence would be the elder man's choice of weapon. Wu'er had still had the pudgy looks of a teenage idol in Beijing despite the fast. He grew fat in exile. His first years in the U.S. are legendary—drunken rock star behavior, unlimited cash, girls, parties, and two-thousand-dollar suits. Talent agencies beckoned. A Hollywood contract to play himself in a movie about Tiananmen was in the offing. But after those few fat years, things began to slide. The money dried up. Exile organizations shunned him. He fainted rather too conveniently during public debates. As with the other student leaders, except Wang Dan, who was still in a Chinese jail, Wu'er Kaixi's image as a sincere freedom fighter had been tarnished.

And now he had married the daughter of a wealthy Taiwanese businessman and worked as a late-night radio disc jockey in Taichung. We met in an American-style hamburger joint. A lachrymose Taiwanese pop song was playing softly. Wu'er ordered a club sandwich. A gray T-shirt was stretched tight over his round stomach. His face had filled out, giving him the look of a dark cherub with soulful round eyes and pouting red lips. He fiddled with a cell phone. A U.S. senator was coming to Taipei and Wu'er was expecting a dinner invitation to come through at any minute. The prospect made him fidgety. The invitation never came.

Despite his sleek and somewhat pampered exterior, Wu'er still has the charm of a born schmoozer, a man who likes to move in public. You could see why the crowds in Beijing listened to him from the moment he clambered on top of a wall and told them to resist the dictators. Wu'er is funny and expansive. He speaks the same almost-perfect American English as Chai Ling and Li Lu: "Those first three or four years in the U.S.? Gee, I should have been put away in an institution." He had been overwhelmed by the experience of exile, of living in a free society. He had needed at least four years to calm down, just to think straight. The greatest problem, he said, was how to cope with disappointed idealism.

Wu'er is a Uighur, the Muslim minority in the far west of China. He looks Levantine more than Chinese. Although his father was a staunch Communist cadre, the family didn't eat pork, and something of the Muslim ethos had survived. Wu'er grew up with a strong sense of right and wrong, he explained, so unlike the Han Chinese, whose values are collectivist, not individual, and that, he continued, is why they lie quite happily to preserve harmony and "face." The idealism Wu'er, or, as he put it, "the Tiananmen generation" grew up with was the last gasp of Maoism. When he was eight, his head was filled with Maoism. But the death of Mao, the arrest of his wife, Jiang Qing, and her cohorts—the Gang of Four—and the opening up of China to the West put an end to all that. Instead, people were encouraged by the new leader, Deng Xiaoping, to get rich quick. Corruption and crime soared. Wu'er: "What we had been taught went against everything we saw with our own eyes." The official rhetoric swung wildly and the wooden phrases of authority almost never matched reality. The realization that they had been lied to, almost universally recognized among intelligent Chinese, fueled the Tiananmen generation's rebellious spirit. But their hatred of authority was mixed, in Wu'er's view, with an "old Chinese intellectual tradition of being responsible for the nation. We thought we could save China."

The massacre on June 4 put an end to that dream as well. As a result, Wu'er explained, people buried their disillusion under a thick crust of cynicism. "It is hard to kill idealism," he said. "But Uncle Sam helped by rewarding extreme pragmatism. The green card is the best way to kill idealism."

I had heard it before, and not just from Chinese: the lack of deep meaning in Western life, the emptiness of American materialism, and so on. Spirituality, or the lack of it, and moral values, or the lack of them, were clearly problems that exercised Wu'er. In his talk, spirituality, idealism, and politics overlapped; they merged into a kind adolescent angst, as they often had in 1989, when Wu'er stood up in the Square, in his jeans and his cowboy boots, an adoring girl usually at hand, and announced that he was not interested in politics but was really an artist. His politics became a form of self-assertion, sometimes expressed in snatches of favorite rock-and-roll lyrics. "I love myself," went one of his lines, "so I say I'm good and I deserve to be happy. I want to live for me. I'm Wu'er Kaixi, not someone else." This was a long way from Maoist idealism. And yet in his comments about Taiwan he could sound almost like a Maoist.

Wu'er pointed out the window of the hamburger joint. "Look at that," he said. I looked, and saw two young girls walking by in miniskirts and T-shirts that left their midriffs bare. "Look at that," he repeated, while looking intently. "You can see everything." The indignation seemed genuine, even though it came from him, the old playboy of the Western world. Just think, he said: Taiwanese girls, "as young as sixteen," who worked in bars and took money for sex, to buy clothes with fashionable brand names. He shook his head as though he couldn't believe it.

The Taiwanese were the luckiest Chinese, he said. They were free. Yet all this had ended in "a collapse of moral values." Uighur morality, on the other hand, was similar to Christianity. Western philosophy, he said, was based on individualism. And so was Islam. But the Chinese—and here he spoke as if they were foreigners to him—didn't think in terms of good and bad on an individual basis. They still had to learn individualism. Not that Wu'er had ever thought of these things much in China: "I developed these ideas after those crazy years in America." And now that he had found himself as a "media person," he wanted to implement those ideas in China. He would revive the idealism of 1989. He wanted to "dream big," work for press freedom, build a "lively civil society." He would have his own radio show in China. No, bigger than that—he would build his own "media empire."

—

Saving China is an old Confucianist project. The China to be saved is often a utopian ideal, defined by cultural rather than geographical borders. Rulers are supposed to be men of superior virtue. If such virtues are lacking in public life, it is the moral duty of gentleman-scholars to restore them. Even without knowing much about the tradition, the former student leaders claim to have been influenced by it, just as their revolutionary parents were. For example, Chai Ling's former deputy, Li Lu, told me: "We thought we could save China because we were educated. It is laughable but also admirable. Like my father, we were typical Confucianists."

Unlike Wu'er, Li Lu comes from a family of intellectuals. His grandfather wrote a thesis at Columbia University in the 1920s, comparing Confucian philosophy with the liberal ideas of John Dewey. An advocate of individual liberty, he died in prison during the Cultural Revolution. Li Lu's father studied science in the Soviet Union and was a good Communist dedicated to the revolution that would save China. But he too was imprisoned for many years in labor camps for being a class enemy. And yet he still tells his son in New York "to be Chinese, to help China, and not be fooled by a foreign country."

Chai Ling has been given to grand statements about saving China as well. At the same time, she describes her American exile as a release, a liberation from that burden. The details of her escape from China in 1990 are still mysterious. She simply arrived in Hong Kong by train one day. There are stories of plastic surgery to disguise her famous face and of help from gangsters, peasants, and even policemen on the way, of being smuggled out in a sealed crate; but none of this is certain. Chai herself has kept her silence. But she told me about her early years of exile, when she lived in Princeton in virtual seclusion. She told me how hard it was to be treated as an icon, when all she wanted was "closure." After Tiananmen, she said, "we were forced to become something we didn't want and do something we couldn't do—find a solution to the ancient problems of China." All she really wanted was to "struggle to be the person I want to be." And it didn't take much struggle to find she was "a born entrepreneur."

While I listened to Chai telling me this happy news in Cambridge, images of a different Chai passed through my mind: Chai holding forth about the future of China on U.S. television shows, Chai talking about being nominated for the Nobel Peace Prize in 1990, Chai posing as the

Goddess of Democracy in New York in 1992, to protest against the visit of Premier Li Peng. And yet I believed her when she said she found it liberating to learn English, to talk to Americans, and to walk around Cambridge and Boston buying clothes, "hanging out," doing what she felt like doing. The propensity to use touchy-feely language about finding oneself, which she shares with Li Lu and Wu'er Kaixi, is not a new affectation picked up in the process of being Americanized; it was already part of the Tiananmen generation. Mixed in with the rhetoric about democratic rights and romantic Chinese patriotism were strong, often barely coherent echoes of European, Japanese, and American revolts in 1968: *"l'imagination au pouvoir,"* sex and rock 'n' roll, "My G-g-g-generation!" The boasting and the braggadocio—Wu'er Kaixi's claims in 1989 that he was better than Lech Wałesa and comparable to Gandhi, or Li Lu's later assertions that the Tiananmen students had lit the fuse that destroyed the Soviet empire—were part of their callow individualism. They wanted to be free to choose their own lives, unmolested by the collectivist pressures of Chinese society and the corruption of China's oppressive politics. Most were already touched by America long before they got there.

The daughter of doctors in Shandong province, Chai Ling had a hard but not untypical childhood for someone of her class and time. She was often left alone to take care of her brother and sister when her parents were ordered to tend to peasants in remote villages. She developed an early aversion to politics, for all too often politics meant being forced to take part in campaigns that were sometimes plainly mad and almost always humiliating. Politics was the reason she was so frequently left alone with her siblings. Life became easier after the death of Mao Zedong in 1976, which is Chai's earliest political memory. Teachers told her to cry, but she felt like laughing instead. She has little recollection of the Democracy Wall movement, which began two years later with Wei Jingsheng. With few exceptions, the students of 1989, who had grown up under Deng Xiaoping's slogan "To Get Rich Is Glorious," had barely heard of Wei. That was a different time—and a very different generation.

Chai was an undergraduate at Beijing University, where, she says, "we all had the American dream." I asked her what that meant. She said: "The America of cowboy movies, where people work their butts off and succeed. I always wanted to come to America. In fact, I was applying for a place at an American school in 1989 when the demonstrations began." The land where people "work their butts off." It was the second time in our conversation she had used that expression. Perhaps you have to grow up in a Communist society, where trying to get ahead through hard work is more often a recipe for trouble than success, to understand that working your butt off can be a form of freedom. From what Chai told me, however, the glimmering of a peculiar American dream, one that combined ambition with a kind of sentimental hubris, came to her as something stranger than cowboy movies: Chai's adolescent dream was to have a television show for parents and children, then to build a theme park and "merchandise" the clothes and toys. Walt Disney was her hero: "He had a passion and made it come true." That was the kind of passion, she says, that went into the Tiananmen Movement.

Disneyland fantasies and starving to save China struck me as an odd combination. But Chai assured me that the hunger strike, too, was all about the love of life. The students loved life so much that they were willing to give it up for others. It was absolutely "sincere," not just a matter of political tactics. "It was meant to overcome politics—the stereotype of politics."

The professions of innocence, of sincerity and youthful purity, tactical or not, were an important part of the students' emotional appeal. They fitted the traditional ideal of selfless love of the nation. But they fitted very awkwardly with the pursuit of American dreams. It was this ill-fitting quilt of traditional Chinese idealism and romantic individualism, inspired by fantasies of Western-style freedom, that the students brought with them into exile. America finally enabled Chai Ling, Li Lu, and others to do what they had always wanted—to make up their own lives and fulfill their ambitions. But as with many immigrants, their new lives magnified some of the weaknesses of the new world as well as those of the country they had left behind. Idealism merged with self-promotion—that is the American way. An instinct for survival and a tendency toward paranoia—that is a legacy from China. After listening to Chai Ling's boosterism of the American way of life, I told her she was the most Americanized Chinese I had ever met. A flash of fearful anger swept across her face: "You must never say that! I am a survivor. If you say that, people in China will hate me!"

She was right. But some of those people, of an older, more battered generation, were living in America too.

———

Liu Binyan was once the most famous journalist in China. In the 1980s, his magazine and newspaper articles exposing official corruption and abuses of power were read, copied, and passed on by millions. Liu was greeted as a kind of savior when he arrived in this town or that to investigate the latest scandal. People camped out in front of his house in Beijing, hoping he might write about their stories of suffering. There were millions, hundreds of millions, of such stories. Liu only had time for a few.

Liu Binyan was a truly Chinese hero, a loyal Communist who tried to live up to the ideals of the Confucian literati. His aim was to uphold the official dogma—that is, Marxism-Leninism—but to keep it pure from human corruption and restore virtue to the men who ruled in its name. But Liu, like all Chinese men and women who refused to surrender their critical faculties, was punished for speaking his mind. In 1987 he was purged from the Party for "libel and slander" and promoting "bourgeois liberalism." It was the second time in his life that this had happened. During Mao's persecution of critical intellectuals in 1957, Liu was stripped of his job and his Party membership and vilified for being an evil "rightist." His children were turned against him, his wife was forced to denounce him in public, and for years he was made to feed pigs and haul excrement. All this because he had dared to criticize the Party leaders, which showed his "insincere attitude" or, worse, his "independent thinking." He was "rehabilitated" in 1961, but persecuted again, this time with even fiercer cruelty, in 1969. Allowed to rejoin the Party in 1980, he had several years of respite, as a star reporter for the the *People's Daily,* the official Party newspaper.

Liu loved the Party but could not refrain from reporting what he saw: Party bosses lining their pockets and abusing women (sometimes in exchange for scraps of food) while people who protested were tortured and killed. "China," he wrote in his autobiography, *A Higher Kind of Loyalty,* "seemed like a monstrous mill, continually rolling, crushing all individuality out of the Chinese character. Every one of your words and deeds, every aspect of your life, had to conform to the norm. . . . The unseen mill ground on relentlessly, silently, trying to wear out all edges and create a mass of people with the same set, ingratiating expression when facing their rulers. The net result was to make a virtue of hypocrisy. Between superiors and subordinates, in relationships with one's own peers, a superficial atmosphere of good fellowship prevailed, while plots and intrigues went on behind your back. But some people, once installed in power, showed their fangs."

Enough, you might think, to destroy a man's faith in communism forever. But Liu still doesn't blame the dogma. He blames the men who perverted it, the people who were corrupted by power. He, like his tormentors, believes that his enemies are imbued with evil motives. And for saying so, he now lives in the small New Jersey town of Plainsboro.

The prim row of new suburban houses in shades of white and beige bears no sign of history or aesthetic tradition; the homes are neat but look flimsy, as though not built to last long. There was no sign of people in the hushed street, just the odd car passing by. Plainsboro felt like a long way from anywhere. I sat down with Liu in his living room one November afternoon. The decoration was sparse: a Chinese calligraphy on one wall, some green plants, and a wooden table covered in clippings from American newspapers and Chinese émigré journals. Liu sat in the shadow of the wintry sunlight that slanted through the window. A tall man with slow, ponderous movements and a leathery northern-Chinese face crisscrossed with deep grooves, Liu looked like a melancholy bear. Speaking in English and Chinese, he told me what he thought of the student leaders of 1989.

"The thing is," he said, "they knew nothing about history. They thought they were the first democrats in China. But their greatest failing was their personal desire for power." I recalled something Liu had written after the Beijing Massacre. He had critized the students for being "the most selfish generation since 1949." He said they had no idea of sacrificing themselves for a larger cause.

I asked him why he thought this should be so. He said it was the influence of the West on Chinese, which is usually negative: materialism, the sexual revolution, that kind of thing. To live in the dark ages and then to be exposed to Western culture too fast—this can only lead to the worst kind of egotism.

So Liu also suspected the students' sincerity. Yet I knew from his book that his first rebellious feelings had not been so different from those of the younger generation he criticized. Some of the sentences in his autobiography reminded me of what I had heard from Wu'er Kaixi. Born in the freezing northeast of China in 1925, Liu had joined the Communist revolutionaries because he wanted to fight the Japanese invaders who ransacked China in the 1930s as well as poverty and injustice. But he also wanted, he wrote, to "liberate myself, to realize myself. I could not say precisely what this 'self' was, but I had a feeling that there was something in me that, though still undeveloped, would eventually blossom, until one day I would do something special."

Liu loved the traditional Chinese theater and read patriotic Communist stories about workers and peasants who gave their lives to the nation. As a young boy, he was inspired by the heroic example of Yue Fei, a twelfth-century military commander whose self-sacrifice is still celebrated in operas and comic books. Yue Fei was one in a long line of Chinese diehards who would not compromise with barbarians at China's gates, in his case nomads north of the Chinese wall. Before going to war, Yue Fei kneeled before his mother, revealing four characters tattooed on his back: "Serve the country to my utmost."

The difference between Liu and the Tiananmen students is that the Communist Party had provided him with a focus for his faith, patriotic ardor, and loyalty. Communism was the correct way to serve China. Unfortunately, however, Liu's other ambition—to "realize" himself—got in the way. That is what made him a "rightist," a "counterrevolutionary," and a "bourgeois liberal"—not despite himself, but because of it. He wanted to believe, but reality kept challenging his faith, and in the end the Party spurned him. The students who came of age after Mao had no such illusions. They had patriotic feelings but no ideology. And they were young enough when they arrived in America to find personal liberation in exile. By contrast, Liu Binyan has found only disillusion. His world has collapsed. He is stuck in an American suburb, because he was betrayed by his own faith at home.

The room went dark as he spoke of his disappointments. Liu had been excited by the Tiananmen rebellion, and in the summer of 1989, when the last vestiges of legitimacy had been stripped from the men in power by their own murderous actions, he expected the regime to crumble. At last he would return home in triumph, to restore virtue to Chinese politics and save not just his country but the best elements of his Marxist beliefs. It never happened. Perhaps Liu's acrimony toward the "selfish" students is a reflection of his despair. They must take the blame for his dashed hopes. He still writes articles for the émigré press and does talks for Radio Free Asia. The station is jammed in China, but people can sometimes hear it, hissing through the airwaves in the early morning or late at night. Liu's name cannot be mentioned officially in China, so he is deeply moved when he hears that people in China "still remember me, still miss me."

I asked him about the hostility within the Chinese diaspora. Why do people hate each other so? He sighed and remained silent, sifting through the newspaper cuttings on the table, trying to find an article about renewed experiments with people's communes somewhere in central China. He wanted me to see the article, because it showed that Maoism wasn't all bad. There were still things worth saving from the wreckage. The peasants in collective farms may not be free, but they had enough to eat and that was all they really needed. Surely the equality of life under Mao had been a good thing. There had to be a middle way between communism and American-style capitalism. He couldn't find the article, but he came around to answering my question. The splits in the democracy movement were not political, he said. Everyone wanted democracy. No, the fights were personal. Too many people wanted to pursue their own profit and fame.

"I think," he said after another silence, "that a lot of this animosity has to do with Han Chinese culture. For two hundred years we haven't produced a great thinker. We have invented many practical things, but we have no philosophers, unlike Germany. And no novelists, unlike Russia. For a thousand years we Chinese have struggled to survive. So we are incapable of abstract thinking for a higher cause that does not concern our own interests. We Chinese are too complicated, too clever at playing tricks. Confucian culture makes people hypocritical. Poor people still sit in the dark, without electricity, brooding on their resentments and ways of wreaking revenge, which makes them cruel. I think we have inherited our problems. They are in our Chinese blood."

It was something I would hear again and again, from Chinese overseas but also in China—this cultural self-loathing, this despair at being Chinese. Bo Yang, a well-known Taiwanese writer, wrote a famous book, published in the 1980s, about the degeneracy of Chinese culture, *The Ugly Chinaman.* In it, he deplores the fact that Chinese cannot "find a common language and are constantly at each other's throats." He identifies a "neurotic virus" in Chinese culture that makes it impossible for Chinese to admit their mistakes and compromise with others.

I suspect that this kind of disgust is born from disappointed cultural chauvinism. And indeed Bo Yang makes the point that "no other nation on earth has such a long history or such a well-preserved cultural tradition, a tradition which has in the past given rise to an extremely advanced civilization. . . . How is it possible for such a great people to have degenerated to such a state of ugliness? Not only have we been bullied around by foreigners; even worse, for centuries we've been bullied around by our own kind—from tyrannical emperors to despotic officials and ruthless mobs. . . ." Bo Yang was jailed for subversion twice—the first time by the Communist government in his native China, the second time in Taiwan, in 1967, for drawing a cartoon that made fun of General Chiang Kai-shek.

"Such a great people . . ." The implication is that China's political problems could stem only from some cultural catastrophe, a noxious virus infecting Han Chinese blood. But the despair of Bo Yang, or Liu Binyan, is more than a perverse expression of cultural chauvinism; it comes from humiliation, the failure to shake off despotism, the indignity of not being free. For a brief moment in 1989, Chinese all over the world thought the mold would finally break and China would be free. Thus the humiliation of the subsequent failure is blamed on the "radical" student leaders, who were either too "selfish" to sacrifice themselves for China or were typical "ugly Chinamen" who refused to compromise and admit that they had been wrong.

—

It was not long after I met Liu Binyan that I heard a former activist now living in the U.S., Gong Xiaoxia, confess that she didn't really want to be Chinese. She didn't "feel comfortable" with her "own race." She wondered how it was possible to spend five thousand years building a civilization only to destroy it in two generations. She, too, lived in a suburban American house, on a quiet, tree-lined street, outside Washington D.C., the kind of street where friendly neighbors exchange news about their dogs and then politely go their own way. Gong Xiaoxia lives there alone with her large dog. She was recently divorced from her husband, whom she had met at university in Beijing and accompanied to Harvard in the 1980s, where they both studied. Gong, thirty years younger than Liu Binyan and ten years older than Chai Ling, works for Radio Free Asia in Washington, where she produces programs in the Cantonese language.

She was at Harvard when the Tiananmen demonstrations began. Like Liu Binyan, she was thrilled. Anything that challenged the Chinese regime thrilled her. But she was also frightened as she watched the drama unfold on television. Gong had lived in China for thirty-one years and was disturbed by the idea of sudden change. It brought back bad memories of Red Guards smashing everything "old"—temples, books, ideas, people— to make a permanent revolution, and of disappointments after rebellions in which she had played a part. She was only a few years younger than most Red Guards. She knew how destructive students of her own age had been when they were led by their emotions. Gong no longer believed in "quick fixes" for China's problems.

She told me her story in a fluent and salty English, pronounced in the harsh, staccato tones of her native Guangzhou (Canton). She liked to talk, at her house, during elaborate Cantonese meals of steamed fish and lemon chicken or in her small office at Radio Free Asia, but she never attempted to charm her listener in the way that the former student leaders Chai Ling, Li Lu, or Wu'er Kaixi did. Indeed, Chai's ingratiating manners were one thing that filled Gong with loathing. "Always making men feel good, goddamnit. I hate that! Why is she always crying? All that talk about 'We poor children.' Goddamnit, she was a married graduate student, not a child. Every time she tried to get sympathy that way, I wanted to say: 'Goddamnit, stand up for yourself! Don't beg for sympathy.' I hate that way of inviting men's cheap sympathy!" I observed Gong during these tirades— with her short-cropped hair, her stocky frame, her sensible trousers and sturdy shoes that still smacked of an earlier China—and realized that she and Chai, though only ten years apart in age, had grown up in different countries.

Gong Xiaoxia was born into a family of intellectuals who paid the price for their pre-Communist education. During the Cultural Revolution, her grandfather was jailed as a counterrevolutionary, her grandmother went mad, her mother was sent to a remote village, and her father was arrested as a Russian spy (he spoke Russian). But Gong's worst suffering came a few years later, in the early 1970s, after she joined an underground group led by former Red Guards who tried to promote a more democratic form of socialism. She described the reasons she had become involved in this highly dangerous enterprise. They were emotional more than political. In fact, using almost the same words as Chai Ling, she told me they were "anti-political." She said: "We had to engage in politics in daily life. You get so tired of that; good people suffer so much, bad people get ahead. So you get involved in the politics of anti-politics, the politics of idealism." On another occasion, she also said something sadder: "Look at the kind of people who join the democracy movement. They all had miserable childhoods. They join out of desperation. Because there is nothing else for them. They are all crazy."

Gong was a misfit, a bookish girl without many friends. During the Cultural Revolution, when books, looted from "bourgeois" households, could sometimes be picked out of the debris left by marauding Red Guards, she came across Solzhenitsyn's *One Day in the Life of Ivan Denisovich*. She was shocked by the realization that her parents, grandparents, uncles, and aunts were not bad people after all, but victims of political madness. And the notion that Stalin had been responsible for so much suffering terrified her. She was like a child who suddenly realizes she can no longer believe in God. She expected to be punished, or her body to change, or to be struck by lightning. But there was no one to talk to. Despair drove her to attempt suicide.

Gong's state of mute shock lasted until 1974, when she read a sensational manifesto tacked onto a wall in Beijing Road in Guangzhou. The text was highly provocative. The Chinese Revolution, it claimed, had never resulted in a true people's democracy. The masses were deprived of their rights to free speech and association, while "fascist" Party bosses ruled like feudal lords. These incendiary words were signed by an unknown figure named Li Yi Zhe—in fact the collective pen name of four local activists, all of whom were to spend years in jail. Gong joined them in a state of excitement; with them at least she would no longer feel alone. She wanted their "intellectual companionship." With them she could speak her mind. It was as though she had found an island of truth in a society of liars. One of the authors of the proclamation, a former Red Guard leader named Chen Yiyang, became her first lover. Like her, he came from a "bad" class background; his father had been an important figure in Chiang Kai-shek's Kuomintang (KMT).

The inevitable happened. The self-proclaimed democrats were crushed. Chen Yiyang was sentenced to fifteen years in jail (his spirit was broken after two, when he was released). Gong spent her twenty-first birthday in solitary confinement. Later, she would spend years working in a candy factory, where she lost a finger in a faulty machine. But the worst thing was not prison or the drudgery of manual work. It was the humiliation that came with her arrest. Gong's parents, who had been so badly damaged by politics themselves, denounced their daughter in public. Her mother wrote letters to the Party, giving examples of Gong's "bad attitude" and "selfish character." Gong's private letters were confiscated and read out loud in public. Every embarrassing detail of her personal life was put on display. Gong prods her eyes with a tissue as she recalls the torment. She never spoke to her parents again.

No wonder Gong, the veteran of persecutions and several failed attempts at radical change, finds the students of 1989 too soft and "goddamn sentimental." She was in Beijing in 1979, when hopes raised by the Democracy Wall were betrayed by Deng Xiaoping, who cracked down on the young activists he had encouraged at the start. Gong thought the Tiananmen leaders, or at least the most "radical" among them, were not only soft but also reckless. Theirs was the recklessness of criminal naïveté, for they had no idea what they were up against. The Communist government is like "a mad beast." It is folly to provoke it, for it will "tear up your flesh." Repeated failure taught Gong Xiaoxia that you have to "play with the beast," compromise with it, nudge it in the right direction, choose the way of slow reform instead of confrontation. This is something the students, in Gong's view, never understood. Whatever it was they demanded, which was never very clear, their demands grew ever more extreme. Like an irresponsible general, Chai Ling led her troops to the slaughter.

I argued with Gong. Surely, I said, it wasn't fair to compare Chai Ling to a general. No one in Tiananmen Square was under any obligation to follow her orders. Chai Ling never led the Square anyway—the Square led her: The people who were still there on June 3, defying government orders to leave, were mostly provincial students, workers, and others who felt there was nothing to gain from retreat. In any case, I continued, the students' demands were never extreme. All they had ever asked for was freedom of speech and association and to be officially acknowledged as "patriots," after they had been described in a *People's Daily* editorial as "troublemakers." And, in any case, they never resorted to violence.

Yes, said Gong, but Chai should have taken responsibility for her actions. Instead, all she thinks about are her own selfish interests.

So it was back to that again: attitude, sincerity, character.

Unlike Liu Binyan, Gong Xiaoxia doesn't feel trapped or marooned in America. For her, as for Chai Ling, coming to America was a liberation. Gong had always felt like an outsider in China, an "uncontrollable kid," a "bull in a china shop." That is why she loves the United States—she no longer feels like such a misfit. "In China," she said, "we had no principles. We were taught how to cheat and to lie shamelessly. To be dishonest was not a problem. People were rewarded for that. So you disconnect what you say you believe and what you really want. Chinese are not disconnected with reality but with themselves. I got much of that back in America."

We were sitting in her room as she spoke, shoeless in the Chinese manner, our slippered feet on a furry white rug, her great dog padding up to lick his mistress. An enormous television set was on, without sound. It was a program about humanitarian aid agencies being aired. Pictures of famished children and tortured bodies flashed silently across the outsize screen.

Gong had left China behind and yet so much about her, from her sturdy shoes to the anarchic way she drove through traffic, from her Cantonese accent to her moral attitudes, was marked by the first thirty-one years of her life. She was not raised with materialist values, she said. She did not understand such things as career moves and publicity. Listening to her speak about the students of Tiananmen, I often felt that what she disapproved of most was their softer ride in life. They had had it too easy—in China, where they had escaped the worst persecutions, and in the

United States, where, after only a year or two, they managed to adopt the behavior of Americans as though they had been born there.

———

Perhaps Chai Ling cried too much. And yet she is also accused of crying too little. For she wants closure, and personal space, and a career. She does not cry in public for the people who lost their lives in June 1989. And this, her critics say, shows her "insincerity." I do not know whether crying is the most reliable sign of sincerity. It is often thought so in East Asia.

The first time I saw Wang Chaohua, she was crying in a documentary, *Moving the Mountain*, made in 1995, about Tiananmen. It was a facile, celebratory film based largely on Li Lu's memoir of the same title. Amid a great deal of talk by Chai, Li Lu, and Wu'er Kaixi about heroism and democracy, Wang Chaohua was the only one who cried. She felt guilty for the people who were killed. And yet it was Wang who had counseled restraint in 1989.

I met Wang in the library of UCLA, where she was studying Chinese literature. A soft wind blew though the cypress trees outside. Tall, soft-spoken, and nearsighted, Wang was watchful and paused to think before saying anything. Her accent was not as American as that of Chai Ling or Li Lu. Premature lines under her eyes and at the corners of her mouth hinted at hardship. There had been a bad marriage in China and she had had to leave her only child behind, out of reach. Because Wang was older than the other student leaders but younger than most Beijing intellectuals who played a part, she was a misfit in the Tiananmen Movement, hesitant to impose herself; yet she was forceful when she felt she had to be. She was one of the few Chinese I met in America who did not denounce the student leaders. People had unrealistic expectations of Chinese exiles, she said, and it was unfair to lump their subsequent behavior in America together with what had happened in Beijing. Not that she especially liked Chai Ling or Li Lu; she said they were "lacking in principles." But her differences with them were not so much personal or ideological as tactical.

Like many of those who were older than herself, she saw the events from the perspective of earlier rebellions. That is why she had favored a hunger strike at first. She remembered from the Cultural Revolution how effective it could be. But she reconsidered when she came to feel that the students' aims were fuzzy and their timing wrong. Wang was furious when Chai Ling and her male coterie had suddenly announced a hunger strike on May 11. Convinced that there was still room for negotiation with the government, Wang screamed at the hunger strikers: They were just doing this out of desperate bravado, to overcome their feeling of impotence. Chai shouted back that she was a student of psychology and didn't need Wang's psychoanalysis. Wang tried to enlist the help of famous intellectuals, such as the journalist Dai Qing, to make the students stop. Dai Qing, a formidable speaker, came to the Square and told the students that they had already scored a great victory. "The students are good," she said. The students were patriots. But if there were any further provocation (or "noise," as she put it) from the students, they risked setting back political progress for twenty years.

There was, however, another reason for Wang's misgivings. She had learned as a Red Guard that nothing succeeds without a solid organization. Lacking that, a protest movement is bound to collapse. So Wang pleaded with the students to go back to their classrooms and consolidate their gains. They should develop independent student unions and branch out from there. Ten years later, she explained her case patiently to me, ticking off every point on her fingers in the Chinese manner: "One: Without organization, you lack proper procedures and radicalism takes over. Two: You need to be able to speak for a constituency. And the students' constituency was on campus. Without that constituency, you had no base to fight the Communists." Procedures rather than drama, consolidation rather than escalation, organization rather than emotion. Anything rather than repeating the bloody chaos of the Cultural Revolution. But Wang never referred to Chai and the hunger strikers as "Mao's best students." She knew the difference, from her own experience. Red Guards fought blindly for idiotic principles. The students, in her view, were driven by vanity. But their vanity was stoked by intellectuals, who used the students to promote their own political views. *They* were mostly to blame for the consequent disaster, not the students, who were "just kids."

The second time I saw Wang Chaohua, she was standing at a slight distance from a Chinese student demonstration outside the Federal Building in Los Angeles on a gray, humid day, with rain threatening to burst from oyster-colored clouds. It was the middle of May 1999, a week after U.S. bombers hit the Chinese embassy in Belgrade, and precisely ten years after the hunger strike on Tiananmen Square. About a hundred Chinese students were singing against the roar of freeway traffic, small figures in a large, indifferent landscape of parking lots and billboards advertising American affluence. This time it was not the "Internationale" or "Descendants of the Dragon" but the Communist Chinese national anthem. There were placards protesting "NATO barbarism"; there were one or two Americans in worn denim jackets handing out leaflets of a Trotskyite organization, and there were a few Serbs, dressed in suits, smiling at this show of solidarity with the Serbian people. But the Serbian people were not really the point of this demonstration. Chinese patriotism was.

I was offered several theories for the bombing of the embassy. A young woman with moist, angry eyes said the U.S. wanted to "keep China down." I said surely the bombing had been an error and the Chinese government was manipulating public opinion. "The Chinese people are not stupid!" she screamed. "Our feelings of sorrow and indignation are sincere!" But President Clinton had just apologized. "Not sincerely!" shouted various students at the same time. "It's the CIA," opined a young man in a blue jacket. "It's Brzezinski," said another. A pretty woman wearing a black armband said the U.S. was trying to divide China. I asked her what she meant by that. "Washington supports Tibetan independence," she explained. Surely not officially, I said. But what about Taiwan? she countered. The U.S. was splitting Taiwan from the motherland! When I observed how close all this rhetoric was to that of the government in Beijing, I was told that this time the Chinese government was on the side of the people: It was allowing the people to show their true feelings.

But these "true feelings" were volatile, swinging from xenophobia to hostility against the Chinese government and back to xenophobia again. Some of the same people standing in front of the Federal Building in Los Angeles had been demonstrating in Tiananmen Square ten years before, demanding to be recognized as patriots. The Chinese government *had* to protest the U.S. bombing. Otherwise the students might easily have turned their outrage on the government itself—for allowing foreigners to humiliate China. When it comes to patriotism, it is never quite clear who is manipulating whom. Only one demand remains constant, whether it comes from patriotic students, intellectuals, or their Communist rulers—the demand for a show of sincerity.

Wang Chaohua was standing quietly on the grass beside the freeway, watching the scene through her thick glasses. I was eager to know what she made of this melancholy affair. She was her usual skeptical self. She believed that the students in China were set up against the foreigners just as the Boxers had been by the Qing government in the 1890s. On the other hand, she thought the bombing surely couldn't have been an accident. There had to be more to it. And besides, she was against using force against force, so the bombing had to be condemned. I disagreed, and told her so. But later that evening I began to understand the source of Wang's deliberate caution and her horror of violence. She had not yet told me the whole story of her life.

Wang was fourteen, a pupil at one of the best schools in Beijing, when the Cultural Revolution began in 1966. Few of her classmates came from a proletarian background. Wang's father was a famous professor of Chinese literature at Beijing University. Naturally, as soon as Mao unleashed the young against their elders, Wang's father was "struggled against" and denounced as a "stinking reactionary." He was beaten and made to kneel while his arms were yanked behind him in an excruciating posture known as the airplane. He was spat on and humiliated for days. Wang's elder brother led a raid on his own father's house with other Red Guards, but then took pity and tried to protect him. But Chaohua, a rebellious teenager, did not. Her rebellion was blessed by Chairman Mao himself. This chance was too good to miss. So while her father was bent over a ping-pong table, she stood there, at the head of a baying mob, screaming examples of his oppressive and reactionary attitudes. For six years she disowned her father, as though he were a piece of dirt staining the revolutionary credentials of his family. She was blinded by "the Red Guard mentality." Later she tried to apologize to him, but her father waved her away. It was all right, he said; she was "just a kid"—the same words she had used about the Tiananmen student leaders.

We were sitting in a Chinese restaurant in Santa Monica when Wang

Chaohua told me this part of her story. After she had finished, she stared silently at the fried squid on her plate, fidgeting with her plastic chopsticks. I remembered the documentary in which I had first seen her face. This was the second time I saw her eyes filled with tears.

———

"What is a dissident?" Dai Qing, the journalist who had pleaded with the students to retreat in 1989, often asked me this, and then she would add, with a mocking smile: "Do you think I'm a dissident?"

I would usually meet Dai Qing in a café on 16th Street, near Dupont Circle, in Washington D.C. We were colleagues at the same research institute. Not that Dai Qing was an exile or a refugee—far from it. She was proud to remain based in Beijing, and, like me, was in Washington only for a year. She rather despised those Chinese who had left China to carry on their dissident activities from New York, Cambridge, or Washington. She thought they were out of touch, too far removed from the cultural hearth. To be away from China was to go soggy, become irrelevant.

Dai Qing has strong opinions. But is she a dissident?

She had certainly annoyed the government enough to be arrested after the Beijing Massacre (for "bourgeois liberalization") and kept in prison for a year. She resigned her Party membership just after the massacre—not, she was quick to point out, as "an anti-Party act" but to distance herself from politics altogether. She had been loyal to the Party, in her own way; but, as with Liu Binyan, her public criticisms of government policies marked her as someone with an independent mind. So the students hated her for trying to muzzle their protests, and the government hated her for being a critic. After her year in jail, which had been relatively comfortable, compared to the treatment of more hard-core dissidents, she was allowed to travel abroad, give interviews to foreign journalists, take up fellowships, and receive foreign prizes, but nothing she wrote could be published in mainland China. Hers was a confusing status, restricted as well as privileged. But then, in a way, it always had been, and Dai Qing was convinced that neither I nor any other foreigner could ever understand China. It was much "too complicated."

And yet time and again she tried to explain what was wrong with

China, with the government, and with the "radical" students, who had, by their "extreme" behavior, made things so much worse than they had been before 1989. She would make a fist of her right hand and smash it into the palm of her left hand, like a boxer. This, she said, is the Chinese mentality, this eternal desire to have all or nothing, this refusal to compromise, this thirst for confrontation, the tendency to do or die. And this is why she blamed Chai Ling and Li Lu, and all the other "extremists," for provoking the bloody debacle on June 4. They had no idea what democracy was. Once more, the fist came crashing into the palm of her hand. Chai Ling "doesn't understand compromise through negotiation. She thinks that compromise is like being a traitor. That is a Maoist mentality." Dai Qing was convinced that the student radicals and the Communist extremists shared similar goals: The students wanted power through revolution.

I watched Dai at the café. She looked out of place in this gay enclave of Washington, a short Chinese woman in her fifties, dressed in sensible Beijing clothes. Her large, curious eyes, set above a small, flat nose, took in the male couples in tight shirts and skimpy shorts walking by with their pet dogs, chattering in the overloud manner of Americans at leisure. She looked amused and utterly detached, like a person gazing at animals in the zoo. America didn't really matter. Although she was physically present in Washington, D.C., her mind was always in Beijing.

Since the early 1980s, Dai Qing had been a reporter for *Guangming Daily,* a Beijing paper favored by intellectuals. She had agreed to work there as long as she did not have to write about government meetings, which bored her. Instead, she would travel and write about what she saw. And what she saw was often not pretty: forest fires run out of control because of official incompetence; demoralized Chinese soldiers from the Sino-Vietnamese war in 1978; shoddy, potentially catastrophic plans to build the gigantic Three Gorges dam on the Yangtze River; and so on. She was brave to write about these things. But it took even greater bravery to dig up, as she did, the histories of early Communists who had fallen foul of the Party and were consequently deleted from history, as though they had never existed. These "historical investigations" made her famous all over China. Her story of Wang Shiwei, a Communist intellectual who dared to criticize the abuses and hypocrisies of Communist leaders before the revolution and was purged, denounced, and finally executed in 1947, caused a sensation. But then, as Dai Qing once said, when all is darkness, the smallest ray of light will cause a sensation.

Dai Qing is a proponent of free speech. This alone makes her a rebel in China. But it does not necessarily make her a democrat. Democracy is of course a much abused concept. Most people say they are in favor of it. Dai Qing, too, claims to want a democracy in China, as do many so-called liberals and reformers inside the Communist Party, but only after a slow process of educating the people, building a "civil society," developing a middle class, all of which will take many years, perhaps as much as a century. Meanwhile, it is best to maintain a regime of benevolent authoritarianism, lest people lose control and bring about violent disorder. Democracy, for Dai and reformers like her, one feels, is a bit like the final dissolution of the state in Marxist utopianism: a fine but distant ideal. China is too big, they say, and the Chinese are too poor. And there are too many of them. Chinese history is too ancient and too complicated for democracy to take root.

The effect of Tiananmen, in Dai Qing's opinion, was to make China's authoritarianism less benevolent. Conveniently provoked by the student extremists, government hard-liners carried out a purge of reformers and liberals. Dai had seen it coming. Indeed, she thought the hard-liners had been manipulating the students to their own nefarious ends all along. That, she says, is why she had wanted the students to stop their provocations. But there was another, perhaps more important, reason for her advocacy of retreat. She put it very clearly in an account of her year in prison: ". . . I feel that revolution—that is, overthrowing a system— is far more frightening than maintaining the present political order, and the damage a revolution would cause to China would be far greater. It is for this reason that from 28 April I advised the students to go back to class. . . ."

Moderation at all costs, avoid any disorder: This is part of a Confucian tradition as much as utopianism—perhaps more so. Extremism in Chinese history is rooted more in folk religions and millenarian rebellions than in the Confucian search for the golden mean. But the problem with moderation at all costs is that it is of limited use if you wish to get rid of a despotic system of government. It can become a form of tortured appeasement.

One night, Dai and I were having dinner at Gong Xiaoxia's house. The news was bad that day. There had been a crackdown on a newly formed political party in China, the so-called China Democracy Party. Several men, who had not advocated violence or revolution but had simply insisted on the constitutional right to free association, were given jail sentences of more than ten years. I asked Dai what she thought of this and was astonished by her reply. It was a very good thing, she stated with an air of supreme confidence, for this way the mistakes of 1989 wouldn't be repeated. This time there would be no extremism, and that would enable reformist policies to proceed. I could not decide whether she was being harsh or simply naïve. Yet naïveté is the last thing I would have suspected. Her background, complicated even for such a complicated society as China, certainly suggests otherwise.

Dai Qing's parents were early Communist intellectuals, and joined the Party in the 1920s. Both were arrested by the Japanese during the war; her mother was released, her father executed. To make life easier for her mother, Dai Qing was adopted by Marshal Ye Jianying, one of the major figures in modern Chinese history, the man who "liberated" Beijing after winning the civil war. As the adopted daughter of one of China's "Ten Great Marshals," Dai entered the highest aristocracy of Chinese communism. She can still remember seeing Chairman Mao push young girls up and down the dance floor, his big feet stomping like a soldier's on parade. She had become one of the chosen few.

Trained as an engineer in the 1960s, Dai worked on intercontinental ballistic missiles before joining the Cultural Revolution as a Red Guard. Her mother was denounced as a traitor, and tortured horribly in struggle sessions. Dai was still full of revolutionary zeal, but seeing her mother's suffering led to a bizarre kind of revelation, rather like Gong Xiaoxia's reading Solzhenitsyn. When her mother was tortured, no one offered any help, even when she was half dead. No one cared, or dared. No one, that is, except for one man, a class enemy, a nonperson, denounced and struggled against himself; he was the only person to offer her comfort. It dawned on

Dai for the first time in her life that "class enemies" could be decent human beings.

In the 1970s, Dai worked on surveillance equipment for the Ministry of Public Security. She became an expert in hidden television cameras. After she secured a job in military intelligence, she also began to write. She joined the Chinese Writers Association and was instructed by her bosses to make contact with foreign, mostly Eastern European, writers and spy on them. This is how she met the American reporter Studs Terkel. She liked his interviewing technique. But her cover was blown in 1982, when a list of spies found its way to the CIA. Dai left the Writers Association, as well as the army, and became a reporter. This suited her. Adopted by the elite, Dai always felt she was something of an outsider, connected to the highest circles and trusted by no one. Now she would be a kind of oral historian, like Studs Turkel, of Communist China. She would try to be independent, without ever quite leaving the fold.

Dai describes herself as a "liberal." Her heroes in history are those who dared to criticize their rulers and paid the price. Chinese history is full of such heroes. The Cultural Revolution was set off by the performance of a play featuring Hai Rui, a noble minister in the Ming dynasty, who lost his position because he presumed to criticize the emperor. Parallels were drawn between Hai Rui and critics of Chairman Mao, and Mao, with his keen sense of history, spotted the danger. The playwright, Wu Han, was denounced and later bullied to death in 1969. This happened soon after Dai Qing, as a Red Guard, wrote an essay about her ardent wish for a science that would enable all young people to transfer their youth to Chairman Mao to give him a longer life. It was perhaps an unconscious variation of Taoist beliefs—held by the Chairman himself—that frequent sex with very young girls adds years to the life of an old man.

I asked Dai what she meant by the word "liberal." She laughed, thought about it for a bit, and then carefully formulated an answer. A liberal, she said, is a person who thinks independently and values free speech more highly than anything else.

In this sense, Dai Qing might be called a liberal, but she also fits an older, more traditional Chinese model: the virtuous Confucian scholar who offers critical advice to his rulers. It can be a noble model, but is almost always a conservative one. The common people are treated with benevolence but are considered too unruly to be trusted to participate in the way the state is governed. This is a caricature, to be sure, but one that fits the period leading up to 1989, the decade of reform, when "liberal" intellectuals, who had been through thirty years of murderous persecution, were at last reinstated by Deng Xiaoping into something resembling their traditional role as advisers, or scholar-officials, contemplating the future of China in think tanks, university seminars, and semi-independent study groups. Their patrons were the reformist Party leaders, first Hu Yaobang, then Zhao Ziyang. They were given back their dignity, their status, even a degree of independence, as long as they did not presume to challenge the political order. It was an ideal period for an intellectual who liked to be at the center of things, patronized and protected by Party leaders, and a critical outsider as well. Ideal, but in the end untenable; you cannot be protected and independent at the same time.

The relatively benevolent though hardly democratic rule of reformist leaders gave "liberal" intellectuals the illusion that incremental change might work, that the Communist Party would gradually open up and reform itself, that intellectual freedom could coexist with benevolent authoritarianism—the word used by General-Secretary Zhao Ziyang was "neo-authoritarianism." You could, in Gong Xiaoxia's words, "play with the beast" and use the Party leaders to change China, but it was a game that exacted murky and illiberal compromises. This is how Dai Qing described it in a speech she made in 1988, to commemorate the men who had tried to change China ninety years before, through political reforms: "You have to negotiate with them, make allies, compromise, make concessions, and even be prepared to sell out your principles for a good bargain. . . ."

The reform movement of 1898, from which Dai Qing drew historical lessons, confronted a situation not unlike China in the 1980s. A corrupt regime was hanging on to power. Nationalism, both anti-foreign (the Qing were Manchus) and anti-government, was rampant. Almost everyone wanted China to change. But how? Some advocated outright revolution. Others urged moderation. But the reformers, as always, were divided: Some rallied around the young "reformist" emperor to instigate radical political changes from the top; others, known as the "self-strengtheners," talked about invigorating China through educational and economic reforms. The young emperor did his best, but his reforms came to nothing. His mother, the ferocious empress-dowager, took power away from him. The self-strengtheners criticized the more radical reformers for being extreme. Some "extremists" were executed, some fled the country. The conservatives around the empress-dowager had won.

It was not the self-strengtheners, however, whom Dai Qing had come to praise in her speech but the radical political reformers. Why? Because they were right, in her view, to seek the patronage of the emperor. She contrasted their wisdom with the recklessness of the revolutionaries. Her point was that benevolent dictatorship should work. Why then did the reformers fail? They failed, she said, because the emperor was too impatient; he should have waited before introducing the reforms, bided his time. She made these points before the Tiananmen demonstrations began. But her basic ideas were the same: Reformers and liberals were on the right track; together with the "young emperor" Zhao Ziyang, they would have succeeded by biding their time. Then the student "revolutionaries" ruined everything. The "empress-dowager" Deng Xiaoping was guilty of murder. But Chai Ling and her allies wrecked the reforms. That is what Zhao Ziyang came to tell them, with tears in his eyes, on the Square on May 19, 1989: "It's too late," he said, "too late." If only they had been more patient, bided their time . . .

And yet the students of Tiananmen were not violent revolutionaries. This is an imaginary role foisted on them for the sake of making up a historical narrative, a neat story of moderates and extremists, radicals and compromisers. It is too pat. To gain a better perspective on the *Rashomon* of Tiananmen it might actually help to forget for a moment about China and its long history. For in a curious way, the interpretations of Tiananmen echo a debate in England more than two centuries ago between John Locke and David Hume: Locke believed that new institutions and new political contracts could set people free, as it were, overnight, while Hume argued that historical arrangements had to be respected and that a bad established order was still better than unpredictable change.

But China being China, such political debates swiftly take a personal turn, and revolve around sincerity, character, and motives. And that is why I found myself, at a café on 16th Street, discussing with Dai Qing not Hume or Locke or the future of democracy in China but gossip that had trickled through the émigré grapevine, such as the absurdity of Chai Ling's pet dog, the fur coat of a political rock star's wife, and the opportunism of Li Lu's finances.

Chapter 2

Waiting for the Messiah

The Chinese Protestant church in Glendale, California, might not seem an obvious place to meet a dissident writer. But I had been troubled by a cliché that kept popping up in conversations about China: the "spiritual vacuum." Again and again, this alleged vacuum was blamed for China's current ills. The Chinese, I was told, were in dire need of religion. Li Lu mentioned it at length in his Madison Avenue office. And so did many other Chinese, as well as foreign experts (who often reflect the views of their favorite sources). Some were a surprise. I met a young veteran of Tiananmen, Richard Li, who was using the Internet to promote Chinese democracy from Washington, D.C. His inspiration had come from reading books about the "new age of global communication" by the futurist John Naisbitt. Li, a cool computer nerd and former Wall Street broker— and hardly a religious crank—explained to me one day that the Chinese could not love one another. The Chinese, he said, lacked a religion that teaches love. The Chinese needed Jesus.

The man in Glendale, California, was named Yuan Zhiming. Yuan was a moderately well-known writer in China and had become sufficiently in-volved in Tiananmen to be forced to flee in 1989. He had written parts of *River Elegy,* a polemical television documentary series broadcast in 1988, a kind of lament for everything that appeared to the authors to have gone wrong with Chinese civilization. There were strong hints in the film that the Communist leaders were as hidebound, dictatorial, and conservative as the semi-divine emperors who had ruled China in the past. The six-part series caused a sensation when it was broadcast. Zhao Ziyang and his fac-tion of reformist intellectuals supported it, but conservatives—that is to say, Party hard-liners in China and Chinese traditionalists overseas—hated it. China's vice president, an army man and Long March veteran named Wang Zhen, also known as "Big Cannon," attacked the film-makers for not "loving China." Big Cannon was proud of never having read a book and was also a strong advocate of violence to put down the student demonstrations. After June 4, 1989, *River Elegy* was denounced as an evil influence on "correct thinking" and partly blamed for the "tur-moil" in Tiananmen Square.

Ten years later, Yuan Zhiming was traveling around America preach-ing the Christian gospel. His aim, he said, was to convert every Chinese to the Christian faith. His message was that China could be saved only in the arms of Jesus. I found Yuan's telephone number and made an appoint-ment to see him at his local church on Broadway, in Glendale.

The church itself was a newish, dull-brick building on a street half an hour's drive from downtown L.A.—not quite louche enough to be Ray-mond Chandler territory, more shabbily genteel. Next to the church was a kindergarten, where Chinese families were finishing their evening meal at a long wooden table. People smiled at me in that beatific way of religious converts. I asked for Yuan and was pointed toward another room. There was no sign of him, but there were others in this sober room with bare white walls, waiting to see a video about Yuan Zhiming's life.

I sat down. Before the show began, a jaunty young minister from Hong Kong, dressed in an open-collared shirt and brown slacks, led the congre-gation in some Chinese hymns, which contained such phrases as "My Lord, my only Lord . . . bless China, and the Gospel in China." He then gave a short sermon about the need to love China, almost as though China were as much the object of worship as our Lord. New members were invited to stand up and introduce themselves and tell us where they were from. Most were from different parts of mainland China: Shanghai, Hunan, Fujian. A few smiled; some looked absolutely miserable. A woman next to me whispered that the congregation used to be mainly Taiwanese but that most recent converts were young mainlanders.

The room went dark, and the video came to life with images of Tiananmen Square—not, however, of the demonstrations in April or the hunger strike in May, but only of the bloody denouement on June 4. The stress, clearly, was on the sacrifice of the innocents. Yuan had been in the Square until June 3, we were told, after which he escaped to Paris. There were shots of Paris, of pigeons fluttering around the Sacré-Coeur. Feeling rejected by his motherland, Yuan went into a deep depression. Images of the massacre haunted him (and kept recurring in the video). Every time the face of Premier Li Peng, the man most people blame for the massacre, appeared on the screen, the audience hissed. Yuan was troubled by his personal life, too. Close-ups of his eyes filled with tears made him look like a *mater dolorosa.*

Yuan's marriage in Beijing had turned bad. There had been violence in the home. Yuan had a brutal temper. But he couldn't bear to be alone in the U.S. He missed his wife. Depression turned into despair until one day he met Chinese Christians, who invited him to "bear witness" and "receive Christ." Despair lifted. Yuan prayed for his family to join him in exile. A miracle happened; his prayers were answered. But the marital problems continued. His wife refused to receive Christ, because, as she put it, reasonably I thought, she had come to America to be free and not to replace one kind of prison with another. There were shots of Yuan praying alone, on his knees, for the salvation of his wife. Again, a miracle. She joined the church, first to learn English and make friends, but then to bear witness, with tears streaming down her face. The marriage was saved. An unctuous Chinese minister in a blue blazer informed us that all Chinese were waiting to be awakened by the Lord. In the last shot, Yuan stood on the Great Wall, during a recent trip to China, gazing blissfully into the horizon, saying: "Where there is God there is freedom."

The lights came on, and there was Yuan himself, beaming behind a pulpit, in a gray tweed jacket, a sleek, handsome man in his late forties with plump red lips, the type of genial vicar female parishioners like to ply with cakes. He talked about China. On his recent trip, he had felt an even greater love for his country than before. But he could not fail to notice the "spiritual vacuum" in the Chinese people, the emptiness in their hearts. He saw the bitterness and hatred that consumed them. This terrible situation could be remedied only by faith in God, for God loves us all equally, and only God would save China. Many of us, he continued, wanted to change China politically, but there was a more pressing task ahead: China had to be changed spiritually, by spreading the word of God.

I was fascinated to know what possessed a dissident Chinese writer to take this particular turn. Indeed, Yuan was not the only one. Of the five authors of *River Elegy*, four had fled to the United States and two became evangelical Christians. One had been sorely tempted, and only one remained staunchly immune to the blandishments of the church. Then there was Zhang Boli, one of the student leaders on Tiananmen, who worshipped at the same church as Yuan Zhiming. And Han Dongfang, who had spoken for the workers in Tiananmen Square. He too had "received Jesus." Chinese friends whom I asked about these conversions cast the usual cynical aspersions on the motives of the converts: They didn't really believe in any of this stuff but were acting out of self-interest; they wanted to get money from the Americans; they wanted power, they were "rice Christians"; the Chinese people were so complicated and double-faced; and so on. I couldn't believe things were quite that simple. There are, after all, tens of millions of Christians in China, in the official Party-sanctioned churches, and many more in clandestine, private "house churches."

—

The last time a serious attempt was made to convert the Chinese people to the Christian God—by native Chinese rather than by foreign missionaries—was in the 1850s. It was a bad time in Chinese history. China had been defeated in the Opium War. The Manchu rulers were hated for being oppressive, corrupt, decadent, and foreign. Time was ripe for another millenarian rebellion. It began after Hong Xiuquan, a failed Confucian scholar, became deliriously ill and saw visions of God and Jesus

Christ. Hong was convinced that he was Jesus' younger brother, enlisted in the war against Satan. Satan was a foreigner oppressing China from the Manchu throne. Hong's aim was to establish the Heavenly Kingdom on earth. The name of his movement was Taiping, or Great Peace. The capital of the Heavenly Kingdom was Nanjing, which the Taipings captured in 1853.

Heaven on earth turned out to be a rather harsh mishmash of Chinese and quasi-Christian traditions. Hong was to be known as Heavenly King, or Lord of Ten Thousand Years, and took on many of the trappings of a Chinese emperor. But there was a streak of egalitarianism in the kingdom, too: Women were told to unbind their feet and were appointed as officers and administrators. Even though the younger brother of Jesus had many concubines, known as princesses, the men of his realm were separated from the women, and those who broke the rules of chastity were clubbed to death with heavy poles. Private property was more or less abolished and replaced by a communal system of ownership. And to make sure people were not confused by incorrect or impure thoughts, Buddhist, Taoist, and Confucian temples and symbols were destroyed. God voiced his approval of these measures in poems handed down through Jesus in fine classical Chinese.

Heaven on earth lasted until 1864. By the beginning of that year, Heavenly troops were being slaughtered by the Qing imperial army all over southern China and the Heavenly Capital was under siege. Food had run out, but Hong told his starving people not to worry, for God would provide manna from Heaven. No one was quite sure what manna was. In any case, it failed to fall from the skies and the Heavenly King himself fell ill and died or, in the Taiping version, ascended to Heaven to join his elder brother. Countless others died as well, their rotting, emaciated corpses covered by a thin layer of earth to ease the passage of their souls to Heaven. Imperial soldiers dug tunnels under the city walls, and hideous underground battles ensued, with soldiers on both sides drowning in sewage or blown up by cannon balls thudding through the dark. By the time the capital had fallen and the Taiping armies were finally defeated, millions of people had died as a consequence of Hong's holy visions.

Karl Marx had followed the Taiping rebellion with a sympathetic eye from London, seeing it as a gathering of dissident forces "in one formidable revolution." And there are parallels to be found in Mao's vision of an egalitarian, puritanical, communitarian utopia. Like Hong, Mao merged Chinese and foreign dreams with bewildering and fatal results. Maoism, too, reflected an ancient Chinese tradition of millenarian movements.

Popular rebellions were no doubt the result of economic hardship, political oppression, corruption of local officials, and the like. But the role played by religion is important. Many uprisings were challenges to the rulers' legimitacy, which is closely linked to religion. The Middle Kingdom was traditionally seen as the center of a cosmological order, and the Chinese emperors were at the apex of this order. Their rule had to be blessed by Heaven. Without this divine mandate, they would fall. The mandate fell only to the virtuous, as defined in Confucian ethics. The scholar-officials were the clergy, who cultivated virtue in themselves and their rulers. They interpreted the dogmas upon which the order under Heaven depended. Any moral challenges from heterodox traditions outside the Confucian mainstream were thus a danger to the regime.

People who joined the folk rebellions were often social misfits and outsiders, indeed they were often men who had failed to make it into the ranks of the scholar-officials. Hong was such a man. Like many of his followers, he was from the community of Hakkas, literally "guest people," who still speak their own language and have their own cuisine and whose ancestors migrated from central China to the south many centuries ago. Hong's plan, like that of other religious rebels, was not just to take power away from the ruling dynasty but to replace one cosmic order with another, by installing an alternative Kingdom of Heaven, and restore virtue to a corrupt world. Attempts such as Hong's—and Mao's—usually end up as distorted replicas of the very thing they seek to destroy. Hence Hong, and indeed Mao, began to behave more and more like a traditional Chinese emperor as his empire grew in power and size.

The makers of the television series *River Elegy* could not have been further removed from the peasant fanatics, oddball mystics, and religious rebels of the alternative Chinese tradition. Or so one might think. They were successful, rather high-minded Beijing intellectuals, who enjoyed excellent relations with the reformists in the Communist Party, including the Party secretary, Zhao Ziyang. The original idea for the film was not even controversial. In 1985, a young television director named Xia Jun was asked to make a documentary about the Yellow River, one of the magnificent, eternal symbols of Chinese civilization, along with the dragon and the Great Wall. But when he began to film the actual river, he was shocked by the misery and poverty he encountered. Magnificent as the idealized Yellow River might have been as a symbol, the ugly reality could not be ignored. And so, out of sheer disgust, the idea was born to use the symbols of China to launch an attack on the actual state of the nation. Since China in the 1980s was going through a fashionable wave of cultural self-criticism, the timing was right.

In one episode, the Great Wall is attacked as a symbol of China's inward-looking, closed, authoritarian xenophobia. "Ah, Great Wall," the narrator cries, "why do we still sing your praises? How could Chinese trade freely behind the walls, trapped in their agricultural society?"

In another episode, the dragon is portrayed as a token of power worship and totalitarian failure. And the Yellow River itself is associated with a sluggish, unchanging history, interrupted only by ghastly convulsions. These symbols—yellow as the earth of China's heartland, isolated, agricultural, conservative—are contrasted to an idealized vision of the enlightened West: ocean-blue, seafaring, mercantile, and free. Images of stagnant China and the rampant West—toiling peasants and ancient monuments on the one side, skyscrapers, ports, and stock exchanges on the other—are spliced together by a narrator's voice, which manages, in the Chinese Communist tradition, to be histrionic and didactic at the same time: "Oh, you heirs of the dragon, what the Yellow River could give us has already been given to our ancestors. . . . What we need to create now is a brand-new civilization. . . ."

And then come the intellectuals. We see, among others, Zheng Yi, a writer who encouraged the students to go on a hunger strike in 1989, dressed in a modish black suit, a cigarette smoldering in his right hand, discussing the relationship between earth and man. But most revealing of the *River Elegy* authors' view of themselves is the text written by Yuan Zhiming, together with another writer now living in America, Xie Xuanjun. Intellectuals, they claimed, had found it hard to "consolidate their economic interests or hold independent political opinions; for thousands of years they have been no more than appendages. . . . Their talents have been manipulated, their wills twisted, their souls castrated, their backbones bent. They have even been murdered. Nonetheless, they hold in their hands the weapon that can destroy ignorance and superstition, for they are the ones who can communicate directly with the civilization of the sea, who can irrigate the yellow earth with the blue waters of the spring of science and democracy."

River Elegy, then, is a battle cry for intellectuals to heal China's ills with their enlightened Western ideas. Every educated Chinese recognizes the phrase "science and democracy." It formed the slogan of the May Fourth Movement of 1919, which began with a patriotic student demonstration at Tiananmen (not yet the monstrously large square it is today) against Chinese territorial concessions made to Japan at the Versailles Treaty negotiations. This became a wider cultural rebellion, not unlike the cultural self-criticism of the 1980s, which called for a remake of Chinese society along scientific, democratic, Western lines. In the 1920s, the great writer Lu Xun denounced the Confucian tradition in masterful essays dripping with cultural despair. (Later, Liu Binyan and Bo Yang followed his example, though with less literary finesse.) Western ideas, often filtered through Japan, were all the rage. George Bernard Shaw came to China in the 1920s and found a receptive audience for his arguments in favor of state socialism. John Dewey spent three years in China and influenced such thinkers as Hu Shih with his pragmatic liberalism. The socialist Chen Duxiu coined the phrase "Mr. Science and Mr. Democracy," and argued that "only these two gentlemen can cure the dark maladies in Chinese politics, morality, learning, and thought." Chen went on to found the Chinese Communist Party but was later brushed out of the history books and vilified as a "Trotskyite" when Mao took "scientific socialism" to far greater extremes.

Confidence in the traditional cosmic order had already begun to show cracks in the nineteenth century, when Western military and technical prowess made China look hopelessly backward. But the sense of crisis in the late Qing era arose from more than technological inadequacy; it was also the result of moral, philosophical—indeed spiritual—despair. Some scholar-officials reacted by advocating extreme conservatism: The Confucian empire had to be sealed off at all costs from foreign contamination (or "spiritual pollution," as Deng Xiaoping would call it a century later). Peasant rebels, on the other hand, reacted by joining cults. And some intellectuals, excited by new ideas from Europe, the United States, and Japan, wanted to dismantle the old order altogether. What all these factions had in common was a holistic attitude to statecraft. Politics, morality, religion, and philosophy were part of the same package, called China. This is what lies behind the radicalism described by the journalist Dai Qing. When all under heaven becomes unstable, there can be no middle ground between iconoclasm or xenophobic isolationism, between building ever higher walls or total destruction.

The makers of *River Elegy* often described themselves as the heirs of the May Fourth spirit—as did the students in Tiananmen Square, all of whom had seen and been excited by the television series. A scholarly adviser to the series, Jin Guantao, told me in Hong Kong that the film was part of China's "second wave of enlightenment." When I mentioned Yuan Zhiming's views on Christianity, Jin reacted vehemently. Christianity was part of the Chinese folk tradition, he said, the "small tradition." *River Elegy* was proposing something quite different. And yet, I think, the leap for Yuan Zhiming from advocating science and democracy to becoming a Christian evangelist was not as great as it might seem, for *River Elegy*, in Jin's words, called "for no less than a spiritual rebirth."

———

I called on Yuan Zhiming at his house in Torrance, not so very far from the church in Glendale. It was a bungalow on a cluttered palm tree–lined street. The houses had seen better days. Paintwork had faded, walls were cracked. Bruised cars were parked in the driveways, some with spare parts strewn carelessly around them. It was a warm spring day. Yuan's cramped living room was still decorated with a lonely Christmas tree. Tacked on the wall were strips of red paper, with Chinese homilies about the importance of sincerity and faith.

Yuan said he had often been plagued by doubts. He began to read Karl Marx after the Cultural Revolution, when he was in the army. The world described by Marx did not correspond to the world Yuan knew. It was the same story I had heard from others who had challenged the official orthodoxy: The gulf between what people could see with their own eyes and the idealized version of reality they were told to believe in became intolerable. After his army service, Yuan studied philosophy in Beijing. When he wrote the text for *River Elegy,* he was an active booster of Zhao Ziyang's policies of freeing the Chinese economy to allow a certain degree of capitalist enterprise.

But what about Zhao's political views? Yuan studied his delicate hands, folded them carefully in his lap, one on top of the other, as though they were a pair of soft white gloves, and answered indirectly. He listed four types of Chinese reformers. Some like the Western lifestyle, he said, but not the system. Some like the economic system but not the politics. Ah, I thought, Zhao Ziyang. Some, he went on, like everything about the West except religion. And some embrace everything, including religion. He himself was of the last persuasion. I thought of the most extreme proponents in the nineteenth and twentieth centuries of westernizing reforms in China, and also Japan, some of whom had advocated abolishing the Chinese or Japanese languages and replacing them with English. Unlike the Tiananmen students of 1989, however, Yuan does not speak much English.

"That is why," Yuan continued, "*River Elegy* was fundamentally superficial. It left out the most important thing, the core of Western civilization, which is Christianity. Without that, you cannot have democracy or human rights. We Chinese studied Western economics and politics but not the deepest thing of all, the Western faith."

I could not presume to know how "sincerely" Yuan believed in Christianity. But listening to him, in his house in Torrance, California, I felt that he was not so very far removed, in manner or thought, from the Confucian tradition that his enlightened, democratic, scientific movement was meant to rebel against. If his Christianity had simply been a personal matter, that would have been one thing. But the desire to convert the entire Chinese people was troubling, for Yuan had discovered a new dogma, a new correct way of thinking to impart to the ignorant masses. That was his way of saving China.

If so, it is an odd paradox, for the main appeal of Christianity, over the last hundred years or so, to many Chinese, Koreans, Vietnamese, and Japanese, is that it provided an egalitarian challenge to the Confucian tradition. It promised to break the hierarchies that dominated East Asian societies. Christian activists like to think that universal and unconditional love are essential to the establishment of democratic freedom. That is why rebellions against dictatorships have often been initiated and led by Christians. Sun Yat-sen, the father of China's republican revolution in 1911, was a Christian convert who believed, as he put it in a speech in 1912, that "the essence" of the revolution "could be found largely in the teachings of the church." The role of the church in the former Soviet empire as a refuge for anti-Communist dissidents hardly needs to be pointed out; it was the one alternative dogma left to challenge the official one. The trouble is that when messianic Christianity is harnessed to political rebellion, it can easily end up replacing one form of oppression with another. The Christian authors of *River Elegy* have not reached that stage. They lack the power. And in fact their zeal, like so much Chinese idealism, is a form of anti-politics. It is more an expression of their despair about politics.

—

The Sheraton Hotel coffee shop in Flushing, Queens, is possibly the only public place in North America where everyone still smokes. There was a blue haze swirling about the place as I walked in to meet one of Yuan Zhiming's co-authors on *River Elegy*, Xie Xuanjun. Xie lives in Flushing, New York City's other Chinatown. While the old one, in downtown Manhattan, retains some of the fetid atmosphere of Kowloon sweatshops, Flushing looks more like a raffish part of Taipei. The smokers in the Sheraton's coffee shop, nursing colorful soft drinks, were mostly young Taiwanese, the men dressed in silky Italian jackets and the women in leather miniskirts. A strong smell of perfume mingled with the cigarette smoke. And the Muzak was unmistakably East Asian—sugary and loud.

Xie is a pale, thin man with the sad eyes of a dog that has had one too many beatings. Like Yuan, he does not speak much English. He makes a living writing articles about economics for the press in Taiwan. His road to Christianity was longer than Yuan's.

Xie Xuanjun's participation in the Tiananmen Movement had been indirect and peripheral. During the 1980s, he was one among many intellectuals in a network of think tanks and research groups who had tried to carve out some room for critical thinking. There was nothing religious or spiritual about his participation in *River Elegy.* Like Yuan, Xie was concerned with economic reforms and "civil society."

Religion, too, began as an intellectual interest for him. Xie read the Bible when he was working in a factory as a twenty-year-old victim of the Cultural Revolution. He was not encouraged at home, for although his mother had been educated in a Catholic school, she believed only in "science and democracy." He began to reflect on the differences between Christianity and Confucianism and Buddhism, and concluded that China lacked a spiritual creed that was suited to life in the secular world. Buddhism was entirely otherworldly and Confucianism purely secular. Only Christianity, it seemed to him, could be both. While he was wrestling with these ideas, he was also haunted by that centuries-old Chinese question: What had gone wrong with China? He read not just the Bible but also Spengler and Toynbee, the twin prophets of Western decline, who have given East Asian intellectuals such solace over the years.

Out of the resulting confusion emerged some interesting explanations for China's decline. First Xie thought it was because of the Chinese obsession with unity. China, he argued in *River Elegy,* had been at its best when it was divided. Look at Europe: Divided since the seventh century, it had flourished. Unity was the problem, unity and the patriarchal system. China, he said, is like a society of monkeys: The dominant males treat the rest as subservient women. It is still like that, even in the overseas Chinese democracy movement: Wei Jingsheng is the man, and others, male and female, are treated like his women. And in Tiananmen Square, many Chinese thought the protest was doomed as soon as they saw Chai Ling as the leader. Westerners like her; Chinese don't.

True or not, these were at least interesting hypotheses. But Xie also had another, more remarkable, explanation for China's decline: the lack of food. "We were in worse physical shape than the Europeans, because we didn't have enough to eat, and that affected our mental health. Chinese dictatorship has to do with being hungry." What about Christianity? I asked, to get him back onto firmer ground. He replied: "I think the Chinese made one big mistake. Instead of learning the ideals from Jesus, every Chinese wants to be Jesus himself."

This, offered without a flicker of irony in his pale, bespectacled face, made some sense. China has no tradition of monotheism. Instead, anything in nature, animal or mineral, can be imbued with a divine spirit. Emperors of China and Japan were gods of a kind. And all East Asian countries have been fertile breeding grounds for self-announced messiahs who promise to save the world if only you will buy their bibles. Xie said too many Chinese want to use religion to change society while what they ought to be doing is changing themselves first.

Xie's conversion came in America. He had been arrested after 1989, for having encouraged the student rebellion as a "liberal" intellectual. In fact, whatever his influence might have been as one of the authors of *River Elegy*, Xie never offered the students direct advice. As it turned out, the government did not regard him as a great danger, either. Released after a few months, he went to Japan as a visiting scholar of comparative religion. While there, he was offered a teaching job at a Lutheran university in Minnesota but was denied a U.S. visa. He read this as a signal from God that he was not meant to become a Christian. When he was finally allowed to enter the United States in 1993, he was miserable. It was the same story as Yuan's: His married life in China had been a disaster, but his loneliness in America was even harder to bear. He was haunted by dreams of dying alone, thousands of miles from home. But then a flash of white light: He was lifted up in the arms of Jesus. It gave him a marvelous feeling, "like floating in liquid." The next day he told Christian friends about his dream and was told he had had a vision of the Lord. Xie was still skeptical. Two more months went by. He fell ill, his temperature soared, he thought he was going to die. In a fit of delirium, he had another vision of Jesus.

This brought him close to conversion. But he was still a deeply troubled man. For even though he now felt Jesus in his heart, he was ashamed to worship a foreigner. Jesus, after all, had been a Jew. Xie thought deeply about this predicament. Then, to his great relief, scholarship came to the rescue. His reading of the Gospels revealed that Jesus had been on earth before Abraham, so he was not really a Jew but the son of God. Only then could Xie fully accept Jesus, for Yahweh may have chosen the Jewish people, but God had chosen Christ.

But still Xie's struggle was not quite over. When his wife called from Beijing, Xie confessed to her what he called his "greatest failure," his conversion to the Christian faith. It was a failure, he thought, because a rational, scientific person should believe only in himself. His wife was surprised to hear the news but told him that she too had been converted, in a "house church." Xie was not entirely convinced of the sincerity of his wife's belief, however, for she still found it hard to believe in the resurrection and without believing in that, he said, you cannot really be called a Christian. Then there was one more thing that bothered him. He raised his doleful eyes, crossed one bony leg over the other, and then uncrossed it again. At another table, a young girl with too much makeup was shouting something in Cantonese into her cell phone. He said his trouble had to do with Tiananmen: "I feel my participation in politics, in the democracy movement, even my historical research, was a sin."

Surprise must have shown on my face, for he quickly tried to explain what he meant. "You see, we said we acted for the good of China and not for our own selfish interests. But in fact we did it to improve our own position. We acted out of pride, for our own honor. And that is to pretend you are God. We were like Satan."

Xie had questioned his own sincerity and found it lacking. This is why he was reaching for a belief in absolute truth—to purge insincerity from his heart. His utopia was a place where people never said anything they did not believe. Some Chinese joined the democracy movement for the same reason. But politics, in his view, was inherently insincere. Even the people in the Chinese democracy movement were just like ordinary politicians; they didn't really believe what they said.

Xie had one person he could turn to with his doubts, a third writer on *River Elegy,* now also living in the United States, Su Xiaokang. Xie told me how Su had struggled with religion too. Su saw that faith had done his friend some good. It had calmed him down. But he wondered how Xie's quest for purity affected his work. The question bothered Xie as well. Su was right, Xie said: "I haven't been able to find a solution to this. When you write and research for a living, you have to consider the marketplace. So to continue in this line of work, you have to say things you don't really believe." Xie looked at me again with those eyes that expected a beating.

—

Before *River Elegy* Su Xiaokang had been a respected reporter at the *People's Daily,* the official Party newspaper, and a lecturer at the Beijing

Broadcasting Institute: in a way, a younger version of Liu Binyan. The film made him a star. He had written most of it. It was Su who wrote that Chinese civilization had "grown old and feeble" and that "a great tidal wave" was needed to flush away the dregs of the old tradition that clogged up the "blood vessels of our people." I had seen film clips of him in Tiananmen Square, telling the students through a megaphone that they were patriots who should guide the Party back to its idealistic, unsullied course. A small, dark, dapper man in glasses, a bit cocky in his manner; in a Western country he would have been a typical media don.

The ambition was still there a few months after the crackdown, when he arrived in Paris as a political refugee. At the bicentennial anniversary of the French Revolution, Su founded the Overseas Federation for a Democratic China with Wu'er Kaixi, the student leader, as vice chairman. Even though he wrote in his diary that he felt "like a tiny boat in a wide ocean, with no idea of the final destination," Su was frantically active, giving interviews here and lectures there, traveling all over Europe, the United States, and Taiwan. This frenzy continued after he moved to the United States, where he was given shelter at Princeton University, together with other political exiles such as Liu Binyan, Chai Ling, Yuan Zhiming, and the scientist Fang Lizhi. Su entered the typical milieu of these exiles, sharing a house with ten Chinese, singing Chinese songs, drinking copious amounts of beer, and talking Chinese politics through the night, endlessly rehashing the failure of Tiananmen.

The one person who could have eased him out of this émigré hothouse was his wife, Fu Li. A physician in Beijing, she had always warned her husband about getting involved in politics. Su needed her advice now. After some hard bargaining—Beijing wanted trade advantages—the U.S. State Department managed to get her out of China in 1991, together with their nine-year-old son. Fu Li told her husband to calm down, learn English, get a job, teach, write, do anything as long as he escaped from the narrow world of political refugees. The worst thing, she said, was to be a professional revolutionary abroad. She was right, of course. But then, one sweltering afternoon in July 1993, everything came unstuck in the most terrifying manner.

Together with another Chinese couple, Su, Fu Li, and their son were heading west along Route I-90 from Buffalo, New York. Su was sleeping in the backseat of the rented Dodge, with his wife on the other side and their son in between. He was a good driver, but a long night's drinking had left him feeling tired, so he let his friend's wife take the wheel. She was not an experienced driver and while passing another car she switched on the windshield wipers by mistake. In a moment of panic, she lost control of the car, which careered across the road and crashed into the barrier; the vehicle flipped onto its side. Su was in a coma for a week. His son was only lightly injured. His friends were all right. But Fu Li was unconscious for three weeks and woke up in a strange country unable to remember anything—not her life in China, not Tiananmen, not her two years in the United States. All that emerged after months of silence were snatches of a nursery rhyme remembered from her childhood, which she repeated softly to herself in moments of distress.

In his despair, Su turned to Christians, Buddhists, and a famous Chinese master of Qi Gong exercises. The master told Su that the crash was punishment for his work on *River Elegy*. Wounded by Su's insults, Chinese civilization had turned into an angry dragon and come back to destroy his life.

I went to see Su at his house near Princeton together with Perry Link, a professor of Chinese literature who had helped give him refuge. I was not expecting an easy interview. Su had become something of a recluse. He told many of his friends that the old Su Xiaokang had died. Although I found a man who sighed a great deal and shivered, like a horse wishing to shake off its burden, Su nonetheless was quite happy to talk. The wooden house was large and comfortable. Piles of books and magazine articles lay on the table, and there was evidence of the teenage son: pictures of American movie stars and rock musicians. Su, who is in his fifties, doesn't speak much English. And his son is bored with his stories about China, a place he can barely remember. Like his mother, though in a different way, the American teenager is living in a different country from his father too.

Su is still haunted by a sense of responsibility for Tiananmen. He told us why in the form of a story. After lecturing about *River Elegy* at a university in New York, he was asked a question by a young student from China. Did he think his film had had a big influence on the Tiananmen rebellion? He said that he thought not, for the students, in his view, were interested in individual freedom, while the documentary was all about the nature of Chinese civilization. The girl was furious and yelled at him that he was irresponsible, like all Chinese intellectuals, who talk big and then duck the consequences of their words. After telling this story, Su sucked his teeth and looked out of the window at the wintry New Jersey landscape. "I still can't figure it out," he said softly. Then, raising his voice, he said: "What she meant is that we fled! We fled!"

He handed me an article he had written for a Hong Kong magazine. When I read it later that day, one sentence in particular impressed me: "We created an atmosphere that encouraged the students to be radical, and then, when they did, we turned around and lectured them about their extremism. That is surely something they will never forget."

I asked Su about the film. What did he think about *River Elegy* now? Here, too, he was critical of his old self. He had made the mistake, he said, of projecting the West as a perfect counter model to China even though he knew nothing about the West. At the time, he had never been outside China. He understood America better now. He still admired the political freedom, but he couldn't get used to the commercialism. His own son was a good example. All he cared about was entertainment. He resisted his father's control: "He wants to be free and all that." As Su spoke, I noticed something moving from the corner of my eye. A pale figure in a track suit shuffled from the bedroom to the kitchen with the help of a steel frame, looking at us with dumb incomprehension. It was as though Su was not aware of his wife's presence. So we politely pretended that she was not there.

Like Xie Xuanjun, Su is a troubled man. Most middle-aged Chinese dissidents in exile are. Their English is poor. They are too old to forget the past and become Americans and too young to retire with their memories. Besides having to look after his wife all the time, Su told me he didn't know what to write about. He was out of touch with Chinese culture and politics. There was nothing much he could do. In fact, he was writing his memoirs. That was at least something. I asked him about religion and about the Christian conversion of his former colleagues. Su looked pained. He said: "We intellectuals in exile all struggled with Christianity.

We all experience a spiritual crisis. I was very depressed after the car accident. I felt I was being punished and I couldn't survive without contact
with God, a Chinese God." So he visited the Chinese church in nearby
New Brunswick, and twice a week an American student came to his house
to read the Bible with him. But he could never quite bring himself to believe.

A common cliché about the difference between East and West is that
Oriental cultures are driven by shame whereas the Judeo-Christian West is
driven by guilt. In the West, God sees our sins even if no one else does, so
we feel guilty. By contrast in the East, which has no God, it is only when
the neighbors notice that one needs to worry, and then one feels shame.
This has always seemed to me a rickety distinction. What troubles Su, Xie,
Wang Chaohua, who once tormented her father, and many other refugees
from China's dictatorship sounds more like guilt than shame—with or
without the all-seeing eye of God. And the guilt goes deeper and back further in time than the events of 1989. Su said: "All of us who went through
the Cultural Revolution feel guilty—of beating our teachers, denouncing
our parents, that sort of thing. At least we intellectuals can talk about it.
Ordinary Chinese have it all bottled up."

So why was it, I asked, that Su ended up rejecting Christianity after all?
His response was a melancholy echo of a distress I would come across
often among the survivors of the Maoist era. He said that since people of
his generation lost their faith in Maoism, they felt like plants cut off at the
roots. It had become impossible to believe in any religion or any ideology,
he added: "I tried hard, but I can't believe in anything at all."

Chapter 3

Stars of Arizona

Professor Fang Lizhi's epiphany, of a secular kind, came to him on December 2, 1979, during a celebration of the Advent of Christ, in King's College Chapel, Cambridge. It was only one year after the famous astrophysicist had first been allowed to travel abroad. And one of his first trips had been to the Vatican to discuss cosmology, a piquant occasion for this Chinese admirer of Galileo, so he was not inexperienced abroad. But Fang was still a Party member, staunchly anti-religious, and unsure of what to do in a church. And his epiphany had a very different character from those of the Christian converts.

The atmosphere in King's College Chapel was strange to him: the slow shuffle of men in white-and-crimson robes on the black-and-white marble floor, the boys' trilling voices echoing from the vaulted ceiling, the light bouncing off dark saints in stained-glass windows. Professor Fang was so moved that he translated the words of a Bach hymn as soon as he returned to his rooms that same night: "A pristine rose has blossomed. . . . Rays from its tender bloom / Light up this cold, cold winter / This dark, dark night." Moved but also baffled, for there he was, in the most famous chapel of an ancient university, known for its scientific bent (and its communist spies); how was it possible that free men of science could sing the praises of Jesus? Science, after all, was not just a secular enterprise, it was the rational alternative to religious superstition. How could an enlightened person possibly believe in both?

Then Fang had his epiphany, the insight that made him see the English dons around him, but also China, in a different, or at least much clearer, light. He realized that Chinese intellectuals had made a big mistake by not paying sufficient attention to the Reformation, which had carried on the humanistic tradition of the Renaissance. Michelangelo, Leonardo da Vinci, and the King's College Choir singing Bach were all celebrating human nature in the image of Christ. The Europeans had humanized their symbols of divinity, turned their gods into men, brought them down to earth.

The story of China, and specifically Fang's story in China, was rather different. Only ten years before witnessing the celebration of the Advent of Christ in Cambridge, Fang had been persecuted in a society where people had turned a human being into a god. They had become worshippers of a divine leader who, in the words of a popular song of praise, rose from the East, like a crimson sun. They sang hymns to him and bore his image, in gold, blood-red enamel, and sometimes porcelain (fearfully, for porcelain was breakable, and at one time a broken image of the deity could mean many years of hard labor).

Fang wrote about his Cambridge experience for a small Chinese magazine called *Life*. The magazine did not survive the article. One can see why. This is how Fang ended his piece: "As far as our 'Hymns' are concerned, with their braying tone and imbecilic lyrics—'The Cultural Revolution is good, oh it's good'—one could only lament the depths to which Chinese civilization had fallen."

———

Fang Lizhi was already a troublemaker as a nineteen-year-old student of theoretical and nuclear physics at Beijing University in the 1950s. Instead of repeating the dogmas of Maoist devotion, he used a meeting of the

Communist Youth League to advocate independent thinking—a heresy. His Party secretary warned him that truths had been settled by Marx, Engels, Lenin, Stalin, and Mao and that it was the duty of intellectuals to come up with fresh ways of restating them.

Fang graduated in 1956. Months later, Chairman Mao decreed that a "hundred flowers must bloom, and a hundred schools of thought contend": Intellectual criticism of Party policies was not only allowed but positively encouraged. It is still unclear whether Mao set a deliberate trap for potential enemies or genuinely thought criticism would be a good thing, but after a month or so of cautious silence, people came forward to say what they thought, in small numbers at first, discreetly, and then in ever larger numbers, ever more vociferously. Some even challenged the right of the Party to monopolize power. Fang was not one of those. A loyal Party man, he simply suggested that scientific research would surely benefit from less political interference. For this, or at any rate for refusing to recant, he was expelled from the Party when, after a few months of criticism, Mao decided enough was enough and critics were to be silenced—many of them forever.

Fang was made to "wear the hat" of a rightist. Wearing a hat meant years of absolute misery for many thousands of people. But at least Fang, unlike others, was neither murdered nor driven to commit suicide. Scientists were too useful to be so casually cast aside. Ten years later, however, when the Cultural Revolution gathered steam, even scientists were no longer protected. "Bourgeois science" had to be eradicated. Barely literate Maoist ideologues were put in charge of scientific departments. Laboratories were ransacked. Research was supplanted by lunatic debates on Maoist doctrine. Fang was subjected to struggle sessions, with baying lynch mobs cursing him as a "reactionary" of the "stinking ninth category." For one year he was locked up alone in a so-called cow pen— reactionary intellectuals were said to have "cow spirits." After that, he was put to work in a mine and, later, on a railroad. Two things happened as a result: For the first time, he began to doubt the benevolence of Mao's leadership, and the lack of a laboratory and scientific books made him turn his attention to the stars. The only book he had managed to keep was *The Classical Theory of Fields,* by the Soviet physicist Lev Landau. So he read it over and over again. And he decided to drop solid-state physics and study cosmology instead.

The way we look at the stars has often been a contentious, and indeed dangerous issue and is intimately linked with religion—and, by extension, with the right to dissent. In Fang's words: "Over history, new cosmologies have more than once led to the downfall of orthodox beliefs." Galileo got into trouble with the Catholic Church for saying that Copernicus was right in his view that our planet was not the center of the universe but only one among other planets revolving around the sun. This was a serious enough challenge to Catholic dogma. Worse was the idea that physical reality could be understood by applying mathematics. What about Genesis, what about God's creation, what, indeed, about the monopoly of truth held by the priests? And so Galileo became a hero to the prophets of scientific socialism, from Engels to Bertolt Brecht.

Chinese astronomers had already started recording solar eclipses more than eight hundred years before Christ. And foreign knowledge, from Persia, India, and later from European Jesuits, influenced Chinese speculations on the workings of the cosmos. And yet, according to Fang Lizhi, Chinese, with rare exceptions, were never interested in finding common laws to explain the natural world. For the natural world, in Confucian eyes, was governed by moral rather than scientific principles. Shooting stars, earthquakes, and the like showed the degree to which harmony ruled in the Chinese cosmos. Since all human relations, including those of the exalted emperors, are subject to moral as well as immoral influences, we cannot expect nature to behave otherwise. The idea of unvarying, scientific laws, then, would have struck traditional Chinese thinkers as absurd.

The Chinese notion of cosmic harmony made astronomy more a matter of political than scientific importance. Court astronomers read the stars carefully for omens, but in Fang's view, the question of what holds up the stars in the sky was not something that exercised Chinese thinkers. He quoted the Tang dynasty poet Li Po to make his point: "Why waste time worrying about the collapse of the heavens, like the people of Qi." Confucius, likewise, thought speculation about the nature of gods was a waste of time: "We have so little understanding of man, how can we possibly understand the gods." A solid basis for skeptical thinking, one might reason. But one could also interpret it as a lack of curiosity about the laws of the universe.

This is what former student leader Li Lu meant when he told me at his office in New York that Chinese lacked a deep understanding of metaphysics. He said the Western fascination with creation had led to modern science. This is why he admired "the mentality" of those Western scientists who wanted to find out the laws of God's creation. Clearly, like many Chinese students of his generation, Li Lu had been influenced by Fang Lizhi.

It is Fang's contention that universal principles inherent in a monotheistic tradition are a necessary basis for scientific inquiry. He does not stop to wonder how the Greeks developed those principles without the benefit of one God. In fact, the Greek view of the universe is similar to that of the ancient Chinese. Plato's idea of the cosmos is profoundly moral. Cosmic harmony is governed by divine causes, and man's duty is to study celestial movements to imitate their innate goodness.

Fang doesn't pay much attention to Taoists, either. This is a pity, for the Taoists represent a dissident tradition in Chinese history. Unlike Confucian mandarins, who supported the orthodox tradition, Taoists were relatively free spirits. They were fascinated by universal principles, and their view of the cosmos was less moral, more individualistic, and thus more inquiring than that of the Confucianist mandarins. They had a mystical idea of universal harmony, which they called the Tao, literally "the Way," but they certainly did not believe in one God. Indeed, thanks partly to Taoist scholars, the Chinese had a more accurate understanding of the cosmos than the seventeenth-century Jesuits who arrived to instruct them. The Jesuits were more sophisticated mathematically than the Chinese, but they still believed that stars were immutable, while the Chinese had observed since the first century that stars were born and died. But European missionaries imparted their scientific knowledge to the Chinese to prove the superiority of their religion, so they disparaged Chinese science and argued that superior Western science was rooted in the Christian faith. One of the ironies of modern Chinese history is how often Chinese intellectuals, especially in moods of cultural self-hatred, reflect the prejudices of Christian missionaries and barbarian conquerors.

In any case, Galileo's problems with the Church came about precisely because of the latter's claim to being the guardian of universal truths. And so did Fang Lizhi's problems with the Chinese Communist Party. For the Party ideologues, whose flimsy knowledge of science was based on what Engels and Lenin had once said, behaved much like the priests who had opposed Galileo. That Lenin and Engels had based their notions of science on Galileo's theories is ironic but irrelevant. The important thing is that Party hacks, like the priests, believed in universal laws, which only they were allowed to interpret. And because of that, they also believed that any challenge to their monopoly of the truth was a challenge to their monopoly of power. So when Fang proposed, entirely in line with modern scientific discoveries, that our universe began with a big bang, this was considered a heresy, for Engels, following Galileo, had believed that the universe was infinite in both time and space.

Fang was replacing the principles of Confucius and Marx with those of modern science. And these he associated with democracy, just as a previous generation had done in 1919, at the time of the May Fourth Movement. Perhaps this explains why so many Chinese scientists became dissidents and reformists in the 1980s. Instead of having a Christian church to rally around as an alternative institution to the Party, with an alternative dogma and an alternative catechism, Chinese scientists had the church of science. The Communist Party itself, as the organized expression of "scientific socialism," had once been worshipped as a product of that church. But by the time Fang came out in opposition to it, the Party had become like the ossified imperial system, jealously guarding its orthodoxy against any challenges, rational or otherwise.

In the mid-1980s, Fang began to make speeches about the need for intellectual and academic freedom. He wanted to "straighten" the "bent backs" of his fellow academics, and argued that "without democracy, the academic community will make no progress." For the first time since the Communist revolution, a prominent Chinese intellectual openly used the phrase that had gained currency during the May Fourth Movement: "total westernization." Nothing less would do. China had to catch up with the Renaissance and the Reformation and have its own Enlightenment. Fang's words were explosive. In December 1986, thousands of students from his University of Science and Technology in Hefei took to the streets demanding democracy, and similar demonstrations spread almost

instantly to twenty other cities. The American journalist Orville Schell remembers seeing wall posters that read "I Have a Dream, a Dream of Freedom. I Have a Dream of Democracy. I Have a Dream of Life Endowed
with Human Rights. May the Day Come When All These Are More Than
Dreams." In January 1987, Fang was sacked from his post as vice president
of the university and denounced for spreading "erroneous statements reflecting 'bourgeois liberalization.' " He became known to the outside
world as China's Sakharov.

The American scholar Andrew Nathan observed, a little waspishly, that
in his speeches Fang often sounded less like the eminently practical
Sakharov than like Dorothy addressing the Wizard of Oz in her decent,
frank, and naïve way. But if some of Fang's statements on politics and science sound platitudinous, his vocabulary reflects an ancient tradition.
From Confucius to Mao Zedong, moral platitudes were always an important part of Chinese political discourse, and Fang's not only carried a high
risk but made more sense than most—and excited all those who heard
them.

—

Xiao Qiang was Fang Lizhi's student in Hefei. Everyone who becomes involved in the Chinese democracy movement overseas knows Xiao, a lanky,
smiling figure with shoulder-length hair, rushing from meeting to meeting, in New York and Washington, D.C., accompanying famous dissidents
here, putting out fires of factional battles there, cajoling congressional
committees, stumping for support for his Human Rights in China organization, talking a streak in fluent English, and surveying the world from the
lofty perch of his office in the Empire State Building. I first saw him in
1997, at the New York Public Library, introducing Wei Jingsheng to the
press just after Wei had been released from jail. Dressed in blue jeans, his
hair flopping about his forehead, he was barking in true northern fashion
at some Cantonese-speaking Hong Kong journalists that "only questions
in English or Mandarin will be tolerated." But the barking manner melted
into the mildest of smiles after a note was passed and a whispered conversation hastily took place. "Well," Xiao burbled, "we are very democratic
here. You can ask questions in any language you want."

In a small delicatessen in midtown Manhattan, I asked him what it had been like to be Fang's student in 1979, the year of the Democracy Wall. The first thing to realize, Xiao said, was how arrogant the science students were. Only the brightest entered the University of Science and Technology (Keda, for short); they represented the best of their generation, indeed the future of science in China. Everyone wanted to be a genius. They all thought they would be an Einstein: "We were so special, so free, and so spoiled." As he said this, I thought of Wu'er Kaixi, who had told me the same thing in the hamburger joint in Taiwan: "All Chinese students are arrogant. . . . We thought we could solve the problems of China." And Xiao was not the first person to mention Einstein, a hero to Chinese dissidents.

One of Fang's closest allies, the distinguished historian of science Xu Liangying, had translated Einstein's writings and kept his portrait on the wall. Shen Tong, one of the student leaders in Tiananmen Square, had named his political talking shop (or "salon") at Beijing University the Olympic Institute, after Einstein's group. Aside from his scientific achievements, Einstein, with his wild white hair and his interest in morality, freedom, justice, and peace, became an almost spiritual figure. It was precisely the linkage in Einstein's thought of spirituality and science that appealed to his Chinese admirers. Like Fang, Einstein was seen as a wise man, a scientific guru. "God does not play dice" was a maxim made for scholars who battled with political superstitions on earth by invoking the higher principles of heaven.

In the early 1980s, Xiao organized a seminar at Keda and asked Fang to talk about philosophy and science. In China, philosophy still meant Marxism. Fang, in his usual sardonic manner, bubbling over with barbed jokes, spoke about the big bang that triggered off our universe and explained that the Marxists, with their nineteenth-century notions of science and their dogmatic insistence on the infinity of time and space, simply had no idea what they were talking about. The students exchanged glances of sheer delight. One of them decided to be direct; he was sure Professor Fang wouldn't mind. So he asked what Fang really thought of Marxism. And Fang answered: "Marxism is out of date." The students burst into wild applause.

Xiao Qiang's epiphany about the true state of Chinese Communist society also came during a visit to a shrine. Like so many people who have grown disenchanted with Marxist dogma and Maoist faith, he was looking for answers in alternative religions. He was in a state of confusion, and hoped to find enlightenment from a spiritual master. So he set off one day in 1980, with a friend from Beijing University, to a famous Buddhist temple that had just been reopened in Anhui province, not far from Hefei.

The temple was new, and looked it; the garish fresh paint still sparkled. The old temple had been demolished during the Cultural Revolution. Xiao and his friend asked the monks if they could stay there and work. They were allowed to sleep in the kitchen. The next day, local people arrived to consult the monks about their problems, as people had done for centuries, for the monks were thought to be learned men who knew how to soothe troubled minds. The harshness of the locals' problems shocked the two spoiled students from the best universities in China. Women had been raped by Party bosses, others were being "squeezed" for money they didn't have, and still others had fathers or sons who had been locked up for years in hard-labor camps without knowing why or having any prospect of being released. The monks, dressed in fine saffron robes, answered by repeating Maoist clichés.

Xiao realized that the temple was a sham, a phony show to attract tourist money, and that the monks were frauds. The whole thing was just "bullshit." It was also then, when the villagers turned in desperation to the two students, that Xiao saw it was not enough to want to be a scientific genius. "The experience," he said, "was a kind of enlightenment. It made me care more about other people."

This was not quite the end of Xiao's spiritual travails. After coming to America in the late 1980s, he spent some time at Notre Dame University learning about Christianity. He also dabbled in Islam and Taoism. There was even a murky episode in Washington, D.C., when he followed a girl-friend into the Unification Church of the Reverend Moon. But back in 1980, when he saw through the useless platitudes spouted by those so-called Buddhist monks, he was at least enlightened enough to see that Fang Lizhi had something important to say of a wholly secular nature. Fang promoted freedom of thought as an essential condition for the practice of science. He also argued that democracy was an essential condition for thinking freely. As he put it in his most famous speech, delivered in

Shanghai in 1986: "Democracy is based on recognizing the rights of every single individual. Naturally, not everyone wants the same thing, and therefore the desires of different individuals have to be mediated through a democratic process, to form a society, a nation, a collectivity. But it is only on the foundation of recognizing the humanity and the rights of each person that we can build democracy."

A year before he spoke these words, Fang had made a similar speech at the University of Zhejiang. It was recorded on tape and one of Fang's students in Hefei spent hours transcribing the words. The student then made two hundred copies of the transcription and sent them to other universities around the country. The speech also found its way to members of the Politburo in Beijing, who were of course outraged. Fang became nationally famous, as well as a marked man. Two years later, he would be expelled from the Party for the second time in his life. But the protest movements of the 1980s had begun. The student who had made those copies and sent them around China was Xiao Qiang.

—

As the plane from Los Angeles to Tucson descended on a clear evening, the orange glow of the sun melting into a warm blue sky, I was getting to the end of a collection of articles by Fang Lizhi, entitled *Bringing Down the Great Wall*. They included his famous letter to Deng Xiaoping, dated January 6, 1989, the fortieth-anniversary year of the Chinese Communist Revolution. Given that it was also the two-hundredth anniversary of the French Revolution, Fang wrote, it would surely be a good idea to celebrate liberty, equality, fraternity, and human rights by releasing political prisoners, such as Wei Jingsheng. This remarkable act of courage marked the beginning of that extraordinary year of protest. Fang's letter provided the first spark. But when the students revolted en masse in Tiananmen Square, he kept a sympathetic distance, for he felt that his direct involvement was neither in his nor the students' interest. In fact, mass movements frightened him. Still, like other liberal intellectuals, he was blamed for the "counterrevolutionary rebellion" as soon as the protest was crushed, and was officially described as "the scum of the intelligentsia." To avoid arrest, he fled with his wife to the U.S. embassy, where he was sheltered for a year, until the Chinese government found a face-saving way to bundle him out of the country. (They said he had a heart problem.) And that is why he was now teaching astrophysics at the University of Arizona in Tucson, where even Jesuits gaze at the stars.

I drove to the university in the morning, passing by low white adobe houses, fat green cacti, as tall as small trees, plush Mexican restaurants, and large billboards bearing such uplifting messages as HAPPINESS IS A HEALTHY CASH FLOW. The sun was beating down; the dry heat was intense. A local country-and-western radio station was playing Willie Nelson and Waylon Jennings. A man in a low, slow, pleasing voice asked listeners who were looking for a job, a good job, a secure job, to call a toll-free number to find employment at one of the fine correctional institutions of the state of Arizona. I thought of questions to ask Fang. The topic I hoped he would talk about was his idea of "total westernization."

Tall, tanned, athletic students walked, cycled, and skateboarded across the campus, dressed in T-shirts, jogging shoes, and shorts. They were from every conceivable ethnic group, except that most were larger, healthier-looking, and better fed than the people on the continents they or their forebears had left behind. Here, on the Tucson campus, you felt you were in the presence of a new breed of physical supermen and -women.

Fang did not look like a superman. His small, intelligent, slightly porcine eyes peered at me watchfully through thick glasses, perched above fleshy cheeks and a generous mouth, at the corners of which white flecks gathered when he spoke. His white sports shirt and gray slacks were rumpled. His office was cramped. The window offered a view of the milk-fed superrace zooming around campus below.

So what about his idea of total westernization? Had he changed his mind now that he had moved West? Fang said he had not. Modern science, he said, was part of the Western "value system" developed in the Renaissance. Nothing like it had happened in China. He didn't really know why. True, Mencius and other Confucian thinkers had put man in the center of their concerns, but that wasn't enough to set off the equivalent of the European Renaissance. It was now up to Chinese intellectuals to start a Chinese Renaissance.

Fang spoke softly, in a northern-Chinese accent. His answers were short. There were awkward pauses. In fact, he was not really in the mood to talk. He was polite but preoccupied; there was no sign of his famous irreverent humor. Perhaps he was depressed by the aftermath of the American bombing of the Chinese embassy in Belgrade. He told me that students of his old university in Hefei had just smashed the local branch of Kentucky Fried Chicken as a protest against "U.S. imperialism." Only a little more than ten years ago, their older brothers and sisters had demonstrated for freedom and democracy by paraphrasing Martin Luther King, Jr. Their teacher's vision of total westernization had excited them. Now students had turned their patriotism against the West.

Fang sighed and said that China had awakened to the modern world only because of European and Japanese cruelty, beginning with the Opium War (1839–1842). So it was always easy to stir up anti-foreign sentiment. Look what happened in 1900, when the Manchu court encouraged the Boxers to attack the foreigners. Not that the Boxers had needed encouragement. They were xenophobic anyway. But as usual in Chinese history, their zeal could easily have been turned against the government, too.

As Fang spoke about the Boxers, I thought of events in the 1980s, which, on a tiny scale, reflected China's perennial xenophobia. Protests had erupted at universities in various cities because African exchange students had allegedly abused Chinese girls. Black students were pelted with ink. The young Chinese students who were inspired by Fang's ideas might in some cases have thrown some of that ink: Visceral resentment of foreigners can coexist with a yearning for Western-style liberties; resentments are often sharpened by the lack of freedom.

Total westernization, in Fang's view, does not mean that Chinese should discard every aspect of their own culture. It means, as he said in one of his essays, "complete openness to the outside world, assimilating all of the cultural advances of the human race." Fang admires "the spirit of the 'complete Westernizers'" both before and after the May Fourth period, who had the guts to call for letting foreign ideas into China, where they could challenge what was not progressive in our culture."

What Fang and many May Fourth intellectuals before him were talking about was a particular road not taken. On this topic, Fang became livelier. He said the response to the Opium War had been all wrong. If only the

Chinese government had done what the Japanese did when Commodore Perry arrived in Shimoda with his "black ships" in 1853, things would have turned out better. The samurai, who were shrewder than the Chinese mandarins about the implications of Western science, saw that it was futile to resist American might. So they started their own Renaissance and imported Western knowledge to modernize their country. The Chinese, however—uneasy, defensive, but still convinced that their empire was the center of the universe, like plump frogs in an old well—reacted to the Western challenge with hostility. They refused to learn from the outside world. China, in short, lacked not only a Renaissance but a Meiji Restoration.

And that was, more or less, were our conversation ended. Fang was weary. He had said what he wanted to say about Chinese politics many times already. He was never an activist. The student demonstrations in 1986 had disturbed him, for he did not want to be responsible for getting young people into trouble. Unlike them, he knew from experience the ruthlessness of the Chinese state. Here in Arizona, he had left politics behind. From time to time he still wrote articles on Chinese affairs for American intellectual journals, and he was a board member of Human Rights in China. But I had the impression he really wanted to be left alone with his research students, and with the stars that sparkled like fat diamonds in the ink-blue desert skies. In a sense, he wasn't really in exile at all.

Perhaps there was one more reason for his reticence. Fang had been criticized by other Chinese for fleeing to the U.S. embassy in 1989 and then leaving his country. After all he had done to stimulate demands for political liberty in China, he seemed to have turned his back and isolated himself in the Far West. Fang himself told journalist Orville Schell that going abroad was a kind of failure, since he had had to leave his friends and colleagues behind, and "naturally my effectiveness will now be marked by this." It was the classic dilemma of exile: freedom gained but influence lost. Fang's escape was widely seen as a blow to the democratic cause. Dai Qing, the caustic journalist, was one of the people who never tired of saying so. "He should never have left China," she proclaimed. "He is useless now."

It is a common accusation made against political refugees, especially when they prosper abroad. Their foreign success is seen as treachery, their freedom to live as they like an affront to those who have to bear the strictures of life at home. Germans who fled the Third Reich in the 1930s were, on the whole, not made to feel welcome when they returned after the war. They had "had it easy," they didn't "know what it had been like." The novelist Milan Kundera was never forgiven by many Czechs for leaving Prague and retiring to his French study to tend to his literary garden. But the absence of freedom forces writers and scientists to lie, and once they lie, their work is worthless. If they choose silence, there is no work at all. Or they risk the silence of prison. That is where Fang would have ended up, heroically perhaps—as a scientific martyr. But martyrdom is not something to wish upon others. Fang had come to America to work, and to get a closer view of the stars.

—

Dai Qing blames it all on Fang's wife, Li Shuxian. She was the "radical." Her influence was always bad. She forced Fang to seek refuge among the Americans. I had heard too many denunciations of this kind before to take this on trust, so I wanted to meet Li Shuxian. A formidable figure in her own right, a physicist like her husband, Li had always been more of an activist. In 1980, the government, in an effort to give more people a minor stake in one-party rule, had allowed elections for local "people's congresses" (like soviets in the Soviet Union). Li won a seat for the Haidian district in Beijing, and irritated the authorities by speaking up for the rights of her constituents. She was also a regular speaker at the democracy salon organized on the Beijing University campus by Wang Dan, the student leader at Tiananmen. And she contributed to the small magazines that flourished in those early years of the 1980s known—much too hopefully—as the Beijing Spring.

To get to the Fangs' house, in the outskirts of Tucson, you have to drive through a quiet stretch of dry, empty desert land, interrupted only by the occasional cactus or dusty shrub. The house stands alone on top of a small hill and is furnished with all the accoutrements of westernized Chinese affluence: a large glass-topped table, a fine calligraphy on the wall, some gilded knickknacks from foreign travels, a pool in the garden. In her sixties, Li is still a beautiful woman. She wore cream trousers and a peach-colored shirt. Her carefully dressed jet-black hair was pulled back, which made her look handsome more than severe. Fang greeted me at the door. As soon as I had sat down with Li, he retreated to his study.

As if she wanted to make up for her husband's diffidence, Li spoke without stopping, in fluent English, which she had learned in school, just before the revolution. It did not surprise me to hear that she was from a distinguished family of landowners. (Fang's father had been a postal clerk.) She had the poise that comes with her class self-confidence, which even years of Maoist torment were unable to wipe out.

First of all, to get that topic out of the way, Li explained why they'd had to leave China. They had not really wanted to leave at all. Indeed, if they had wanted to come to the West, they could have done so before, under better circumstances. There had been no lack of offers. Anyway, the day after the Beijing Massacre, they were staying at a hotel, the Shangri-La, since their house was under constant police surveillance. Fang was about to go to work at the Beijing Observatory. But students had phoned to tell him that both he and his wife were on the most-wanted list and would certainly be arrested. So Li decided it was time to get out of the country. She thought Fang might be killed. He agreed. They applied for a U.S. visa, and asked whether the embassy could offer them temporary shelter. The embassy, not sure what to do, suggested they might apply for refugee status. They declined the offer and returned to their hotel. But after midnight, they were picked up as "guests of President Bush," escorted out of the hotel through the back gate, and driven away in a black car by the head of U.S. embassy security. For more than one year they were virtual prisoners inside the embassy.

Since I knew Li had been close to the students, especially Wang Dan, I asked her where she stood in the debate about Tiananmen. Had the student leaders been too uncompromising? Should they have backed down?

"They were too young. They didn't know history. They were simply too young." Unlike their elders, who had suffered for years under the Communist regime, they didn't understand the true nature of the Party, she continued. They thought they could imitate Gandhi. But you couldn't be a Gandhi in China. Gandhi's opponents represented a constitutional democracy. China was too big and had too long a history of tyranny. China's problems couldn't be solved in a few days. The students would be crushed. That is why she went to the Square on May 5 and tried to persuade them to retreat. They wouldn't listen. It was the last time she saw Wang Dan in China.

Li and Fang were colleagues at Beijing University when they married in 1961. Like her husband, she had been in deep trouble several years before that. But she had begun as a passionate supporter of the revolution, celebrating the "liberation" in Shanghai. A Party member and a patriot, she believed in social equality and restoring greatness to her country. When Mao invited criticism in 1957, she talked to fellow students at Beijing University about writing a letter to Party headquarters. This was not an act of rebellion. In fact, she believed that the greatness of China would be enhanced if students were encouraged to think for themselves instead of following Marxist-Leninist dogma without question. The letter was never actually sent. But rumors of her intention were enough to brand her as a "rightist" when the crackdown came, and she spent the next two years feeding pigs in a tiny village northwest of Beijing.

Li probably never stood a chance anyway. Perhaps she is lucky to be alive, for her family background was all wrong. Her father, who died in a car crash before the revolution, had been a surgeon and had served with the Kuomintang during the war. Her mother came from a family of rich landlords. There were relatives in Taiwan. Thus Li was never trusted. During the Cultural Revolution, she was tormented as a "stinking reactionary" even as she was about to give birth to her second child. Her first son, an eight-year-old "Little Red Guard," publicly railed at his mother for being unfit to bring him up. After further denunciations and struggle sessions, she was sent to the countryside once again, this time to labor in a mine.

Li was matter-of-fact about all this, as though these events were a normal part of everyone's life. The tragedy is that such a life was indeed normal for a person of Li's background. She was one of many victims of Mao's loathing of upper-class intellectuals. During a rare moment of silence, we both looked through the window into the blinding afternoon sun. A white shaft of light cut into the room like a knife. Still gazing into the sun, which lightened her brown eyes, Li suddenly said softly, almost as if she were speaking to herself: "The worst thing is that they control our memories." I looked at her, waiting for more. "Especially when they have done something terrible, they hide history or force people to forget. Even my son doesn't know what happened in those days. That is why we must educate people, step by step, about the truth."

Li had always been ambitious. Her mother had taught her never to depend on a man. Anything a man could do, she could do better. She was the brightest pupil in her high school class in Shanghai. After she graduated in 1952, her teacher asked her what she wanted to do. She replied that she wanted to study the most difficult subject there was so she could prove herself to be as good as any man. He said physics was the hardest subject. So she studied physics. But then, branded as a rightist and a class enemy, Li was unable to have a career in scientific research and took up teaching instead.

Her husband had the career she had aspired to. She became the politician; he was the scholar. She claims she was glad when Fang was sacked as vice president of his university in 1987, for then he could concentrate on his scientific work. And she was happy when he was expelled from the Party. History would prove him right anyway. It was his scholarship that should come first.

And now they were in America, where he could finally work in freedom. After thirty-two years of struggle in China, defeated in their efforts to build a better society, they had started a second life. Arizona was good for Fang, Li said. I thought I detected a wistful note in her voice, and I asked whether it was good for her, too. Her mouth tightened. She felt homesick at times, she admitted. Her mother and brother had died after she and Fang moved to the West. She would love to go back to China, but on her own terms—openly—and not furtively, after cutting some shabby deal with the Party. Li repeated: "This is a second life for us." She silently smoothed her slacks with both hands. And with an air of resignation—not anger or resentment—she said: "You know, I used to be a good teacher, but here there is no one for me to teach. Now I am finally free to talk, but there is no one for me to talk to."

———

After leaving the house of Fang Lizhi and Li Shuxian, I decided to go for a drive through the desert landscape down to the Mexican border. The road to Nogales passes through several Native American reservations. Here and there, minute specks in the shimmering horizon suggested human dwellings; the rest was empty, dry land, with no Native American in sight. I saw a sign to the Intercontinental Ballistic Missile Museum and made a note to swing by on my way back.

Something Fang had said came back to me: "I am anti-religion. Modern science is part of the Western value system." He implied that science was able not just to supply explanations for the natural world but also to tell us how to live. Through science, social harmony could once again match the mathematical harmony of the stars. It was a Platonic, as well as a very Chinese, notion.

—

The political scientist Yan Jiaqi, who was trained as a mathematician at the University of Science and Technology in the 1960s, went one step further. (He went many steps further than Fang in several ways. In May 1989, he openly supported the students in Tiananmen Square while also denouncing Deng Xiaoping as a "senile dictator" who should be brought down.) When I saw him in his apartment in Brooklyn, a month before visiting Arizona, amidst the usual émigré clutter of newspaper cuttings and unfinished articles, he told me why he hadn't become a Christian. It was "because I'm a scientist. I can use science to explain the world. I want to know God through science." He gave me a small book he had written, which I read afterward. Science, he wrote, was "the wellspring of human optimism." Why? Because "with the use of science, people can create the conditions or alter existing conditions in order to deal with the concrete problems they need to solve." In other words, for Yan, and perhaps Fang, democracy is more than a flawed system that works better than others: it is the only scientifically correct system.

Chineseness is not an adequate explanation for why many dissidents in China are "scientists," those who believe in science as an alternative to religion. For almost a hundred years, scientism was in fact part of a deliberate attempt to get away from Chineseness. To make sure China would not be humiliated again by superior Western powers, Chinese reformists in the early twentieth century wanted to modernize China by adopting the "scientific spirit." They felt that China had been held back for centuries by hoary philosophy and spiritual flimflam. The new scientific spirit would sweep the cobwebs away, free the Chinese from their shackles, and invigorate the nation. The debates in those years leading up to May 4, 1919, were not so different from similar arguments between "ancients" and "moderns" in seventeenth-century Europe. Then, too, some wanted to forge ahead by exploring the outside world by scientific means, while others put their faith in cultivating the self by studying the classics. The difference is that science in twentieth-century China was associated with Western thinking, and philosophy with the ancient Chinese classics. Science was modern; philosophy was history. That is why "scientists," or even scientists, were quickly associated with "total westernization," although they did not necessarily wish to destroy all Chinese traditions.

Cultural conservatives saw modern science not only as a Western but also as a purely materialistic enterprise. Matters of the spirit, or the soul, belonged to the ancient tradition. Since the late nineteenth century even reformers made the distinction between Chinese learning to cultivate the spirit and Western learning for practical use—to build guns, say. The Chinese "scientists," including Fang Lizhi, tried to break away from this distinction by identifying science with values, or indeed with a "spirit." This is difficult to grasp without knowing the Chinese context. For Chinese scientism is not quite the same as Einstein's moral concerns. The "scientists" are optimists and believe that science will lead to enlightenment and truth, whereas Einstein worried that people would not use scientific discoveries responsibly. As he observed: "Our entire much-praised technological progress, and civilization generally, could be compared to an ax in the hand of a pathological criminal."

Einstein's quote was not really on my mind when I drove up to the gate of the Intercontinental Ballistic Missile Museum. But it is hard not to reflect on the dangers of pure science when you enter the museum, which is really a silo containing a gigantic Titan nuclear missile once aimed at several sites in the Communist world, perhaps even Beijing. From this spot in the desert, forces could have been unleashed that would have killed millions. The missile still stands underground, like some malign giant phallus. But the exit has been sealed.

I bought my entrance ticket from a woman in her sixties. Her hair was painted a light shade of blond. She spoke rather brusquely in a German accent—a former GI bride perhaps? I joined a group of tourists, mostly young people, of various nationalities. Our guide was a roly-poly man with a ready smile and a baseball cap perched above a beefy face. The cap identified him as BOB. Bob was a retired military man who had worked on the Titan when it was still operational. Another tour group emerged from an elevator that had come up from the underground control center. Their guide was an equally jolly-looking figure; PETE according to his cap.

Aboveground, Bob informed us about the various technical details of the Titan—how much fuel it took, its weight, its speed, and so on. He pointed out the various devices to camouflage the Titan's location from prying enemy satellites. He told us everything except how much damage the phallus would have done in the event of its deployment. Perhaps it was squeamishness or perhaps he simply did not know. Psychiatrists have identified a kind of numbing effect on scientists and soldiers who deal with death on a massive scale. It is difficult to be morally engaged and think of the possible consequences of your job. It is at any rate not easy to imagine the death of millions.

Down in the bowels of the Titan missile complex, dozens of feet underground, we entered the control room through a long succession of thick steel doors, which clanked shut with a peculiar hissing sound, as though sucking the air from the tight little spots we found ourselves jammed in. Bob showed us the control panel with the buttons, in red, yellow, and green, that would have set the missile off. A middle-aged lady in tight shorts and Nike running shoes was invited to assist Bob in a mock-up nuclear attack. She giggled as Bob led her pudgy finger to "Target One." I asked him what the targets were. He said that was something they were never told. Not knowing, he said, made the job easier.

Was this the nightmare side of the Enlightenment? Had Bob and Pete been the pawns in a game of science gone mad? Is the human capacity to blow up our world an argument against pure science? On my way back to Tucson, with the evening sun bathing the Native American reservations around me in a warm pink light of extraordinary beauty, I could not think of any rational reason why man's freedom to explore the nature of our world, and the universe beyond our world, should be shackled. The question is how we use these inquiries. The nuclear bomb was developed by refugees from Nazi Europe and used on other human beings by the most democratic nation on earth. This was a terrible thing. But if Hitler's scientists had gotten the deadly new weapon first, the results surely would have been worse. The problem, then, is not science as such. Nor is it the artificial and fruitless battle between "materialist" science and "spiritual" tradition. The problem is the nature of the society in which the fruits of science are employed. It is absurd to expect scientists to be more moral, responsible, spiritual, or wiser than the rest of us. That is where the "scientists" are wrong. And the notion that science supplies moral truths is equally wrongheaded. But it is not scientists who must be chained, but governments. We need ways to stop our rulers from ruling arbitrarily or absolutely. The first principle of good science and good governance is the freedom to be critical. In this respect, Fang Lizhi and his fellow dissident scientists are an example not just to China but to us all.

Chapter 4

Mr. Wei
Goes to Washington

It was, as far as Washington, D.C., news goes, not a major incident. Indeed, it was barely reported in the American press, which was, in the freezing month of January 1999, still dominated by details of President Clinton's sexual transgressions with a lovestruck young woman on the White House staff. But for Chinese living in exile in the United States it was a big event, discussed with great gusts of emotion in émigré journals and on Internet websites.

It all began when Wei Jingsheng, together with several other Chinese dissidents, was invited to testify before the United States House of Representatives' Committee on International Relations. Wei, the author, in 1978, of the democratic manifesto that got him jailed for fifteen years, was neither a Christian nor a blind disciple of Mr. Science. The occasion was prompted by the arrests in China of a number of people whose crime was to have founded the so-called China Democracy Party. Their aim had not been to overthrow the government but to take part in legitimate local elections. But since unofficial parties threaten the Communist

Party's monopoly on power, this initiative was swiftly dealt with: the Democracy Party was banned and its leaders put in prison. One was a veteran activist named Xu Wenli, who had already been driven to the limit of his endurance in the early 1980s, when he was locked up for twelve years, much of the time in a kind of concrete cage that was too small to stand up or lie down in. His hair turned white; he lost his teeth, and almost his mind. In 1998, this gentle magazine editor, who had always advocated socialist reform, not revolution, was sentenced to another thirteen years in jail.

I sat directly behind Wei in a large room inside the Rayburn Building, where congressional hearings are usually held. Hideous oil paintings of former U.S. congressmen added a somewhat contrived democratic gravitas to the clubby wood-paneled walls. The starched Stars and Stripes stood out boldly against the sea of sky-blue curtains. Facing us, on an elevated stage, rather like judges in a courtroom, sat the committee members. They included a Democrat from San Francisco, who told us that the Chinese sitting before them were the "heirs" of the liberties imparted to "our great country" by "our Founding Fathers," a Republican, also from the West Coast, who got very red in the face and said the dictatorship in China was "evil, just as the Nazis were evil," and a large, smiling Samoan Democrat in a string tie, who reminded us of the human-rights abuses in the United States, beginning with the slave trade two hundred years ago and continuing in our time with discrimination against Pacific Islanders. The Democrat from San Francisco nodded wisely and added something about women. The testifiers, some of whom had only just arrived from China, where they had been kept in prison until the day they left, looked mystified.

But not Wei. I noticed his broad back stiffen as he drummed his fingers on the arms of his chair. Tufts of short-cropped black hair stood up in little spikes around the collar of his blue open-necked sports shirt. Wei had heard this kind of waffle before and was itching to speak. I could just make out, over his shoulder, his pointed chin jutting toward the committee members. I was reminded of the photographs taken of Wei during his show trials in Beijing, in 1979 and 1993, when he was charged with "conspiracy to subvert the government." His head shaved, like a monk's, he had had that same look of determination, of knowing what (and who) is right and wanting to tell the world all about it: a man with a mission.

Although the questions from the congressmen were addressed to Wei as well as to his colleagues, Wei did most of the talking, while the others peered around and took in their strange surroundings: the flag, the portraits, the large foreign men and women looking down on them, smiling with an air of what might be described as parental pride. Later, also in the Rayburn Building, I was in an elevator with Wei when the bluff Republican chairman of the House Foreign Affairs Committee stepped in with a colleague. He wrapped a big, blue-blazered arm around Wei, patted him on the back, and boomed that here was the greatest human-rights activist from China. "Now, tell me, how long were you in jail for?" Eighteen years, said Wei. "Oh my goodness! God bless you, sir."

In the Beijing courts, in 1979 and 1993, Wei had had the marvelous effrontery to lecture his judges calmly on human rights before they put him away—on both occasions for more than ten years of prison and hard labor. His remarks in Washington, spoken in purring northern Chinese, showed the same self-assurance. Wei leaned forward as his words were translated to the committee, nodding vigorously as though to drive each point home with his chin. People in the West may think that human-rights conditions in China were improving, but in fact, he said, this assumption was absolutely incorrect. The recent arrests showed clearly that the Chinese Communist Party was not about to relax its grip on power and that only constant pressure from the West would force the government to make any concessions. He himself probably owed his life to such pressure. He added, for the benefit of the Democrats on the committee, that every nation, including the United States, had a history of human-rights abuses. The American slave trade had been an appalling thing, to be sure, and the situation in places such as Burma and East Timor may be very bad too. But China was different: China was bigger, more powerful, and thus more dangerous. And it was, in any case, morally wrong, as well as misguided, to criticize smaller, weaker nations while not daring to speak out against China.

Wei's testimony was an astonishing performance: a model of concise analysis, which made the rhetorical preening of some of the congressmen look fatuous (C-SPAN cameras were on hand to provide live television coverage to the voters back home). And here was a man who had spent much of his adult life in solitary confinement, with only police interrogators and hardened criminals, ordered to beat him up, for occasional company. (In the cold, bleak fastness of a labor camp in western China, Wei was once given the rare privilege of being allowed to keep a rabbit, a source of profound happiness; but with a change of guards, the privilege was swiftly taken away.)

The incident that sent such ripples across the Chinese political diaspora occurred only seconds after the hearing was over. The cameras were still running, red lights blinking. But the committee members had already risen from their chairs and were slipping their papers into blue plastic folders. Suddenly a voice cried out in Chinese from the back of the chamber: "You are not representative of the Chinese people! How dare you speak for the democracy movement! You insulted Xu Wenli! You are beneath contempt!"

A man in a shabby blue suit rushed forward to where Wei was standing. One of the congressmen tapped a microphone and asked: "Can we have a translation please?"

The man in the blue suit became more and more agitated and made as if to attack Wei physically. Another Chinese man, dressed more expensively, in a brown silk suit and shiny crocodile shoes, was watching the commotion. As Wei, who remained silent, was eased out of the room by his supporters, a third Chinese man, in a thick gray sweater, began to shout abuse: "He is scum! My wife is still in jail in China and nobody says anything about that. But everything that motherfucking scoundrel says is reported in *The New York Times*!" Then he turned to a pale, thin man in the audience. "And you," he shouted, jabbing his finger into the thin man's chest. "If you can't stop bad-mouthing Xu Wenli, you should go back and rot in jail!"

When the police finally arrived, the man in the crocodile shoes said, "Enough," and the rumpus died almost as quickly as it had started. Only the man in the shabby blue suit raged on for a bit and had to be restrained by his friends. He had an odd face, slightly horsey, with large eyes and a sharp nose, features more common among some of the ethnic minorities than the Han Chinese. And I suddenly remembered where I had seen him before.

Earlier that year, I had attended a rather melancholy gathering of exiled Chinese activists in what was still the Portuguese colony of Macau. This was just after the fall of General Suharto in Indonesia. There was a sense of futility about the meeting: people who had once been important in China sounding off to an indifferent world. And there, in that hot and airless schoolroom, rented for the occasion, this man had stood up to make an emotional statement about solidarity with the Indonesian democrats: Today Jakarta, tomorrow Beijing! It was a noble gesture, especially in the somewhat rancid air of Chinese self-absorption. His name was Wang Xizhe.

———

At one time, Wang's heroic status had matched that of Wei Jingsheng. Wang was one of the authors of the famous manifesto posted on a wall in Guangzhou (Canton) in 1974, signed Li Yi Zhe, demanding democratic rights and criticizing the Party bosses (though not Mao) for being corrupt bureaucratic fascists. It was Wang's group that Gong Xiaoxia, my friend in Washington, D.C., had joined, thrilled to find an oasis of serious debate in a brainwashed society. The group would meet every week in a one-room apartment to discuss Marx, Engels, Lenin, and Mao—and also Solzhenitsyn, John Locke, and Max Weber. Wang, taller and more forceful than the others, had stood out even then. He liked to be the center of attention.

The Li Yi Zhe essay, which went on for sixty-seven densely written pages, was the first major attack on the Communist regime from the Cultural Revolution generation. It was an attack from the left: The revolution had reneged on its promise to give power to the people. Instead of socialism, Chinese Communist rule had imposed a more ferocious form of feudal despotism. The particular tone of this attack, its revolutionary passion, had everything to do with the authors' experiences as Red Guards.

Wang had been a student in Guangzhou when the Cultural Revolution began. Full of enthusiasm to "make revolution" and smash "bureaucratism," he joined the second wave of Red Guards in 1966, the so-called rebel faction, which concentrated on purging Party cadres. Mao, supported by his wife, Jiang Qing, and her extremist group, the Gang of Four, had deliberately incited the first wave of students—mostly children of the Party elite—to attack their elders, drag them out of their offices and homes, force them onto their knees, beat them, spit on them, torture them, daub them with ink, put dunce caps on them, and make them confess their heinous political crimes. If the "capitalist roaders" and "stinking reactionaries" should die in the process, then so be it. This was Mao's way of breaking the power of Party bureaucrats and thus ensuring the continuation of his absolute rule.

This first wave had included Wei Jingsheng, the son of a high official. The second wave was less rooted in the Communist upper class. Neither Wang nor his friends, such as Gong Xiaoxia's lover Chen Yiyang, were from the elite. On the contrary. They were sometimes from the wrong class—that is, their parents were educated people tainted by the ancien régime.

Hierarchies were turned topsy-turvy. Rebellion was blessed. Mao was God. But when the students began to develop their own ideas, roaming around the country in armed gangs, threatening to rush beyond Mao's grasp, and fighting one another, first wave against second wave, army units against Red Guards, faction against faction, they too had to be crushed. In 1968 Mao's erstwhile "little generals" were hunted down by the police, arrested, and sent to remote villages to "learn from the peasants." This is what happened to Wei Jingsheng. It is what happened to Wang Xizhe and Chen Yiyang and the rest of their group.

The sense of betrayed expectations is palpable in the Li Yi Zhe manifesto: "The freedom of speech, the freedom of the press, the freedom of association, which are stipulated in the Constitution, and the freedom of exchanging revolutionary experience, which is not stipulated in the Constitution, have all been truly practiced in the great revolution and granted with the support of the Party Central headed by Chairman Mao. This is something which the Chinese people had not possessed for several thousand years, something so active and lively; and this is the extraordinary achievement of the revolution. But our Great Proletarian Cultural Revolution has not accomplished its tasks because it has not enabled the people to grasp the weapon of mass democracy."

It is a slightly odd statement to read now, long after the event, since the quasi-religious worship of Chairman Mao can hardly be described as "freedom." Yet the violent anarchy of the 1960s gave millions of young people their first taste of attacking state authority, or indeed any authority except Mao's. As a result of the manifesto, Wang and his colleagues were denounced as "reactionaries" and forced to do hard labor in the countryside. Under the Gang of Four, the reactionary label was often a death sentence. Wang Xizhe survived his time in detention but was sentenced again after Mao's death in 1976. This time, absurdly, he and his friends were charged with being counterrevolutionary followers of the Gang of Four and maintaining clandestine links with Taiwan and Hong Kong. After a year in a detention center, he was freed. But worse was still in store.

Even as Wei Jingsheng was causing a sensation in Beijing in 1978 by posting his manifesto, advocating the Fifth Modernization (democracy), on the Democracy Wall, Wang was busy writing political essays in Guangzhou, which he sent by mail as mimeographed "newsletters"—a crude harbinger of the e-mail networks that were to come twenty years later. Both men said they wanted democracy, but their politics were not at all the same. Wang had begun to recognize Mao as the monster he was. He described him as a typical Chinese peasant rebel who founded a new dynasty and ruled as a traditional despot. Mao was not a true Marxist in Wang's view. But Wang still was a Marxist, and like most dissident intellectuals, including Xu Wenli, who later founded the China Democracy Party, he believed that a reformed Communist Party could deliver a better society. Since Deng Xiaoping had also been purged during the Cultural Revolution and was now promising new liberties, he should have the benefit of the doubt. Deng, so Wang believed, offered the best chance of achieving real democratic socialism.

Wei disagreed. Almost alone among his fellow activists of the Democracy Wall period, Wei warned that without radical political change, Deng would turn out to be a tyrant just like the countless Chinese despots who had preceded him. Without the freedom to criticize and vote, there could be no check on absolute personal power. Wei turned out to be right.

Deng, just as Mao had done so often before, used the free-spirited young before turning on them. He needed the support of Democracy Wall activists to oust the remnants of the Gang of Four and take power himself. Once he ruled China, he got rid of his critics. Wei Jingsheng, who had caused the greatest offense by attacking Deng by name, was the first to disappear into the Chinese gulag. Others quickly followed. But even then Wang Xizhe did not see what was coming. He thought Deng was being indiscriminate in his crackdown on Democracy Wall but that the arrest of Wei was defensible. "Some people," Wang wrote, "criticize Deng for sentencing Wei Jingsheng simply for having spoken up. I disagree. Deng's main problem was to keep the situation under control after a long period of repression. Both history and common sense show that social upheavals that are too radical often alienate the people."

It was the classic line of the reformist intellectual, to be repeated by many others: avoid chaos at all costs, give "the doves" in the Party some time, democracy can wait, maybe socialism can still be saved. In 1989, the journalist Dai Qing used more or less the same argument to attack the student "radicals." Not that it helped Wang when the despot's eyes came to rest on him. For Deng did not give *him* the benefit of the doubt. In 1981, Wang too entered the dark maw of the Chinese prison system, where he was locked up for long spells in a solitary cell. A former inmate of the same prison remembers being spooked at night by Wang's lonely howls echoing through the corridors. Wang did not reemerge into the light until 1993. Like Xu Wenli's, his hair had gone white.

—

Here they were, then, Wang and Wei, brave and damaged veterans of the Chinese gulag, face-to-face in a government chamber in Washington, D.C., one man screaming in rage, the other silently turning his back. Why were relations so venomous between men who should be allies? Did it go back to old differences?: Red Guard rivalries between snooty, northern Beijing and despised Guangzhou, or quarrels about tactics, radical democratic change as opposed to slow, Party-led reform? Was it guilt, perhaps, or resentment to do with Wang's defense of Wei's arrest in 1979? Or was it simply a matter of jealousy and frustration?

Wei, after all, was still being described as the "father of Chinese democracy." He still had the ear of foreign ministers, American congressmen, and Washington columnists, while Wang had become a shadowy figure since his arrival in the U.S., one of many dissidents trying to find a role, attracting attention by periodic hunger strikes, attempting to join the Kuomintang (KMT) in Taiwan (unsuccessfully), or trying to enter China without any chance of success. Just before the Washington incident, Wang had been on a brief hunger strike in front of the United Nations in New York. A pamphlet handed out at the occasion concluded: "We wish that our voices be heard by the entire world." They seldom were.

I remembered a conversation with the former student leader Li Lu, who was of course a generation younger. After Tiananmen, Li had been through feuds of his own, between "moderates" and "radicals." He offered a cultural explanation. Chinese culture, he said, produces either a slave mentality or extreme individualism. Those who refuse to be slaves are fighters. And the first to rebel expect to be leaders. The fighters in exile live in a small Chinese ghetto, where everybody knows everybody. And so they fight one another.

The picture Li paints of life in the "ghetto" is plausible. These are all damaged people, prone to expend their frustrated energies on devouring each other. But there is more to it than psychological trauma. In the absence of an institutional mechanism, such as the vote, to resolve political conflicts and give legitimacy to leadership claims, feuding and intrigue take over. This is not only true of politics in exile but of politics in China itself, or indeed in any dictatorship. If the people cannot choose their rulers, the rulers will decide on the pecking order themselves, through patronage, family connections, and raw, sometimes murderous skulduggery. Joseph Conrad caught the poisoned atmosphere of late czarist Russia perfectly in *Under Western Eyes,* his novel about the treacherous student, Razumov, living among revolutionary exiles in Geneva: " 'Oh, we are great in talking about each other,' interjected Razumov, who had listened with great attention. 'Gossip, tales, suspicions, and all that sort of thing, we know how to deal in to perfection. Calumny, even.' "

The pecking order among the exiles revolves around a key phrase: *zige,* meaning "credentials" or "qualifications." To be a leader you need *zige,* indeed more *zige* than any rival. It is one of the most common phrases of abuse or dismissal: He has no *zige* to . . . speak for the democratic movement or to organize a conference or to lead a party or to testify to a congressional committee. *Zige* can be earned in various ways and played like a trump card in an elaborate game whose rules are necessarily vague. Wei's eighteen years in jail would have awarded him more *zige* than Wang's fourteen. But Wang could claim to have been an activist longer than Wei. The Li Yi Zhe poster went up when Wei was still an obscure electrician.

There is also something less tangible and perhaps more traditionally Chinese that determines the degree of *zige,* something closer to the Confucian idea of moral character. This became clearer to me as I was standing outside the Rayburn Building on that wintry day in Washington and talking to the man in the crocodile shoes. His name was Dr. Wang Bingzhang (he had been a medical doctor in China), and his claim to *zige* was based on his having founded the first overseas Chinese democratic association in 1982. An ill-considered clandestine trip to China, which led to his expulsion, did nothing to enhance his *zige,* however. There was a slightly louche air about Wang Bingzhang, a hint of the smooth operator. After I talked to him the next day in the lobby of the Willard Hotel, he insisted on posing with me for a photograph, as though he were a politician on the stump.

Dr. Wang prided himself on being a religious man. He was worried about the loss of "values" in China, about that notorious "spiritual vacuum." And like so many others, he saw Christianity as the essential vehicle for "saving China." He first saved himself by converting to Christianity while living in Toronto in the early 1980s. Without Christianity, he told me, people cannot control themselves. And that was the problem in China. People were corrupt. They could not control their greed. All because of the destruction of traditional values by communism.

There was, however, no mention of God in the pamphlet Dr. Wang pressed into my hand on the steps of the Rayburn Building. It was an open letter to the chairman of the House committee, written in awkward English and filled with the denunciatory phrases in which Communist Chinese is so rich. The letter explained why Wang Xizhe and Dr. Wang

Bingzhang should be testifying to the U.S. Congress instead of the "ill-cultivated bubble-star" Wei Jingsheng. For they had supported Xu Wenli and his fellow members of the China Democracy Party, whereas the "bubble-star" had been consistently hostile to Xu. It was indeed true that Xu had received money from Dr. Wang. And Wei had criticized the fledgling party as a hopeless project: The timing was all wrong; it was bound to fail. In fact, Wei went further and saw sinister motives at work. Xu Wenli, he ventured, had probably made a secret deal with the Chinese government. After a year or two they would let him go to America, where he would use his dissident credentials to undermine Wei. Poor Xu, rotting in jail, was denounced by Wei as a government agent.

Given the length of Xu's jail sentence, this accusation was absurd. It was the kind of suspicion that might easily arise in the mind of a man who has spent eighteen years trying to outwit interrogators bent on his destruction. But one senses that the real quarrel here was not about spies or politics but about *zige*, character, recognition, mutual insults—in short, about who is to be boss.

That is why Wei was described in the pamphlet not only as a "bubble-star" with "poor vision" and "moderate IQ" but as "rootless in the entire Chinese dissident community in China." Wei was not the "father of Chinese democracy," as some foreigners said, but a "self-esteemed phony 'leader,' " created by the Western media, which are obsessed with celebrity and ignorant of the real dissidents working inside China. Wei and his supporters were "acting like cancers in the exile dissident community. . . ." The conclusion: "To have bubble-stars monopoly all the creams while leaving nothing to those hard workers is just part of the soap opera culture."

The meaning of "bubble-star" can be guessed. Wei is accused of being just another meretricious celebrity. But one wonders what was meant by "the creams." Money from government agencies and private funds? Invitations to testify in Washington? Interviews in the mass media? Probably all of these things. Sadly, Wei was as wild in his denunciations as his critics. Not only did he see conspiracies behind Xu Wenli's arrest, but he told me later that Wang Xizhe was also most probably a secret agent in the pay of the Chinese government. Where else did he get his money from? After all, he had no *zige*. His views were discredited. He was a failure in the West. Yet there he was, living in comfort, bad-mouthing Wei. There could surely be only one explanation.

When I asked Dr. Wang about this, still standing on the steps of the Rayburn Building, he repeated all the allegations against Wei, but then said something curious. He had urged Wei, as well as Wang Xizhe, to go to church, a Christian church, to have "a direct experience with God. Before our Lord, everyone must be humble." After that he set off into the icy streets. His light-brown crocodile shoes had gone dark and soggy with slush.

—

It is sometimes tempting for the outside observer to wish a plague on all their houses. In periodic fits of disgust with the sheer bloody-mindedness of exile paranoia, I would recall one of Gong Xiaoxia's remarks: "Look at the kind of people who join the democracy movement. They all had miserable childhoods. They join out of desperation. Because there is nothing else for them. They are all crazy." I once asked her how much she thought life in prison had warped men such as Wang Xizhe and Wei Jingsheng. She replied that she was always surprised how little they had changed.

The other temptation for the outsider is to pick sides, to become an advocate for one figure or faction or another. The result is always deadly. You begin to see the world through paranoid eyes, and the person whose cause you seek to champion will inevitably resent you, too, for no apologetics can ever be wholehearted or effusive enough. It is amazing how many disillusioned foreign fans, experts, and groupies the overseas dissidents leave in their wake.

And yet it is wrong for an outsider to act as a moral judge. For however much they might set upon one another, men such as Wei Jingsheng and Wang Xizhe still deserve respect—not just because of their suffering, but because they chose to face the consequences of speaking out in circumstances that are hard for us even to imagine. They defied orthodoxy at the risk of their lives. To persist in doing so during long years of torture, buried alone in filthy, concrete vaults, where mind and body are systematically broken by brutal experts, takes extraordinary strength of character.

Wei was locked up in stinking death cells, interrogated day and night for months, had his teeth smashed and his health wrecked, and when he staged a hunger strike in desperation, he was hung upside down, his mouth wrenched open with a steel clamp and hot gruel pumped into his stomach through a plastic hose. When Wang Xizhe went on his hunger strike, he was force-fed through a bamboo tube rammed down his throat.

Wei's friend and supporter Liu Qing, who was jailed for having published the transcripts of Wei's first trial in his samizdat magazine, was forced to spend four years sitting absolutely still on a tiny stool made of hard rope that cut through his buttocks. No books, no exercise, no conversation. Every day for four agonizing years. And while he sat, privileged criminals ("trusties") were ordered to surround him in shifts, to beat him if he so much as moved. To come out of that without going mad, you have to be stubborn to the point of madness.

Liu Qing had also been present in the Rayburn Building when Wei was accosted. Indeed, it was Liu who was cursed by the agitated man in the gray sweater and told to go back to China and rot in jail. But this kind of madness, this embittered émigré frenzy, is not the kind of cussedness that kept Wei or Liu, or even Wang, from cracking in jail. Wei especially was driven by something else, more like an absolute conviction. After having been mentally swindled once into a blind belief in orthodoxy, Wei decided he would never again give up the freedom to think for himself. He changed his mind about communism, found another truth to replace it, and never wavered. The harder the authorities tried to break him and make him recant, the harder this conviction grew. The freedom to state the truth as he saw it became absolute in Wei's mind. On this point he is utterly uncompromising, a quality so rare, and dangerous, that it could be easily mistaken for madness.

———

One way to get the measure of Wei Jingsheng's character is to take a ride in his car. It is a disconcerting experience, not because he is ignorant of the traffic rules, but because he chooses to make up his own. Perhaps because of all those years of forced immobility, Wei is happiest when he is in motion and, above all, when he can control that motion himself. Impediments such as red lights are to be ignored. When Wei gets behind the steering wheel, he is a free man. Streets are taken in great bursts of speed. When the car must stop, to avoid instant death, he will slam on the brakes at the last possible moment. The point is to keep moving, moving, moving. A one-way street? Lesser men might be impeded. But not Wei. Impossible to turn left or right? Wei will decide about that. I never witnessed him being stopped by the police, but I can imagine his indignation.

There was some talk of my driving across America with Wei. He was keen. I was looking forward to it, with some trepidation. But the trip never came off. Wei was in Paris that week, or Bonn, or Taiwan, or Berkeley, or . . . Motion was perpetual, and stretched across continents. After eighteen years in a cell, the man with a mission could not bear to sit still.

It was never even clear where he lived. When he had a scholarship at Berkeley, he was hardly ever there. He kept an apartment near Columbia University in Manhattan, but his sister had moved into it with her daughter. Relations were not always good. There were times when Wei, rather than go home, would drive around New York for hours, aimlessly, just to keep moving.

One afternoon, in the living room of a mutual friend, Wei explained his attitude to rules. He said that societies where people stick to the rules are stable societies. When nobody obeys the rules, society breaks down. And yet, he said, to be creative, you have to break a few rules. A society in which everyone followed the rules would be boring and dead. So to liven things up, some people must ignore the rules, at least some of the time.

I first met Wei at a dinner in Washington. The other guests were a well-meaning but rather pompous State Department official and his somewhat formal wife, several academics in the China field, an expert on military affairs, and the odd journalist. It was, as Washington dinners go, not a stuffy occasion, but it was clear from the moment Wei appeared, wiping his eyes after a late afternoon nap, that he liked to present himself as a bit of a bad boy who had no time for petty conventions. For one thing, he refused to wear socks or shoes. For another, he not only smoked incessantly, which is perfectly normal in China, but insisted on blowing smoke into the eyes of the official's wife. And the more the Americans lectured him about the perils of smoking, the greater the relish with which he lit up another cigarette and another, stating that, on the contrary, smoking was very good for him. His round baby face widened in a grin of deep satisfaction.

Wei delights in exaggerated displays of proletarian mannerisms, rolling his trousers up above his knees when he feels hot or letting out trumpeting farts in public. There is an element of playacting in this. The trickster's chuckle is never far away. But I really understood the true nature of Wei's manners only after reading his prison letters, which he had managed to keep, and later publish, by refusing to leave jail without them.

In 1982, in a letter to his brother and two sisters, Wei discusses a movie about an eccentric Song-dynasty poet named Lu You. The poet is conventionally described as a "mad genius" who flouted the Confucian conventions of his time by living with his lover without marrying her, and so on. The point, writes Wei, is that he wasn't really mad at all. Since feudal customs were intolerable, it was "more convenient to move about under the cloak of 'madness' in order to resist these customs or simply to numb oneself to them." Wei continues: "The fact that traditional China could be so dictatorial and at the same time pass down so many anti-feudal elements in its literary classics has a lot to do with literati intellectuals feigning madness in order to resist social mores, as well as an increasing aspiration and admiration for the 'famed mad genius' style."

In another letter, Wei reminds his brother, Taotao, of the time they were sent down to their ancestral village during the Cultural Revolution. Rural life was still in a state of shock. After Mao's catastrophic economic experiments of the Great Leap Forward in the late 1950s, two thirds of the villagers had died of starvation. People had been forced to eat their neighbors' children (even in desperation it was too painful to eat your own). But revolutionary extremism had not dented the stubborn rural conservatism of the survivors. "Taotao," writes Wei, with an air of big-city arrogance, "do you still remember how the two of us acted back when we were staying in our ancestral hometown? I had grown disgusted with the false niceties and affectations of southerners and began self-consciously modeling myself after the 'famed mad geniuses' of China and abroad."

Wei continues to do so today—self-consciously, that is. For he is not an idiot savant or a simple worker whose thirst for freedom is instinctive and unschooled. Even though he was once an electrician, like Lech Wałesa, he is also the son of highly educated Communist cadres and went to the best school in Beijing. And like many former Red Guards, including his rival Wang Xizhe, he used his years of aborted education to read widely. Since he was born into the Party elite, he had the run of restricted libraries. So Wei not only worked his way through the Communist classics, but by the late 1970s he had become a self-educated expert on thinkers of the European Enlightenment as well.

In a sense, perhaps, Wei's personality—like that of Mao Zedong, whom, in his total self-belief, he resembles—is artistic more than political. It does not take much prompting for his mad-genius side to come out. When I was in Washington, he would often drop in at my friend's house, arriving from New York, Copenhagen, or wherever he happened to be that week, to cook steaming pork dumplings, roll up his trousers, take off his socks, hang them on the chair beside him, and hold forth in a bizarre, sometimes utterly wrongheaded, but often brilliant torrent of words.

He had thoughts about everything. "Western debate," he opined, was all based on rhetorical "trickery." Look at the O. J. Simpson trial; whoever has the better lawyers wins the argument. "Orientals," he professed, are much more honest in debate: "We learn how to establish the truth through argument at a very early age."

I expressed some skepticism, and said that I didn't know about the Chinese, but the Japanese were hardly known for their debating skills.

Wei waved his hand as though my remark were a noisome fly. "The Orient," he said, squinting through a curtain of cigarette smoke, "is China. Japan is just an appendage."

Wild denunciations of fellow activists were made without any evidence. Western experts on China, who had sometimes dedicated themselves to helping Wei's cause, were dismissed with "You foreigners can never understand China." American policy was described as "pro-Communist." And all this with unshakable conviction. But as with the cigarette smoke blown into the Washington lady's face, you were never quite sure about the degree of deliberate provocation. He liked an argument for the sake of it, just to test your mettle. And he would always claim victory at the end.

———

If the world of intellectuals can be divided, as Isaiah Berlin once argued, between foxes, who know many things, and hedgehogs, who know one big thing, Wei is clearly a hedgehog. The one conviction he guards like a precious jewel, and about which he is lucid, always serious, and willing to stake his life, he had already expressed clearly in his 1978 manifesto on the Democracy Wall in Beijing. It goes to the heart of the Chinese problem. "History," he wrote, "shows that there must be a limit to the amount of trust conferred upon any individual. Anyone seeking the unconditional trust of the people is a person of unbridled ambition. The important thing is to select the right sort of person to put one's trust in, and even more important is how such a person is to be supervised in carrying out the will of the majority. We can trust only those representatives who are supervised by us and responsible to us. Such representatives should be chosen by us and not thrust upon us."

Wei Jingsheng was twenty-nine when he wrote that. Memories of Mao worship and its millions upon millions of victims, humiliated, maimed, and tortured to death, were still raw. The statement is as simple as it is true. And Wei has stuck to it. He is often accused of being out of touch with developments in China, of not recognizing the changes that economic reforms, carried out while he was in prison, have brought. But if one believes, as Wei does, that only political change which guarantees the right to criticize and to vote will do, such reforms are beside the point, for they fail to address the main problem. He argues, simply, bluntly, doggedly, at times megalomaniacally, that without democracy—not "socialist" democracy or "people's" democracy—the Chinese cycle of violence, followed by tyranny, will never be broken.

The way a former Maoist fanatic arrived at this conclusion has been described by Wei himself, as well as by his perhaps too admiring biographer, the German journalist Jürgen Kremb. That he was once a fanatic is clear from his own account: He had wrecked "bourgeois" homes, dragged out "rightists" for public interrogations, and spouted devotional Maoist maxims ever since he was a child, when his father made him learn a new page of Mao's writings every day. Wei was among the first wave of middle school students to become a Red Guard but also, it seems, among the first to have doubts. Some of the stages of Wei's intellectual journey from total belief in communism to total disbelief have taken on an almost mythical status. Most poignant, perhaps, is Wei's glimpse of the naked girl.

To make it easier for the young to spread revolutionary terror all over China, Red Guards were allowed to travel by train free of charge. Wei hopped on a train sometime in 1966, bound for the northwest. When the train pulled into the city of Lanzhou, he was shocked to see children swarming outside the window begging for food. A middle-aged man, sharing his compartment, said they were probably children of landlords, "rightists," and other "bad elements," and deserved to starve.

The barren northwestern landscape became more desolate by the mile after the train left Lanzhou. It stopped at a windswept little station so insignificant that it did not even have a platform. Again, the crying and whimpering of beggars drew Wei's attention. He leaned out of the window. One girl, of about seventeen, her face covered in soot and her long hair caked with dirt, raised her arms, begging for something to eat. She appeared to be dressed in a filthy rag. The middle-aged man sniggered and said girls like that would do anything you fancied for a few crumbs of food. Suddenly Wei pulled back from the window in shock. What looked like a rag was nothing of the kind. The girl was covered in nothing but her own matted hair. Wei was overcome by a wave of disgust—with the obscene, sniggering man, the starving, naked girl, the stench of urine and excrement, the simmering violence among the Red Guards, and the bony arms outside clawing the ground for scraps of food. And he asked himself: Was this the "fruit" of socialism?

There were more shocks to challenge the official version of reality in China. On a trip to the far west, he saw families living in holes in the ground, sharing one warm garment against the freezing winds; he met "rightist" intellectuals there who had been banished in 1957 to do hard labor without a chance of ever going home. In the early 1970s, Wei met his first girlfriend, Ping Ni, the daughter of a high-ranking Tibetan Communist living in Beijing. Her family story was enough to drive away any illusions he might still have had.

Ping's father was a staunch Maoist, even during the bloody suppression of the Tibetan revolt in 1959. But someone had to be blamed for the escape to India in that year of the Dalai Lama and a hundred thousand followers. So one night in the spring of 1960, when Ping Ni was six years old, there was a knock on the door. Her father was taken away to spend the next twenty years in prison. Six years later, the Red Guards came for her mother, who, in full sight of her daughter, slit her veins with a razor. With blood spurting from her wrists, she was dragged downstairs by the teenage revolutionaries and bundled into a truck. Ping Ni's last sight of her mother was of her legs kicking before the door was slammed and the truck drove off into the dark.

Wei came to the dangerous, and for him almost fatal, conclusion that "a foremost characteristic of the Communist Party is lying, very effective lying, lying all the time and about everything. It is not easy for ordinary folks to see through this. As the youngest in the [Red Guard] leadership, I saw it clearly, all the cruelties, which totally destroyed my previously conceived impressions of the Communist Party."

This in itself did not make him an original thinker. Many intelligent Chinese had reached similar conclusions. More unusual was his view that communism was absolutely incompatible with democracy, and there was nothing to gain from making concessions to the Party. This is what drove him to the Democracy Wall.

—

Beijing in 1978, when it all began, was a city in chaos. The winter was unusually cold, with winds from the Gobi Desert howling through the broad, empty avenues around the Forbidden City. Thousands of jobless former Red Guards were returning every day from the countryside. Many of them hung around the streets with nowhere to go. Thousands more victims of recent upheavals, ex-prisoners, desperate people labeled as "rightists," orphans of murdered parents, all the human ruins of Maoist lunacy, arrived by bus or train or even on foot. They came to petition the government to get their innocent relatives out of jail, or to find jobs, food, or indeed any means of survival.

There was also a sense of political and cultural excitement in the air, as though a thick layer of ice that had muffled free human expression were gradually melting. Independent journals were founded. Artists experimented with new forms. And apart from the many pathetic petitions plastered on the Democracy Wall, in Xidan, a busy junction not far from Tiananmen Square, there were poems and political tracts. A young poet named Huang Xiang wrote about Chairman Mao's war on the Chinese people, a war that was not yet over, despite the Great Helmsman's death:

> The war goes on in everyone's facial expression.
> The war is waged by numerous high-pitched loudspeakers
> The war is waged in every pair of fearful, shifting eyes.

But most of the political writing on the wall was supportive of Deng Xiaoping, and couched in careful, reformist, Marxist language. The term "human rights" was not yet used. Dissidents talked about "citizens' rights" instead. All except for Wei. That is why the appearance on the dawn of December 5 of the Fifth Modernization caused such a commotion. Crowds gathered around Wei's wall poster, shoving one another to get a better view. Volunteers read the words out loud so others could hear. Word got around, and crowds kept coming and coming. The message, expressed in simple, lucid prose, that Chinese should be masters of their own destiny, that they had no more need of gods and emperors, and that the only form of modernization worth having should bring democracy and freedom, was so unusual, so fresh, and so extraordinarily bold after thirty years of leaden propaganda that it packed the emotional force of great poetry or beautiful music. People burst into tears.

Not only had Wei said in public what he thought; he had signed his name to it, too. His own recollection of this act of almost suicidal courage is already encrusted in legend, but it is a legend wrapped around a psychological truth. In 1999, Wei explained to some Chinese journalists why he had done it. He said it had been a matter of pride. He recalled that in November 1978, Deng Xiaoping had issued an order to stop the protests on the Democracy Wall. A notice duly appeared on the wall saying that Comrade Xiaoping's words should be heeded.

The popular reaction, according to Wei, was one of disgust: "As soon as this notice was posted," he remembered, "citizens all over Beijing were critical: 'The Chinese are simply inept, and spineless. Just imagine, after having been free for only a couple of days, and able to speak out, they now want to retreat because of a little directive from someone. What a bunch of spineless weaklings. There is no hope for China.' "

Wei goes on: "After I heard such commentaries, I was particularly saddened. I felt that not all Chinese were spineless. Certainly my thoughts, and my ideas, with years of deliberation, had long been stored in my mind. I decided to utter them, to do something. The primary motivation was to prove to everyone that not all Chinese were spineless. So I posted the Fifth Modernization."

It is a neat little story, with a fine mythical resonance. In fact, Deng had not forbidden postings on the wall in November 1978. On the contrary, he told a Canadian journalist that the Democracy Wall was "good." The Fifth Modernization manifesto was posted in that short period of calculated tolerance. The trouble actually began early in the following year, when Deng had defeated the hard-line Maoists and was embroiled in a messy war with Vietnam—described in the official press, rather quaintly, as "the self-defensive counterattack." It was only then, in March 1979, that Deng decided to crack down on liberals, reformers, and dissidents. And Wei responded, in a typical act of political bravado, by attacking Deng for being just another Chinese despot. That manifesto was called "Democracy or a New Dictatorship?"

But the historical sequence is less important than the underlying sentiment. Wei was touched, as were so many modern Chinese rebels, including Mao himself some fifty years before, by the pain of Chinese humiliation, by the abject feeling of impotence and submission to bullies and tyrants, foreign or homegrown. It is the sentiment that sparked almost every revolt in China in the twentieth century, from Sun Yat-sen's anti-Manchu revolution in 1911 to the May Fourth Movement in 1919 to the Communist revolution of 1949 to Tiananmen in 1989. When they took part in the Tiananmen demonstrations, Li Lu, Chai Ling, Wu'er Kaixi, and their fellow students knew virtually nothing about Wei Jingsheng or the Democracy Wall. And yet Li Lu used almost the same words as Wei to describe the actions of his generation. He said: "In 1989, the people discovered that they had lived like slaves. And they risked everything to rebel. I believe that the sense of humanity that emerged in 1989 had been buried. But once it came alive, that feeling of human dignity, you were no longer a slave."

The deep sadness of modern China is that every generation has had to learn the same lesson, over and over again, a lesson written in great lakes of blood.

—

One of the most indelible images of human dignity is that of Wei Jingsheng reading his defense statement during his first trial, in October 1979. I am moved every time I see it. The photograph is simple, with no great dramatic action. Wei stands in the foreground, looking young and thin, fragile almost, in his shabby convict's clothes, one buttonless sleeve hanging loosely around a slender wrist. His shaven convict's head and calm, studious expression make him resemble an earnest monk. Behind him is a blur of faces. Two people appear to be picking their noses, several blink up in a bored, distracted manner, and a few look at Wei with curiously froglike expressions, caused by the harsh television lights bouncing off their glasses. They are all identically dressed in Mao uniforms, these provincial policemen and prosecutors summoned to Beijing to learn how a show trial should be staged.

Yet this was no ordinary show trial. For Wei's speech was every bit as devastating as his Democracy Wall manifestos. He made a simple, beautifully argued case for the right to criticize. The logic was so impeccable that it embarrassed the judges, who shuffled their papers, cursed the defendant's impertinence, and called for an early lunch. One of the things Wei said was: "The Constitution grants citizens the right to criticize their leaders, because these leaders are human beings and not gods. It is only through the people's criticism and supervision that those leaders will make fewer mistakes, and only in this way that the people will avoid the misfortune of having their lords and masters ride roughshod over them. Then, and only then, will the people be able to breathe freely."

Wei was sentenced to fifteen years for "betraying the motherland," because he had mentioned the name of a Chinese general fighting in Vietnam to a Western journalist, and for writing "reactionary articles," as well as propagating "counterrevolutionary propaganda and agitation," all of which constituted "a serious counterrevolutionary crime of the most heinous nature."

In fact he was lucky to have gotten away with his life. Deng Xiaoping is said to have wanted him shot. The fact that we know what happened during the trial is one of the reasons he was spared. Wei's defense was published all over the world, and the trial, held less than a year after Deng won American hearts by wearing a cowboy hat in Texas, had become an international cause célèbre. The man who smuggled Wei's words out of the courtroom and thus helped to save his life is an artist now living quietly in a terraced house in a southern suburb of London. His name is Qu Leilei.

Qu, a neat man with small laughing eyes and a craggy face, is the same age as Wei. They first met in 1966, at the house of a distinguished older writer, who patted the top of Wei's head and pronounced that this young man would one day be a great theorist. After that they lost touch. Qu was sent to the countryside and, like Wei, served some years in the army. He became serious about art sometime in the 1970s, when he saw for the first time a book of French Impressionist painting. After years of nothing but Soviet socialist realism and Maoist propaganda, this first, unforgettable glimpse of European art was a revelation that paralleled the discovery of Yeats and T. S. Eliot by young Chinese poets, or Wei's reading of Locke and Montesquieu.

Qu was working as a lighting technician for China Central Television when Wei was arrested. And by sheer chance he was ordered to attend Wei's trial as a member of the television crew. When the leading dissidents Liu Qing and Xu Wenli heard that a sympathizer was going to be in the courtroom, they called on Qu the night before to ask whether he would be willing to make a secret tape recording. Qu agreed, and the next morning he smuggled a small cassette recorder into the courtroom in his bag and placed it as close to Wei as he dared. During the lunch break, he met Liu and Xu in a secret place to quickly exchange the recorded tapes for fresh ones. The tapes were transcribed that same night, and the next day Wei's defense was posted all over the Democracy Wall.

But nobody dared to publish it—nobody, that is, except Liu Qing. Liu told me in New York, where he works in the Human Rights in China office, that other editors would not touch the speech, because Wei was considered "too radical" and "too dangerous." In fact, Liu himself did not share Wei's radical views, either, but knew that his friend had not had a fair trial. And he realized that if the government got away with this, it would be "Wei today and me tomorrow." So, well aware of the risk he was taking, he printed fifteen hundred copies of the trial transcripts, which were quickly picked up not just by Chinese readers but by the international press. Liu would pay a terrible price, but his action saved Wei's life. And if the truth had not been told, thanks to Liu, Qu, Xu, and others, Deng Xiaoping's cynical prediction that no matter what happened to Wei, no one would remember him in ten years' time would almost certainly have come true.

Liu does not look like a tough guy. Unlike Wei, who has the stocky frame and expansive manners of a street fighter, Liu looks like an intellectual: slim, a little owlish behind his spectacles, hair plastered across a high, pale forehead. His strength seems to be entirely mental. When he was made to sit on the punishment chair for four years, he developed a regimen of imperceptible muscle movements: pressing the floor with the balls of his feet, flexing his arms ever so slightly, muscle by muscle, as though physical exercise were almost entirely in the mind. He would try to think through scientific problems, such as the nature of black holes. Or he would build houses and construct bridges. Liu was an architectural engineer by training.

But these methods, extraordinary though they are, do not reveal the source of the man's inner strength. Like most people of my generation, born just after the war in a country that had been under Nazi occupation, I have always been haunted by the moral dilemmas we never had to face. How would we have behaved? Would I have risked everything? Would I have broken under torture? There is no answer to these questions, but still I looked for hints in men such as Liu and Wei, not so much to understand my own morbid preoccupations as to gain some larger insight into human nature.

Liu said he had been able to stand his torments because he believed that what he did was right. That was of course precisely the spirit his jailers meant to crush. The Chinese penal system is designed to break the prisoner's will, to force confessions of ideological "crimes." "Re-education though labor" may be a Communist innovation, but public confession always was of prime importance in Chinese justice. The object of punishment is the mind. Humiliation is the key. Liu's interrogators had wanted him to tell lies. Yet he resisted. "They can control your body," he said, "but they can't control your thinking." Even, he might have added, if they drive you insane. For insanity is the final refuge, where a person is beyond the reach of even the most skilled and brutal interrogator.

Liu, and Wei too, reminded me of stories I had read about religious martyrs, men and women who would rather burn than stamp on an image of Christ. During the Nazi occupation, the Resistance had a strong religious component, which often seems the source of greater resilience than more secular convictions, patriotism, say, or human rights or scientific truth or democracy, though the line between secular and religious is not always easily drawn.

Wei denied that religious faith had ever played any part in his life. He understood its power and conceded that it might help other people to survive in prison. But in fact he had never seen any evidence of it. Chinese, he said, had other ways of standing the pressure. One day, after a lunch of dumpling soup, which he had cooked in haste before rushing off to Paris via New York, Wei mentioned a short story by Lu Xun that every literate Chinese knows. It is called "The True Story of Ah Q."

Ah Q is a village vagabond, uneducated, unscrupulous, and sly, a kind of rural Chinese Everyman, who grovels to his social betters the more they abuse him. But Ah Q has one line of psychological defense. In his tortured mind, he manages to turn every misfortune into an imaginary blessing. After being robbed by village ruffians, he walks away, slaps his own face, pretends it was meant for one of the ruffians, and soon believes it was so: ". . . it was just as if he had beaten someone else—in spite of the fact that his face was still tingling."

Lu Xun's point was to criticize the abject passivity of Chinese people, their unwillingness to fight back or do anything to improve their fate. He wrote the story in the early 1920s, when China was at the mercy of predatory warlords and foreign imperial powers. Ah Q was, in fact, a study of Chinese humiliation.

Wei understood the story very well but gave it a peculiar twist of his own. He said Chinese had been like Ah Q for centuries. But the same psychological mechanism that turned Ah Q into a slave could also be turned to a more positive end. Wei's prison guards used every means to break him down, not just by brute force. They were especially good at demoralizing a political prisoner by pointing out kindly that all resistance was futile, nobody outside cared, people were getting richer all the time, and they no longer even knew his name. "They use your own regrets and human weakness to torture you." Wei coped with this in a way that he claims is traditionally Chinese. It is not through controlling desire, as in Buddhism, but by shifting its focus. Wei kept on telling himself that he was freer than his jailers, for unlike them, he could say what he really thought. "Because I could speak the truth, I had more integrity than they did. Their official position may have made them better-off, but I was happier, for I could live life as it is, not life as we are told to think it is."

Wei, in other words, had used Ah Q's method to overcome humiliation, or, better still, to humiliate his torturers. That is why they were unable to break him. He could not afford to let them do it. For it was a game of all or nothing. The smallest concession, the tiniest dishonest "self-criticism," would have turned the prisoner into a slave.

As Wei spoke, I studied his face, the sharp stubborn chin, the spiky hair and tobacco-stained teeth, and the dark eyes that were always watchful even when dancing with laughter. And I think I could see why this enormously attractive man had so many enemies. Resistance heroes rarely make good diplomats or politicians. Having defied for eighteen years the attempts of prison interrogators to make him budge, Wei is not about to fudge or compromise now that he is free. This makes it difficult for him to work with others; he would have to concede too much. Wei is an admirable dissident, a moral symbol of defiance whose vision remains unsullied, but these qualities are not necessarily suited to the give-and-take of democratic politics. Deals and messy compromises are more in the line of smooth operators like Dr. Wang Bingzhang.

This is not to condemn Wei, or indeed Dr. Wang. A democracy movement needs dissidents as well as operators. Without the purity of vision of the former, the latter would soon degenerate into mere contenders for petty power, with *zige* as the only political currency. And as long as there are no democratic institutions in China, the scope for democratic politics is limited anyway, since it is impossible to organize political parties at home and they have little meaning abroad.

So to say that Wei should be more compromising is to miss the point of him. The importance of Wei Jingsheng is the clarity of his principles. As long as he is there, no one can say that Chinese don't care about freedom or that it is an alien concept which has no place in an ancient, non-Western civilization. For here is a man who was prepared to die for it. Whenever operators and politicians, in Washington, Beijing, or anywhere else, claim that authoritarian rule is best suited to China, Wei is there to offer an alternative view. I know from conversations with people in China that this view, though only heard by few, still offers some comfort to those who cannot yet freely express it.

The last time I saw Wei, as I write, was in London, on the television news. The sky was a pale wintry blue. Flags of Britain and the People's Republic of China were snapping in the blustering wind. And there, clattering along the Mall, in the direction of Buckingham Palace, was the queen of England in a gold coach, accompanied by President Jiang Zemin, smiling vacuously, his mouth half open, at the sparse crowds waving paper flags handed out by Chinese embassy staff. President Jiang had come to London for a state visit. Economic deals were promised. And the British were aware that protesters irritated the Chinese president. When some Tibetans had been able to get into his line of vision during a recent visit to Switzerland, Jiang told his hosts that they had just lost themselves a good friend. The British were determined to stop a similar mishap from upsetting their distinguished visitor.

On that sunny, windy day in London, then, the television cameras were focused on the royal coach, the queen waving and her guest smiling, when suddenly there was a commotion. The camera turned to a scuffle in the crowd. A middle-aged Chinese man in an anorak was being wrestled to the ground by British policemen, who then dragged him off with his arms pinned behind his back, almost as though they were forcing him to adopt the "airplane" position. It was Wei Jingsheng. He had tried to draw Jiang's presidential eye to a large white sheet of paper held in his hand that read RELEASE ALL POLITICAL PRISONERS.

I would like to have spoken to Wei and shared my outrage with him about his reception in tolerant Britain. But the next day he was out trying to catch Jiang's eye again, in Cambridge. And the day after that, he would be in Paris, and then in Spain or Tokyo or Los Angeles or . . .

Chapter 5

China in Cyberspace

The problem of exile is that it becomes increasingly hard to go home. You might eventually be able to return physically, but not to the country you left. Too much will have happened in the meantime. Those who stayed behind will have changed, but the exile, because of his peculiar experience, will have changed even more, marked by exposure to an alien world. There are cases, it is true, where exiles have gone back to be leaders. At the beginning of the twentieth century, Sun Yat-sen plotted the Chinese revolution in Tokyo, London, and Honolulu, and he returned in 1911 to lead the Chinese republic. But this is rare. Former exiles are not usually welcomed back to the fold. Like Brahmans who leave India, political rebels tend to lose their aura once they step away from the native soil. I once asked an academic in Hunan, who was critical of the Communist regime, what he thought of overseas dissidents such as Wei Jingsheng and Fang Lizhi. He replied that once a dissident leaves China, "he has no right to speak out anymore." This was not an isolated opinion, which, by the way, is never expressed about overseas Chinese who get rich.

"All the nobodies who cannot return are going home." This line is from a poem by Yang Lian, a writer from Beijing now living in London. He carries a New Zealand passport and lived in four different countries before arriving in England in 1993. His flat is on the third floor of a redbrick early-twentieth-century apartment block. All his neighbors are Chasidic Jews, who speak Yiddish and wear clothes reminiscent of eighteenth-century Poland. Exiles of a different kind, they regard Yang Lian and his wife You You as exotics. Yang wrote that poem in London. Those who live abroad become nobodies. Home is a land of their own invention.

Yang was once one of the "Misty Poets," caught up in the excitement of the Democracy Wall, when young artists were discovering that there was more to art than socialist realism and more to language than Maoist jargon. They were no longer interested in "art for the masses"; official populism was tainted with too much blood and misery. Instead, they tried to pick up the fragments of traditions that they themselves, as Red Guards, had helped to destroy, to forge new forms of art that were linked to the past without being mere re-creations. Modernism suited them— T. S. Eliot was the Misty Poets' favorite master—because they tried to reinvent "China" in a cultural and linguistic wasteland, by scraping off the grime of propaganda and creating a language that felt authentically their own.

I first met Yang in 1985, in a smart, Western-style hotel in Beijing. He looked the same then as he does now: a tall, slim figure in jeans and shoulder-length hair, the epitome of a bohemian aesthete, the antithesis of an official hack. He did not speak English yet, and my Chinese was rusty. But we understood each other. I mentioned the title of a famous Ming-dynasty pornographic novel, long forbidden in Communist China. Yang's eyes lit up. "Very interesting!" he said. I was impressed. What I didn't know then was that one of his own poems, celebrating, in the name of a Tibetan deity, the reawakened vitality of street people and young hoodlums, had been banned for being too obscure, too esoteric, "ideologically unhealthy," and, of course, "pornographic." Yang left China with his wife a few years later, before the Beijing Massacre made exile a more or less permanent condition.

Once, Yang was taken by a Scottish poet to see the ruins of a castle said to be Macbeth's. Yang took in the green, windswept Highlands landscape and the ancient stones and observed to his host: "I've almost forgotten the feeling of being a poet who lives in his own country." Yang does go back to China now and then, to see his family and travel, to sniff the familiar smells and be shocked by the changes in his native Beijing, but it no longer feels like his country. He calls it his "own foreign country."

Like many Chinese overseas, Yang is haunted by the idea of "China." He has often talked to me about this, in his redbrick flat in the Chasidic street in north London, sitting at his dinner table with Peking duck, served with dark, sticky hoisin sauce, like sweet tar, on our plates and Miles Davis blowing from the CD player. He is interested in politics but rejects it as a theme for his poetry, which he sees as too personal, too private to accommodate the language of public affairs. The idea of being a Chinese poet, rooted in a tradition, or seeking roots, bores him too. In an essay, entitled "Poet Without a Nation," Yang wrote that he was not born into a "motherland" or a "tradition," but that they are born in his poetry. Chineseness, he said, "depends on my discovering it again and choosing it again."

Yang Lian's "China," then, is a private place that exists in his own poetic Chinese language. And yet the paradox of many poets in exile is that they are lost to their readers "at home." Presented as those of a "Chinese poet" at international poetry festivals, Yang's words are heard most often in translation.

"In this world no-one comes from 'China.' I came from 'The People's Republic of China,'" Yang Lian has written. " 'Chinese' has no other significance for me." But this is not quite true. The great advantage for Chinese writers living abroad, compared to Czechs or Poles or Japanese, is that the written Chinese language transcends national borders. There is a Greater China on paper, stretching from Beijing to Vancouver. Yang Lian's poems are published in Hong Kong and Taiwan, and sometimes even in China. He recognizes that a shared knowledge of history, literature, and even of exile from mainland China enables Taiwanese or Hong Kong Chinese to have a deeper understanding of his poetry than what can be expected of Europeans or Americans. Yang Lian's poems are a tiny part of a culture that crosses the internal borders of Greater China. Kung-fu novels and movies, mostly produced in Hong Kong—the latter starring such diaspora heroes as Bruce Lee (born in San Francisco), who flatter ethnic myths by defeating large, villainous white men or demonic Japanese—are part of that culture. So are Cantonese pop songs and Taiwanese soap operas, and fried noodles and duck with sweet sauce. An avant-garde poet from Beijing with a New Zealand passport and a home in London may play only a peripheral, even marginal, part in that China, but as long as there is a Chinese language, that part remains. Words are his umbilical cord.

Life is more difficult for a political activist, for literature is private, and at its deepest level universal, while politics is public and resolutely local. To engage in politics, you need a political community, a nation with shared political institutions and public opinion expressed in a shared press. A dictatorship is still a political community, even though the mass media are used for propaganda and critical opinions can be voiced only underground. Exile for an activist means to be cut off from that community, no matter how many slots there are on Voice of America or Radio Free Asia. Though exiles from mainland China can publish their ideas in Hong Kong and Taiwan, they cannot do so in their homeland. To be sure, their voices had been muffled in China, too, especially if they were in jail. But their presence, even as martyrs in solitary cells, was still felt. Once abroad, many of them flounder, as lost men in search of a phantom society, fighting other lost men, hanging on desperately to the few remaining threads tying them to the world they left behind. This is why his rivals in exile accused Wei Jingsheng of being "rootless" in China. To lose your roots is to have no *zige,* no credentials.

And yet, perhaps, the way we define political communities is changing a bit. When we think of China as a political community, there are two Chinas, and, if we include Hong Kong, three. The millions of people outside these three places who still think of themselves as Chinese have diverse political loyalties or ignore politics altogether. Their "China" is cultural, linguistic, or sentimental: those fried noodles, ancestral memories, and kung-fu movies, but not a political community. Politics has drawn the Chinese diaspora together only under exceptional circumstances: the war against Japan, or the Tiananmen Movement in 1989. But the idea of nationhood has been shifted somewhat by the extraordinary nature of new information technology. "China" has been changed by the Internet.

———

China, as an imagined political community in which all Chinese can take part, albeit without common institutions, now exists in cyberspace— indeed, it exists only in cyberspace. The idea of electronically linking the various parts of a notional empire, like so many lights on a Christmas tree, is sentimental too, of course. The pioneers in this field were the Germans, during World War II, who hooked up field telephones and radio transmitters for special Christmas broadcasts: "Hello, here is Berlin . . . Riga . . . St. Malo . . . Kiev . . . Benghazi." When the linkups didn't work, they would fake it. But the significance of Cyberspace China is not just sentimental. There, for the first time, Taiwanese, mainland Chinese, Hong Kong Chinese, and overseas Chinese can talk about politics every day. The Internet has become a forum of worldwide Chinese opinion, posted on websites, transmitted by e-mail, debated in chat rooms. Geographical borders no longer count in the same way they did. Even minor barriers to smooth communication, such as the different ways of writing Chinese characters in mainland China and other parts of the Chinese-speaking world, can be overcome with a simple change of font.

Cyberspace China is also where religion gets a boost from science. New, Buddhist-inspired religions have always spanned the various parts of Greater China; now they can spread instantly through the Internet. Most recently, Falun Gong has spooked the Communist government sufficiently to become an international cause célèbre. What began as a loosely organized group of people in northeast China expanded into an international organization with millions of followers all over the world. Without the World Wide Web and e-mail, it would never have happened. And no matter how many adherents are arrested, tortured, and killed in China, the movement stays alive, both in the streets, where believers continue to volunteer for martyrdom, and in cyberspace.

Surfing the Chinese websites, many of them set up in North America, is a bit like delving into the conscious, rational mind of a nation as well as the dark unconscious, filled with delusions and paranoia, sexual fantasies, religious longing, and smoldering resentments. The Internet lacks a superego that filters the monsters arising from the lower depths. It is where the wildest conspiracy theories are aired. It is also where people are denounced as spies, whores, gangsters, Communist agents, ass-licking dogs of the American imperialists, and much, much worse. Feuds between different factions of the overseas Chinese democracy movement go on and on, often expressed in terms more commonly used on the walls of public lavatories. One search for the names Wei Jingsheng or Wang Xizhe will reveal file upon file about their hostile encounters, posted by acolytes, enemies and hangers-on, from Boston, Hong Kong, or Shanghai. The Internet has the effect of making the private public; malicious gossip is instantly shared by millions. But since much of this is posted on the Net anonymously or under false names—and some of it planted by government agencies—you never really know who is saying what, and why. Entering some websites is therefore a surreal experience, like visiting a mental institution with thousands of insanely chattering voices.

On the question of Taiwan, for example, there is at one level a great deal of interesting debate on the Internet about the meaning of popular sovereignty, the relative importance of history and culture on political affairs, and the nature of the Communist Party compared to the KMT. Opinions tend to reflect the origins of those who express them—that is, native Taiwanese, whether they are living in Taiwan, the U.S., or elsewhere, promote Taiwanese independence more than do those with a background in mainland China. But not always. Wei Jingsheng has stated that Taiwanese sovereignty should be a matter of popular choice. He doesn't advocate independence, indeed he warns against it, but if most Taiwanese choose independence, it should be up to them to decide.

However, if you were to read other opinions posted on bulletin boards to encourage debate, you would plunge straight into the soil where more primitive weeds flourish. I found the following argument on Taiwanese independence expressed in broken English on a website called Free Talk: "Fuck UR mother. I fucked 17 mainland whores." Whereupon another debater on the same issue responded: "Fuck you! Fuck you! Fuck UR Taiwanese mother. Taiwan is China province." The peculiar nature of the insults clearly reveal the writers to be Chinese, though in this case they are expressed in English, the lingua franca of habitual Internet surfers. Similar insults are also posted in Chinese, sometimes by official sources. The crudest language is said to come from Public Security agents in Beijing.

It is not always easy to combat Internet abuse without resorting to the kind of censorship that Chinese dissidents are trying so hard to resist. On the tenth anniversary of Tiananmen, Wang Dan, the former student leader, now living in Cambridge, Massachusetts, led a signature campaign through the Internet to press Beijing to revise its verdict on the events of 1989. His website was quickly filled with obscene messages and insults, some perhaps sent from sources connected to the Public Security Bureau. But out of deference to the principles of free speech, Wang was reluctant at first to object. Nonetheless, like hecklers at a meeting, this cyberspace graffiti became such a menace that a warning had to be issued. Profanities and incitements to violence and hatred would no longer be tolerated: "We have a responsibility to remove your posting, if you do not follow these simple rules, and we will."

Politics are local. Few Taiwanese Internet surfers are interested in the feuds among political refugees from mainland China, while the internal politics of Taiwan or Hong Kong are of interest mostly to people living there. But certain symbols and historical events speak to the heart of all "descendants of the dragon": tragic defeats, heroic rebellions, and permanent enemies. Two events stand out in Cyberspace China: the Nanjing Massacre of 1937, when Japanese troops killed and raped many thousands of unarmed citizens, and the Beijing Massacre of 1989. The first turns shared feelings of outrage outward, against Japan, for its "refusal" to apologize, compensate, and atone for its war crimes; the other focuses on the crimes of the Chinese government itself, but also on hopes for a freer, more dignified, more open China, in which all Chinese can take pride.

Rage against foreign aggression and homegrown tyranny are linked, by patriots quick to criticize their government for not "loving China" enough. The language used in both cases, by writers from all parts of Cyberspace China, is similar. Phrases like "wipe out the shame" and "blood for blood" crop up frequently. And readers are sometimes addressed as "brothers and sisters," as though all Chinese were family. At least one website is called the Family of the Chinese People (*Huaren Yijia*). It is certainly the case that when Japanese do anything to stir up Chinese emotions—a conservative politician justifying the war, or right-wing zealots occupying a tiny disputed island in the South China Sea—the Internet starts to hum with Chinese voices that can agree at least on the point of Japan's eternal iniquity. The same patriotic solidarity was expressed in 1989, when Chinese everywhere sent money to the students in Beijing, linked to the world through a fax machine. The Internet should be an even more effective tool for organizing a worldwide Chinese community.

The Internet has created a new species of dissident, too. In the 1990s, bands of cyberspace guerrillas, or hacktivists, with names like the Cult of the Dead Cow—so named because its founders used to hang out in an abattoir—hacked into official Chinese government websites sabotaging their operations. The so-called foreign minister of the Cult of the Dead Cow is a former Chinese U.N. consultant who goes by the Internet name of Oxblood Ruffin. The leader of the gang is called Blondie Wong; he is an astrophysicist who recalls seeing his father being stoned to death by Red Guards. It was the sight on American TV of tanks rolling into Tiananmen Square that prodded Ruffin into action.

Li Hongkuan, or Richard Li, or Richard Long (aliases proliferate on the Net) lives in Washington, D.C. Li is not a hacker, but his activities in a one-room office stacked with laptops and CD-ROMs have been more influential than the exploits of the Internet guerrillas with rock group names.

We would meet, during the winter and spring of 1999, at a coffee shop near Dupont Circle. A vibrant, round-faced figure in his late thirties, who could pass as a sharp financial trader, Li decided in 1997 to edit a website called VIP Reference News, or Dacankao. The name is a witty borrowing of the official term for uncensored "internal" information, often foreign news, circulated only among Party cadres: Real news is privileged; the common people have to make do with propaganda. Li decided to change that by making the news available to all. He provided a daily newsletter excerpting many of the papers and magazines published in China, Taiwan, and Hong Kong, as well as Chinese dissident journals abroad, and, of course, information about Tiananmen and the Nanjing Massacre. There were links to bulletin boards, which function like an electronic Democracy Wall, plastered with e-mails instead of wall posters. And all this was financed by Li's own savings, accumulated by a stint on Wall Street.

Li's first political act was to join a pro-democracy demonstration in

Shanghai in 1987. As a graduate student in biochemistry, he was inspired by a speech given by Fang Lizhi at the Chinese Academy of Sciences. But worship of science cannot have been his only motivation. For this was the same Richard Li who told me that Chinese hate one another because they lack a religion that teaches them to love. The Chinese, he said, did not know the difference between right and wrong. Everything in Chinese life depended on connections. If someone knew you, you would be treated well. But they hated you if you were a stranger. And that, he concluded, is why Chinese might be in need of Christianity, to learn to love without condition.

The coffee shop where we met was noisy. Rock music, clinking glasses, and a buzz of conversation made it difficult to hear exactly what Li was saying. He spoke fast, sometimes in English, sometimes in Chinese, and drank several cans of Budweiser in quick succession. Li had the kind of transparent self-regard I often noticed in active Chinese men. He liked to make claims that he was "the only one" to do this or that. He had the "biggest database" of e-mail addresses in China. Nobody else was reaching out to China the way he was. The stars among the exiled dissidents, Wei Jingsheng, Chai Ling, Liu Qing, they were all pretty useless. As I made notes, he smiled with satisfaction. I asked him whether he was a Christian. He said he was not. With his background in science, how could he be a believer? So was it Professor Fang who had first turned his mind to politics? No, that was not it either.

As a biochemistry student in Nanjing during the early 1980s, Li had come across a book that changed his life. *Megatrends,* written by John Naisbitt, the American futurist guru of global networking, was strictly for "internal" distribution among Party cadres. Somehow Li managed to get hold of it. Before turning to Naisbitt, Li told me he had been an avid reader of Victorian fiction—he mentioned *Jane Eyre*—and a keen student of Chinese sexual customs. But through Naisbitt he was introduced to the idea of a world without frontiers, with every citizen connected through the wonders of technology. This, Li said, "really blew my mind."

Like many students of the Tiananmen generation, Li had benefited from Deng Xiaoping's reforms. Born in 1963, he has only hazy memories of Maoist persecution, but he can still recall his confusion when he saw his grandmother being spat at and forced to clean the streets. Her sin was to have married a landowner before the revolution. Because of this, the family lost all social benefits, and Li's mother cursed the old woman for their misfortunes. But by the time Li himself went to school, things had become easier, and he graduated from university without any trouble in 1984. Instead of taking a government-assigned job, however, Li decided to apply for postgraduate studies in Shanghai. That is when he began to read John Naisbitt, as well as books about the May Fourth Movement and by intellectuals of the 1920s and 1930s.

When the Tiananmen Movement began, Li was teaching chemistry in Beijing. He went to the Square more as a sympathetic observer than an active participant. On the evening of June 3, he left the Square to go home. Only hours later, when he realized how serious the street battles between soldiers and demonstrators had become, he tried to return but could not press his way through the crowds. He heard gunshots and screaming. Suddenly there were people lying on the ground, covered in blood. He managed to load some of them onto pushcarts so they could be rushed off to a hospital.

Li is modest about his role in 1989. He does not claim to have been a leader. His activism began only after he had managed to get a research job at the Albert Einstein College of Medicine in New York and joined an organization of overseas Chinese scholars. It was there that he found a way to marry his love of technology with his interest in politics, or what he calls "humanities." While taking part in discussion groups on the Internet, he noticed that the most active participants were scientists, who were experts at using the Internet but had little idea of politics. In 1996 the discussion groups began to attract people from China, too. That is when Li decided to follow Naisbitt's ideas and use the Internet to carry on, as he puts it, "the unfinished revolution" of 1989.

———

It is a curious paradox of contemporary Chinese politics that Beijing insists on one China, including Hong Kong and Taiwan, even as it tries to stop people in the various parts of China from communicating with one another through magazines, newspapers, television, and now the Internet.

Beijing faces a dilemma: It wants China to be "wired," to become a modern economy, while at the same time wishing to restrict the information that new technology can provide. This problem is hardly new: how to gain knowledge from barbarians without being polluted by their ideas. The phrase used at the end of the nineteenth century was *ti-yong,* "essence" and "practice"—that is, Chinese learning for the spirit and Western learning for practical use. Chinese learning used to mean Confucianism. Now it means socialism with Chinese characteristics. However, it is no longer the barbarians who are most feared but other Chinese.

In a perfect reprise of the nineteenth-century *ti-yong* debates, President Jiang Zemin warned against spreading "sham science" and "unhealthy trash," while also talking about "positive use" of the Internet to promote "healthy information."

So far, in 2001, about 14 million people in China have access to computers, but the number just about doubles each year. One computer has many users, especially in such places as Internet cafés, so it is impossible to say how many mainland Chinese go on-line. By the end of 2002, it should be more than 30 million. Since e-commerce is still undeveloped in China, where credit cards barely exist, most Internet users are interested in other types of information. Many are scientists and entrepreneurs, who look for technical or business news. This is leavened with the kind of thing mainland newspapers now increasingly offer their readers, to sweeten the wooden propaganda: movie star gossip, local scandals, or lifestyle advice. Unbiased news about Taiwan or Tibet cannot be found on official websites, and political criticism, though not unheard of, especially in the academic corners of cyberspace, is limited. And yet information is exchanged in chat rooms, and critical voices are heard. Banned writers post articles on websites, which might be shut down, but they are swiftly replaced by others. How can the government make sure that millions of people limit themselves only to what it wants them to know? The point of the World Wide Web, after all, is that it is open to everyone. The answer is that the government cannot. But there are various ways it can try. One method is to make it so expensive and burdensome to get access to an Internet service provider that only a trusted few can afford it. But for the equivalent of less than one U.S. dollar, anyone can use the Internet for an hour at an Internet café, or *wangba.*

Around 1996, when the Internet began to take off in China, you still had to fill in complicated identification forms and present police records to show you were an obedient citizen, even in Internet cafés. You had to swear not to read, reproduce, or transmit material that was pornographic or damaging to public order or state security. Damage to state security includes anything that might encourage "division of the country" (meaning Tibetan or Taiwanese independence) and is, of course, forbidden, as is the spreading of "falsehoods." It is up to the government to decide what is true or false. This is why readers of Li's VIP Reference News are advised not to send it on to others by e-mail. Still, there are free service providers in China that do not require much paperwork. And the rules on registration in cafés are rarely enforced.

A more serious threat to freedom of information is the so-called firewall. By making it illegal to log on to the global Internet through other than official Chinese portals, the government tries to block unwelcome websites. The official networks connect with the Internet through one gateway, which is controlled by the Ministry of Information Industry. Control over foreign websites is spotty, however. Anyone who speaks English and can afford the price of an expensive local call and a cup of coffee can usually log on to foreign newspaper sites and get all the news in the world. What the government would really like is an insulated Chinese Internet, which has all the advantages of speedy communications (good for business, as well as the security agencies) but protects the purity of the Chinese spirit behind an electronic wall.

But the Chinese wall is full of holes. One way to penetrate it is through so-called proxy servers—that is, overseas servers that can bypass the Chinese gateway. Proxy-server addresses are passed around among friends, and sometimes even provided at Internet cafés. And no matter how hard teams of technicians from the Public Security Bureau try to do so, they cannot block all of them all the time, for there are simply too many. And since many of these servers are connected to overseas universities and other institutions that help keep Chinese scientists up-to-date, it would harm the national interest to close them all down anyway.

Spamming, or sending e-mails to a vast number of people at the same time, is a technique normally used by advertisers. Li Hongkuan uses it to transmit his VIP Reference News, which is, naturally, a banned website, but he has collected about 250,000 e-mail addresses in China, some of them from businessmen, who swap data with him. Spamming is not a method everyone approves of. At least with proxy servers, a person can choose what to read. But spamming has great advantages. Though e-mails can be intercepted by the government, and read, most of them get through, and Li makes things harder for the censors by daily changing the address from which he sends them. Recipients can honestly claim that the material was unsolicited. E-mails between individuals can also be made illegible to third parties by encryption, ensuring privacy by encoding and decoding messages. The best the government can do is to intimidate potential readers by making examples of a few.

In March 1998, Lin Hai, a thirty-year-old computer company owner in Shanghai, was arrested in his apartment by twenty plainclothes police officers. His computers, phones, printers, business cards, and books were confiscated, and his wife, Xu Hong, was briefly detained as well. After sitting in jail for almost a year, Lin was sentenced to another two years. His alleged crime was "incitement to undermine the government" by giving thirty thousand e-mail addresses to VIP Reference News. Lin was not a dissident, but he had been unable to sell his addresses to legitimate businesses. His wife made the reasonable point that "e-mail addresses are public information, just like telephone numbers." But that was to miss the point. Lin's case was an example of what Chinese call "killing a chicken to scare the monkeys."

In September 1999, Qi Yanchen, an economist, was arrested at his house in a small city in Hebei province. No one is quite sure what prompted the arrest. But printouts were found in his office of VIP Reference News, and he is said to have been working on a book, entitled *The Collapse of China*, which he had planned to distribute through the Internet. Qi might also have been involved with an electronic magazine linked to a banned, nongovernmental organization in Hong Kong. He was known for his strong views on the environment and political reform. In any case, Qi was charged with breaking a law that forbids communication with "foreign individuals or organizations."

Then, in the summer of 2000, a schoolteacher was arrested for posting criticism of the government from an Internet café in Sichuan, named Silicon Valley Internet Coffee. He was charged with "incitement to overthrow the government." Another man in Sichuan, who ran a website that tracked down missing persons, including many abducted children, was jailed for having articles on his website about the June 4 massacre. His last message was: "Good-bye, police have come to take me away for questioning."

But these desperate measures cannot stop thousands of others from surfing forbidden areas in cyberspace. Nor can the government stop people from talking to one another on the Internet, wherever they might physically be. New religions, like Falun Gong, are not the only organizations that use the Internet; new political parties do the same. That is how Xu Wenli and others managed to organize their China Democracy Party in 1999 without the government knowing about it. Like Falun Gong, the CDP has been driven underground, but that underground is "wired." CDP supporters everywhere, in China and outside, remain in touch and could organize again at once.

Chen Ziming, a well-known dissident in Beijing, who set up a highly respected independent think tank for political and economic reform in the 1980s, was arrested in 1989 as a so-called black hand behind the Tiananmen demonstrations. He was jailed for six years but now lives at home, under permanent house arrest. He cannot speak to people on the telephone, receive visitors, or even go for a walk. He can only read, talk to his wife, watch television, work out on an exercise machine, and use his computer. Cut off from the world physically, he is still linked to the world electronically. E-mail is his lifeline.

Access to news or electronic links alone will not bring democracy to China. New technology can be used to good or bad purpose, for linking dissident groups and for invading their privacy. But an authoritarian system based on secrecy and national isolation becomes vulnerable once the walls that contain the secrets come down. The myth of one China, where people live in harmony and dissent is denounced as "anti-Chinese," has been shattered by the electronic revolution. For the democratic cacophony of voices posted on the Internet shows clearly that China already exists as a pluralist society, not only in Taiwan and Hong Kong, but in cyberspace. And however much Beijing tries to stop it, mainland Chinese are now members of that society, too. All that remains is to bring it down to earth.

Part II

Greater China

Chapter 1

Chinese Disneyland

Lee Kuan Yew's Singapore is a post-Maoist model of the Chinese future. To lapsed Communist Chinese rulers, heirs to the scientistic myths of May 4, 1919, and the autocracy of imperial China, a society that manages to combine the riches of capitalism with the harsh discipline of a one-party authoritarian state would seem progressive and reassuringly traditional at the same time. That, and the superb food, are the main reasons I keep returning there. Singapore gives you an idea of "China," reflected in a distorting mirror. Yet this remarkable Singaporean creation was the work of men who were not all ethnically Chinese, were largely ignorant of Chinese history, culture, or tradition, and whose chief architect was an English-educated barrister, who fought all his life against communism. The result owes little to Karl Marx, a bit more to Lenin, and a great deal to the accumulated instincts of mandarins, bureaucrats, and Party cadres who have ruled for centuries in Confucius's name.

It is not so easy, however, to define the Chineseness of Singapore or of its main ruler, now senior minister, with precision, for it is distorted by another tradition, whose roots are Western, not Oriental. Harry Lee Kuan Yew comes from a typical colonial Straits-Chinese family. His grandfather, a gentleman of the old school, who never took off his collar and tie in the noonday sun, thought the British were always right about everything. And Harry, who adored his grandfather, was sent to an English-language school to be equipped, as he put it in his memoirs, entitled, rather grandly, *The Singapore Story,* "to go to an English university in order that I could then be an educated man—the equal of any Englishman, the model of perfection."

Lee's obsession with discipline and cleanliness, and his horror of tropical sloth and native corruption, reflects his colonial education. And so, perhaps, does his conviction that power is the monopoly of superior men, whose virtues should be an example to lesser breeds, convictions that match older Chinese ideals of scholar-officials, selected on the basis of their rote learning of Confucian classics. They were thought to embody a higher morality, based on an orthodoxy that it was their duty to instill in the common people.

Singapore's superior men no longer learn the classics; they are technocrats, who think in terms of human "digits," to use one of the senior minister's phrases. Their superiority is less the product of Confucian virtues than of a perverted rationalism or technocratic skill. But they are still selected through examinations that test their political orthodoxy as well as their academic learning. To enter a university in Singapore in the 1960s and 1970s, a student needed to have a "suitability certificate," to prove that his family had the correct political leanings. Like the Chinese Communist Party, Lee's People's Action Party (PAP) seeks to control every aspect of society—not just the way people behave, but how they think—and it cannot accept the idea, let alone the necessity, of loyal opposition. Since mandarins or cadres are held to be virtuous and their rule benevolent, critics by definition are morally deficient, and thus must be eradicated, lest they infect the healthy social organism.

In theory, in imperial China, even rulers had to obey the moral dogmas laid down by the ancient sages, and if they departed from Confucian ethics, it was the duty of scholar-officials to show rulers the error of their ways. Singaporean officials, too, accept criticism, and sometimes even say they welcome it, but they call it "feedback" or "constructive criticism." By this they mean technocratic advice, filtered through the PAP, on how to make the government system work even more efficiently. What they do not want is criticism of the way they use the system to keep themselves in power.

Nothing is more Chinese about Singapore than its punishments. Caning offenders and minor criminals is a legacy of the British empire as much as the Chinese tradition of corporal punishment. But the use of public confession is an old Confucian practice. It shows that the critic has submitted to orthodoxy. It has to be imposed to enforce obedience or, as Lee would have it, "social cohesion." The orthodoxy of Lee's Singapore, sometimes called Asian values, since it cannot be identified as "Chinese" in a multiracial state, is that collective interests, as defined by the government, come before individual rights and that liberal democracy and human rights are Western "values," which do not apply to Asians.

What confuses the outsider in Singapore at first is the institutional layer of Britishness that lies on the surface: the constant talk about the rule of law, the rituals of judicial and parliamentary procedure, even the style of the government-controlled English-language press, which reflects the priggishness—though not the quality or the relative independence—of the 1950s BBC. Bit by bit, however, Lee's PAP has removed the more liberal aspects of British institutions: trial by jury, freedom of the press, adversarial politics. You might say, then, that Lee Sinified the Raj, even though he did it in the English language and his main adversaries were Chinese speakers. He imbued the most authoritarian aspects of British colonial rule with an autocratic Chinese spirit.

Lee's version of this Chinese spirit is at the very core of the nation's foundation myth, promoted in theme-park panoramas, television soap operas, National Day speeches, school textbooks, and history museums. In the middle of the old colonial center of town, now an area of carefully preserved museums and churches, is the National History Museum, a handsome, classical building, in the colonial style, with a white dome, colonnades, and verandas. Its "mission," so the museum pamphlet informs us, is to "explore and enhance the national identity. . . ."

On the ground floor is a series of dioramas showing Singapore's history until 1951. We see the early settlements of Malay fishermen, the arrival of Sir Stamford Raffles in 1819, the growth of Chinese trade under the British, the first rubber plantations, and the wartime Japanese occupation. All this is done sketchily; the real foundation myth is yet to come. For that you go to the top floor, to an exhibition called "From Colony to Nation."

It is the story of a nation that became prosperous, clean, orderly, and almost perfectly governed after a succession of enemies had been cleared away. The enemies outside are the Malays, in Indonesia and Malaysia, the teeming millions, poor, brown-skinned, backward, barely civilized, but always liable to run amok and cross the borders. The enemies within are the Communists and the pro-Communists. Old black-and-white photographs are shown of rioting Malays in Jakarta and Kuala Lumpur and of students and trade-union activists in Singapore being pursued by policemen brandishing sticks. The message is clear: Dissent means violence and disorder. The rooms in which these pictures are displayed are cluttered and murky. After that come the lighter rooms, celebrating in full color the achievements of the PAP, which brought order, security, and prosperity. The message is emblazoned on the wall: Singapore's economy developed "in leaps and bounds" under "political stability" and "strong leadership."

Here it is, then: a rich and orderly society protected by strong and benevolent rulers from the ever-threatening chaos of barbarians and domestic rebels. The ancient paranoiac notion of China surrounded by barbarians has been transplanted to a tiny Chinese enclave in the swamps and jungles of Southeast Asia. There is no room for critics or dissidents here, for they are, at best, misguided losers, too stupid to understand the necessity for "strong leadership," or, at worst, dangerous "Communists" who would plunge the land into chaos and darkness. The fact that dissidents are called Communists in Singapore and counterrevolutionaries in China is incidental; the underlying sentiments of the rulers are the same.

—

Chia Thye Poh speaks very softly, almost in a whisper. Like Wei Jingsheng, Chia has spent most of his adult life in prison, with no one to talk to but interrogators trained to break his spirit. Until a few years ago he was one of the longest serving political prisoners in the world. What makes Chia's story so remarkable is that he was a prisoner in the richest, technically most advanced, and socially most efficient part of the Chinese-speaking world.

We faced each other in the winter of 1999 at a Formica table in the clean, warm, but rather institutional canteen of a research institute in the Netherlands. Chia had received a scholarship to study the politics of economic development, a safe enough topic, in a safe enough country. He was, he said, "the oldest student in the building."

A slim, frail-looking man in his early sixties, with large black-rimmed glasses and brown sun spots on his sallow face, he smiled politely whenever a fellow student greeted him. Often he would get up to shake hands. A hearty Japanese clapped him on the back and said: "My friend." Chia just smiled. He worried whether I had had enough coffee or that it had gone cold. Even though I protested that I was fine, he would rush to the coffee machine to fill up another Styrofoam cup, and return with a packet of cookies or a bar of chocolate.

Chia had endured twenty-three years in a Singapore prison, mostly alone in his cell, merely because of his politics. He never cracked. I looked for hints of steeliness, something that might reveal a clue to Chia's mental resilience beneath his whispering, solicitous manner, and could surmise only that soft-spoken courtesy can be as effective a shield against continuous mental aggression as a more swaggering posture. Or perhaps Chia was just behaving like someone who had learned the hard way to value discretion. In this respect, he could not have been less like Wei Jingsheng.

Although he was now a free man living in Holland, he did not want me to quote his views, which were unfailingly moderate. He was afraid the Singaporean government would make it impossible for him to go back and find a job. They might accuse him of being a "Communist," as they did a few years ago, when he criticized an old colonial law that allows the government to detain people indefinitely without trial. He was in no hurry to go home. He had been robbed of an active life. His health was ruined. There was talk of another scholarship, in Germany perhaps. But he thought he eventually might go back. It was, after all, his country.

Then he told me his story—a very Singaporean but also very Chinese story. Chia was born in Singapore. His paternal grandparents had come from Hokkien (Fujian) province, in China, as had his mother, who was illiterate. His father worked in an ice factory before the war and later as a vegetable salesman. The colonial Chinese community made up about 75 percent of the population; the rest were mostly Malays and Indians. Some were educated in English, therefore closer to the British masters, and thus part of a colonial elite. Most, however, spoke Hokkien, the dialect of Fujian province. Chia attended Chinese primary and secondary schools. And since he was keen on science, he chose to study physics at the Chinese-language Nanyang University. Like all Chinese institutions for higher education, Nanyang was influenced by the May Fourth Movement, and Mr. Science and Mr. Democracy were both much in evidence. The founder of the university was a famous tycoon named Tan Lark Sye. Far from being the stereotypical Chinese businessman, "only interested in money," Tan encouraged students to take an interest in politics and society. He saw political activity as the mark of good citizenship. Politics in Singapore in the 1950s meant the struggle for independence. Democracy, it was hoped, would follow from that.

Many Chinese speakers in Singapore were inspired by the "liberation" of China in 1949. This was partly a matter of ethnic pride, but also a victory for anti-imperialism. The British were accused of running Singapore as a police state. The British colonial administration responded by closing down some Chinese high schools, which were mostly financed by tycoons but also from donations by taxi drivers and even patriotic nightclub hostesses. This caused increasing agitation against the preferential treatment of English education.

One of the early fighters for independence and democracy was a young lawyer, then still called Harry Lee, who, despite his ethnic origin, did not yet speak Chinese. He was, in his own words, a typical "Anglicized Chinaman." Later, after he had studied Chinese to appeal to Chinese-speaking voters, he became better known as Lee Kuan Yew. As prime minister of Singapore, he would advance the British policy of Anglicization by abolishing Chinese higher education altogether. But that is getting ahead of the story.

Chia Thye Poh returned to Nanyang University as a graduate assistant after teaching science and mathematics at a Chinese high school. He was not an activist. His main interest was science, and he was planning to study abroad. But then came 1963. It was a tense time: Singapore was about to merge with Malaysia, and the Indonesian government, under Sukarno, was trying to intimidate Malaysia through aggressive "confrontation." Lee Kuan Yew's People's Action Party (PAP) was running for election against the only serious opposition party, the Socialist Front, or Barisan Sosialis. Lee was also a socialist at this time, but he had convinced the British that only he could stop a Communist revolution. Some of Lee's opponents, mostly trade-union members, Nanyang University faculty, and members of various Chinese civic associations, were accused of having pro-Communist sympathies. Lee did everything to stoke such suspicions, and just before the elections, in an early morning sweep called Operation Cold Store, all of Lee's main political rivals found themselves in jail, without charge, as national security risks. This was easily done under the so-called Internal Security Act, instituted by the British in case of Communist insurgencies; Lee gratefully inherited the law to eliminate his political rivals. His word for this was "fixing." He fixed the Communists, the Chinese-speaking schools, the opposition parties, the independent Law Society, the churches, all in good time, until only the PAP was left in charge.

Inspired by Tan Lark Sye's views on good citizenship, Chia decided to run as a Barisan candidate. It wasn't easy. Everything was done to make it impossible for Barisan to put on an effective campaign: printing plants were closed suddenly; permits to hold rallies failed to come through; radio time was denied. And so on. Chia won his seat nonetheless, together with twelve other opposition members. But thirteen opposition members in Parliament were too many for Lee to stomach, so three were arrested immediately; two, who were about to be taken in, just managed to escape overseas. To make sure that even an emasculated assembly would not cause him any trouble, Lee kept it in almost permanent recess. And as punishment for financing Barisan candidates, Tan Lark Sye was denied Singaporean citizenship.

This might strike one as odd behavior in a Cambridge-educated, socialist prime minister who had made his name as a fighter for freedom and democracy, but times had changed. Lee was in power now, and the specter of communism continued to justify his tightening grip. He explained his position in 1960, when he said that "all this talk of democratic rights, laissez-faire liberalism, freedom and human rights, in the face of the stark realities of an underground struggle for power, can only confuse the English-educated world." The implication, which would be regarded as racist if it had been uttered by a white man, was that Chinese speakers were unsuited to democracy and should be treated ruthlessly. And Lee's own "English-speaking world" should not be confused by half-baked Western ideals.

Under these trying circumstances, then, Chia began his life as a member of Parliament. There is no evidence that he was ever a dangerous radical, let alone a Communist. But he did believe in parliamentary procedures, so when Lee chose to ignore the legislative assembly, even on such a vital issue as Singapore's merger with Malaysia, Chia resigned in protest with his fellow Barisan MPs. A few weeks later, in October 1963, he was in jail. The pretext for his arrest was a protest demonstration against a planned visit to Singapore by the U.S. president, Lyndon B. Johnson. Like most people on the left, Chia was opposed to the Vietnam War. But he was not officially charged with anything. Nothing was ever announced. Chia simply disappeared from sight. He was only twenty-five years old.

Chia was locked up in a narrow cell, about the size of a toilet cubicle, in a nineteenth-century brick building called Moon Crescent Detention Center. Without light and with a very high ceiling, it was like being buried in a tomb. The only sound that penetrated Chia's chamber was the stamping of military boots and the muffled screaming of a prisoner in another cell. Chia was told that after a few days in this dark dungeon most men went mad.

Chia was lucky in a way. Unlike some political prisoners, he was not badly beaten or half drowned in a toilet bowl or tortured by electrodes clipped onto his genitals. To have a chance to get out, all he had to do was sign a confession that he was a Communist infiltrator. This would serve to confirm Lee Kuan Yew's propaganda about a Communist conspiracy. Others had done it, usually after they had been deprived of sleep and beaten into submission. The Barisan leader, Lim Chin Siong, a highly popular figure among the Chinese speakers and by all accounts a rousing public speaker in Hokkien, agreed to sign in 1967, after he had failed to hang himself in his cell, but begged Lee to be spared the humiliation of a televised confession. Lee refused. After two more years in prison, Lim was a broken man.

Pressure was put on Chia's parents to convince their son to sign. His mother, frantic with fear, had several strokes. Chia was interrogated day and night, while being forced to stand naked in a freezing room with the air-conditioning going full blast—a peculiarly Singaporean method of torture: a modern luxury turned into a torment. For the first few weeks in his dark cell, Chia really did think he was going insane. But somehow he held on, and was taken to the Whitley Road Detention Center, a bunker-like prison built especially for political prisoners, hidden behind the palm fronds in a plush, green suburb not far from the beautiful main road to Singapore International Airport.

Alone in his cell, often without anything to read, even a censored newspaper, Chia had to wait until 1985 before a charge against him was made public: membership in the Communist Party of Malaya, a party that was all but defunct. By then he was forty-four. Again Chia was pressed to confess and promised his freedom in exchange. And again he refused. He sent a letter to the authorities saying that the charge was entirely fictitious.

I asked him why he had persisted. What had given him the strength to resist for so long? He gazed at me through his glasses with an expression of surprise. He was much too polite to say so, but it was clear my question had baffled him. I wished I hadn't asked. "How could I have signed?" he said, very softly. "It wasn't true."

Chia did not boast of his defiance. It was for him the natural thing to have done. Any other course would have broken his spirit. He would have ended up like Lim Chin Siong, an embittered man staring into space. He did not talk about his life in prison as though it were of any particular significance. On the contrary, he apologized for telling me an old story and worried that it would be of no help to me.

I was struck by the way he referred to Lee Kuan Yew by his first name, Kuan Yew, as though they were close friends. It said something about the smallness of Singapore, a city-state of barely 3 million people, where everyone knows everyone else. Or perhaps a sense of intimacy builds up between a prisoner and his chief jailer, especially when the prisoner refuses to give in. Wei Jingsheng, too, spoke about Deng Xiaoping as though they were intimates, two stubborn adversaries worthy of each other. But perhaps Chia used Lee's first name only to show that unlike most Singaporeans, he did not fear him.

After Amnesty International began to pay serious attention and his case received publicity in 1985, Chia's continued incarceration became an embarrassment. One day in the late 1980s, Chia asked to see a doctor. Having spent so much time in the dim light of his cell, his eyesight was failing. He was taken to see an eye doctor in town. On the way back, his jailers decided to give him a little tour. They drove him downtown, where the new high-rise buildings stood, in shining chrome and gold, with logos of Japanese corporations and international banks winking in the neon sky. They pointed at the fine new Sheratons, Hyatts, and Hiltons, and the flashy new department stores on Orchard Road, where thousands of young people, dressed in the latest fashions, bought the world's most desirable products. And they drove him to his old constituency in Jurong, with its new supermarkets and government-subsidized public housing, all perfectly organized, with civic organizations, sports clubs, schools, cultural associations, and excellent public transport facilities—everything, in short, that a person might need from cradle to grave, all controlled by Lee Kuan Yew's People's Action Party. And Chia's jailers said to him that all his years in prison had been for nothing. Nobody even knew his name anymore. Singaporeans were prosperous and content, thanks to the PAP. That is why they voted every five years to keep the PAP in power. Chia had fought for a lost cause. He was irrelevant now. Why resist any longer? Why not just sign and be done with it? Then he, too, might be able to enjoy his remaining years as an obedient citizen of the Garden City.

Chia didn't sign, and in 1989 he was finally released from jail. Even then, his punishment was not quite over. He was put on the ferry to a small island called Sentosa, meaning Isle of Tranquillity. Before Singapore was founded, the island was known by the Malays as Pulau Blakang Mati—Isle Beyond the Dead. In World War II the Japanese used it as a POW camp. Now Sentosa is best known as a theme park called Discovery Island, with rides and pools, a musical fountain, a golf course, and an

"Asian Village," with fast-food restaurants, one for each ethnic group—Malay, Chinese, and Tamil—panoramas showing colorful "Images of Singapore," and, especially for Japanese tourists, a museum of waxworks showing the British surrender of Singapore in 1941: a bull-necked General Yamashita sitting opposite General Percival, whose spindly legs stick out awkwardly from a pair of faded khaki shorts. This was to be Chia's permanent home. He was the only resident on Sentosa, confined to a one-room guardhouse. For two years he was not allowed to leave the island without permission. It was the final, exquisite cruelty: the man who had dared to resist Lee Kuan Yew reduced to a lone shadow among the attractions of a theme park.

———

Singapore has been called Disneyland with capital punishment. A cliché, but not a bad description. I have often wondered about the taste for theme parks that have sprung up like bamboo shoots in the last twenty years, especially in Japan, the south coast of China, and Singapore, even as the few remaining historic buildings were being bulldozed, as though they were leftover rubbish to be disposed of in the quest for more prosperity. Perhaps the two phenomena are linked, the bulldozing and the re-creation. The theme parks—miniatures of historic Chinese cities and "traditional" Japanese towns, as well as imagined foreign locales, with a profusion of Eiffel Towers and small-scale Bavarian castles—compensate for the loss of visible history.

Or maybe people prefer it that way: a sanitized version of the past (or of destinations abroad), safe and clean, with fun rides for the kids, instead of the actual clutter of history or the hazards of foreign travel. Chinese have built, destroyed, and rebuilt their cities for thousands of years. What matters is not the actual age of a building but the location. A new concrete temple on an ancient site is considered "old," or at least historical. It is the association, the genius loci, that counts.

The problem for Singapore is that its genius is so recent, and its past so thin. Almost everyone came from somewhere else. Yet that is also its fascination. Like Los Angeles or Miami, Singapore bears all the marks of recent invention. It is an Asian New World.

One of the first things Lee Kuan Yew did after becoming prime minister in the early 1960s, was to launch a campaign against "yellow culture." This included brothels and hot cabaret shows, of course, but also juke-boxes, for which the prime minister felt a peculiar, personal horror. (A fastidious man, he was reputed to have had his prime-ministerial swimming pool drained after an Indian dignitary had used it. Apocryphal, perhaps, but not implausible.) One place in particular embodied yellow culture: a narrow strip in the center of town called Bugis Street, where pretty prostitutes and often even prettier transvestites of all ethnic origins danced nightly to attract their international clientele, mostly drunken sailors, who would climb on an old urinal to watch the show. Bugis Street was eventually razed. But in the 1980s, in an effort to attract more tourists, and stung by a report in *The Economist* that Singapore was "boring," the authorities decided to build the street up again as a perfect replica, without transvestites this time, but with the promise to offer "the quaint and the queer" of exotic Asian nightlife. This was vice as theme park, a simulacrum for family entertainment.

Most of old Singapore has been torn down, like Bugis Street. But there are still pockets of history—a row of nineteenth-century Chinese shophouses here, an Indian street there. Few people actually live there anymore, but they are polished, dolled up, garnished for the tourists, and for Singaporeans, too, to give them at least an idea of the fairly recent past, as synthetic, as clean, and as organized as the "Asian Village" on Sentosa Island. This is not unique to Singapore. You see the same in China and Japan, not to mention the United States. But since the PAP government is forever tinkering with culture and language—launching campaigns to "Speak Mandarin" or to clean up the English language or to abolish local Chinese dialects, or to study Confucianism—culture and language in Singapore have a stilted, theatrical feel to them, something officially acquired secondhand, like the folk-dancing festivals in Communist states.

Nothing in this small, rich, claustrophobic city-state is left for the people to work out for themselves, and consequently nothing feels quite authentic. Abolishing provincial Chinese dialects has had a particularly devastating effect, for they were the richest, liveliest modes of expression in a country of immigrants. But the dialect of Fujian or Hokkien, or even

Cantonese, was considered to be too vulgar and provincial for a successful city-state. Like the old Bugis Street, it had to be replaced by something more respectable, more "rational" and businesslike. The officially approved languages, apart from Malay, are a pseudo-BBC English and Mandarin Chinese. To acquire the latter has become fashionable, especially among the English-speaking elite, as a badge of ethnic identity. You hear the official languages spoken on television, correctly but stiffly, even mechanically, not unlike the voices that emanate from computers.

What makes theme parks in general so interesting, and also a little sinister, is the utopian illusion of technical perfection. Theme parks represent the dreams of their makers. They are usually extremely clean and even a bit puritanical, like Disneyland itself. I was shown around a theme park in Japan once, a model Dutch town, located near Nagasaki. The owner was a Japanese businessman who had dreamed of the perfect city, clean, crimeless, with a pleasant veneer of historical detail, a city without the messiness of human habitation, even though, paradoxically, he also had hopes that some people might actually want to live in his toy town. He showed me the splendid replica of the Royal Palace, the fake seventeenth-century town houses, the canals, and the authentic little tulip fields, but what filled him with the greatest pride, what almost made him cry with emotion, was the spanking-new sewage plant, which turned human waste into the purest drinking water.

Lee Kuan Yew's Singapore, once a dirty, bustling, crime-ridden port city, is now a bit like that. Cleanliness is almost a fetish; gum chewing and spitting are illegal. "Educating Singaporeans on the importance of discipline" is Lee's proudest achievement. And Mr. Science has triumphed in a twisted kind of way, for everything in society is reduced to a technocratic problem. When Lee Kuan Yew became interested in gene pools and the prospect of more efficient ways to make sure educated Chinese married their own kind, he set up a "Social Development Unit." He proposed to restrict nongraduate mothers to two children. "Creativity," too, became a government project, when it was suggested that Singaporean students were dull. Committees of PAP cadres drew up plans to make them more "creative." The plans, which do not allow for nonconformity, have yet to bear fruit. No wonder Lee once spoke of his citizens as "digits." And the digits are perfectly comfortable, until one of them decides to be less dull and question the authorities; then, like the proverbial nail that sticks out, it will be hammered down with great force.

———

So why do some digits continue to get out of line? The rewards of conformity are, after all, considerable. It is an odd sensation, driving around this suburban paradise, with its silky green golf courses, splendid public libraries, superb tennis courts, lavish shopping malls, excellent housing, and fine restaurants, trying to meet the tiny awkward squad. But in fact the material comforts of Singapore make the reasons for dissent more interesting. Many Singaporeans, from either fear or complacency, will tell you that there is no need for opposition in the Garden City, that it is of no use and only causes trouble. By contrast, the few open dissenters are forced to justify the value of dissent itself. I had met some of them before, in the late 1980s and mid-1990s. In 1999 I paid them another visit.

My first appointment was at six o'clock in the evening on the corner of Serangoon Road, in the heart of the Indian district. The air was hot and clammy, after late-afternoon rains had brought a temporary relief. It was November, the eve of Diwali, when Hindus celebrate the Festival of Lights.

Serangoon Road, a strip running through Little India, dotted with restaurants serving hot, runny curries on floppy green banana leaves, was packed with well-dressed people carrying cameras and shopping bags, marked BENETTON, GAP, or BALAKRISHNAN SHOPPING EMPORIUM. They were tourists, but also Indians, who had come in from the affluent suburbs to sample the traditions of a country their parents or grandparents had left long ago. Smells of sweet incense wafted from souvenir shops and the two Hindu temples. In the larger one, with its façade of gods and goddesses, their tongues out, writhing and wriggling in a brightly colored stuccoed mass, I watched men kneeling on the shiny marble floor to an image of Kali, the terrifying mother goddess, who was wearing men's severed heads around her neck and plucking the entrails from their bodies. The wailing sound of South Indian musical films playing on cassettes was everywhere. And in the midst of all this, the milling crowds, the wailing music, and the sweet and pungent odors, stood a small, portable wooden table with a pile of booklets and papers stacked on top. Three men, one Indian, the others Chinese, stood around the table trying to sell the papers. The Indian kept repeating the words "Don't be afraid. Don't be bullied by the PAP. Buy our paper. Don't be afraid."

But his voice was largely drowned out by the music and the chattering crowds, who passed the table by without a glance. They seemed less afraid than indifferent. There was an air of futility about the three men selling papers nobody wanted, and yet there was more to this scene than was immediately apparent. For one of the Chinese, a trim figure in his thirties, wearing a neat white shirt and glasses, looking rather like an accountant on his day off, was Chee Soon Juan, the secretary-general of the tiny Singapore Democratic Party (SDP). Before turning to politics, he had been a neuropsychologist. Apart from the veteran chief of the Workers' Party, J. B. Jeyaretnam, Chee is the only leader of an organized opposition left in Singapore. His story is all the more remarkable because he is the perfectly placed Singaporean, ethnically Chinese, English-educated, bright, enterprising, eminently respectable. He could have joined the elite, if only he had played the game. And yet here he was, almost penniless, sacked from his university job, without a seat in Parliament, continually harassed with lawsuits and arrests, hawking unread leaflets in the streets.

The leaflet in question was not a revolutionary tract. Called "The New Democrat," it had on its cover a picture of Chee, grinning in a blue suit and tie, shaking hands with Jimmy Carter. Readers were invited to join the SDP to "ensure transparency and accountability in the PAP government." Cases were mentioned of alleged government blunders, which a lively press would surely have exposed. And there was a note of protest against the way PAP candidates, including the prime minister, Goh Chok Tong had threatened people with dire consequences if they voted against the PAP. But most of the paper was taken up with a defense of freedom of speech, as though its value were not self-evident. The authors argued that speaking out freely did not mean riots in the streets. "Freedom of speech," they said, in perfect Singaporean technocratese, "generates an open and thinking society which is the corner-stone of a knowledge-based society." That this passes for subversive literature in a sophisticated city-state is both bizarre and sad. Chee's books are filled with similar sentiments, and although they are not exactly banned (only deemed "undesirable"), book-shops are afraid to stock them.

When Chee tried to sell his books in the streets, he was arrested for il-legal hawking. When he tested his right to express his opinions in public by making a speech in a busy shopping center, he was arrested, jailed, and later fined for failing to apply for a permit. And when a reporter for a Western news agency asked people what they thought of this, he was told (by a young financial consultant): "The government cannot please every-one. [Chee] is only saying bad things about the PAP. You must admit we have a good life under the PAP." At dinner with an intelligent, successful Singaporean businessman who had little sympathy for the government, I mentioned Chee. He thought Chee was wasting his time. Admirable, to be sure, but also a bit of a fool. "What's the use?" he said. "Debate, politics, not practical, *la,* no use, *la.*"

Chee and I sat down in a "hawker center" off Serangoon Road, an open place filled with Chinese, Malay, and Indian food stalls. Chee ordered some Malay and Hokkien snacks. He ate his thin fried noodles with fiery red chili sauce and helped me to some creamy white bean curd dunked in a sweet peanut paste. When I asked him how things were going, he pulled a face, and waved his hand in the direction of the crowds. "Tourists," he said. Nobody was from the district. Normally, Indians were receptive to the SDP. Many were not as well off as the Chinese, and were more outspo-ken in their views. But not today.

Again I sensed an air of futility, of fighting a losing battle. Arguments I had heard or read played through my mind: Liberal democracy is a West-ern value, most Asians care only about order and a full bowl of rice; men like Chee are westernized, confused, and out of place in their own cul-ture. . . . Just then, a Chinese man shuffled up to our table, dressed in shorts and a dirty, torn T-shirt with a beer brand stamped on it, a worker from one of the food stalls, perhaps. He reached into his pocket. Chee looked up, as though to shoo him away. "Chee Soon Juan?" asked the man, and bared a row of broken red teeth. "Yes, I am." The man's red mouth opened wider and he said in Hokkien: "Sir, you're a great man. I'd like to help you out." And he shook Chee's hand after handing over a grubby bit of plastic. It was a half-used telephone card. Chee turned to me with a smile, his spirits visibly revived, and said: "It happens all the time."

I had met Chee once before, in 1995, at the Singapore Sheraton Hotel. He struck me then as an amiable if slightly naïve idealist, a do-gooder, the kind of clean-cut young man who volunteers for campaign work during elections in the United States. The meeting had an air of absurdity. We sipped cappuccinos while a man in a lime-green tuxedo played Mantovani favorites on a grand piano. Well-dressed yuppies were ordering salads and Perrier and chatting loudly into cell phones. The air-conditioning was turned up to just the chilly side of cool. This could have been anywhere— Sydney, or Tokyo, or Atlanta. Chee spoke earnestly about the importance of free speech. And around us, sitting amid the huge tropical plants, were three silent young men in polo shirts, trying to look nonchalant. Each was carrying a black bag with a neat little hole drilled into the side facing us. "Cameras," said Chee.

Now, four years later, Chee told me his life story in more detail. We had agreed to meet in the office of the Indian who had helped hand out leaflets in Serangoon Road. It was located in a row of shabby two-story Chinese shophouses, with a pawnshop on one side and a little store selling dumplings on the other. Inside the house, on the wall, was a large picture of Sai Baba, a plump Indian guru with a necklace. The owner's wife was a follower. On the second floor I met Chee's Taiwanese wife, who was cradling their baby. She spoke in Mandarin to Chee, though he is more fluent in English. He grew up speaking the Hokkien dialect with his parents but still has trouble reading Chinese. He said he was taking lessons.

Like Chia Thye Poh, Chee was not a natural activist. Although he had been a rebellious student at his Methodist secondary school, he never really thought much about politics. After all, he was being groomed for success. And politics in the 1970s was for "losers." Unless, of course, you joined the PAP. But when Chee was a university student in 1981, something happened that changed his life. Perhaps people were getting tired of being nagged by the government. For the first time since the country's independence in 1965, a member of an opposition party had managed to break the PAP's absolute monopoly in Parliament. A local by-election in a district called Anson was won for the Workers' Party by J. B. Jeyaretnam. It became a legendary event. At last there was a voice of opposition. What is more, it was an eloquent voice. Trained as a barrister in England, Jeyaretnam, a Sri Lankan Tamil, spoke the queen's English, with an even plummier accent than Lee's.

Everything was done to reduce Jeyaretnam to silence, first by ridicule and abuse, which declared that he was immoral. When he won for a second time, in 1984, the tactics were harsher. Charged and subsequently convicted for irregular campaign financing, Jeyaretnam was disqualified as an MP and barred from practicing law. Though the Privy Council in London—still the court of final appeal in those days—judged him innocent of all charges, the government refused to give him his seat back in the assembly. The Singapore Law Society decided he could resume his work as a lawyer. (From that moment, the Law Society, too, was marked for "fixing.") Jeyaretnam managed to return to politics a few years later but faced an endless barrage of lawsuits and other chicaneries, which virtually bankrupted him. But this man who would not shut up inspired a new generation of Singaporeans, including Chee Soon Juan. The more the government bullied Jeyaretnam, the more Chee liked him.

Soon after the famous by-election, Chee left for the United States to study neuropsychology in Georgia and Pennsylvania. In the vast American continent, Singapore politics receded. But Chee preferred not to stay in America. He went home in 1990 and became a lecturer in the department of social work and psychology at the National University of Singapore. He had a nice house, a good car, a high salary. He was a member of the elite. Yet he had doubts about the way that elite was formed. These doubts were not overtly political. They had more to do with his own area of professional expertise. He was disturbed by the education system, which divided children into winners and losers from a very early age. Children who had not made it to the top stream were treated as if they were crippled. The obvious thing to do, he thought, was to express his views in a letter to the *Straits Times,* the main English-language newspaper. This seemed pretty safe. He was not challenging Lee Kuan Yew. But it upset the head of his department, who warned Chee that it could seriously affect his career. Why didn't he join the PAP and get into the PAP Youth League? He had everything going for him. Why ruin things for himself now?

Chee refused to listen. Instead, he decided to join the Singapore Democratic Party and run for office. He told me he would never have gone into politics in a democratic country. His main interest was science. But after a group of young Christians and social workers got into trouble in 1987 for advocating civil rights, the government announced that those who wished to "dabble" in politics should join a party, and do it full-time. So, like Chia Thye Poh a generation before, Chee felt it was his civic duty to enter Singaporean politics. To shut up and play the game, as most people did, would be too humiliating. And that is when his troubles began. For the government challenge was disingenuous. The only party that could offer its activists a decent living was the PAP. If you chose an opposition party and wished to survive, you had to keep your regular job.

Soon after Chee put up his name as an SDP candidate, he was sued by the head of his department for misusing university funds to mail a personal document. It was an extraordinarily petty charge. But Chee lost the case and his job. His allegation that the charge was politically motivated was dismissed, and he was forced to pay $235,000 (U.S.) in damages. A hat was passed around for donations from wealthy Singaporeans who had often grumbled about the government in private. But they turned away now, as though Chee had a contagious disease.

Chee had to sell everything he had. More lawsuits followed, as well as problems with the tax authorities. Though he is the only qualified neuropsychologist in Singapore, no one will employ him. The promising young man had lost his caste, and would now live on the margins. Officially, he had become a bad character, a threat to the common good. Former colleagues refused to return his calls. Fear of contagion from a political dissenter is physical as well as mental. Chee had become literally untouchable. He told me that people who bought his book in the streets would throw money at him so as to avoid direct contact—and these were, presumably, sympathizers. Prime Minister Goh Chok Tong crowed that "we annihilated him."

Chee reminded me of another Chinese Singaporean, about ten years older. I had met Ho Kwon Ping several times, in his office and for dinner in Chinese restaurants. He had been a journalist for the same magazine I had once worked for in Hong Kong. But he was a grander figure now, a star of the Singaporean elite: chairman of a large corporation founded by his grandfather, a property developer, chairman of Singapore's power utilities, chairman of the Speak Mandarin campaign, host to ambassadors, tycoons, and prime ministers, and a popular speaker around the region, especially adept at promoting "Asian values" to an international audience. Handsome, smooth, and well dressed, Ho would arrive for our dinner appointments in a white Mercedes-Benz with his beautiful wife, one of the nine members of Parliament to be officially appointed instead of elected.

It was hard to imagine that this son of a former ambassador, alumnus of international schools and Stanford University, this sleek personification of Asian success, had ever been a rebel, and yet, in his fashion, he had. In the 1970s Ho wrote critical articles about Singapore for the Hong Kong magazine. Lee Kuan Yew decided to scare him. He was arrested, together with a colleague, under the Internal Security Act, accused of being a Communist, and jailed for two months. He can laugh about it now, and make self-deprecating references at public functions to the naïve idealism of his youth, so long ago. But he did what Chia Thye Poh refused to do, and made a full confession on television. Having survived this rite of passage, he was able to resume his climb to the top, a destination almost guaranteed by his family background. His colleague, who was of Indian origin and from a more modest family, did not come out of it so well. For many years he was deprived of his citizenship.

Chee was never accused of being a Communist. After 1989, such an accusation had become absurd, even in Singapore. But he is a political outcast. In our conversation, Chee kept returning to a single question: If the government is so sure that everyone is happy, why then should it want to do everything in its power to stop a lone critic from being heard?

It is indeed odd. I think the answer lies in a paradox that almost all authoritarian states have in common but one that is especially acute in Singapore, with its colonial British patina. The governing party wants to have complete control over the public and, where possible, even the private lives of its citizens. But it also wants a Potemkin democracy, a semblance of political liberty, parliamentary window dressing for a virtual one-party state. This puts political opponents in a bind, for if they manage, against the odds, to be elected, they will always be in a minority that lends legitimacy to a system in which they can never win. Opposition parties have no access to the mass media. Their campaigns are sabotaged and their candidates harassed, all strictly according to the law, of course, through petti-fogging rules or lawsuits (defamation, usually), which the government always wins. If an opposition party still does well in an election, the electoral districts are redrawn to stop it from happening again. Because of all this gerrymandering, only two members of opposition parties managed to get elected in 1997—though more than 36 percent of the people voted against the PAP. The other non-PAP members in an assembly of ninety MPs were appointed, and knew better than to speak up.

"I'm damned if I'm going to be an opposition like that," said Chee, in a sudden burst of passion. And that is why he and Jeyaretnam are still hounded for their refusal to be controlled. They are a bit like Chinese exiles living in the West, free spirits who pay for their relative freedom with impotence. I asked Chee what kept him going. He sighed and said: "People sometimes come up to me and tell me I could surely be doing something better than hawking books and papers in the streets. But what else can I do? I still want to be heard. If I felt I had enough people with me, I could go on. But perhaps something serious has to happen here first, before there can be any change."

I thought of the Chinese man in the market off Serangoon Road, one of many Singaporeans who did not necessarily feel best represented by the PAP. I thought of the 36 percent who voted for the opposition, people from all ethnic groups who, for one reason or another, did not like being mere digits in an authoritarian social scheme. And I thought of the students in Jakarta, and other Indonesian cities, who had demonstrated for democracy and brought Suharto down. Compare them to the neat young Singaporeans, chatting in English and shopping for Western fashions along Orchard Road. It made nonsense of "Asian values." Who were the Asians? What were their values?

Chee looked down at his shiny black shoes and said, to himself as much as to me: "I must give it a shot. Giving up now would mean failure. I must go on. At least then, by the time I am too old, I can look back and say that I tried."

Because I knew he had been educated by Methodists, I asked Chee whether he was religious. He told me he had joined the Brethren, an Evangelical church, as a teenager. This is not uncommon in Singapore. Every week there are announcements in the newspapers of Christian meetings of one kind or another. They are especially popular among the affluent young, the bankers, managers, and stockbrokers, who gather in the function rooms of expensive hotels, dressed in suits and ties, singing hymns in English, rather stiffly, while someone plays an electronic organ. After a while, depending on the skill of the preacher, they slowly unwind, and, more often than not, end up falling to the carpeted floor, babbling incoherent phrases, while the preacher hollers about salvation.

Chee no longer attends services with the Brethren, and feels let down by them. The head of his department at Singapore National University, the man who sued him, was a fellow of the Brethren too. And so was the dean. They had held religious meetings in Chee's office on Friday afternoons. And yet they didn't hesitate to sue their colleague. Chee was disgusted that Christians would do such a thing.

When I asked him whether his political activism had been influenced by his religious beliefs, Chee hesitated. He had thought about that question a lot when he was in prison for having spoken in public without a permit. It was true that Jesus ate and drank with prostitutes and ministered to the poor, yet Chee was not a supporter of liberation theology. The church was not a political institution. But if he had one belief, it was this: "A human being should have the right to choose his own destiny. Why otherwise should God have granted Adam and Eve a free will? If God allowed our ancestors to choose for themselves, who has the right to stop them?"

—

The popularity of Evangelical Christianity in Singapore is not difficult to understand. It is a way to relieve the stress of constant striving for material success. And it offers an alternative dogma, something beyond the reach of worldly powers. It is the one area of life that the PAP cannot really touch, even though it tries to all the time.

I had visited Singapore in 1987, just as a group of young people were being arrested for organizing a "Marxist conspiracy to overthrow the government." The alleged ringleader was a Catholic lay worker named Vincent Cheng. The members of the "plot" included several young lawyers, a playwright, the owner of a printing plant, some social workers, and a number of priests, who were living abroad, out of reach of the Internal Security Department. Most, though not all, were Christians. The Singaporean archbishop, Gregory Yong, had shown some sympathy for them. He demanded proof of a plot, but this was slapped down as a kind of impudence by Lee Kuan Yew. That shut the archbishop up.

Lee's views of the Catholic Church are eccentric, to say the least. During a visit to the Vatican, Lee was so impressed by the spectacle of the pope carried about on a palanquin, with attendant nuns "almost fainting with joy," that he decided to introduce certain Church practices into the PAP. Henceforth, the central leadership would be chosen by top PAP cadres, appointed by the prime minister, just as the cardinals elect their pope. The Catholic Church, Lee pondered, must have done something right to have survived for so long. Survival, of races and institutions, was always something of an obsession with Lee, hence his interest in theories of climate, genes, and the quality of glands in various racial groups. The Chinese, being a hardy race, have good genes and fine glands, in Lee's opinion. Malays and Indians, being used to a softer life in warmer climates, are not as blessed. The Catholic Church, however, does not score high. Lee has argued that celibacy cuts down the number of bright children in the Catholic world, because too many clever young men become priests. But the Church can be a rival institution in a virtual one-party state. And priests can be troublesome, especially when Marxism touches their theology. This, evidently, is what Lee feared in 1987.

No evidence of a Marxist plot was ever revealed. The main crime of the playwright, a young woman named Wong Souk Yee, was to have written a satire on the ill-treatment of Filipina maids in Singapore. The social workers were guilty of advising poor Filipino workers about their legal rights. One lawyer had neglected prospects of a more lucrative practice by advising a Catholic student union—a sure sign, in official eyes, of Marxist tendencies. Two other lawyers had enraged Lee by criticizing his attempt to stop the Singapore Law Society from expressing independent views. And the lawyer representing them was arrested for "plotting" with "foreign powers" to interfere in Singapore's internal affairs—again, an uncanny parallel to the methods used to crush critics in Communist China. The latter's crime, apart from representing political detainees, was to have established contacts with an American diplomat and foreign human-rights organizations. He also happened to be president of the Law Society. Communism was only a pretext, of course. The fix was in for the Church and the legal profession.

The plotters, arrested under the Internal Security Act, were taken to Whitley Road Detention Center and subjected to the usual treatment. Thrown into dark solitary cells, they were told that they would be held indefinitely, like Chia Thye Poh, if they didn't confess. They never saw Chia, but his name was a warning. He was the chicken who had to be killed in order to scare the monkeys. They were stripped naked, made to stand in freezing interrogation rooms, slapped, and abused, some of them for seventy-two hours without food or rest.

They were not as tough, or as cussed, as Chia—this was a different generation, used to a softer life. One of the detainees was reminded of the Hollywood movie *Midnight Express;* it was her only experience of this kind of thing. So the detainees signed a confession, and appeared on TV. When they were freed, they told friends that they had done so under duress. News leaked out to the foreign media. Pressed to repeat their complaints in public, they did, and were taken back to the detention center for another round with the same officers they had accused of maltreatment. After several more days of standing naked in an ice-cold room and being screamed at by officers, they signed a "statutory declaration," which stated that their allegation of torture had been "a political propaganda ploy to discredit the government." Since it is an offense to claim that such a declaration is false, that was the end of the affair.

Most of the detainees returned to their jobs. One left for Hong Kong. Their lawyer remained in jail for two months, then ran for Parliament as an opposition candidate, won a seat, was immediately hounded by tax officials and government lawyers, and now lives in the United States. The Law Society no longer voices critical views. A law was passed in 1990 to allow the detention without trial of clergy and laymen if they should pose a threat to national security. The chief interrogator, who had used all his dubious skills to extract the confessions, is now chief executive of the news group that owns the *Straits Times.*

Meeting some of the "plotters" in 1987 was both heartening and depressing. They were funny, ironic, outspoken, fearless. They were also patriotic. They stressed how passionately they felt about Singapore. Unlike their grandparents, they were not immigrants. Singapore was their home; they wanted to be citizens. J. B. Jeyaretnam's electoral success was an inspiration. The other was the government's switch in rethoric in the mid-1980s. A new generation of PAP cadres was being groomed to take over. There was talk of new winds about to blow. PAP leaders openly worried that Singaporeans had become too passive. People should be more engaged, even critical—as long as they were "constructive." And this group of young Singaporeans answered the call. But it was depressing to see how quickly their initiative was crushed and budding citizens were turned once again into passive subjects—not, of course, through massive purges and bloodshed, as in China under Mao, but by the deft use of intimidation, just enough to scare others off.

I saw Teo Soh Lung in 1999 at her law office, located in a cluster of new high-rise buildings in the old Chinatown. There were still some two-story shophouses left, brightly colored in salmon pink and custard yellow. And there was a sign to mark the spot where Japanese military police had rounded up Chinese men for execution in 1941. The Japanese military secret police had set up their torture chambers in the same neighborhood, but the building had been torn down. Teo was one of the lawyers who had dared to criticize Lee Kuan Yew on television when he challenged them to a debate about the Law Society's role. Lee did not really mean to debate. What he had in mind was a stern prime ministerial lecture—a theme-park debate. Teo's effrontery had sent Lee into such a rage that his crimson face had to be toned down by broadcasting technicians.

Teo is a small woman with short hair flecked with gray. Narrow eyes blinking through her steel-rimmed glasses give her a quizzical look, as though she never quite believes what she is told. She shares her tiny office with Patrick Seong, another of the 1987 detainees. I had seen such offices in other parts of the world, a generic dissident lawyers' office: Martin Luther King, Jr.'s "I have a dream" speech tacked to the wall, a bookcase containing works on Nelson Mandela, American and British history, Third World problems, Asian politics, British jurisprudence, Salman

Rushdie's novels, and Edward Said's *Orientalism*. Various human-rights journals lay scattered about. And a poster supporting the Burmese opposition leader Aung San Suu Kyi hung near the door. We were joined by Patrick Seong, who had not changed much since I had last seen him in 1987—a thin man who made sardonic jokes in a soft voice.

I had been told by others that things had got worse after 1987, that the government's intimidation had worked. Teo sat down at her desk, put a few papers in order, and mused with Seong about their time in jail. The memories made them giggle, as though they were part of a private joke, which in a way I suppose they were. Teo remembered how she could hear loud screams coming through the walls of the room where she was being beaten by male as well as female ISD officers. These eerie sounds were almost certainly a recording, she now thought, and laughed. She also recalled that the interrogators were very superstituous. She would warn them about the ghost of her grandmother, who was buried in a cemetery behind the detention center. It had made them visibly nervous. According to Chinese tradition, in July, the "month of hungry ghosts," the ISD officers would buy expensive charms to bring them good luck and huge amounts of charcoal, known as black gold, to protect them from malevolent spirits.

I suspect there was an element of class involved in such stories. The interrogators were less educated than their prisoners. But Teo and Seong are victims of a different kind of fear—the fear that stops people from hiring them as lawyers, the fear of their contagion as former dissidents. And this fear is far less amusing. Unlike the rich property developer, who resumed his road to the top, the two lawyers still live on the margins. Corporate clients will not go near them. And neither, of course, will anyone with links to the PAP, which most Singaporeans have. The lawyers embarrassed the government. They had made the PAP "lose face." So they scrape by on small cases or on solicitors' work.

"Controversial"—that is to say, political—cases are wholly out of the question. J. B. Jeyaretnam asked Teo to represent him, but she refused. It would have made her practice even more marginal. In fact, however, she is thinking of giving up the law altogether, to "do my own thing," live on a farm, somewhere abroad perhaps. The dream of active citizenship, then, is over.

Talking to the former detainees, you sense not only disillusion—a shrug of the shoulders, the giggling acknowledgment that to struggle is hopeless—but also a lingering feeling of betrayal. One of them compared the PAP's admonishments in 1986 to come out and be critical to Mao's Hundred Flowers campaign in China. It was the old tactic of "charming the snakes from their holes" so they can be trapped more easily. This is not how they saw it at the time, of course. The only friend who advised caution and talked about the Cultural Revolution was one who had had a Chinese education. The others were all educated in English. A few used their time in solitary confinement to practice Chinese.

As can be guessed from his name, Patrick Seong is a Catholic. But that was not the main reason for his involvement. He had been a bit of a dreamer at school, with an idealistic view of the rule of law, which he thought protected people's rights. But he was not a political activist, and even the ISD did not think he was a Marxist. Seong simply got in their way. Through his connection with the Church, he knew some of the accused social workers. Since no other lawyer in Singapore would represent them in court, he felt duty-bound to do so. Seong knew at the time that this would damage his career. But he had not expected to be locked up and humiliated.

I said, a bit fatuously, that at least he was still a free spirit. This was easy for me to say. Seong answered that he was not sure his children would see it that way. His daughter was doing well at school. She had already entered the "express stream," which meant special privileges but also heavier doses, even at her age, of PAP orthodoxy. From an early age, children are taught about the need for "permanent vigilance" and "discipline," and about the "constant threat of danger" from external and internal enemies. But if she continued to do well and stayed out of trouble, she would be comfortable; her "lifestyle" would be "upgraded" at every step. Who knows, she might even end up as a government minister. Seong told me all this in his soft, ironical manner.

—

Intimidation in an authoritarian state works in insidious ways. I often noticed how people were afraid even when there was no ostensible reason. Fear gnaws away at people until it manifests itself in unthinking reflex responses. It actually seems to be worse in Singapore than in China, because the place is so small that you cannot avoid scrutiny. Singapore can feel like a boarding school run by a terrifying headmaster, who is constantly drawing up new, arbitrary rules while warning of the dire consequences of infringement. You never know when (or even why) you might be punished. The reflexes are often physical, like those of dogs expecting a beating. A British academic at Singapore National University once told me about a political scientist there who turned and ran when my friend showed him a faxed article from a British newspaper critical of Lee Kuan Yew.

I returned to my hotel, after seeing Teo Soh Lung and Patrick Seong, pondering the effect of intimidation. I was thinking of my e-mail exchange with Chee Soon Juan a few weeks before I left for Singapore. He had asked me to give a talk to a group he had formed with Jeyaretnam, called the Open Singapore Center, which held regular meetings and invited guests to speak. It was informal, innocuous, and, I thought, worth supporting, a small drop of plain talking in a sea of shifty conformism. So I accepted. A week later I received another message from Chee. Since government permission was required for such gatherings, could I please send my passport number, date of arrival, and so on. Suddenly, I too felt the clammy chill of possible trouble. Would I still get my visa? Would I be stopped at the airport? Would I be followed?

I canceled the talk. And I told myself that I had acted wisely. My purpose, after all, was to find out what Singaporeans had to say, not to hold forth. But I took no pride in my decision. I was reminded once again of the traveling writer's odd position. The privilege of a foreign passport and the detachment of a temporary visit place a glass wall between him and the people he meets. The risks are all theirs. All the writer can hope to come away with is a deeper understanding.

Entering my comfortable room, the air-conditioning set at a perfect temperature, I saw the red light blinking on my phone. It was a message from Teo Soh Lung. She had a package for me. Could I please come and pick it up at her office? This sounded mysterious. I wondered what documents it might contain.

Teo was not in her office. The package was on her desk, a slim brown envelope. I opened it and found, somewhat to my surprise, one page, photocopied from a famous book by the British poet D. J. Enright, entitled *Memoirs of a Mendicant Professor.* Enright spent much of the 1960s teaching English literature in various parts of the world, including Singapore. Almost as soon as he got there, he ran into trouble. It happened during Lee Kuan Yew's war against jukeboxes and other forms of "yellow culture." Enright, the new professor of English Literature, gave an inaugural address, in which he pointed out, politely, that culture flourished when people were free to create and enjoy the arts as they saw fit. Culture, he observed in a memorable phrase, could not be produced from a test tube.

In what came to be known as the Enright Affair, these remarks were pounced on by the government and the local press as a neocolonialist intervention in Singapore's internal affairs. Enright himself described the affair in an amusing and lighthearted way in his memoirs. I cite the page that Teo left for me almost in full, because it is such a melancholy testament to the thwarted aspirations of Singapore's brightest, liveliest, most decent men and women:

> The Communist is accustomed to a party line and to obedience and to the idea of public confession. Unless he is a pure fanatic, he doesn't find it overwhelmingly difficult to change his line from Communism to anti-Communism; and having recanted, having faced the mild ordeal by television in which he will play the hero as much as the villain, like a backward boy, previously despaired of, who has suddenly passed all the examinations, then often he will serve his new masters well. But the liberal, the man who believes in truth and justice, or in fairness and decency, he cannot be trusted. He is the enemy of all doctrine. . . . His politics were shifty to begin with and they will continue to be so. He sees good in practically everything, he sees bad in practically everything; he grants you your point, and then expects you to grant him a point in return. He cannot be relied on, he is undisciplined, unrealistic, ungrateful, and he pampers his little private conscience. Prison is his proper place.

One question continued to bother me in Singapore: If the PAP rulers had managed to turn Singapore into a theme-park version of Chinese authoritarianism, what about the people they governed? Does the sterile air of discipline and conformity have anything to do with the fact that almost 80 percent of the population is ethnically Chinese and thus heir to a Confucian tradition, as Lee Kuan Yew thinks? I was shown a newspaper clipping in Chee Soon Juan's office, dated March 1985, in which Lee said: "Had the mix of Singapore been different, had it been 75% Indians, 15% Malays, and the rest Chinese, it would never have worked." But then one would expect him to say that.

It is, after all, the basis of PAP orthodoxy that obedience to an authoritarian state, also known as "consensus" or "society above self," is an Asian virtue, while those who resist and continue to advocate more liberal politics are deluded by Western notions. Malays and Indians are Asians, too, of course, but for Lee they lack the Confucian values. Perhaps that is why a disproportionate number of lawyers in Singapore (half the members of the Law Society, in fact) are Indians. And yet Lee himself began his political career as a proud Cambridge double-first with Western democratic ideals. Perhaps he would argue that he gradually liberated himself from his colonial education and learned to think more like a Chinese. But then how do we explain Chia Thye Poh and his fellow Nanyang University graduates who opposed Lee?

Being Chinese in Singapore is in any case anything but straightforward. For many people, especially among the lower, commercial classes—hawkers, shopkeepers, artisans, taxi drivers, minor civil servants—it is a matter of food, language, and vaguely remembered customs: burial rites, annual festivals, and family relations. Cultural identity is not something most of them are likely to worry about. They take it for granted. If anyone frets over identity it is the highly educated, English-speaking, westernized elite. It is they who want their children to learn Mandarin, take classes in Confucian ethics, and talk obsessively about being "Asian."

A few doors down the road from my hotel was a Chinese bookstore stocking works from China, Hong Kong, and Taiwan—novels as well as essays, biographies, and classics such as *Dream of the Red Chamber* and Confucius's *Analects*. There were also CDs with folk songs and operas, and scrolls of rather mediocre landscape painting in the classical Chinese style. There were Chinese-English dictionaries and textbooks for learning Mandarin. And yet the predominant language among the Chinese customers was English. I watched them leafing through picture albums and glossy books imported from the People's Republic of China that celebrated its fifty years: President Jiang Zemin beaming at a reception for African dignitaries, Mao Zedong pointing at a glorious sunrise, Deng Xiaoping inspecting a gigantic dam project. And I thought of the Chinese-speaking men and women who had resisted the PAP some twenty years ago and were punished for being "Communists."

—

I set off in a taxi to have lunch with J. B. Jeyaretnam in the Malaysian border city of Johor Baru. He can no longer afford to live in Singapore. The driver, a Chinese, speaking in a Hokkien accent, offered the list of complaints one often hears in the safe cocoon of a taxi. People say Singapore is rich. Well, it may look that way to you, he said, but life for ordinary people, especially taxi drivers, was very hard. It was okay for the higher-ups, always telling people what to do, but they don't have to drive a car all day long for a pitiful profit, which is all spent on ludicrous taxes anyway. Now, his son, he was very smart. He was in England, studying to be an engineer. Hull University. He would do well out there, make money, and maybe not come back, *la*. You couldn't blame him. Singapore was no good, too many rules and regulations, and too small, *la*.

Borders are often symbolic of the countries they divide. This one was no exception. On the Singapore side is a kind of high-tech medieval fortress, huge, gray, forbidding, with turrets and what look like stylized watchtowers at odd angles from a roof, which bristles, like a monstrous porcupine, with antennae of all sizes. Customs officers take an inordinate amount of time scrutinizing cars, especially those coming in from Johor, but also those belonging to people wishing to leave the Garden City. The other side is a different world. The smooth, clean, velvety roads running straight through the dense emerald-green landscape of Singapore become, on the other side of the causeway, a jumble of potholed streets filled with honking cars. Old ladies with heavily painted faces, Malay and Chinese, squawk at the men passing by the peeling shophouses and ask them to come upstairs for some fun. Dogs poke through the litter. And the stench of rotting food mingles nicely with the smells of cement, fried chicken, and diesel fumes. It all comes as something of a relief.

Jeyaretnam was waiting in the lobby of the large hotel where we had agreed to meet. He is over seventy but wears his years lightly. After taking me to task for refusing to speak at the Open Singapore Center, he suggested several places where we might have lunch. Indian? Malay? Chinese? European? J.B., as his friends call him, is a caricaturist's dream, a dark Victorian gentleman, with long, gray side-whiskers sprouting from his chocolate-colored cheeks, a hawkish nose with large nostrils, and eyes that change color according to the light, from gray-green to the purest blue. He was dressed casually in a blue polo shirt, slacks, and sandals.

Although I had hoped to engage him on the topic of race, the Chinese compared to the Indians, he was more interested in straight politics. Unlike Chee Soon Juan or Chia Thye Poh, Jeyaretnam is a born politico, eager for a good fight. The last election, in 1997, was a scandal, he said. He had been robbed of his seat. Though there were enough uncontested seats to ensure a PAP victory, they still could not let his party win. I had heard the stories before—how the prime minister, Goh Chok Tong, threatened that votes against the PAP would turn a district into a slum; how J.B.'s fellow Workers' Party candidate, Tang Liang Hong, was accused—in a heavily Catholic area—of being an "anti-Christian Chinese chauvinist"; how, after Tang filed a police report protesting such false allegations, he was sued by Goh, Lee Kuan Yew, and other PAP ministers for defamation, which effectively bankrupted him, since he was ordered to pay $5.65 million; and how J.B. himself was forced to pay $59,000 in damages because he had mentioned Tang's complaint in an election speech. J.B. had not yet been able to pay. Bankruptcy would mean the end of his political career.

J.B. ate in the way he spoke, slowly but with enormous gusto. More and more food arrived at our table: fried chicken, fish swimming in flaming red chilies, fresh green cabbage with bean curd and sliced eggs, chunks of suckling pig basted in a sweet mango sauce. His nostrils widened with each new dish. And his eyes gleamed when he spoke of the next election, which would probably be his last. Here was a man who called himself a political animal but who had been battered all his life fighting in a system where the odds were stacked against him. In the ideal Chinese authoritarian state, a man like J.B. is not supposed to exist.

I remembered another sensualist at odds with a society created in the puritanical image of its first prime minister. He was David Marshall, an

Iraqi Jew born in Singapore, a hard drinker and a ladies' man. Marshall had been a heroic figure in his day: a tireless fighter against British colonial rule, he was the first elected chief minister in 1955 and founded the Workers' Party in 1957. Lee feared him as a rival, and then, after Lee had acquired almost absolute power, despised him—for being too full of life and for lacking the ruthlessness that Lee prized above all other qualities. To get rid of him, Lee made Marshall his ambassador in Paris, a seductive option, but a bittersweet end to Marshall's political career. When I last saw him, not long before he died, Marshall, who had once fizzed with vitality, looked exhausted—not only because he was already very ill, but because he felt his battles had all been in vain. He felt, like Lee himself, that Singapore was a Chinese creation, and he feared for the future. The Chinese, he said, were brutal in their politics. They had no understanding of democracy. They killed their enemies. With the deep melancholy of personal defeat, Marshall said: "With the ebbing of American influence, and the flowing of Chinese influence, we see an extension of nails in our [Singaporean] coffin, and an expansion of our ruthlessness."

J. B. Jeyaretnam did not talk like that. Instead, he reminded me that his supporters in the 1981 Anson by-election had been mostly Chinese, even though his opponent from the PAP was also Chinese, and the nephew of a cabinet minister to boot. In fact, he said, Chinese in Singapore—bus drivers, taxi drivers, hawkers, and so on—constantly came up to him to shake his hand. J.B.'s eyes shone when he said this: "They tell me I am a great man. I'm not great, I tell them. I just say they must all do their bit."

And yet J.B. knows he does not stand a chance. He would like to live out the last years of his life in peace. So the next time around he would tell people that if they wanted the PAP, then so be it. He had done his best. And he had paid a high price for it. I asked him what the worst of it was. He said, after a long pause, that he had lost everything—his apartment, his money. Because of his opposition to the PAP, his law practice had floundered. "I've never praised the system," he said, "and that is why, Mr. Buruma, people don't come to me. They assume I will be treated differently from other lawyers in the courts. They avoid me like the plague."

But, he continued, there was something worse than that, something infinitely more painful, and that was the suffering of his wife. She had been diagnosed with cancer in 1977 and had died in 1980. If he had stepped back from politics and gone to live in England, well, then perhaps she would have lived. A tear trickled from his pale blue eyes. Perhaps it was his neglect of his private life—the bane of every political animal— that haunted him more than the remote chance of his wife's survival. But for an instant I felt something of the loneliness of being a dissenter in Singapore, of being on the edge of society, always hounded, ridiculed, and made to feel small and pointless in a place one had fought all one's life to improve.

I knew that J.B. was an Anglican. Even so, his religious feeling took me by surprise. When I asked him what had kept him going, he passed his hand down his face, as though in a gesture of ritual cleansing, and said: "I suppose its my Christian faith. I suppose we are made in the image of God. That is what we are taught to believe. I feel very strongly about the dignity of the human being. Jesus spoke about that, you know."

The influence of faith as an alternative to political orthodoxy shouldn't be underestimated, even though the institutions of Christianity in Singapore have been cowed into silence, and even, sometimes, into active collaboration. That is why J.B., like Chee Soon Juan, refuses to attend services at his church. But what was it about Christianity in particular that sustained these men and women? The Christian faith, especially Roman Catholicism, was neither liberal nor democratic, except perhaps in the sense that all men are equal in the eyes of God. I recalled my conversation with David Marshall, who had been born in the East but had lived some of his life in the West, an Oriental Jew whose native home was among Malays, Indians, and Chinese. Did he feel closer to the European tradition? He opened his dark eyes wide and said in his broken voice, which had once boomed from the hustings, that most certainly he did: "The brotherhood of man, equality, what a beautiful concept! What a beautiful thing: a religion that makes brothers of all men." Egalitarianism as a universal idea was of course inspired as much by the French Revolution as by the Judeo-Christian God, and an idea, moreover, that in Marxist garb had once swept across the Chinese empire too, and burned almost everything before it.

———

According to the *Straits Times,* more than 90 percent of Singaporeans whose opinions were polled said they wanted the government to censor the Internet: not families, teachers, or "communities," let alone individuals, but the government. The worry was pornography, as well as religious cults and other "undesirable" stuff that might be downloaded from cyberspace. I mentioned this to a sociologist born in China and living in Singapore. He took a rather macabre interest in what he called the "experiment" of the PAP state. He admired it as an exercise in sociopolitical skill; otherwise he found it stifling. He was not surprised by the result of the opinion poll. Since people assume there is a government line on everything and individuals cannot always be sure what it is, they consider it safer to leave such matters up to the authorities. Did this seem sad to him? "No," he said. "Since I am not a Singaporean and have no intention of changing anything, I cannot muster enough emotion to find it sad."

Teresa Ma (not her real name), an old friend, is a regular visitor to critical websites on the Internet. She refuses to be intimidated. She simply behaves as though she lives in a free country. This gets her into trouble, but she still has her pride. Being the way she is, she has developed a fine nose for the pockets of freedom that open up here and there, little oases that allow a person to breathe—in cyberspace, but also in real life.

The last time I was in Singapore, she had taken me to the Boom Boom Room, a nightclub on the second floor of a corner house on Bugis Street. The main attraction was a brilliant entertainer called Kumar. Tall, Indian, male, and dressed in an extraordinary array of shimmering saris and glittering evening gowns, Kumar sashays onto the Boom Boom's stage like a breath of fresh air. Screeching in Singlish, the Singapore street language, mixing English freely with Malay and Chinese, Kumar says things that no one is supposed to say in Singapore: He makes fun of ethnic stereotypes, laughs at the prissy, Boy Scoutish respectability of PAP orthodoxy, and is merciless to the buttoned-down yuppies who make up most of his audience. The atmosphere in the club is not entirely different from that at gatherings of evangelicals in expensive hotel function rooms. People come to shed their social straitjackets, if only for an hour or two. Kumar became so popular that he was offered a slot on television. The show was quickly taken off the air.

This time Teresa had another enthusiasm, a young theater group called ACTION Theatre. This, she said, was something really new in Singapore, a breakthrough of sorts. It showed that young Singaporeans were cutting loose. ACTION Theatre did plays that were quite close to the knuckle—about sensitive social problems, about sex. Naturally, I wanted to see this phenomenon for myself.

ACTION Theatre was to perform in a lovely colonial villa, about a five-minute walk from Bugis Street, in a kind of designated "cultural" area, subsidized by the government, which had become increasingly concerned about "creativity," or the lack of it, and culture. Next door was a dance studio, and next to that you could take classes in Chinese calligraphy. Around the corner were most of the city's main museums. And there were coffee bars, done up in tasteful re-creations of the colonial style, where young people in Japanese designer clothes sat around discussing the latest trends in London and New York over their café lattes. I saw the director of ACTION Theatre, an affable young man from Thailand named Ekachai. He kindly gave me an invitation to the first night of the group's next performance, a short play entitled *Viva Viagra*.

If I had paid closer attention, I could have picked up the tone of the occasion from the invitation card itself, which mentioned that the dress code would be "resort gear or smart casual." It also announced that the guest of honor would be Professor Tommy Koh, ambassador-at-large. I had never met Professor Koh, but knew of him. A bit of a liberal in his youth, like the property developer—although never, so far as I know, arrested—a man who had once had democratic ideals, Koh had become a prominent PAP mandarin; having also been an ambassador in Washington, he was an academic with a taste for the arts, an ex-chairman of the National Arts Council, and an active spokesman for "Asian values." Some might say Tommy Koh had sold out. Others might call him a liberal, perhaps even a "reformist" inside the establishment, a man of culture, indeed a traditional type of Chinese intellectual, who advises his rulers and spreads the orthodoxy.

The drinks party before the performance of *Viva Viagra* was civilized enough. People in smart casual resort gear drank chilled white wine and nibbled on non-fattening Vietnamese snacks. There were serious-looking women in black, a few homosexual couples in dark Kenzo T-shirts and heavy boots, and there was Tommy Koh, wearing a very smart casual blue-and-purple batik shirt, and modishly long gray hair wrapped carefully around his ears, smiling and chatting and working the room.

The play itself was a kindly satire on modern Singaporean sexual politics. A young woman is shy about having sex with her boyfriend and shocked that her widowed mother should still have sexual feelings at all. The mother's lover is too proud to take Viagra. Two young men take too much. But, partly thanks to the wonder drug, all ends well for everyone.

More interesting was the speech by Tommy Koh before the play began. He spoke in English about his pride in being Asian. He pointed out that bureaucrats were not always "bad guys"; they could be "good guys," too. This splendid new theater was made possible, was it not, by the active support of the Singaporean government. The audience applauded. A blue spotlight, bouncing off Koh's glasses and the gray-blue highlights in his perfectly coiffed hair, gave him a weird shine, as though he were polished with wax. Many people, he continued, perhaps a bit incongruously, said that it would take many years to recover from the Asian economic crisis. But he didn't share that pessimistic view. The Asians were clever and industrious, and they had pulled off miracles in the past. A new economic miracle was now just around the corner. However, the next step in the Asian miracle would surely be cultural. After Asian economic power, there would be Asian cultural power and, so Koh was happy to tell us, the whole world would sit up and take notice. Indeed, it was already happening now, in Singapore.

More applause. Ekachai, the ACTION Theatre's director, professed how moved he was, thanked Koh for all his help, and said there was a surprise in store. The lights dimmed, Koh blinked, and from the back of the theater about fifteen actors and actresses came in, carrying a huge cake and singing, "Happy birthday to you, happy birthday to you, happy birthday, dear Tommy. . . ." Ekachai was smiling, Koh was smiling, everyone looked happy, and by the time they began to sing "For he's a jolly good fellow, for he's a jolly good fellow . . ." I thought here was an example of what was wrong with Singapore.

It was trivial, of course, compared to being locked up for twenty-three years, or being worked to death in labor camps or tortured to denounce one's parents or forced to worship a leader as though he were God, but it was an example of how some of the best and brightest are co-opted into an oppressive system even as others are crushed.

I asked Ekachai the next morning what he had really thought of Tommy Koh's speech. He shifted a little in his plastic garden chair, looked at me with a degree of suspicion, and said: "Which part of his speech?" The whole speech, I said. And Ekachai, a lively, intelligent Thai, began to formulate an answer that sounded curiously like an opinion column in the *Straits Times*.

Tommy was really quite liberal, he said. And anyway, he, Ekachai, was happy to receive the "hardware" from the government as long as he could choose the "software." True, he still had to submit work in advance to the censors. But in fact *Viva Viagra* was really quite risqué for Singapore.

Really? I asked, thinking of Kumar's act only a few streets away. Well, he said, maybe not to him or me, but I should understand that the Singapore government was concerned to reflect the views of the majority of Singaporeans, and most Singaporeans are still very conservative. I was about to open my mouth, but he waved his hand as though to indicate that he already knew what I was going to say. Of course, the arts had to be a bit adventurous, but one should not be out of step with the people. And besides, while the government was loosening up, one didn't want to go too far. It might "scare" them.

Ekachai's impassioned apologia had the sweet sound of reason and moderation. But it also had the deadening ring of submission to the paternal, authoritarian state.

Sitting in the air-conditioned bus, almost soundlessly rolling along the perfectly paved coastal road to Changi International Airport, past the skyscrapers with their blinking neon lights, past the golf course, past the junction leading to the Whitley Road Detention Center, hidden behind the tall green trees, past the pastel-colored Housing Development Board apartment buildings, I thought again about Tommy Koh and Ekachai, and reflected on the sheer waste of talent and enterprise when there is no room between conformity and marginality. An artistic, intellectual, or political rebel would have to plump for marginality, of course, but here the margins were too ruinous. Ekachai's fear of "going too far" and Koh's talk about Asian "cultural power" were two sides of the same melancholy coin: energy misapplied, originality stifled, and liberty killed at birth. For most people, the suffering involved may be minor and may perhaps even pass unnoticed, soothed as most people are by material comfort. But it was there all the time, hanging in the air of almost every encounter I had in Singapore—the fear of authority and the anxiety to appease it.

In the opulent splendor of the airport, I went through some of the items I had clipped from the Singaporean newspapers. One in particular, which had caught my eye, perfectly illustrated that pervasive Singaporean mood, a faint echo, muffled in affluence, of the same thing I had noticed in other parts of Greater China, and sometimes even in Japan.

It was an article in the *Straits Times* about the new Madame Tussaud's that had just opened in Singapore, featuring wax models of Einstein, Michael Jackson, Bill Clinton, Marilyn Monroe, and many other celebrated figures, including, of course, Lee Kuan Yew. There was a photograph of the waxen Lee standing stiffly, small, stern eyes staring glassily ahead, the prominent southern-Chinese jaw clenched tight. At his feet was a middle-aged woman. She was kneeling to smooth the knife-sharp crease in his dark-blue trousers. Her name was Karen Toh, a business manager. "I admire him a lot," said Ms. Toh, "and have no chance to see him personally. The figure is just like his real person. I feel happy to be able to touch him and not be afraid he'll get angry with me."

Chapter 2

Not China

Kaohsiung, a port city on the southern tip of Taiwan, is no more or less ugly than most East Asian cities; that is to say, it is for the most part hideous, in the concrete bric-a-brac style of postwar Japan. It has none of the manicured slickness of Singapore. And what goes for the architecture applies to the politics, too. The Japanese actually built much of Kaohsiung, or Takao as they called it, when Taiwan was part of the Japanese empire, between 1895 and 1945. Before World War II, the new, prosperous parts of Takao were Japanese, with Japanese houses, Japanese department stores, Japanese inns, Japanese shrines, Japanese banks, and Japanese movie theaters. (Most Taiwanese lived in shabbier areas, filled with low houses, built along rank-smelling canals.) But so little is left of the prewar city that a group of elderly Japanese tourists staying at my hotel could no longer recognize a single street. They stood around the marble lobby shaking their gray heads and emitting throaty little sounds of disbelief. Like most East Asian cities, Kaohsiung has been totally transformed at least twice during the last hundred years.

Kaohsiung today is an urban sprawl, some of it built on reclaimed land between the South China Sea and a ridge of green hills that is often hidden behind a shimmering screen of industrial pollution. It looks much like a large, provincial Japanese city in the southern palm-tree zone: the same jumble of quasi-Western-style buildings—raw concrete if built in the 1960s; steel, glass, and granite if built in the more prosperous 1980s. There are the same garish advertising banners with Chinese characters splashing down from roofs or strung across the streets and the same higgledy-piggledy skyline bathed in bright neon, which looks especially fine at dusk. And yet there is a roughness, a loudness, and a hint of rebelliousness to Kaohsiung that is more typically Taiwanese.

You notice it in small things as well as large. The "elevator girl" working the lifts in a new Japanese department store in the center of town wore a Japanese uniform of white lace gloves, beret, high-heeled shoes, silk stockings, heavy white makeup, skirt just above the knee, all prim, cute, and proper. She was trained to move in the precise, oddly stylized manner of the typical Japanese elevator girl: gloved hand pointing up or down, falsetto voice announcing the different floors, forty-five-degree bows to customers entering and leaving. But where the actual Japanese elevator girl is drilled to be virtually indistinguishable from a mechanical doll, and would rather die than display a flaw in her dress or demeanor, everything about the girl in Kaohsiung was slightly out of kilter: her shirt was stained, her hat askew; she lifted one foot to scratch the back of her other leg, twirled a chunky jade ring around and around her little finger, and grinned at me as though to show how ridiculous this prissy Japanese charade really was.

The Kaohsiung elevator girl was almost certainly a "native Taiwanese." Most people in Kaohsiung are. They call themselves native because their ancestors moved to Taiwan from the China coast before 1945, often as long ago as three hundred years. The "natives" make up about 85 percent of the population. Taipei, where the government is located, is home to many Chinese "mainlanders," who came over only in the late 1940s, with General Chiang Kai-shek's army, after the Nationalists had been defeated by the Communists in the Chinese civil war. Until recently, mainlanders dominated the ruling party, the bureaucracy, and the armed forces. Their children, born in Taiwan, are still referred to as mainlanders. Standard Mandarin Chinese is their common language, spoken on state radio and television stations. In Kaohsiung most people speak the dialect of their Fujian forebears, like many Singaporeans.

Most native Taiwanese are in fact from the same Hokkien stock. But while the Singaporeans have been browbeaten into political submission, the Taiwanese have rebelled against autocracy and established the first democracy on Chinese soil. The south of Taiwan is their stronghold. Some would say the democratic revolution that led to the first free presidential elections in 1996 began in Kaohsiung, on Human Rights Day, December 10, 1979. Political opposition to the Nationalists, or Kuomintang (KMT), came to a head that day in a violent clash between activists, mostly native Taiwanese, and the police. It was a chaotic demonstration, with people gathering in different parts of the city, singing patriotic songs, making speeches, and demanding democracy and independence. Violence threatened from the start. A number of activists had been tortured at a local police station. Demonstrators came armed with sticks. Riot police charged. Street battles ensued. Every major opposition figure was there, from underground journalists to members of the legislature, and almost all were arrested. After a much-publicized trial, some were sentenced to life for sedition.

The "Kaohsiung Incident" was, in a way, the Taiwanese Tiananmen. The confrontation resulted in failure. Freedom came later, after martial law was lifted in 1987 and after President Chiang Ching-kuo, like a Taiwanese Gorbachev, helped to dismantle the system that had given him absolute power. He had done so for various reasons. Pressure from the United States was one. His realization that the KMT government, in order to survive, could not rest on brute force was another. He needed the consent of most native Taiwanese, and elections seemed the best way to secure it. Also, the KMT, unlike the Chinese Communist Party, was founded by Sun Yat-sen in 1912 as a democratic party. Regardless of how it later functioned in practice, its roots were democratic. It came to power in China in 1913 through a national election. But pressure from dissidents, at home and abroad, was also an important factor, and the Kaohsiung Incident was, many still believe, the moment the KMT dictatorship began to show cracks.

———

Some of the veterans of 1979 were hanging around the Kaohsiung election headquarters of the Democratic Progressive Party (DPP) in the winter of 1996. I was greeted at the door by a small, dark-brown man in a blue suit. His tie was a riotous affair in red, purple, and pink. "Welcome," he said in English, and invited me to sit down for a chat on the second floor of the gray two-story building, decorated everywhere with the DPP symbol—a blue map of Taiwan in the shape of a whale. Sounds of honking, moaning whales wafted through the open windows from loudspeakers outside. A middle-aged woman whose teeth were stained red from chewing betel nuts offered me a plate of fresh pineapple chunks and spat a crimson gob on the concrete floor.

It was, in fact, an extraordinary occasion, for this was the first time in history that a Chinese people was freely electing its own president. General Chiang Kai-shek, and then his son, Chiang Ching-kuo, had ruled Taiwan as dictators. After Chiang Ching-kuo's death in 1988, party chairman Lee Teng-hui, a native Taiwanese, became president. He carried Chiang's political reforms even further. Now he, too, had to run for election. Even the fact that the People's Republic of China had decided, in a spasm of belligerence, to shoot off missiles across the Taiwan Straits didn't dampen the mood of celebration. On the contrary, it seemed to have pulled the Taiwanese together in a spirit of defiance. They would have their democracy, whether Beijing liked it or not.

All over Taiwan, streets were festooned with banners and posters bearing the portraits of candidates: smiling, pink-faced men in blue suits and party badges, rather like provincial bank managers—a world away from the stern Generalissimo Chiang Kai-shek (the "Gimmo"), who ruled Taiwan as a martinet after 1949. The airwaves were filled with political chatter: call-in radio shows, interviews with politicians, debates between experts, journalists, professors, pop stars, and whoever else thought he or she had something to say. Every taxi driver seemed to be tuning in. I picked up snatches of radio conversation about the future of the KMT and the interference from mainland China. Taxi drivers explained the political demographics of their hometowns. Men and women who had been in jail as political dissidents only a few years before were now openly discussing their views. Like a political Rip Van Winkle, Peng Ming-min, the DPP's presidential candidate, had come home in 1992, after twenty-two years of exile in the United States.

Memories of political violence were still raw in 1996. Less than two decades earlier, one of the opposition leaders, Lin Yi-hsiung, had lost his mother and small twin daughters—stabbed to death by unknown assailants—while he was in jail as a political prisoner. In 1981, an academic named Chen Wen-cheng, visiting Taiwan from the United States, was found dead on the lawn of Taiwan National University, with thirteen broken ribs and ruptured internal organs. The police claimed they had had "a friendly conversation" with the professor. In 1989 an elderly opposition politician in Kaohsiung County, Yu Teng-fa, died in a pool of his own blood. He had been about to take his bath. There was a nasty gash in the back of his head. Perhaps it was an accident. His family suspected foul play. The wife of Chen Shui-bian, the dissident lawyer who was to become the first DPP president of Taiwan in 2000, was paralyzed by a hit-and-run accident in 1985. An accident, possibly, but Chen suspected the worst; during election campaigns, his wife would be wheeled onto the speakers' platform as a reminder of the pre-democratic past. These cases were never cleared up. But the point was less whether the deaths were in fact due to political violence than that people automatically believed they were. Paranoia was the legacy of years of terror.

Violence still flared up here and there in the cauldron of politics and crime; in Kaohsiung a politician was killed in a nightclub by a colleague with gangster connections. But in 1996, the official terror was over. Like South Korea and the Philippines, Taiwan had made the transition from military rule to democracy, a feat received in other parts of the Chinese world with a degree of churlishness, even pique. So-called liberal officials in Hong Kong had told me that Taiwan was sliding into "chaos." In Singapore, too, Taiwanese democracy was not hailed but seen as an affront: It made the "Asian values" propaganda seem absurd. There were various reasons that China decided to herald Taiwan's first free presidential election with a missile launch, but anxiety about a fledgling democracy on what China regarded as its national soil was surely one of them.

The brown man in the blue suit and the riotous tie was named Huang Hua. He swiftly launched into a story of hardship and sacrifice that one came to expect in DPP campaign offices, and yet the cumulative effect of these stories was humbling. Huang had been arrested three times between 1963 and 1975, for promoting Taiwanese independence. He spent ten years on Green Island, a grisly camp for political prisoners, where he was locked up for much of the time in isolation, reading British history, Gibbon's history of the Roman empire, and biographies of U.S. presidents. Huang said the governers of Green Island were not educated enough to understand the political content of these books. He was finally released in 1986, the first year an opposition party was allowed to take part in national elections. Peng Ming-min, the DPP leader, who had spent all those years in the United States fighting for Taiwanese freedom, was his "teacher," he said.

Mr. Huang was not a famous or glamorous figure but an obscure university librarian. His story of a lifetime of sacrifice dropped into a casual conversation was typical of many I heard in Taiwan, but it was the kind of story one would like to blast into the ears of all those who say that "the Chinese" don't care about politics. Once again I marveled at the tenacity of people like Huang. His passion for national sovereignty was undimmed by the years he spent in prison. Even if China were to become democratic, he said, Taiwan should still be an independent country. He viewed the dissidents from China with suspicion. They were not to be trusted, for whatever they said about Taiwan now, their ultimate aim was to build one China. If they ever came to power, Chai Ling or Wei Jingsheng or Wang Dan or whoever, they would be just the same as Chiang Kai-shek or Chairman Mao. Clearly, one of the things that kept Huang and others like him going was a deep-seated animus against mainland China, an animus born in the violence and terror of the early years of KMT rule.

I wanted to hear more, but that was the last I saw of Huang. We were invited to join the parade on the way to the DPP rally, and as soon as I stepped outside, I lost him in the crowd. The street was blocked by jeeps, taxis, tractors, and forklift trucks, all bearing the white-and-green banners of the opposition party. There was a deafening racket of car horns, firecrackers, men shouting through megaphones, campaign jingles, and the chanting of party slogans. Revving cars and motorbikes created a blue, dusty haze that hung heavily in the stifling subtropical air.

Someone shoved me into one of the taxis, and that is how I met Kathy.

Sitting in the front seat. She turned around, smiled, and said: "Hi, I'm Kathy with a *K*."

A wiry bundle of nervous energy, in her early thirties, Kathy Wei had short hair and a long, thin face. She spoke fast in an American accent, which she had picked up at college in Binghamton, New York, and later, working at a local TV station in California. The cars began to inch forward, honking their horns and adding their fumes to the haze, which gradually took on a sulfurous orange color as the afternoon wore on. Along the route, men and women, many with children in their arms, held up three fingers: the number of the DPP on election forms. Kathy jiggled her knees, looking this way and that, humming with excitement. She told me about her life in America and her job at the TV station, where she had worked with Taiwanese and Chinese from the mainland. Her feelings about "the Chinese" were mixed. She wept when she watched the crackdown on Tiananmen Square, yet she found mainland Chinese difficult to get on with, lazy and resentful of Taiwanese wealth. The Taiwanese, she said, were more like Americans, industrious and self-reliant. A Taiwanese friend had told her to ignore the Chinese. "We cannot change them," she'd said, "so just don't let them change us."

We stopped near the small park where the rally was to take place. There was no chance of getting through the traffic. Green flags and green-and-white party banners fluttered lazily. The noise of campaign songs, car horns, and amplified voices was enervating. Because of the muggy heat, we walked into a 7-Eleven to buy bottles of water. A young man in a white T-shirt, carrying crates, put down his load as soon as he saw me, thumped his chest, and exclaimed: "I am Taiwan man! China no good! We don't want China!"

The park was actually a glorified playground, a scrubby place roughly the size of a baseball field. (The main stadium of Kaohsiung had been reserved that night for the KMT rally, for which thousands of people had been bused in from other areas, to watch a show of professional singers and dancers sweating it out amidst clouds produced by dry ice.) A smell of fried squid came from the food stalls that had been set up by enterprising vendors. People of all ages were milling around aimlessly. Two men dressed in cotton undershirts came up to offer me their views. One, a gaunt, toothless figure in his sixties, was a former dockworker, the other a plump primary-school teacher. Soon the group expanded to include at least ten people, their earnest brown faces glistening in the early evening light. Kathy translated from the Fujian dialect, which I could not understand. Was I aware of all the corruption? asked the former dockworker. And vote-buying by the KMT? Did I know about that? Kathy was stamping her feet with impatience, her eyes darting about the field. The dockworker, pressing his fingers into my arm, said that the Taiwanese people had been humiliated by official corruption, but now the truth would come out, for people were free to tell it at last.

A brass band, playing with more vigor than skill, struck up the party anthem. The microphone was being tested by a man who seemed to be emitting amplified burps. Lights flickered on and off. There was a sudden hush, followed by loud cheering. I had lost Kathy for a moment and found her in the thickest concentration of people, near the entrance of the park, where she was leaping up and down, like a young girl, trying to get a better view. A spotlight hit the middle of the commotion. I could just see a group of men in suits and pale blue baseball caps being hustled through the crowd by younger men in flak jackets. Someone nudged me and mentioned the name Peng Ming-min. Then I saw him, the DPP presidential candidate, a tall man fixing a glassy smile on nothing in particular, his skin waxy with fatigue. Kathy reached out to one of the men in Peng's entourage. He failed to notice her and swept past, looking straight ahead. Kathy turned around. Her eyes filled with tears. "This is the happiest day of my life," she said softly. "Now I see him as a man."

It was a puzzling statement. Whatever did she mean "see him as a man"? Peng was speaking into a microphone, sounding hoarse and oddly hesitant; clearly, he was not a born public speaker. Then Kathy explained. One of the men with Peng, the one she had tried to touch, was her father. He had fought all his life for this moment, abandoning his family, living in exile in the United States, thinking only of "the cause." And there he was now, standing on the platform a little behind Peng, supporting his party in a free election. Once an absent father, now a vindicated man of flesh and blood. I saw him in the distance, a bland-looking figure blinking into the spotlights through a pair of steel-framed spectacles. His name was "Ben" Wei Rui-ming.

Kathy sketched an outline of her life the next morning. She was calmer now. Some of her wiry tension had worn off. Her story was as much about her father as about herself, the typical story of a native Taiwanese family.

Kathy had been born in Kaohsiung, but spent her first few years in Japan, where her father was a law student. The family was supposed to have returned to Taiwan when Kathy was four, but after Kathy went home first, with her mother and elder brother, plans began to fall apart. Her father, having become involved in an organization that promoted Taiwanese independence, was unable to go back without being arrested. So he went to the United States instead, on a scholarship to study theology. Like many Taiwanese since the late nineteenth century, Ben Wei was a Christian, a Presbyterian. He had intended to become a minister.

Back in Taiwan, Kathy's family was under constant police surveillance. There were humiliating interrogations. When the family applied for permission to go to the United States, their passports were taken away, and gradually Kathy's father became a distant and resented figure, visible only in a black-and-white photograph taken in Tokyo, which Kathy kept. He was blamed for abandoning his family: His wife's parents, as well as his own immediate family, believed that paternal duties should never be sacrificed for a political cause.

There was another—historical—reason for family resentment. After the Japanese defeat in 1945, many native Taiwanese intellectuals had become involved in politics, hoping to be able to run their own affairs. Then the KMT officials began to arrive from the Chinese mainland, together with the gangsters and carpetbaggers. In Taiwanese eyes, these newcomers were primitive, lawless, disheveled, corrupt, arrogant, and often violent. The economy soon suffered, and comparisons with the immediate past were inevitable. The Japanese may have been harsh, but at least they had brought order, modern facilities, and a degree of civility. The mainland Chinese appeared to be bringing nothing but hardship.

Tensions between Taiwanese and mainlanders exploded on February 28, 1947, when KMT troops fired into a crowd of protesters in Taipei. Taiwanese all over the island rebelled, which resulted in martial law and a ferocious military crackdown. In every city and town people were massacred. Students, journalists, doctors, academics, and other suspected rebels, branded as "communists," disappeared in the night, many never to come back alive. Bodies wrapped in jute bags floated down the Tamsui River in Taipei.

More than twenty thousand Taiwanese died as a result of the "2-28 [February 28] Incident," souring relations between Taiwanese and mainlanders ever since. Kathy's maternal grandfather had been a schoolteacher under the Japanese and had grown used to their sense of order. Many of his friends were killed in 1947. From then on, like most Taiwanese, he decided to retreat from politics into a sullen colonial acceptance of mainlander rule as the only way to survive. His son-in-law, Ben Wei, had decided otherwise, however, and brought trouble upon his family. So as Kathy was growing up, her father's name was not to be mentioned.

One day, when she was fourteen, her father called from the United States. He had married another woman by then, a pharmacist in Flushing, Queens, and had abandoned his plans to become a minister. While helping his new wife run the pharmacy, Ben Wei became deeply involved in the Taiwanese independence movement.

Kathy's feelings were complicated. Her father's life may have been a source of bitterness in her family, but she also heard many complaints about the government mentioned in private. Like all Taiwanese children, she was subjected to daily KMT propaganda in school: reverence for Sun Yat-sen, the "Father of the Nation," reverence for Chiang Kai-shek and his struggle to reclaim China. This was the dogma, the "correct thinking," to which all Taiwanese had to conform. In front of every school or public building stood a statue of Sun or Chiang and a yellow map of China, denoting the ultimate defeat of Red China. "We were always told that the KMT was good," Kathy said, "but I have eyes and ears. I could see that bribery went on, and people were frightened."

One day, Kathy's urge to rebel was activated by something of no great importance, a routine event in fact, but it is often just such small things that inspire resistance. The students were assembled in her classroom and told to come forward, one by one, to pledge their loyalty to the KMT. Kathy didn't know what to do at first. When it was her turn, she was angry and nervous. On a sudden impulse, she ran away and locked herself in the dormitory. I asked her why she had done this. Was it out of loyalty to her father? No, she said. It wasn't that. She may have resented her father, but she remained intrigued by him. "No. I guess I did it out of loyalty to Taiwan."

When she was finally permitted to go to the United States, as a student, Kathy got to know her father for the first time. They had much catching up to do. But he was a busy man, always going to meetings or traveling to Washington. He became even busier after 1978, when President Carter recognized the People's Republic of China and severed diplomatic ties with Taiwan. For years, Taiwanese dissidents in the United States had been trying to lobby Washington, but as long as Taiwan had to be cultivated as "Free China," they met with little success. After 1978, however, the thuggishness of the KMT government was becoming embarrassing, even in Washington. The overseas dissidents, galvanized the following year by the Kaohsiung Incident began to have more influence. President Chiang Ching-kuo came under pressure to grant some liberties. In 1987 martial law was lifted. In 1992, Kathy went home. Her father returned two years later. It was the first time he had seen Taiwan since 1963. He arrived at the airport in Taipei with Peng Ming-min. Twenty thousand people had come out to welcome them. It was a tear-filled event. Kathy was there, too. But he didn't even notice her.

—

I flew from Kaohsiung to Taipei the day after the presidential election. Most of the posters and banners had been cleared off the streets during the night. Here and there countrywomen, shawls wrapped around their faces, were still busy sweeping up pictures of those pink-faced bank managers in blue suits. I thought of Kathy. I knew how unhappy she would be with the result. President Lee Teng-hui, the KMT candidate, had soundly beaten the DPP. The KMT still had the money and the networks, cultivated over many years of patronage, to bring out the votes. The only consolation, perhaps, was the fact that President Lee was not a mainlander but a native Taiwanese, and he had done much to promote democratic reforms.

When I went to see Ben Wei in the half-empty rooms that had served as Peng Ming-min's campaign office, he was smiling. Chinese and Japanese often smile to hide their embarrassment or a misfortune. But this wasn't like that. Wei, a studious man with a stubborn jaw and soft, delicate hands, looked genuinely happy. He said he had gone to a church the night before that had been full of DPP supporters, many of them crying. Wei, however, saw it as a kind of victory that there had been an election at all. He spoke softly, with frequent pauses, sometimes in English, sometimes in Japanese, which came to him more easily. I told him I had seen Kathy.

"You know," he said, "I am sixty now, and I have been part of the movement since I was a student in Japan. I suffered a lot for our cause. I couldn't see my daughter, Kathy, for fifteen years. But I don't feel any regret. If I were born again, I would do the same. For I have no choice. I don't know how long I will live, but I'll do my best to educate people, to teach them to take the future of Taiwan seriously. To be annexed by China would be a great tragedy for the Taiwanese people."

Wei saw the election as an enlightening process. He wanted to instruct young Taiwanese about constitutional law. But he kept returning to the price he had paid for his life in exile. His son still had not forgiven him. Wei mentioned a film—he couldn't remember the title—about a political prisoner whose daughter visits him in jail and tells him that she respects his ideals but then asks why, if those ideals were so important to him, he brought her into this world. Wei had seen the film in America, with Peng Ming-min, who had also left his children behind in Taiwan, and together they had wept in the dark. As soon as the movie was over, Wei rushed to a public phone to call Kathy and tell her how sorry he was. He apologized again when he picked her up at the airport in New York. "When I saw her at Kennedy airport . . ."

The memory stopped him in mid-sentence. He pulled out his wallet and produced a crumpled black-and-white photograph of his family, taken in Tokyo, when Kathy was three. A woman and two children were looking solemnly at the camera, Tokyo's version of the Eiffel Tower looming fuzzily behind them.

Wei suggested a Japanese restaurant for lunch. After a short gap in our conversation, while we both chewed on our pork cutlets, Wei suddenly said: "I kept going. I never thought of giving up." I asked him why. "Maybe because I'm a Christian."

He mentioned his grandfather, who had taken part in a failed rebellion against the Japanese back in 1896. His grandfather hid in a Presbyterian mission, whose missionaries, mostly from the United States, were sympathetic to the Taiwanese and made many converts. Wei continued: "From the very beginning I had hoped to build a nation that was different from China. Most intellectuals in Taiwan are Christians, about 90 percent of them Presbyterian. We believe that every man was created equal, and we have the right to choose what kind of society or nation or system we think is best. That would certainly be different from Chinese society. For we believe in freedom and individualism."

Wei doesn't like China. He went there once, in 1993, for a visit and was shocked by the crowds, the filth, the coarse manners, and the general dishonesty. Everywhere he went, he said, he was cheated. It was a common reaction of Taiwanese in China. Even though Taiwanese dissidents had often been called "communists" by the KMT, their contempt for the Chinese Communists ran as deep as their hatred of the KMT, for both pretended to represent One China, of which the Taiwanese wanted no part.

I reminded Wei that the Generalissimo had been a Christian, too. Wei smiled: "Well, he had a right to claim he was a Christian. But he killed so many people in an un-Christian way."

———

Killing on a massive scale is one of the foundations of modern Taiwanese nationalism. Most nations have a founding myth of martyrdom. They are myths not because killings did not take place but because bloody events are given a coherence in retrospect, turned into a story, and encrusted with symbolic meaning that pulls people together in a shared memory of collective suffering. The 2-28 Incident is a myth of that kind, the founding myth of a democratic Taiwan.

Memories of the killings in 1947 were so painful and left such resentment that it was not permitted to mention them under the old, predemocratic KMT regime. They were officially buried, erased from the public memory, just as positive memories of the Japanese empire were to be expunged. For many years Japanese films were banned in Taiwan lest they provoke nostalgia. Instead, the KMT promoted its own myth of martyrs, who had struggled heroically to save China from the Japanese and then from the "Communist bandits," a myth whose theme was of returning one day to the Chinese motherland. There was no mention in any Taiwanese textbooks of the 2-28 Incident, no memorials, no streets named after it, just a chilly blanket of official silence. The memory lived on only in frightened whispers among trusted relatives and intimate friends.

I met one old dissident in Taipei who used a metaphor to explain what it had been like to grow up in the shadow of 2-28. A woman he knew had joined a religious cult. She was seduced by the cult leader. The woman's young daughter soon noticed what was going on. When the cult leader realized this, he told the little girl that she had seen nothing. She was forced to blot it from her memory, or otherwise terrible things would happen. "I later met this girl," the dissident said, "and she was pretty messed up."

When I first visited Taiwan, in 1982, the symbols of the KMT were everywhere: the yellow maps of One China, the busts of Sun Yat-sen, founder of the KMT, of Chiang Kai-shek, looking stern and patriarchal, and the admonishment, written on posters and scrolls, never to forget the motherland, harking back to Ming-dynasty loyalists who hoped to reclaim China from the Manchu invaders in the seventeenth century. Every train station, school, and public building displayed them. By the mid-1990s, however, when former dissidents were serving as DPP legislators or city mayors, most of the busts of Chiang had disappeared. I wondered what had happened to the thousands of stony heads of the Gimmo. Had they been pulverized, or was there some giant vault somewhere containing the detritus of KMT dreams, or a dumping ground, perhaps, like the one in Delhi where statues of British viceroys gather dust?

A large avenue in Taipei that used to be named after Chiang Kai-shek now bears the name of an aboriginal tribe (after a suggestion to call it Marilyn Monroe Avenue had been rejected). And in the center of town is 2-28 Park. In the middle of the park is a new memorial, a kind of pagoda done up in black granite, set in a pool of water. Near the memorial is the 2-28 Museum, housed in a biscuit-colored colonial-style building that used to be a propaganda broadcasting station, first for the Japanese and later the KMT, and was the first building taken over by the Taiwanese rebels in 1947. In front of the museum is an abstract modern sculpture, a line of large stone blocks. The precise meaning of this composition escaped me, but the title read THE SOUL OF TAIWAN.

The museum is a shrine to the 2-28 Incident, containing blurred, blown-up photographs of the martyrs—doctors and students and intellectuals, some of them dressed in formal Japanese kimonos, others in neat linen suits—together with historical documents, and various relics: fans, letters, eyeglasses, guns, pamphlets, pens, radio sets, and threadbare clothes. Displayed in one glass case is a black Japanese-style student uniform with brass buttons on a torn jacket encrusted with dark stains. It had once belonged to a provincial student, who found himself stranded in Taipei when rail services were suspended after the events of February 28. He had entered the Railway Administration Building with other students, to inquire when services would resume. It was the last time they were seen alive. All students were suspect: the railway director's private guards murdered them in a matter of minutes.

As told in the museum, the story of Taiwan, including the 2-28 Incident, is as formulaic in its way as the old KMT myth of Nationalist martyrdom. A short historical overview explains how the Taiwanese—that is to say the Chinese who arrived in Taiwan three centuries ago—were always oppressed by foreign conquerors: first the Dutch, then the Portuguese, the Japanese, and finally the KMT mainlanders. This, one is told, fostered a unique love of freedom and a rebellious spirit. But the story had a typically Taiwanese post-colonial twist. Hindsight has given Taiwanese a rosier view of Japanese rule, which, though harsh, also brought many benefits, such as universities, science, railways, and electrification. The KMT, on the other hand, brought only violence, poverty, and corruption. The loathing of aliens that once bound Han Chinese together against the Manchu invaders is replicated in the Taiwanese hatred of mainland Chinese.

The story of 2-28 itself, as described in books, comics, videotapes, photographs, prints, posters, and textbooks, invariably goes like this: On February 27 agents of the Monopoly Bureau, who were little more than mobsters on the government payroll, assaulted an old lady who was peddling cigarettes in Taipei. One of the agents beat her over the head with his pistol. Crowds gathered to protest. The agents, panicking perhaps, began to shoot and killed one of the demonstrators. More people were gunned down the next day, with internationally outlawed dumdum bullets, which rip the body open. The rebellion spread all over the island. Radio stations and government offices were taken over. People suspected of being mainlanders, in or out of uniform, were attacked and sometimes clubbed to death with sticks.

In 1947, Taiwan was a province of China, which was still ruled by the KMT. A meeting was convened between Chen Yi, the KMT provincial governor, a brute with Shanghai gangster connections, and members of the Taiwanese elite. Civil liberties were promised in exchange for a return to law and order. But as soon as more KMT troops arrived from China, the "white terror" began: Martial law was declared and mass arrests, torture, rapes, disappearances, and executions followed. Within about two months, much of the native Taiwanese intelligentsia was wiped out. Many people were so badly tortured that they had to be carried to the execution grounds. Eventually, after he had lost the civil war in China and retreated to Taiwan, Chiang Kai-shek made a gesture to appease outraged Taiwanese feelings: In 1950, after a splendid fireworks display, Chiang's old friend Chen Yi was executed for being a "traitor."

As I wandered outside the museum, past the granite blocks expressing the "Soul of Taiwan" and the young people posing for pictures in front of the 2-28 Memorial, I thought about the melancholy fact that the foundation of modern nations is almost always soaked in blood. There is a strong nineteenth-century whiff about the Taiwanese story, an air of neighing horses, heroic martyrdom, and fine Enlightenment ideals of freedom, national independence, and democracy. The same ideals had also been aired in China at various stages of its modern history, yet they had failed to take root. Why had they succeeded in Taiwan? What was it about Taiwanese nationalism that brought freedom and democracy, while Chinese nationalism resulted in tyrannies on the mainland and in the Chinese Republic on Taiwan?

I was struck by an odd wooden sign, written in Chinese, near the 2-28 Museum: ROAD TO HEALTH. Behind the sign ran a narrow, ten-meter strip made up of small, black sharp-edged pebbles, stuck vertically in the surface, rather like a fakir's bed of nails. Next to the strip was a pair of Nike running shoes, placed neatly together, with a pair of white socks tucked inside. And there, on the pebbled Road to Health, was a young man with a crew cut, walking slowly up and down in his bare feet, his back straight, his arms swinging like a soldier's, his face a picture of forbearance. Up and down he went, along the stony road leading to the 2-28 Museum, up and down, up and down.

—

Almost every Taiwanese over a certain age has a personal 2-28 story to tell, a remembered fragment of the bloody national myth. "Mark" Chen Tan-sun remembers the murder of a respected local doctor who lived in a small town near Chen's home when Chen was twelve years old. The doctor, having protested against a venal and incompetent KMT mayor, was dragged behind a car to the county capital; there, he was made to kneel, and his brains were blown out. Chen can remember listening to rebel radio broadcasts inciting Taiwanese—in Japanese, the lingua franca that mainlanders did not share—to rise up against the KMT. He remembers the excitement. But he also remembers the fear that came afterward, when friends and relatives began to disappear.

I met Chen for the first time on election night in 1996, and saw him again three years later. Like Ben Wei, he had returned in 1994, after nineteen years of exile in the United States. Now he was magistrate (or mayor) of Tainan County, near the village where he was born, one and a half hours by train from Kaohsiung. To get there you pass through some of the ugliest industrial landscape on the island: drab cement works, steel plants emitting green and yellow smoke, and small factories in rinky-dink buildings of corrugated iron. Squat concrete apartment buildings rise out of flat, emerald rice paddies, lined with dusty palm trees. Billboards advertising yet-to-be-developed real estate—high-rise buildings with Spanish-style balconies and phony Chinese roofs—promise a future of opulence and ease.

Mark Chen spoke excellent English and Japanese, as well as Mandarin and his native Taiwanese dialect. A large office in the county hall was filled with mementos of his American exile: baseball pennants, and signed photographs of Senators Ted Kennedy and Claiborne Pell posing with

Chen and beaming with avuncular goodwill. There was also the usual collection of gifts and testimonies to high status: diplomas, prizes, sporting trophies, calligraphies, a Japanese doll in a glass case, and elaborate ornaments of jade and gnarled wood.

Chen, still a tall, handsome figure with a thick head of hair dyed black in the common style of no-longer-young East Asian men, was ecstatic about the democratic changes in his country. It was marvelous, he said, marvelous. By the way he was bouncing in his chair, barely able to contain his excitement, you would have thought his party's candidate had won the presidency, not Lee Teng-hui. There was only one issue left to be resolved, he said, and that was Taiwanese independence. This was an absolute necessity, for, as he put it, "we can never trust the Chinese." The Japanese, he said, created a "clean environment" in Taiwan, but "Chinese culture" changed all that.

The contrast between Japanese cleanliness and dirty, double-talking Chinese corruption had no doubt grown sharper over time as memories of Japanese brutality faded in the light of later Chinese betrayals. The first thing Chen did after being elected as county magistrate was to erect a monument in memory of those who had died in 1947. Then he told the education department to revise the textbooks to include the history of 2-28.

Chen grew up in an atmosphere of bitterness and evasion. Before 2-28, he said, people talked about politics, but afterward there was silence. He was always conscious that Taiwanese were treated as second-class citizens in their own land and punished for speaking their language at school, but the worst thing, in his recollection, was the corrosive effect of mainlander rule on what he called the Taiwanese mentality. "People used to be honest, but after Chinese culture was forced on us, we changed. Nobody told the truth any longer. It was too dangerous." Again that question of truth and the humiliation of being forced to live a lie. And again the idea, expressed by a Chinese, that other Chinese cannot be trusted, that, in Chen's words, the Chinese are "tricky people."

Chen studied mathematics and did his military service in Taiwan. He left for the United States in 1964—not to be a political activist, but because all the good jobs were taken by "those Chinese," meaning mainlanders. In the U.S., Chen became an American citizen, but like many others, he drifted into the politics of Taiwanese nationalism. This wasn't an easy cause. But the dissidents bided their time, writing anonymous articles (to avoid trouble for their families on Taiwan) and arguing their case against the KMT. And they quarreled, as overseas dissidents do, in their various émigré organizations, splintering into this faction or that. Some advocated violent rebellion; others took a more evolutionary view. There were rumors of mishandled funds and sexual improprieties. Leaders were deposed and reputations damaged by allegations of spying. And yet, compared to the mainland-Chinese dissidents today, the Taiwanese held together, mainly because, whatever their differences, they were united by the aim of national independence.

Little by little, they began to be taken more seriously, by liberals such as Ted Kennedy, but also by members of the Republican administration under Ronald Reagan, when U.S. policy moved away from automatic support of anti-Communist allies and toward the encouragement of democracy. The People's Republic of China had been officially recognized by Washington in 1979, when Taiwan was still under martial law. Promised elections were suspended. The Kaohsiung Incident, on December 10, 1979, got international attention. And a series of political murders, including the shooting of Henry Liu, a dissident journalist, in San Francisco, gave the Taiwanese regime an increasingly seedy reputation. Liu had written a critical biography of President Chiang Ching-kuo, the Generalissimo's son and successor. Liu's killer was a Taiwanese gangster, but the orders had allegedly come from the Taiwanese security police, led by another Chiang—Ching-kuo's son, Hsiao-wu.

When Mark Chen was finally able to go home, at the age of fifty-nine, Taiwan had become a democracy. The way he moved about his large office, his easy but firm manner of talking to his staff, and his obvious enthusiasm for solving local problems gave him the air of an aristocrat restored to his rightful place—the lord who came back to his manor. But of course he was not a lord; he had been freely elected. I asked him about his children, whose photographs I had noticed on his desk: three smiling young men with their father's thick eyebrows. "Well," he said, with a quick intake of breath, "they are in the U.S. They came to see me here, once . . .

to eat the food. They like Chinese food. But they don't speak the language. They can't really adjust to the life out here. They are Americans now."

There are others like Chen who came home alone, leaving their children in the U.S. or Japan. Not all of them fitted in as easily as he seems to have done. After those heady times in the mid-1990s, the DPP was soon taken over by men and women who had stayed in Taiwan all along. Many had spent long spells in prison. After a period of polite respect, to give them "face," old exiles like Peng Ming-min were slowly eased off the scene. Their role as keepers of the flame abroad had been played out. Some of them found it hard to adjust to a country that had changed almost beyond recognition. I thought of the mainland Chinese exiles I knew, Wei Jingsheng, Liu Binyan, Chai Ling, Li Lu, Su Xiaokang, and the others, and wondered whether they would ever return in triumph before retiring as has-beens, no longer at home abroad, but estranged from the country they had grown up in.

———

The man who is now director of the Taiwan Association for Human Rights in Taipei once tried to assassinate Chiang Ching-kuo in New York. He suddenly turned up in Taiwan in 1996, after spending thirty-two years abroad, much of that time in hiding. No one quite knows how he entered Taiwan without a passport. All he will say is that he didn't arrive by spaceship. Officially, he is not even there. But since his botched attempt at assassination occurred in 1970, he can no longer be charged in Taiwan, where twenty years is the limit for criminal prosecution.

"Peter" Huang Wen-hsiung is altogether a mysterious character. But this much we know: He was born in a small town near Taipei in 1937. So he was ten at the time of the 2-28 Incident. Like Mark Chen, he recalls the festive first days of rebellion. Everyone seemed to be happy. The Taiwanese were in control of much of the island. At night you could hear gunfire. During the day things were quiet. But everything changed when KMT reinforcements arrived from China. Names of people who had been executed were posted at the railway station. Friends were taken away, their hands tied with rope. People went mad with fear. After that you had to pretend that nothing had happened.

I was having lunch with Huang in a small Japanese-style coffee shop, which served sweet soft drinks, ice cream, and lukewarm spaghetti; some plump young girls were eating all the various offerings at the same time. I wanted to know what had driven this soft-spoken, articulate, highly educated (Pittsburgh and Cornell) man to attempt such a desperate measure as shooting the future president of Taiwan. Strands of thin gray hair sprouted on the sides of an otherwise bald head, giving him a monkish look, and a pair of steel eyeglasses rested on the tip of his nose. Only the occasional baring of his teeth, rather like a wince of someone who has just been punched in the face, offered a hint of obduracy or perhaps aggression.

"I was never a so-called good boy," he said. He had what might be called "an authority problem." Trouble began early on, when he was kicked out of five different schools. In one case he had found evidence that a particularly unpleasant civics teacher had once been convicted for bribery. He posted evidence of this on the blackboard, whereupon the school authorities panicked. Huang's class was made to stand outside in the sun until the culprit confessed. After standing for hours in the exhausting heat, Huang decided to come forward. "That," he said, "is the trouble with this country. You cannot use knowledge to show disrespect to your elders."

Like so many Chinese rebels, Huang believes there is something basically wrong with his "culture." He believes that Asians are, as he puts it, "underindividuated" (Huang studied sociology). "The social roles always overwhelm the person. That is partly what I rebelled against. Since I was always marked as a maverick, I got used to it and began to enjoy it." This was the first time I saw him bare his teeth in that slightly wolfish manner.

He says he would never have gone after Chiang Ching-kuo if he had been the citizen of a Western democracy, where there are institutional ways for one leader to succeed another without bloodshed or coercion. But in Taiwan, Chiang Kai-shek had instituted the "barbarous dynastic practice" of grooming his son, Ching-kuo, to take his place. Different factions inside the KMT had been "pacified," and in 1970 the Chiang dynasty was set to rule for many years. Killing the heir apparent, therefore, made sense, for it would create divisions in the ruling party and thus, Huang hoped, offer more scope for democratic change. It had to be done by a Taiwanese and not a hired gangster, and it had to be accomplished without killing innocent bystanders, for that would have made the democracy movement "look bad." Finally, it would be best if it were done by a person who had little to lose—no children or career or anything of that sort. Huang, a bachelor, a maverick, and an active figure on the anti–Vietnam War scene, was the perfect man for the job.

So there he was, with his sister, his brother-in-law, and a semiautomatic gun, waiting outside the door of the Plaza Hotel in Manhattan, where Vice Premier Chiang Ching-kuo was speaking to a group of businessmen. The plan was to get close enough to shoot him in the stomach, for that way no one else would get hurt. It was, as it turned out, a flawed plan. Chiang emerged from the revolving door, and Huang lunged toward him with the gun, but before he was able to get sufficiently close, he was wrestled to the ground by two security guards. The gun went off, and the bullet lodged in a slab of marble above the entrance to the Plaza.

What followed was in a sense even more extraordinary than the deed itself. A collection among Taiwanese living in the U.S., mostly poor students, quickly produced the $190,000 required to get Huang out on bail, and he became a celebrated figure, lecturing on democracy at university campuses and organizing rallies for Taiwanese independence. But the idea of being jailed in America, which was bound to happen sooner or later, was "against [Huang's] principles," because the U.S. government was protecting the Chiang dynasty, so Huang used his contacts in the anti–Vietnam War movement and went into hiding.

The hardest thing about living away from one's native country for so long is that it becomes a place of memory, an abstraction more than a living society. To stay in touch, Huang would occasionally emerge to join Taiwanese tour groups, posing as a tourist. But still, when he returned in 1996, Taiwan had become a strange place. He spent months just traveling up and down the island. Once, a friend took him up in a private plane, and Huang was shocked by the changes he saw. The countryside he had known as a young man had become industrial zones, and villages had grown into cities.

Huang's brother-in-law had not been able to escape a jail sentence. After his arrest for assisting in the failed assassination, he fled to Sweden but was extradited to the United States, where he served his time in prison. Now he was back in Taiwan, too—legitimately, and running for the legislature as a DPP candidate. Huang was asked to support him. He smiled at the thought, a little wistfully, but also a little sardonically, in the manner of the young boy with an authority problem. Many people had asked him for his support, he said. "I guess, to many people I am what you might call a national hero. But I've deconstructed that. I don't think heroes are very good for democracy."

—

The 2-28 Incident could be spoken about in public only after martial law was lifted. It reached a kind of iconic status in 1989, when a Taiwanese movie entitled *City of Sadness* won the Golden Lion at the Venice Film Festival. Hou Hsiao-hsien, the director, had started making serious movies in the Taiwanese language during the early 1980s, when the cultural and political climate began to loosen up. But 2-28 was still too delicate a topic to broach in those early days. Perhaps Hou's film would not have been shown even in 1989 if it had not won a famous international prize. Banning it would have made the KMT government look worse.

Hou is too subtle an artist to divide his characters into heroes and villains. The violence of 2-28 and the "white terror" that followed, are observed through long lenses: figures being killed in a green, mountainous landscape. Shots are heard in the background, rattling in the night. Some Taiwanese, more ideologically driven than Hou, mistook subtlety for softness; they wanted anti-KMT propaganda. Hou's film is much better than that. Shot in dark, muted colors, it reveals how a small-town Taiwanese family is torn apart by history—first by the war and then by its aftermath, including 2-28. The violence ebbs and flows, sometimes instigated by gangsters, sometimes by government troops; there is little difference. Two of the brothers have died by violence, one as a Japanese soldier during the war, another killed by mainland mobsters. A third brother goes mad after being tortured by the KMT as an alleged Japanese collaborator. The only survivor is a kindly deaf-mute, who runs a photographic studio. His best friend, Hinoe, takes to the hills as a revolutionary but is caught. The mute marries Hinoe's sister, Hinomi—a Japanese name, like her brother's. It is no coincidence, of course, that the main surviving witness of the calamities should be mute. Then, he too is taken away by the police.

City of Sadness was shot on location in Rui-fang, a small town on the east coast of Taiwan. After the success of the movie, Rui-fang became a popular destination for Taiwanese tourists, eager to soak up something of the almost vanished atmosphere of an older Taiwan, before the mainlanders came and before industrial transformations of the 1980s obliterated most historical traces on the island. I had seen the film and I had seen images in tourist folders of Rui-fang, with its old houses and narrow streets, descending like stone ladders toward the sea. Finally, in the spring of 1998, I saw the real thing.

I was actually on my way to a city named I-lan, where I wanted to visit a museum of the Taiwanese democracy movement. The fact that political events of the late 1970s and 1980s were already featured exhibits in a museum in 1998 showed how quickly things had changed. I was taken by two friends, a chatty Romanian stockbroker named Norman and his Taiwanese wife, Fu-mei, who worked as an editor for a soft-porn publication. Both in their twenties, they played loud CDs in their car as we wound our way through a landscape of dark-green pine trees, lush gorges, and mountain peaks knifing into the misty air.

As I had half expected, Rui-fang was a kind of open-air museum of the pre-KMT past, full of quaint tea shops, stores filled with overpriced, mediocre antiques, and dainty restaurants, all dolled up to look traditional. We pressed on to I-lan.

Inland from the coastal road, the country becomes glassy and flat: watery rice paddies with new, two-story farmhouses in their midst, like islands. There is something bleak and isolated about I-lan, hidden between mountains and sea; it was the kind of place, I was told, where people keep to themselves. Fu-mei told me that I-lan people are known for their independence. Even the Japanese had found it hard to control them.

The museum, which was in fact more like an archive, was in the center of town, on a dusty street, with some uninviting shops and the odd noodle restaurant. There were few people about. The museum looked barely finished. Inside was a strong smell of paint. We were greeted by a man in a red baseball cap, his face creased in a toothy grin. White tufts of hair protruded, like whiskers, from his nostrils. Could he have my visiting card? Since I assumed he was part of the museum staff, I shook his hand and handed him one.

Tapes of old political songs were playing in the basement, where a permanent exhibition of dissident journals and documents was stored. The songs sounded to me remarkably like the marching music favored by wartime Japanese and Communists on the Chinese mainland. We walked past the displays of photographs and papers, and I suddenly realized that when I had first visited Taiwan in the 1980s, most of the people in these pictures had still been in exile or jail. And many of the magazines and pamphlets, now neatly exhibited in glass cases, had still been forbidden materials, including a full set of issues of *Formosa* magazine, around which the opposition was formed in the late 1970s.

There was also a famous cartoon, drawn in 1968 by Bo Yang, of Popeye and his baby son trapped together on an island. Popeye says: "So you are the prince?" Baby son cries: "I want to be president!" To which Popeye replies: "You talk very big for such a small child." For this innocuous little satire on the Generalissimo and his son, Bo was jailed for nine years. It could have been worse. His offense of "slandering the head of state" still carried the death penalty then.

As we were about to leave the premises, we were stopped by two women, who introduced themselves as members of the museum staff. They looked worried. Did we know the man in the red baseball cap? Was he a friend of ours? I said I thought he worked for the museum. Now they looked distinctly queasy. I should never have given him my card, they said. He might have been a government agent. This was two years after the first presidential elections in Chinese history. Taiwan was free. The dissidents in the photographs displayed in the museum were now running cities, and soon would perhaps run the country. But traces of the old paranoia remained.

On the way back to Taipei, Fu-mei played some more of her Taiwanese rock CDs. Taiwanese identity, she told me, 2-28, and all that bored young people now. "Identity" belonged to the 1980s. Today's kids cared about more universal things: love, sex, et cetera. And yet . . . Fu-mei played me one CD by a local singer, wearing moody black clothes and dark glasses. It was an agonizing song about belonging to "the yellow race." "My home is in Beijing," he sang, sounding like a man in despair, "my home is in Hong Kong, my home is in Taipei, my home is in Lhasa. . . ." Another singer lamented "ancient China" and the sadness of "people who cannot go home."

I felt there was a confusion here, which Fu-mei, dressed in black, like the rock singer, did little to clarify. She was a native Taiwanese, born in Taipei. The rock singer was a "mainlander," also born in Taipei. I asked Fu-mei whether she ever listened to mainland Chinese rock music. "Never," she said, with a hint of indignation. "Their culture is totally different. We have nothing in common with them." Surely, I said, trying to press her on this matter, mainland Chinese culture was still closer to Taiwanese sensibilities than British or American culture. "No!" she said, very firmly. "It has nothing to do with us."

Perhaps she was right. For in Taiwan, the narcissism of minor differences counts. Anglo-American pop culture is exciting, apparently universal, and unthreatening to the Taiwanese sense of themselves. Mainland China is a threat, because it is too close, too big, and too powerful. To maintain a sense of their uniqueness, Taiwanese have to reject the Chinese colossus, whereas mainland Chinese can enjoy and mimic Taiwanese or Hong Kong culture with no trouble at all. To them it is all part of the same cultural empire; and they are its center.

What goes for rock music and fashion goes for politics, too. Mainland Chinese dissidents speak enviously of the "Taiwanese model" of democracy and would like to adopt it themselves. But when the students defied their government in Tiananmen Square, few Taiwanese students came out to voice their support. Let the mainlanders take care of their own affairs, they seemed to say. For Taiwan could only be free in isolation—not from America or Japan, but from China. I thought of Kathy's friend, who had said: "We can't change them. So just don't let them change us."

There is nothing like the shared sense of victimhood to draw people together. And that is why, despite what my friends in the car had said, 2-28 will not go away, even now. I sometimes grew bored with the air of self-pity. It is, of course, easy for an outsider to be impatient when others wallow in collective misery. It is also easy for an outsider to grow tired of

Taiwan's willful provinciality, of the insistence of the Taiwanese that theirs is a small island, separate from the cultural motherland. In fact, you don't have to be a foreigner to feel weary. Many children of mainlanders have left Taiwan for the United States—not just because they felt like strangers in a Taiwanese society, but because Taiwan felt like a backwater.

And yet I think the rejection of mainland China has been a vital element in Taiwan's liberation. By looking away from China and the weight of its "ancient history," Taiwanese are freed from the awful burden of having to carry its destiny. They don't have to "save" China. Their indifference to "Chineseness," even their active hostility to it, is parochial, but it also provides room for maneuver. Having chosen to remain firmly in the periphery, they don't need to hold the center. And being excluded from government for so long, even as advisers, Taiwanese intellectuals were never tempted to become official scribes upholding an orthodoxy that was never theirs. No matter how much the KMT dogma, based on recovering the Chinese motherland, was drummed into them by political cadres, at schools, universities, or in the army, few of them would have felt "unpatriotic" by rejecting it.

Taiwanese nationalism, with all its resentments, had another important political effect. It forced the KMT, a Leninist party, much like the Chinese Communist Party, to make concessions. The mainlanders never made up more than 15 percent of a population of more than 20 million. To remain in power, the majority had to be appeased, first economically and later politically. Taiwanese farmers benefited from land reforms in the 1950s, but Taiwanese landowners were richly rewarded as well. And as a kind of compensation for accepting mainlander rule, Taiwanese businessmen were allowed to thrive and, indeed, dominate the economy. So while mainlanders for many years held power in the civil service, the legislature, and the armed forces, the Taiwanese had most of the wealth. But in the long run, acquiescence was not enough. More and more Taiwanese were brought into the KMT. Taiwanese candidates outside the KMT, known as the "outside party," were allowed to run for office in cities and counties and, from the 1960s, to a very limited degree, in the central government as well.

The president responsible for lifting martial law, one year before his death, and finally allowing opposition parties to compete in elections, was Chiang Ching-kuo, the man who had narrowly escaped assassination. He was not a natural democrat. A remote and unprepossessing figure, with a notorious record as the former security chief, Chiang Ching-kuo nevertheless understood that Taiwan could be governed in the long run only with the consent of the Taiwanese. He also knew that recovery of the Chinese mainland was but a dream. It took a bit more than benevolence at the top, however, to test that consent in a truly open and democratic system.

———

The transition from dictatorship to democracy in Taiwan was captured most succinctly in an extraordinary black-and-white photograph. It was taken not at the time of the first free elections, which came sixteen years later. But it is an image of supreme defiance, and it showed everyone who saw it that the old regime was on the defensive. And almost everyone in Taiwan did see it. In a moment of censorial absentmindedness, the government allowed it to be published in all the newspapers. The picture is of the trial, in 1980, of the "Kaohsiung Eight," the organizers of the rally for free speech and democracy in Kaohsiung on December 10, 1979.

The composition of the photograph is awkward, even naïve, as though the photographer were not aware of the message it conveyed. Behind four of the eight defendants are four police officers—three men in white helmets and one young woman; their youth (as well as the period) is accentuated by the policewoman's uniform, a miniskirt and black leather boots. Three of the defendants, casually dressed in jeans and open-necked shirts, look a bit apprehensive. But one, standing slightly behind the others, with his hands in his pockets, looks up with a broad smile on his handsome, mustachioed nightclub singer's face. Since he, like the others, was being tried for a capital offense (sedition), the smile might strike one as a trifle unhinged. In fact, it is not. Neither is it exactly a smile of mockery, although it has a certain schoolboyish quality. It is rather the expression of a man who refuses to be intimidated, the kind of smile that enrages authorities, since it robs them of their most trusted tool, fear. And this was a man who had already spent fifteen years in prison. He knew what the authorities could do to him.

The smiler was Shih Ming-teh, the main organizer of the Kaohsiung Incident. The photograph still hangs in his office in Taipei, nicely framed, above a signed baseball, next to a plaque of the Rotary Club. Shih escaped the death penalty but was sentenced to life. Some of the time, he was in a tiny solitary cell; at other times, as a kind of cruel jest, he was locked up with a dangerous mental patient. Three times he went on hunger strike. And twice he refused to be pardoned, because that would have been an admission of guilt. In 1990, he was finally freed, by which time he weighed less than a hundred pounds.

When I first met him in 1998, Shih was a DPP senator. He rather enjoyed being called Taiwan's Nelson Mandela. Indeed, he brought it up himself, with a roguish smile that was meant to convey a degree of charming self-mockery, which was not entirely convincing. Shih had the look of a nightclub entertainer: perfectly coiffed hair, expensive Italian ankle boots, a collarless white shirt, and a blue silk suit. His teeth looked unnaturally white, but then I remembered what had happened to his real teeth: smashed by the boot of an interrogator. Shih may be vain, but he is also brave. Altogether he had spent twenty-five years, almost half his life, in jail.

I asked him about the picture. Shih laughed, caressed the sharp crease in his trouser leg, and began to speak softly in heavily accented Mandarin Chinese. The photo was taken during the first day of the trial, he said. He was aware that everyone in Taiwan would be watching it on the television news. He also expected he might die. So he decided to put on a show of dignity. Dictators, he said, "don't want to create martyrs, so you must show your will. If you weaken, they will kill you."

The photograph and the television images of Shih smiling in defiance had such a powerful effect in Taiwan, and created so much sympathy for the defendants, that broadcasts of the trial were immediately stopped. But Shih thinks the watershed for Taiwanese democracy had already been reached a month earlier, in Kaohsiung, where all the opposition leaders, "outside-party" moderates as well as more radical activists, had come together to demonstrate for political rights. Their arrests, and the trial of the Kaohsiung Eight, galvanized Taiwanese organizations abroad and stirred up public opinion at home. Before the trial, many people might still have believed the propaganda that opponents of the KMT were all "communist rebels." But after they had heard the defendants talking reasonably in court about the need for free speech and general elections, few people believed the propaganda any longer. "After Kaohsiung," said Shih, "people lost their fear. And the trial gave them a valuable lesson. It made them aware of their rights."

It is easy to be charmed by "Taiwan's Nelson Mandela." Even his love of showmanship is endearing, if perhaps lacking in the gravitas many people expect from a professional politician. But then Shih, though a senator, is not really a professional politician. He is a romantic rebel whose heroics are no longer required in a democracy. When I talked to him, he seemed a bit bored by his present job. He said he was not really interested in campaigning. It was too tiring. He had resigned his position as chairman of the DPP two years before. Mere ambition, after all, is not fit for heroes.

Shih was born in Kaohsiung in 1941. Close friends and relatives still use his Japanese nickname, Nori. He says he can remember the city being hit by American bombers at the end of the war. But his first vivid memory of violence was an execution he witnessed during the white terror, following 2-28. A man was made to kneel in the street near Shih's house, opposite the main railway station, and executed by a shot in the neck. One eyeball lodged, like a shiny marble, on the branch of a tree close to where Shih was standing.

It was at this time that Shih's father, a Roman Catholic and a practitioner of traditional Chinese medicine, was arrested. After two months of interrogation, he came home a broken man. He said the Taiwanese would never be free to control their own destiny. Shih read books about great military heroes—Napoleon, Hannibal, and Alexander the Great—and dreamed of dying for his country.

It was unusual for a native Taiwanese, and a rather bookish one at that, to choose a career in the army, though Shih's worship of military heroes may have had something to do with it. After graduating from the military academy, he was sent to serve on a small island near the Chinese mainland. Life on such island bases was tedious and the soldiers spent much of their time raising pigs. It was there, in 1962, that Shih's troubles began, when he was arrested and accused of plotting sedition. The interrogators cited conversations going back to his high school days. Every indiscreet re-mark had been reported; every bit of youthful bravado was on record. He was told to confess to being a member of a revolutionary group called the Taiwan Independence League. Shih admitted he had had conversations with friends about independence, among other things, but denied ever having been engaged in a plot to overthrow the KMT government.

The most notorious place of detention for political prisoners was the Garrison Command Security Center in Taipei, where such well-known techniques as the "toothbrush torture" and the "airplane torture" were employed to extract confessions. The first involved scraping female geni-tals with a hard brush. In the airplane treatment, a prisoner was hog-tied and suspended in mid-air from a pole. Shih was beaten so badly that his spine was damaged and he lost all his teeth. He received a life sentence, his first.

But the lowest point of his incarceration between 1962 and 1977 came after a failed escape attempt by several prisoners. Shih took no part in what he regarded as a hopeless venture, but he knew who the organizers were. He refused to give up their names, however, even when he was forced to live in a solitary cell that was too small for him to stand up or lie down in at full length. Shih's mother died while he was inside, and his wife left him for another man.

When Shih received amnesty in 1977, under pressure from President Carter's human-rights policies, Taiwan was a different place from the country it had been at the time of his arrest. It was much richer, of course, but the political climate had begun to change as well. Local elections for city and county magistrates had been held since the 1950s. And there had also been elections for the provincial government of Taiwan and a few outlying islands. The national government, however, whose legislature was still filled with old men who had received their mandates in China be-fore 1949, was the exclusive domain of the KMT. But in 1969, the first "outside-party" member, Huang Hsin-chieh, was voted into the national legislature. He was joined in 1973 by another outside-party legislator, Kang Ning-hsiang. And in 1977 the outside-party candidates in local and provincial elections won 38 percent of the votes.

It looked as though Taiwan might be evolving slowly into a democracy, even though political parties, apart from the KMT, were still banned, martial law was still enforced and political gatherings were forbidden. But as memories of 2-28 lost their fearful edge, Taiwanese intellectuals were becoming more politically active. Opposition journals began to appear. The number of seats up for election in the national government was limited. Opposition publications were usually swiftly banned. And it was almost impossible for outside-party politicians to beat KMT candidates who had the money, the connections, and the party machine to back them. But it was a beginning.

Things began to look even better when President Chiang Ching-kuo allowed supplementary elections in 1978 for the national legislature—again, after pressure from the Carter administration. Opposition leaders used informal occasions—weddings, funerals, graduation ceremonies—to meet and organize across the nation. A non-KMT Kaohsiung County magistrate, Yu Teng-fa, the man who later died under peculiar circumstances in his bathroom, put up money for a group to help opposition candidates. Yu was the chief of a political clan that had provided local bosses since the Japanese days, and perhaps even before. Such chiefs acted rather like old-fashioned mafia dons; regardless of who happened to be in power, they cut the deals and took care of their people. Yu was very much in that mold, a square-faced gambling man who wore loud suits and refused to take orders from anyone.

And then things suddenly came to a halt. Without a warning to the Republic of China on Taiwan, U.S. relations with Beijing were normalized in 1979 and official relations with the ROC were terminated. Days before polling day, the KMT government decided to abort the national elections. Yu Teng-fa announced that he would attend a rally in Kaohsiung to protest this decision. This led to the old man's arrest. Dissidents from all over Taiwan, including some elected officials, gathered for a public demonstration. More arrests were made. The scene was set for a serious confrontation.

The rallying point for all dissidents on Taiwan was the journal *Formosa*, founded in August 1979. By December it had reached a circulation of more than 100,000. The general manager was Shih Ming-teh. Every major city in Taiwan had a *Formosa* office. Known as "service stations," they were actually offices of a nameless, unofficial political party. Demonstrations became more frequent, often accompanied by violence—provoked, perhaps, by turned ex-Communists, who were used by the government as goons. Shih Ming-teh decided that December 10, universal Human Rights Day, would be a good occasion for a large rally in Kaohsiung.

Exactly what happened that night is still a matter of debate. No one disputes that two men, connected to *Formosa*, were arrested on December 9 as they drove a sound truck through Kaohsiung to announce the time and place of the rally. They were picked up at the police station the following day, and rushed to the hospital. Torture, said the *Formosa* people; resisting arrest, said the police. Shih had ordered the purchase of 130 wooden stakes—for "self-defense," he said. The government spoke of an armed rebellion. Permission for a rally was first denied and then granted, but not at the place where the organizers had planned it. So the crowd built up in front of the *Formosa* office and in a nearby park. The police got jumpy. Torches lit up the evening sky. The crowd sang Taiwanese songs and "We Shall Overcome." The police tried to block the people in the park from joining the others. Scuffles broke out, and policemen were attacked—by agents provocateurs, said the organizers; by rebels, said the police.

Stirring words came through the megaphones that had not been heard in public before: "Oppose one-party dictatorship! Long live the people of Taiwan! Long live democracy!" For twenty minutes, a well-known feminist, "Annette" Lu Hsiu-lien, made an emotional speech: "My dear fellow Taiwanese," she cried. "If you are Taiwanese and you are not with us here today, you will not have a clear conscience later. . . . Have we ever had a time when we ourselves were masters in our own house? Isn't it true that we have always been slaves, subject to the whims of others? We have never overcome." Annette Lu was one of the Kaohsiung Eight and received a twelve-year jail sentence.

During her speech, riot squads began to menace the crowd. Shih Ming-teh desperately tried to keep things under control and begged the police to back off: "This office of *Formosa* magazine," he cried, his voice breaking, "is the sacred ground of the Taiwanese people. Please stop here. Taiwanese soldiers, lay down your arms! You Taiwanese soldiers are all our brothers and sisters."

Similar words were spoken at Tiananmen ten years later, when students and citizens of Beijing appealed to the patriotism of the People's Liberation Army soldiers. But the police in Kaohsiung moved in with tear gas and batons, not tanks. The crowd fought back with fists and sticks. How many policemen got hurt—many, said the police; not so many, said the organizers—and how many demonstrators—none, said the police; many, said the organizers—is still unclear.

All the main organizers, *Formosa* editors, and other dissidents were immediately arrested. Shih Ming-teh did the traditional Taiwanese thing and sought refuge in a Presbyterian church, where he was hidden by a minister. A dental surgeon and *Formosa* colleague tried to disguise his features by performing crude plastic surgery on his jaw. It was not a success. Shih was soon betrayed to the police by two men who had been in prison with him. They disappeared and were never heard from again. The amateur surgeon later became the mayor of Taichung, the third largest city in Taiwan.

—

The arguments about what precisely happened on December 10, 1979, are entangled with a debate about the effect of the events. Shih and other witnesses were caught up in the same embittered arguments I had heard about Tiananmen: journalist Dai Qing's criticism of the "radicals" who had recklessly provoked the Communist autocrats, and student leader Li Lu's defense that the Chinese people after Tiananmen were no longer slaves. Dai Qing is still convinced that Tiananmen set back the cause of "liberalism." Li Lu thinks it exposed the government's moral and political bankruptcy. "Reformist" intellectuals say direct confrontation was naïve, and irresponsible. Chai Ling, Li Lu, Wu'er Kaixi, Wang Dan, and other former student leaders say they may have been young and naïve, but they wonder where their elders were when it was time to stand up and be counted.

Kaohsiung was of course not Tiananmen, and the KMT in 1979 was not like the Chinese Communist Party in 1989. But the arguments are strikingly similar. Shih says: "Sure, we lacked experience, but who dares to say they had more? And where were those who thought they had more experience anyway? Of course we could have done better. But why did those who think they could have done better not join us and lead us?" The "reformists," on the other hand, think Kaohsiung was a serious setback. After all, they say, Taiwan had been slowly evolving toward a democratic system. The editor of *Formosa*, Chang Chun-hung, said: "I never wanted to go to prison. It was Shih Ming-teh who got me into trouble."

Annette Lu was going to run for the legislature, and she likes to say that she would have won if only she hadn't been arrested. But she can hardly blame Shih for her disappointment, for the elections were suspended months before the rally in Kaohsiung even took place.

I had heard a great deal about Annette Lu while traveling in Taiwan. I had heard how she had started a feminist movement in the 1970s. And people spoke in awe of her Harvard law degree. In 1992 she was at last elected to the legislature. When I visited Taiwan six years later, she was mayor of Taoyuan County. I made an appointment to see her at her county seat, about a hour's drive from Taipei. I wanted to ask her what had happened all those years ago in Kaohsiung and what she thought about it now.

Taoyuan has a reputation for racketeering and violent crime. A crime syndicate, protected by local KMT bosses, monopolized garbage collection and transportation, and when there were challengers to this arrangement, the mob made sure that garbage piled up for two months. Annette Lu was elected as county chief after her predecessor was murdered, along with seven other people. The case was never solved.

Taoyuan, like so many Taiwanese towns, is a jumbled place, with messy streets and market stalls selling phony French handbags, betel nuts, electronics, and sexy lingerie. Narrow lanes are lined with massage parlors, with blinking fairy-lights and barbershops and karaoke bars, thrown together in cheap materials of pink and baby blue. Girls totter about in high-heeled shoes, and young men in white suits chatter on their cell phones.

The cleanest, most impressive—indeed, monumental—building is the new county hall. I had noticed this elsewhere in Taiwan. The new democracy—or perhaps it was just a sign of new Taiwanese wealth—was heralded by gigantic government buildings, many of them done up in a neoclassical, quasi-Mussolinian style: too many Greek columns, great domes, and vast roofs.

Annette Lu's office was of gigantic proportions, with an enormous desk at one end. On the wall, above the usual knickknacks of high office, including a large gold clock of truly extraordinary ugliness, hung a huge photograph of the beaming mayor herself, framed in elaborately worked gold. Like many middle-aged ladies in Taiwan, she wore a great deal of makeup and jewelry. I hoped to break the ice by remarking on the size of the new government buildings. This was met with a look of undisguised disapproval. She tugged, a little impatiently, at the sleeves of her cream-colored jacket and looked at me severely through a pair of gold-rimmed glasses, waiting for me to begin.

I asked about her childhood. She was born in Taoyuan, the daughter of a self-educated businessman, and she grew up idolizing both her father and her elder brother. Her father made it clear he wished she were a boy, and she tried her best to be like her brother. They encouraged her to read the newspapers and practice her skills as a speaker. She was told stories about great historical figures, all men. Whatever her brother did, she would do as well, indeed better. So when he studied law, she did the same, and graduated at the top of her class. In the early 1970s, she went to the United States for further studies and became a feminist. The problem with Taiwan, she concluded, was the patriarchal Chinese society. She returned to Taiwan in 1978 to join the opposition.

She had told the same story often. I had read it before in newspaper clippings, a standard tale of political awakening. There was no tentativeness in her manner of speaking, no moment of doubt or reflection; there was not enough time for that. She seemed irritated when I asked her about Kaohsiung. "I delivered the most important speech that night," she said, and reached for a book on the shelf behind her desk. It was her biography. "You can read it all in here."

I asked her whether the demonstration had promoted or retarded democracy. She said she "would have been able to do more for Taiwan" if she had not been involved in the Kaohsiung Incident. She said that if "people like Shih Ming-teh" had not been in charge, "things would have been different. He had no idea what he was getting into. It was a trap set up by the KMT to crack down on the opposition. Unfortunately, he had not been aware of that."

Then, suddenly she drew herself up and said: "Look, I'm a very busy woman, and I have no time for trivia. What is it you want to know?"

My mouth went dry. I realized I had badly misjudged the occasion. The interview had turned into an embarrassment. I had no idea what else to ask her. She was a professional dealing with the complicated daily affairs of a difficult region. Kaohsiung was history. A romantic, like Shih Ming-teh, might bask in past heroism and reflect on its meanings, but Annette Lu had no time for such things. After one or two more perfunctory questions, I decided I had better leave, whereupon her face lit up in the radiant smile of her official portrait. She asked me to repeat my name, took up a gold pen, and signed her book for me.

On my way back to Taipei, I thought about the difference between Shih and Lu—the romantic rebel hero and the ambitious politician; the "radical" who dreams of dying for his people and the feminist who wants to succeed in a world dominated by men. It is in the nature of any dictatorship to want to divide its opponents. And the natural gulf between reformists, who try to work inside the system, and the rebels, who feel more at home in the streets, is the easiest thing to exploit. It was easier to like Shih Ming-teh than Annette Lu. Rebels usually have more charm. But the importance of Kaohsiung was that for a moment these divisions were forgotten: radicals, reformists, sympathizers, fellow travelers, inside and outside the system, all came together in a gesture of defiance. This, as much as slow negotiation, is a necessary condition for change. Without it, a dictatorship, or a one-party state, will try to drag its feet forever while the reformists blame the radicals for their frustrations.

And in fact change did come to Taiwan. The elections for seats in the national government took place in 1980. The Kaohsiung Eight could not run for office, but their wives and lawyers did. One of these lawyers, Frank Hsie, eventually became the DPP mayor of Kaohsiung in 1999. Another, Chen Shui-bian, later became mayor of Taipei, and later still, in 2000, the first president of Taiwan. His vice president was Annette Lu.

———

There was something reassuring about the sheer wackiness of the election campaigns in 1999. The euphoria of 1996 had faded. The mayoral contests for Kaohsiung, Taipei, and the legislative elections throughout Taiwan were almost politics as usual—that is to say, marked by the nonsense, calumnies, and froth that go with campaigns in most democracies. In front of the same DPP headquarters in Kaohsiung where three years ago I had heard harsh stories of punishment and sacrifice, I stood in the afternoon sun looking at a bizarre float called the "King-tanic." It was a contraption on wheels made up to resemble a cruise ship. (The movie *Titanic* had been a big hit in Taiwan as well as in mainland China.) On board the "King-tanic" stood various candidates in fancy dress, some of them well-known ex-dissidents, who had spent many years abroad or in prison. There was Hsu Hsin-liang, a veteran activist, dressed in a white admiral's costume and mugging like a nightclub entertainer. Another DPP candidate, made up to look like Popeye, was sucking on his pipe, flexing his arm, and rolling his eyes. And while the candidates made faces at the cameras, a group of male dancers in sailor suits and dyed-blond hair gyrated to a song by Madonna. Taiwan, I thought, has finally joined the free world.

Contentious political issues, such as Taiwanese independence, were buried during the campaigns under a highly personalized politics. The people around Frank Hsie, the DPP candidate for mayor of Kaohsiung, had released tape recordings of his opponent, a married man, having an intimate telephone conversation with his mistress. His phrase "I love you" was much quoted, as if this were the height of caddishness—in a country where most men with means keep at least one mistress. Frank Hsie, in his turn, was accused of defending a kidnapper who had killed the daughter of a well-known show-business figure. The tearful parent, who happened to be close to the KMT, declared in a widely distributed videotape that a man who would defend such a vicious killer must be a very bad man himself. Rumors also abounded of Frank Hsie's curious religious predilections. He was said to worship an impostor who had sent out photographs of himself with a faked halo.

There was a peculiarly lachrymose quality to the campaigning, especially of the DPP. I followed one candidate in Kaohsiung, whose sound truck blared out an endless tape of a woman crying and wailing. It was the candidate's wife, I was told, begging the voters to elect her husband, because he lost the last time and to lose again would break his heart.

But I had come to Kaohsiung to see the grandson of Yu Teng-fa, the old local patriarch who had died so messily in his bath. The Yu family was still the boss clan of Kaohsiung County. The old man had been succeeded as county chief by his daughter-in-law, Yu Chen Yueh-ying. After she retired, her son took over. Her other son, the one I wanted to see, was running for the legislature, and so was his sister. The mother supported her daughter. I had met Yu Chen Yueh-ying a year before at her headquarters way out in the countryside. She was still a formidable figure, running affairs as though she were still in office. I spoke to her in Japanese as she pressed her crimson seal to a huge pile of documents lying on her desk. The phone rang continuously. Men scurried in and out of her office in peculiar cringing postures, as though they were permanently bowing. Outside was a line of supplicants, dark-skinned men and women in badly fitting clothes, clutching petitions.

A plump woman in a colorful silk dress and glasses encrusted with what looked like tiny gems, Mrs. Yu proudly announced that she had been called Taiwan's Mrs. Thatcher. I knew she also had another name: Ma Zu, after the mother goddess worshipped by Fujian fishermen and in shrines all over Taiwan. (Her daughter was running her campaign for the legislature as "the daughter of Ma Zu.") She explained that a political career had never been her choice. It was the old man who had made her run for office. She had just been a "bourgeois girl" who played the piano. Still, it was her duty, as a member of the Yu clan, to take care of the people of Kaohsiung County. Just before it was time for me to leave, she barked an order at one of the cringing figures in her office. He disappeared for a few minutes and came back with a neat little box marked PIERRE CARDIN. It was for me. Mrs. Yu took both my hands and said: "We must work for international friendship." I opened the box later. And there was the gaudiest tie I had ever seen, a kind of overripe fruit salad printed on a shiny, synthetic material. Pierre Cardin had nothing to do with it.

I had been driven to Mrs. Yu's office by Kathy Wei. The nervous tension she had shown three years ago was gone. These were more placid times. We spoke in the car about her father, and Kathy asked me why I was so interested in dissidents. I had often wondered the same thing. I mumbled some platitudes about the importance of freedom. Yes, she said, politely.

Sure, of course. But I felt I owed her a better answer. And I said it was partly because I was fascinated by people who were prepared to sacrifice everything for their freedom. I could not imagine being that brave myself. I wanted to describe people who had the courage to choose prison or torture rather than submit to the servility, the double-talk, the evasions and dishonesties of life in a dictatorship. I knew that many of these people were flawed, wrongheaded, and perhaps intolerant in their own ways, but I admired their sheer cussedness. I was haunted by the idea of tyranny, just as it has haunted many people of my age who were born in Europe not long after the war and the end of Nazi occupation. We were never put to the test.

Kathy and I had dinner with Yu Jeng-dao, Mrs. Yu's son, in a Sichuan restaurant in Kaohsiung. Even his name, Jeng-dao, meaning Way of Politics, showed the traditional occupation of the Yu family. He was a baby-faced man in his thirties, with thick, soft hands and excellent American English. Yu had gotten a master's degree in public administration at the University of Southern California and was clearly of a different generation from Mark Chen or Shih Ming-teh. He had no Japanese nickname or memories of 2-28. He had gone abroad not to escape prison but to get a better education. "My generation," he said, "is able to think freely."

But he did remember his grandfather, the patriarch who had brooked no contradiction—not from KMT officials, and certainly not from his own family. Even his daughter-in-law, the formidable Mrs. Yu, had obeyed the old man's orders. "My grandfather," said Yu, "represented authority. When he made up his mind, we were not expected to oppose him. You see, he liked the way the Japanese governed Taiwan. They were just and well organized." I recalled something Shih Ming-teh had told me. He said he still worried about the "political culture" in China and Taiwan. It was vital to build the right system, he said, for otherwise the DPP might become as dictatorial as the KMT had been.

In 1998, Yu Jeng-dao had shaved off all his hair, which flattened his features, giving him a pink, egglike appearance. As we made our way in a green-and-white sound truck through the dusty flatlands of Kaohsiung County, with its banana groves, tobacco plantations, rice paddies, and small, industrial plants, Yu told me something about his politics. It was his aim as congressman, he said, to protect the local farmers from American pressure to open the Taiwanese market. Even though Taiwan was a small country, the U.S. had no right to push it around. This was not the kind of thing you would have heard from older dissidents, who tended to look on the U.S. as a political savior. It was more what a young student at USC would have picked up.

Yu also told me a great deal about KMT corruption, how votes were bought for about NT$500 (roughly U.S. $15) per person. And he spoke about the politics at Taiwanese universities, where students of his generation had tried to get rid of political cadres from the KMT, mostly retired army people, who had to make sure the students had the correct line on things. After an hour or two of driving around in the sound truck and stopping at various points to shake hands with voters and hand out leaflets, I was bored and decided to leave for my hotel. Yu told me to come back in the evening. There would be a rally in the courtyard of a Buddhist temple outside Kaohsiung.

It was dark by the time I got there. Taiwanese pop music was wailing from CD players in the market stalls outside the temple. Inside the courtyard, there was an overpowering smell of sweet incense billowing from a large bronze burner, and of barbecued squid skewed on bamboo sticks. The temple, with its southern-style curved roof, like a dragon's back or a lobster claw, had thick vermilion pillars in front and thousands of gold lacquered Buddhas inside, gleaming in the spotlights. Every time a new speaker was announced, there was an explosion of firecrackers and the sound of marching-band music coming from the speaker's platform.

The scene was a bit like a medieval pageant. Candidates would enter the temple compound, followed by a retinue of men carrying tall banners announcing the candidate's name. One trick to attract attention was to parade in front of the platform and shake the banners whenever a rival speaker was about to hold forth. The only language spoken was Taiwanese. None of the candidates, even those from the KMT, bothered to use standard Mandarin in Kaohsiung. Yu's sister, the "daughter of Ma Zu," who had the misfortune to arrive without her retinue of banner-men, shouted that "the KMT is a party of foreigners. The DPP belongs to us." Yu himself had a surprisingly strident manner of speaking for such a mild-mannered person; he hollered and shrieked, repeating the same slogans over and over, mostly about KMT vote-buying.

I left for the market street outside the temple compound, to get a snack. For about half a mile the street was lined with food stalls, their wares set out on tables lit by naked bulbs: piles of squid, octopus tentacles, endless varieties of shellfish, buckets full of pigs' innards, intestines, raglike stomach linings, fatty livers and succulent hearts. I settled for a bowl of fried noodles and squid. When I was halfway through my meal, I noticed the familiar sight of green banners coming my way. Yu and his banner-men were moving from stall to stall. At each one he shook hands with the owner and the customers. When he spotted me, he had a quick word with the owner, told him he would pay for my noodles, and slipped him a handsome tip that amounted to quite a bit more than the price of the meal. Things had changed a great deal in Taiwan, but I was happy to note that some traditions still remained the same.

———

I left Taiwan feeling elated—not so much because of the election results, which were mixed. Chen Shui-bian lost in Taipei; Frank Hsie won in Kaohsiung. Yu Jeng-dao won a seat in the legislature; his sister lost. It would be a bit more than a year later that Taiwan passed the real test of democracy: a peaceful transition from one party to another. In March 2000, Chen Shui-bian was elected as the first DPP president of Taiwan, breaking the KMT monopoly on power.

But in many ways the test had already been passed. The Taiwanese had shown that Chinese people could establish a democratic system and sustain it. They also made nonsense of theories one still heard in other parts of the Chinese-speaking world, which, more annoyingly, were often repeated as superior wisdom in the West: that "the Chinese" didn't care about politics, that political freedom would only lead to social chaos, that firm, authoritarian leadership was more suitable to the "Chinese mind," and that any suggestion otherwise was a form of neocolonial arrogance. Democracy in Taiwan was not a Western imposition, even though it had been encouraged, rather belatedly, in Washington; it had been created by the Taiwanese themselves—and not only by the "native Taiwanese" but by enlightened members of the KMT as well, starting with the late President Chiang Ching-kuo and continued by his successor, Lee Teng-hui.

The history of modern Taiwan showed something else as well. Until the 1980s, Taiwanese dissidents abroad were as impotent and as easily dismissed as irrelevant and quixotic as the mainland dissidents are today. But when Taiwan politics began to turn after the Kaohsiung Incident in 1979, the overseas activists had the international contacts, the expertise, and the financial resources to play a vital role. They knew how Washington worked. Above all, despite their feuding and their occasionally wild and desperate actions, they had kept the flame alive during the dark years, rather like governments in exile, offering hope that one day change would come.

And yet the case of Taiwan sits oddly within the history of China, for Taiwanese freedom was built in defiance, not only of the People's Republic of China but of the idea of One China. I was often struck by the Japanophilia among the older dissidents and their contempt for "those Chinese" on the mainland, and I assumed it was a necessary defense against the official propaganda of reuniting the motherland. As a gut feeling or prejudice, anti-mainlander feeling can be disturbing. But the belief that the ancient Chinese drive toward central power over a vast land has been inimical to political freedom is surely right. For democracy to succeed, "China" probably needs more Taiwans.

Just before leaving Taipei, on my way to Hong Kong, I went to see John Sham, an old acquaintance. Famous as a comedian in Hong Kong, John had become a ubiquitous figure during the Tiananmen demonstrations in 1989 when he helped channel money and other goods from Hong Kong to the students in Beijing. You would see him on the television news, in his T-shirt and with his wild, bushy hair, leading demonstrations in Hong Kong, cracking Cantonese jokes, and making speeches. And you would see him on the Square in Beijing, talking to Wang Dan, Wu'er Kaixi, or Chai Ling, a man who liked to be at the center of things. He once boasted to me that he was so famous that "everyone with a yellow skin knows me." After the crackdown, John had helped some student leaders escape to Hong Kong. As a Hong Kong show-business figure, he had many contacts, some of them in the shady world of criminal triads, without whom the students would never have been able to get out.

John was now living in Taipei, running a cable television company. "Quite a show, huh?" he said when I walked into his office. We could hear the noise of an election campaign going on outside his office. Yes, I said, quite a show.

I was interested to know what John made of Taiwan and its new democracy. I knew that the Hong Kong perspective was complicated. During the first presidential campaign in 1996, I had watched a rally in Taipei together with a group of Hong Kong democrats. Lawyers, legislators, and academics, articulate in English and Cantonese, smartly dressed, and mostly rich, they were amused by the rustic manners of the Taiwanese, their gaudy taste, their odd superstitions, their loudness, and their crass sense of style. But there was some discomfort, too, for when it came to politics, these same crass, vulgar, rustic people were clearly way ahead of Hong Kong.

So I asked John Sham what he made of the Taiwanese. He lit a cigarette, threw up his arms, and sighed. The Taiwanese were pretty much like the mainland Chinese, he said. All that talk about "native Taiwanese" was nonsense. Only the aboriginal tribes were native to Taiwan. Culturally, Taiwan was part of China, and culture, in terms of race, was the strongest basis for an independent state.

Was he in favor of unification, then? Yes he was, and yet, he said, he was very "westernized" himself, much more so than most Chinese dissidents. So much so, in fact, that he often found it difficult to communicate with them or with the Taiwanese. Taiwanese, mainlanders—they were part of the same culture. That is why it was difficult to relate to their idea of democracy. "What are we talking about when we say 'democracy'? Are we talking about the same thing? The Taiwanese vote in large numbers, sure, but do they really understand what democracy is about, in the way British people do? I doubt it. Look at the way they drive, without any consideration for others or any idea that one should stick to the rules. This is all very different from Hong Kong. In Taiwan and China, people behave as though individuals don't count. . . ."

I told John of my conversations with older Taiwanese, who had pointed out what a difference Japan had made to Taiwan and who maintained that the Japanese sense of law and order was what distinguished Taiwanese from the mainlanders.

John waved this away with his cigarette, trailing an arc of smoke through the room. No, no, he said. "We are different in Hong Kong. We are westernized. There is no spitting in the streets, we abide by the traffic rules. We take individualism seriously. The thing is, when we look at a problem, we try and find a legal, sensible, humane solution. To the Taiwanese, that makes us look as though we are lacking in human feelings, because we put law and reason in the first place. And why do we do that?" I raised my eyebrows in the shape of a question, even though I could easily guess the answer. "Because we Hong Kong people were ruled by the British."

Chapter 3

The Last Colony

In Hong Kong it usually rains in spring and summer, the typhoon season. It rained when the Chinese government declared martial law in Beijing, in May 1989. A real typhoon rain, loud and thick and fast, with driving winds and lightning bolts fizzing off the spiky top of the Hongkong and Shanghai Bank building. Shops and schools were closed. People were told to stay at home and bolt their windows, yet fifty thousand people forced their way through the typhoon gale to Victoria Park that night in support of the students in Beijing. They sat in the open air, buffeted by the storm, soaked through and through, singing the patriotic hit song of the day, "I Am a Chinese." Martin Lee asked people to put up their umbrellas, but nobody did, just so everyone could have a clear view of the stage: They were in this together—the very feeling many Taiwanese chose to reject. Later that night, several hundred people stood outside the office of the New China News Agency (the unofficial Chinese embassy) in an even heavier rainstorm and sang the Chinese national anthem, a patriotic gesture both ironic and deeply felt. The following day, a million people came out in the streets.

It rained again on July 1, 1997, the night of Hong Kong's "return" to China, when Prince Charles, with perfect British sangfroid, pretended not to notice the steady stream of rainwater cascading, absurdly, off the peak of his cap to the tip of his nose. It rained so hard you could barely get into town that week. Avalanches of liquid, toffee-colored mud were blocking the roads.

It rained solidly every day, from morning to night, during the legislative elections in May of the following year, the first after the handover. In some places, people had to wade through water that reached their knees to cast their votes. Old people in the villages were carried to the voting booths. And yet they came, in larger numbers than had ever turned out to vote before.

But on June 4, 1999, the tenth anniversary of the Beijing Massacre, it merely drizzled, softening the hot and humid night in Victoria Park, where some seventy thousand people had gathered to remember. It was dark when I arrived from the neon-lit malls of Causeway Bay. Everything in the park was wrapped in a steamy gauze: men, women, and children sitting in neat rows, as they always do in Hong Kong, holding candles; the spotlights picking out the Pillar of Shame, a truly hideous sculpture made by a Dane, named Jens Galshiot, to commemorate Tiananmen, something between a totem pole and a turdlike ice-cream cone, showing emaciated figures writhing in death agony; the flames leaping from a bronze torch; the replica of the Goddess of Democracy, which had been crushed by tanks in Beijing ten years before; the white column with the words "The spirit of democracy martyrs will live forever"; the huge video screen showing blurred images of students on Tiananmen Square, of young people covered in blood being rushed away on carts, and of tanks rumbling along Chang'an Avenue; and onstage, the activists, the politicians in white T-shirts, and the singers of patriotic songs. Once again the plaintive sound of "Descendants of the Dragon" filled the night, again and again. The chief executive of Hong Kong, the successor to the British colonial governors, a former shipping tycoon named Tung Chee-hwa, had warned of "chaos" and told the Hong Kong Chinese to put the "baggage" of the past behind them. He did not like these gatherings, because he didn't want to upset the new colonial power in Beijing. In fact, he had no taste for any kind of protest. If it were up to him, he would run Hong Kong along the lines of Singapore. But it was not entirely up to him. Opinion in Hong Kong was still supposed to be free.

The atmosphere in Victoria Park was actually anything but chaotic, a memorial service rather than a political rally, a tearful celebration of martyrdom more than a cry for action. Blood, real spilled blood, as well as metaphorical blood, in the sense of ethnic kinship, set the tone. A local artist, Andy Kwong, had doused the Pillar of Shame with two buckets of red paint, after mixing it with his own blood. This, he explained, symbolized the blood of the students who had died in Beijing. He was arrested but soon released on HK$1,000 bail. (Not long before that, an artist from mainland China had expressed his anti-colonial sentiments by flinging a pot of red paint at the bust of Queen Victoria located in the same park. Hong Kong people criticized this as an act of vandalism or, worse, as deeply passé: Queen Victoria was no longer a hateful symbol; British colonialism was now beside the point.)

The main speaker among the politicians and activists onstage, magnified on the video screen, was a bespectacled man in his late sixties, a rousing Cantonese orator and Democratic Party legislator, Szeto Wah. He wore a white T-shirt that displayed the words DON'T FORGET in large Chinese characters. Szeto speaks little English, unlike most of his colleagues in the democratic camp. They are mostly middle-class lawyers and other professionals; he is a former teacher and union man, a "man of the people." Szeto knows how to work a Hong Kong crowd. It was Szeto Wah who, in 1989, founded the Hong Kong Alliance in Support of the Patriotic Democratic Movement in China. Ten years later he lit the flame of remembrance, squinted at the Pillar of Shame, and said, or rather, declaimed in the manner of an official mourner: "Do you hear our cries? May your heroic souls descend here—the only piece of Chinese soil where we can gather to remember you in public."

The crowd did not shout or cheer, but was quiet, quite unlike the frenzied crowds I had seen in Taiwan. This was typical of Hong Kong, people said: Cantonese with British restraint. Perhaps that was it. But people also looked genuinely sad. Some were in tears. The candles softly swayed. This was a solemn occasion. I was reminded of another date, which marked my childhood in the Netherlands: May 4, Commemoration of the War Dead. During the day, our teachers talked about the war. At six o'clock, the entire country would come to a standstill for a minute of silence (and woe betide the hapless German tourist who kept on talking or driving). Church bells would ring all over Holland. And a procession would set off for that quiet place in the dunes, near The Hague, where members of the Resistance were taken to be shot by the Germans. Shared remembrance of suffering, of heroes and enemies, pulled the nation together in a ceremonial moment of patriotism, dignified but also sentimental. It is during such moments that tribal feelings stir.

There is something of that feeling in the yearly remembrance of Tiananmen in Hong Kong. It is when "Hong Kong people" or "Hong Kong Chinese" tell pollsters that they feel most "Chinese." Memories of that particular martyrdom forged the main emotional link between the former British colony and the Chinese mainland. The notion that Hong Kong is "the only piece of Chinese soil" where the bloodshed can be remembered in public makes for a bitter pride. It means that Hong Kong is not a mere colonial appendage, despised as a gaudy marketplace, dedicated to nothing but horse racing, nightclubs, and the pursuit of wealth. Hong Kong, the city of refugees from Chinese tyranny, is also part of China, the freest part, where people still have the dignity of free speech if not a fully democratic system.

Szeto Wah had one other thing up his sleeve, one more ceremonial link between Hong Kong and the rest of the Chinese world, a patriotic link in time instead of space. Wang Dan, the former student leader in Tiananmen Square, had been invited to speak in Hong Kong on this occasion. But the Hong Kong government decided not to grant him a visa. So he would speak via satellite from San Francisco, known to Chinese as Old Gold Mountain. As his image was projected on a video screen his mother, the historian Wang Lingyun, would speak from Beijing on a cell phone, since her own phone had been disconnected by the authorities at 5 P.M.

"The good mother and the good son," announced Szeto Wah in sonorous Mandarin. Once they had all been hooked up, the Old Gold Mountain, the former British colony, and the capital of the Chinese empire, Szeto Wah invited the good son to speak to his good mother. But

Wang Dan, a man of northern-Chinese reserve, was shy of such mawkish gestures and said he would prefer to speak to his mother in private. Instead, on this occasion, he told the Hong Kong crowd to remember that "the dead have paved the way for democracy." And his mother asked "the younger generations" to "have a sense of historical commitment and social responsibility. They should all pursue democracy, freedom, and learn well."

It was banal, perhaps, and a little gimmicky, and yet moving too. Most modern nation-states have been founded on myths of martyrdom and bloodshed for freedom. So it has been with the modern Chinese states, built on the foundations of one the oldest nations in the world. Communist China has its myths of martyrdom; so did Taiwan under the Nationalists; and so does Taiwan under the Democratic People's Party today. A democratic China recalling the myth of 1989 is yet to be born. But it is the hope of that China which moves the people who gather each year on June 4 in Hong Kong. The descendants of Chinese refugees, who are still shielded by a fortified border from the Chinese state of which they are officially a part, are the patriots of a China that as yet exists only in the mind.

The shipping tycoon who replaced the British colonial governors told these people to forget about the past. He likes to make speeches about traditional Chinese values. Like Lee Kuan Yew, a leader he much admires, Tung Chee-hwa is a believer in "Asian values." Chinese patriotic pride is often invoked to bolster his shaky credentials (he was essentially handpicked by Beijing). But remembering what happened in 1989, openly, truthfully, is the one thing that makes many people in Hong Kong feel proud to be Chinese. That is why people lay wreaths every year at the foot of the Pillar of Shame, bowing three times out of respect to the "martyrs," while he, their governor, would rather that damn thing disappeared from sight forever.

Two days after the ten-year anniversary of Tiananmen, an article appeared in the *South China Morning Post,* Hong Kong's main English-language paper. PILLAR OF SHAME SPLITS CAMPUS said the headline. The split was between students and university authorities. After the official ceremonies on June 4 were over, four hundred students of Hong Kong University returned with the Pillar, which they proceeded to put up on campus. The university's External Affairs Office protested that this "unauthorized move" was "a danger to public safety," and it reserved the right "to take appropriate action to remove the statue. . . ." The students, in language no less wooden, but inspired by nobler sentiments, declared: "We are of the view that the students' decision to have a long-term erection of the sculpture was made in accordance with a complete democratic mechanism."

The poor Pillar had actually been on an odyssey ever since the Danish sculptor donated it to Hong Kong in 1997. First it was displayed at Chinese University, then transferred to another college, and then to six other universities, but no one wished to be responsible for giving it a permanent home. A request in 1998 to place it among other sculptures in Kowloon Park was rejected by the municipal committee, because it was of "poor artistic value." This judgment, not in itself absurd, might have carried more weight if other public sculptures in Hong Kong had been of greater merit. Another official took the view that only works by local artists would be acceptable. Democrats protested. There were heated public meetings. The Provisional Urban Council Committee referred further discussion to the government's Recreation Committee. Pending a decision, moves were made to put the Pillar in the New Territories, a newly urbanized area north of Kowloon. But protests from local villagers put a stop to that. Bad feng shui, some claimed. Too politically sensitive, said others. And so the Pillar was passed around, ferried from place to place, without reaching a final destination. The last I heard, it was languishing in a remote container park, somewhere in the New Territories. Tsang Kinsing, a spokesman for the Hong Kong Alliance of the Patriotic Democratic Movement in China, called the lack of a permanent place for the Pillar "the sorrow of Chinese."

———

In Hong Kong, the June 4 anniversary of Tiananmen signifies a kind of Chinese unity, but it is the unity of dissidents, democrats, and citizens who value their freedom, not of governments. The patriotism of this imaginary China, celebrated in Victoria Park, is the antithesis of the official patriotism promoted by the Communist government. And yet a closer look at the staging of the event shows subtle fissures running through the ranks of the unofficial patriots. For some of the most famous democratic politicians in Hong Kong, such as Emily Lau, the feisty leader of the Frontier Party, are nowhere to be seen. And the most famous democratic politician of all, Martin Lee, does not appear with his Democratic Party colleagues onstage but sits among the people, facing the stage, albeit in the front row. He is there, but not, as they say, in "an official capacity"; involved, sympathetic, but at an angle, away from the center.

Lee and Lau, and others like them, well-traveled, fluent in English, many of them educated in Britain and America, could be described as Hong Kong patriots. Pan-Chinese patriotism, inspired by a shared sense of national humiliation and the martyrology of 1989 or the 1937 Nanking Massacre by the Japanese is not what drives them. In the spring of 1999, dignified, lawyerly Martin Lee, as leader of the Democratic Party, had to march through the streets in a headband to protest the NATO bombing of the Chinese embassy in Belgrade, but he looked uncomfortable, as though he would rather not have been there at all (yet he had to be, lest he be branded "anti-Chinese"). When right-wing Japanese politicians deny Japanese wartime atrocities, as they sometimes do, Lee is not given to venting his rage.

It is not that he doesn't care about the Japanese war record; his father fought the Japanese as one of Chiang Kai-shek's generals. General Li was a Chinese patriot, who refused to register his son Martin's birth in Hong Kong lest he be classified as a British citizen. When the Japanese invaded, Li's children were smuggled to Guangzhou in baskets, carried across the border by coolies. Nor is Martin Lee indifferent to what happened in Tiananmen Square. He led the Hong Kong protest demonstrations in 1989. But he would prefer Hong Kong to be left alone as a fully democratic, sovereign city-state ruled by law. He does not want to be governed from Beijing any more than from London. Hong Kong may have been better off as a crown colony of democratic Britain, but it would be better off still if it were independent like Taiwan.

Hong Kong was never like Taiwan, however, and even less like Singapore. Taiwan was split between the heirs of the Chinese republic and the former subjects of the Japanese empire, while Hong Kong was in some respects the successor of old Shanghai, that glittering den of thieves, businessmen, and dreamers, shielded by Western colonial privileges and legal institutions from the harsh authority of the Chinese state. Shanghai in the 1920s and 1930s was not a democracy, to be sure, but there were other freedoms—economic, social, intellectual, and artistic—that allowed Chinese to flourish. Shanghai was the conduit for modern ideas, from Europe or the United States, sometimes via Japan. The indistinct outline of a modern China, commercially vibrant, intellectually on fire, inspired by Marx, Chaplin, Lu Xun, Tagore, Spencer, Mill, Hu Shih, and John Dewey, a China of contending literary magazines, lively newspapers, American movies, jazz music, horse racing, and public libraries, a China, in short, that was crushed on the mainland but whose pale shadows lingered on in Hong Kong, first took shape in Shanghai. The key to these freedoms was a degree of legal protection.

The topography of Hong Kong shows marked similarities to that of Shanghai. On one side of the bay is Kowloon, the "Chinese city" as it were, much of it a frenzied souk of tenements and street markets, brothels and gambling parlors, teahouses and short-time hotels, and crowds, endless, teeming, buzzing crowds, which fill the narrow streets and neon-lit boulevards day and night. On the other side is the more sedate, more "Western" business district, called Central, a bit like the Bund in Shanghai, with its banks and law firms, its solid, neoclassical Legislative Council building, and its cluster of skyscrapers all vying for attention, one more sleek and wondrous than the other, some upholstered in the gaudiest shades of gold, like towering blocks of bullion. Old Shanghai department stores, such as Wing On and Sincere, still thrive in Hong Kong, as do such purveyors of Western luxuries as Lane Crawford. English and American books are still sold at the old Shanghai firm of Kelly and Walsh. The culture of Hong Kong, the source of its energy, is the amalgam of East and West, just as it was in old Shanghai. The difference is that Shanghai was not only the cosmopolitan center of Chinese intellectual life but a city in China, attracting people from all over the country, while Hong Kong was a British colony, cut off from China and populated mostly by refugees, or children of refugees, most of whom were Cantonese. Patriotism in such a place could only be a vexed affair.

John Sham, the Hong Kong show-business entrepreneur now living in Taipei, was right. Hong Kong is the most westernized part of China, and Martin Lee is a typical product of it. But Western influence, too, has never been straightforward. Hong Kong has some highly skilled fakers of European luxury items. I used to know a man who went from office to office selling almost perfect imitations of Swiss watches. You could tell that the fine Rolex he held in his hand was fake only when you had opened it up to examine the Japanese-made mechanism. Political institutions never pretended to be replicas of Westminster, yet they too were enveloped in make-believe. Even though British governers ruled with almost absolute power, the issues of the day were debated in a Westminster-type legislature, of which no member, until the last few years of British rule, was directly elected. Jan Morris caught the atmosphere of the colony nicely in her book *Hong Kong,* where she described the British legislators (there were Chinese, too) as "able but sufficiently ordinary Britons, to be encountered, one might think, any day on a stockbrokers' commuter train into Waterloo, transformed into Honourable Ministers on the other side of the globe." What Hong Kong had, then, was a kind of spectacle of democracy without democracy itself.

And yet the British did build a framework upon which a democracy could be built, a relatively free press, and a legal system, which, however imperfect in practice, was still based on the principle that the rule of law applied equally to all. The same system was handed down to Singapore but was undermined by Singaporean politicians almost as soon as the British left. In Shanghai it was crushed altogether. Martin Lee's mission, carried out with an almost religious passion, is to prevent this from happening in Hong Kong.

He has been accused by Beijing, and by his enemies in Hong Kong, of being both a "radical" and a "pro-British" colonial and thus, by implication, "unpatriotic," even "anti-Chinese." He is in fact much more complicated. When the British still ruled Hong Kong, Lee was not really a dissident in any philosophical sense. He did not disagree with the British ideal of liberal government and free commerce. He was, if anything, a conservative. But he wanted the substance, not the show. While most of his fellow members of the colonial elite, the "Sirs" and "Dames," who sat in appointed councils and committees and showed off their finery in the glossy magazines, knew how to work the colonial system to their own advantage, Lee wanted what almost none of them, whether British or Chinese, had in mind: a real democracy in Hong Kong. For he knew that once Beijing took over, civil liberties and the rule of law would be impossible to safeguard without it.

Martin Lee is not an easy man to interview. Not that he is unfriendly, difficult to meet, or unwilling to offer a good quote. Quite the contrary. He is unfailingly courteous and eager to offer his views. But he is also a traditional British-style barrister, with the dry manner and rather pedantic diction of his calling or, given his school education, a Jesuit priest. That is why he has always looked ill at ease in street rallies, in T-shirts and headbands, trying to be a man of the people. A tall, thin, somewhat owlish man, born in 1938, Lee looks more comfortable in his customary dark gray double-breasted suits. He can be a precise and persuasive guide to the intricacies of Hong Kong's constitutional arrangements. One always comes away from his neat, wood-paneled law firm with a better understanding of the Basic Law (Hong Kong's new constitution), the struggles over the Court of Final Appeal, and the vital importance of maintaining an independent judiciary. But he is not one to put his passion on display.

If Hong Kong had remained a British colony, Lee might never have become involved in politics at all. He had a successful law practice, made "more money than I needed," and was a settled member of the Hong Kong elite. He, too, appeared in the social pages of the Hong Kong glossies, at this ball or that function, in formal evening dress. Until the early 1980s, there was no reason for him to be interested in politics. He might even have believed, as did most of the local elite, that politics was not suited to Hong Kong, that stability was the thing, that Chinese people were too immature and too excitable to be trusted with democratic rights, and that, in any case, since they lacked a democratic tradition, they were not interested in politics. What changed his mind, around 1982, was the looming threat of being ruled by Beijing. He noticed that many of his friends were now talking about getting foreign passports. Refuge in Britain or Canada would have been a soft option for Lee as well; an easy escape was one of the perks of privilege in Hong Kong. But somehow this didn't feel right. He describes it as a guilty conscience.

In 1982, Lee visited Beijing as chairman of the bar association. The question of future sovereignty came up—this was two years before the British agreed formally to the handover in 1997. Speaking to his Chinese hosts, Lee used a gardening metaphor. He said: "If you see a lovely rose growing in your neighbor's garden, and you pluck it and put it in a vase, it will die in a few days." It was not an especially subtle reference to the precarious status of Hong Kong. Nor was the answer it provoked: China would have to resume full control over its territories.

That is when Lee decided to become a politician—not to save the British empire, but to safeguard some of its institutions. First he was elected to the Legislative Council by his colleagues as their representative of the legal profession. Later, in 1991, when some seats were contested in direct elections for the first time, he was elected by popular vote.

I knew that Lee was a devout Catholic, educated by the Jesuits: another Chinese activist with Christianity in his background. So I asked him one day, in his office, whether religion had influenced his politics. He thought for a bit, and said: "I often think that if you are a member of the Chinese Communist Party, it would be perfectly logical to be corrupt. Why not? Everybody is doing it. Christianity is good, because it gives you a reason to be good and not corrupt. I always believe that somebody up there is in charge." And then, as though unwilling to dwell on such personal matters, he quickly changed the subject: "The most important thing is the rule of law. . . . But if you want to keep the rule of law, you can't just depend on the judges. You need an elected government." This was vintage Lee: dogged, precise, a bit plodding, yet wholly admirable.

It would be easy to describe Martin Lee, with his faith in God and the rule of law, as a typically Anglicized Chinaman (to use Lee Kuan Yew's phrase), born in the dusk of the British empire, a pinstriped anachronism, out of touch with the culture of his race. This is more or less how his political opponents choose to see him, those "patriotic" businessmen and politicians who travel back and forth to Beijing (where Lee is barred from going), promoting a Singapore-style paternalistic authoritarianism in the name of stability, economic development, and Chinese values. Most of these people were as westernized as Lee. Many of them proudly bore their British titles and attended every function at the Governor's Mansion, or, indeed, Buckingham Palace. Some of them pleaded with the British to continue their colonial rule. But when they saw the British game was up, they became instant Chinese patriots, dropped their titles, spoke of Chinese values, and attended every function at the New China News Agency, or at the Great Hall of the People in Beijing. The one thing they did not have to change was their conviction that democracy was unsuited to Hong Kong.

———

Northern Chinese in general and Communist mandarins in particular regard the Cantonese, and especially the Cantonese in Hong Kong, as crass, loudmouthed merchants, people without culture, who will eat anything that flies, walks, or swims and have but one talent, which is to make money. The Chinese government has no intention of crushing the despised Hong Kong merchants in the way the Shanghainese were crushed in the 1950s. On the contrary, Hong Kong is supposed to remain a "commercial city," managed like a giant business, unhampered, so far as possible, by politics, which is why a shipping tycoon was put in charge.

One of the oddest, most ironic accusations lodged from Beijing against the British in their last years of rule was that a proposal to improve the welfare of poor pensioners would "undermine capitalism" in Hong Kong. And not only that: The pro-Beijing trade unions are set against the right to collective bargaining, while the much weaker and poorer independent unions are in favor. No wonder, then, that Hong Kong tycoons find it congenial to be "patriots," for their kind of patriotism comes with fat profits. All this gives a new meaning to the distinction between right and left: The right is largely on the side of the Communist government in Beijing; the left is the common enemy of Party cadres and patriotic tycoons.

There is in fact a history of leftist patriotism in Hong Kong, much of it organized from Beijing, part of the united front, which tacks to every wind blowing from China. But there is also a genuine leftism, rooted in Hong Kong's anti-colonial Chinese schools, student unions, and independent labor unions. During the Cultural Revolution anti-colonial rage threatened to roll over Hong Kong. Most of this was highly orchestrated: employees of mainland-owned stores waving Mao's Little Red Book, pro-Beijing newspapers fanning anti-British sentiment, and so on. But it all began with a protest against deplorable labor conditions in a plastics factory. Left-wing patriotism, though still marginal, became more interesting in the latter half of the 1970s, when democratic activists began to stir in China. And it came to a climax in the spring of 1989, when a million people hit the streets in solidarity with the students in Beijing. Szeto Wah comes from this tradition, and so does an extraordinary man named Lau San-ching.

I came across Lau several times after 1997, sometimes in person, sometimes in press reports. Small, bespectacled, and rather shabbily dressed in a cheap cotton shirt and sandals, Lau looked like one of those boys who attract the attention of school bullies, get beaten up, and come back for more, bleeding from the mouth, glasses cracked. You would see pictures of him in the papers, his face contorted with anger or pain as the police tried to stop him from protesting against this or that. Lau makes a modest living helping mental patients and has organized a union of social workers. When I met him for the first time in the late 1990s, he was exercised about the negative effects of "privatization" in China: Tens of millions of laid-off workers were roaming the cities in search of survival. All the Communist Party cared about was money, he said. And the so-called liberals in Hong Kong, including Martin Lee, were supporting privatization, too. In the transition from Maoism to raw capitalism, he warned, the workers were being crushed.

A do-gooder, then, an old-fashioned lefty, harmless, noble, an oddball in relentlessly capitalist Hong Kong. Nevertheless, Lau San-ching is a rather heroic figure. For he is one of the very few people in Hong Kong who actively tried to promote democracy in China long before 1989. He told me parts of his story on various occasions, once at an expensive coffee shop at the Mandarin Hotel in Central Hong Kong, once outside a conference hall in Macau, then again at the Mandarin. Looking a little incongruous in the midst of blue-suited businessmen and obsequious waiters at the Mandarin, Lau always spoke softly, in a Cantonese accent. There were details he left out, but he pointed me to a website that carried an account of his life, written by a human-rights activist, Kate Saunders. Gradually, I was able to piece his extraordinary story together.

Lau was born in Hong Kong, the son of poor immigrants from

Guangzhou. His father worked in a factory. Chinese patriotism was not something Lau encountered at home or at school. School was solidly colonial in sentiment. And his parents, having once had patriotic hopes for the Chinese Communist Party, felt that their patriotism had been betrayed and wanted nothing more to do with either China or politics. To them, as to most first-generation immigrants, colonial Hong Kong was a safe haven from Chinese politics.

It was only at university, where he studied physics and mathematics, that Lau took an interest in politics. He was an active member of the student union. Some of Lau's fellow students were official patriots, who supported everything the Beijing government said or did. Since this was in the early 1970s, when Mao and the Gang of Four still ruled, these patriots were ardent Maoists. Most ended up doing very well in Hong Kong. Several ex-Maoists would go on to become senior figures in the government after 1997, advising the former shipping tycoon how to run Hong Kong as a "commercial city." Lau thinks they had been groomed for this task all along.

Lau was not a Maoist but a Trotskyite, a "romantic revolutionary" in his own words, a member of the Revolutionary Marxist League. He wanted real socialism in Hong Kong, a quixotic aim. But in a mixture of patriotism and religious zeal, he also wanted to promote socialism in China. And he thought he saw a glimmer of hope in 1974, the year when the famous Li Yi Zhe wall poster went up in Guangzhou criticizing Mao's Cultural Revolution for being anti-democratic. Two years later, masses of students demonstrated in Beijing, honoring the memory of Zhou Enlai. The armed militia cleared the square with water cannon and truncheons. Lau named his group of activists in Hong Kong after the date of that crackdown: the April 5 Action Group. In 1979, hope was rekindled by the Democracy Wall and the little magazines and underground pamphlets and manifestos published by the likes of Wei Jingsheng, Xu Wenli, and Wang Xizhe, one of the original authors of the Li Yi Zhe poster.

Lau decided he had to go to China. He doesn't like to be called a patriot, because he sees himself as an internationalist; patriotism smacks too much of being a government toady. Nonetheless, he was fired by the same spirit that drove a million Hong Kong people into the streets in 1989. He took the train to China, not, as he puts it, "as a Hong Kong person, but as a Chinese." He felt that if he did not go, mainland activists "would say we had no guts." His was a typically Hong Kong brand of unofficial Chinese patriotism, born of a sense of colonial inferiority.

In Guangzhou, Lau established contact with Wang Xizhe and his friends. He smuggled overseas publications to China and mainland activist publications to Hong Kong. Back and forth he went, in an increasingly risky enterprise. As a kind of corollary to his economic reforms, Deng Xiaoping decided he had to stamp out the democracy movement. Both Wei Jingsheng and Wang Xizhe were thrown in jail. The underground magazines were more or less killed. When Lau set off once again for Guangzhou on Christmas Day, 1981, his girlfriend, Christina Tang, feared the worst. She told him not to go. Lau didn't listen. (He now admits he was guilty of "adventurism.") Winters are cold even in southern China. Lau wanted to give Wang Xizhe's wife a sweater to pass on to her husband in jail. She looked shifty when she saw Lau, told him to wait, left the house for twenty minutes or so, and came back in tears. That night Lau was arrested.

Lau was given a choice: He could confess to his "counterrevolutionary" crimes against "socialism" or risk having his mind and body broken in jail. He spent the next year and a half locked up in a dark cell, the size of a toilet stall, freezing in winter and stifling hot in summer. He had nothing to read, no one to talk to, and barely enough food to stay alive. It was the first of the three extended periods he would spend in solitary darkness. The second time, which lasted two years, he was shackled in a dark and filthy cell with blood on the walls and cockroaches scooting around a hole in the concrete floor that served as his toilet. Swarms of mosquitoes made sleep almost impossible. Criminal inmates were ordered to watch his every move day and night and report on what they saw. They are known as *ermu*, "ears and eyes." The only escape from this torment was to "confess." Lau refused, and gradually lost his capacity to tell day from night. He still didn't confess, but admitted to having been "uncooperative." Finally, he was released from his dungeon and put in a marginally better cell.

Things could have been even worse. Lau recalls a mentally retarded man who was too feeble-minded to "confess" to anything. He was locked up alone in a dark cell, his hands and feet in shackles, and never let out. He could not wash. For years he was in there, howling to himself in the dark like a caged beast. One day, he found the desperate strength to break the door with his bare hands. He was beaten up, put in chains, and thrown into an even more isolated cell, where his cries could no longer be heard. When the prison authorities, after ten years, wanted to hand this human wreck back to his family, they refused to have him, so he was left to rot in his dark cage.

Lau spent his last period of solitary confinement in a labor camp. Wang Xizhe was in the cell next door. They managed to communicate by talking, or "telephoning," through the wall. Or sometimes they would climb to a tiny window at the top of their cells and catch a glimpse of each other. This was called "faxing." Despite this relief, Lau and his fellow inmates had a hard time surviving. Wang would often let out a piercing howl that went on an on, like a police siren. Another former activist started babbling about an invasion by space aliens. Lau was tortured by terrifying nightmares. He tried to remain sane by concentrating his mind on the moment only: Never think back, never think of the future, for that would provoke longing. Once you did that, you were done for.

I tried to imagine what Lau had gone through. It was of course beyond the scope of my imagination. I watched him drink his cappuccino and eat his Danish pastry at the Mandarin Hotel coffee shop. A large silver Rolls-Royce glided by outside. People around us were setting up lunch appointments, talking on their cell phones. A waiter came over to ask us discreetly whether we would like anything else. There were many things I wanted to ask Lau. I wanted to know what it meant to go through hell. But I knew he couldn't answer that question. He could only describe it, in his soft Cantonese voice, and smile.

Instead, I asked him about his relations with the mainland dissidents. He said they had always been difficult, for the activists of the 1970s were from a "lost generation." They were damaged by the Cultural Revolution. Lau picked his words with tact. He said: "This may be difficult for Westerners to understand. But, you know, the way they grew up, they cannot have nice personalities. They have strong characters, but in some sense they are not so honest."

Lau was finally released on the day after Christmas, 1991. He still had not confessed to his "counterrevolutionary" crimes. When he arrived at the Hung Hom railway station in Hong Kong, he was greeted as a hero. It is extraordinary that he had survived at all.

The last time I spoke to Lau, in the summer of 2000, once again at the Mandarin coffee shop, he was better dressed. He looked less out of place this time, wearing a gray cotton jacket and chatting on his own cell phone. Lau had joined the Democratic Party now. I was a bit surprised to hear this, for he had often spoken of the "liberals" with disdain. He said he was still a Marxist, though not an orthodox one. He believes in "science and objectivity," but agrees with "Marxist theory about economics and capitalism."

I am not a Marxist and have little sympathy for Trotskyites, yet when I think of Lau San-ching, who spent ten years in prison and still cannot visit China because of his "crimes against socialism" and then think of his old fellow students, the Maoist patriots who now advise the former shipping magnate on how to keep Hong Kong safe for bankers and property tycoons, it is hard not to feel enraged by the sheer hypocrisy and mendaciousness of Communist Party rule in China—and of their proxies in Hong Kong.

Looking up from his cup of coffee, blinking through his glasses in that curious mixture of good nature and hard resolve, the unsettling look of the total idealist, he said something that bordered on desperation about China and its history. And yet despair is the one thing a total idealist can never afford to give in to. Lau said history always goes in cycles: His parents liked the Communist Party but felt betrayed by it. His own generation tried to accept the Party but felt betrayed by the Gang of Four. And now, the young generation was trying to follow the Party once more, all in the name of patriotism. Patriotism, Lau said, with the sweetest of smiles, is the nightmare for each new generation of Chinese.

———

The Mandarin Hotel lobby on the morning after the handover of Hong Kong, on July 1, 1997, was a ghostly place. There, hovering around the reception desk, making quiet small talk or, in some cases, carefully looking away when political opponents threatened to come into view, were the British players of the last twenty years or so in Hong Kong's colonial drama. Two former foreign secretaries were there guarding their suitcases, waiting for attendants to whisk them away. A former governor of Hong Kong was studying the morning's paper, waiting for his wife and children. Media stars and press moguls stood about, looking lost. Former colonial secretaries, Legislative Council (LegCo) members, Special Branch officers, Government House employees, and press spokesmen hung around waiting for transport to the airport. There was nothing more to do. The party was over. This place was no longer theirs. They looked oddly diminished on that gray, drizzly morning.

The occasion was made even more macabre by a pumped-up jollity, a contrived festiveness, going on at the same time. Middle-aged men and women, many of them Europeans, some Chinese, dressed in Chinese fancy dress, complete with silk hats and false pigtails, danced in the lobby to an orchestra playing jazzy versions of Chinese folk songs. The orchestra members, too, were decked out in red, blue, and yellow silk robes. The dancers were mostly businessmen and their wives, the kind of people who kept on telling reporters that Hong Kong was a "commercial city" and would be absolutely fine.

I had seen other people celebrate the night before: beefy young "expats," wearing Union Jack hats, vomiting in the streets in Lan Kwai Fong, and Hong Kong tycoons, in evening clothes, toasting Communist officials in broken Mandarin at lavish and largely untouched banquets. Like the new buildings in China, everything was on an outsize scale. On the day of the handover, there was an auction of an enormous painting of little girls in tutus handing flowers to the Chinese leaders Li Peng, Jiang Zemin, and Deng Xiaoping while Hong Kong's patriotic worthies, including the former shipping tycoon, looked up at the Chinese leaders with smiles of almost hysterical delight. It went for almost U.S.$300,000 to a Hong Kong company whose founder had just been convicted of insider trading. A Shanghai millionaire was devastated to see his bid for "the best painting in the world" topped. All this celebration made for a curious and melancholy contrast with the passive, even apprehensive attitudes of most ordinary citizens of Hong Kong. "It's nothing to do with us," taxi drivers said with depressing predictability whenever I asked them. "We are just ordinary people."

I was waiting in the Mandarin lobby for Emily Lau, who had been a directly elected member of the legislature until midnight of June 30, when the elected LegCo was abolished in favor of the "provisional legislature," appointed by Beijing. The last bill to be passed by the elected legislature was to limit the right of the police to tap people's phones. One of the first measures of the new, unelected LegCo would be to repeal it.

While waiting for Emily, I recalled a conversation the night before with a distinguished British newspaper columnist, Simon Jenkins, who had arrived in Hong Kong for the occasion. He did not know the place but had gotten around a bit, talked to a few people, had lunch with some old chums, and after a day or so in the territory decided that people in Hong Kong did not really want democracy. The last British governer, Chris Patten, had done everything he could to expand their democratic rights, it is true, but Jenkins was skeptical about all that: No point annoying Beijing unnecessarily; this wasn't Europe or America, you know. "I really wonder," he said in his pleasantly polished voice, redolent of comfortable leather chairs and good cigars. "I really wonder if these people understand politics. It's awfully hard to know *what* they think, really."

Emily walked in from the soft rain, dressed in blue jeans and a red T-shirt, pale and drawn, still tired perhaps from the last all-night session of the elected LegCo, which had ended in tearful embraces. I thought of all the years I had known her, first as a colleague at the *Far Eastern Economic Review,* for which she had covered Hong Kong. It was then, in the mid-1980s that she became politically active, arguing for more democracy in Hong Kong. Educated partly in Britain and the United States, she shared the humiliation of those who knew the West well enough to see through the hypocrisies of colonial rule. She made speeches and wrote passionate articles and had daily conversations on the phone with Martin Lee and other democrats. Her nickname in the office was Basic Lau, for banging on so much about Hong Kong's constitution. In those days there was a shrillness in her tone, an edge of hysteria almost, in her denunciations of British policies and British grandees, who would come to Hong Kong for twenty-four-hour visits to say that everything would be fine. But shrillness is a minor vice in a just cause. When Margaret Thatcher visited Hong Kong after the deal with China had been done, it was Emily who stood up at a press conference to ask her how she felt about handing over a free city to a Communist dictatorship. Mrs. Thatcher stared at her with almost pitying disdain and drawled that the young lady was surely the only person in Hong Kong to feel this way. Emily Lau went on to become the most popular politician in Hong Kong.

We sat down at the Mandarin bar, to be out of sight of the fancy-dress revelers. I asked Emily how she felt now that British rule, which she had resented so much, was finally over. She shrugged her shoulders and said she was worried about the future. The opposition did not have enough money to keep going. Hong Kong, unlike Taiwan, lacked a culture of democratic opposition. The Chinese government, the new masters, would surely crack down anyway. Perhaps she would go on vacation with her husband, a successful lawyer. She would go to Italy. And after that? After that, she would just have to keep going, wouldn't she? I looked through the door, toward the sound of Chinese music. And Emily said: "I'm glad it rained. At least it spoiled China's party."

China's party, in both Hong Kong and Beijing, had been drenched in official patriotism. But for a Communist government, which sees itself as the proud heir of the May Fourth spirit of Mr. Science and Mr. Democracy, or at least of scientific socialism "with Chinese characteristics," it was a peculiarly touchy, sentimental kind of patriotism, in which imagined "Chinese characteristics" overwhelmed anything that might have been described as either scientific or democratic. The kind of patriotism promoted in Hong Kong—and in China—that week goes back a little further in time than Mr. Science and Mr. Democracy. It, too, was largely imported from the West. The term for it, a character combination coined by the Japanese, is *minzu zhuyi,* literally "racialism," or "Volkism," a romantic notion of national or racial destiny, determined by history and culture. Some of its symbols are ancient, but it is firmly rooted in the nineteenth century, when national consciousness was forged out of a double sense of humiliation: imperial government by corrupt Manchus and military defeat at the hands of superior Western powers.

Song-and-dance troupes, performing on the night of June 30 in Beijing, set the tone. The humiliations of modern Chinese history were rehearsed with an almost masochistic zeal: the Opium War, the unequal treaties, the Boxer War, and the sacking by foreign troops of the Summer Palace in Beijing. The Great Wall, that great symbol of ancient oppression and modern national pride, was assembled out of thousands of half-naked bodies moving in unison to the beat of martial drums. Never again would barbarians assail China. In seconds, the human wall changed into a massive red flag: Under the leadership of the Communist Party the Chinese people had risen!

A new film, apparently the most expensive ever made in China, opened in Hong Kong for the occasion. Chief Executive Tung attended the premiere, as did Chinese officials from the New China News Agency. *The Opium War* had all the stock images and characters of modern Chinese Volkism: treacherous Manchu officials, venal Cantonese traders, villainous British capitalists, and heroic Chinese patriots. The story is repeated in textbooks, popular comics, patriotic museums, and political speeches all over China: Western capitalists sold opium to the Chinese to weaken the Chinese people and rob them of their wealth. The Manchus were too effete to resist. A patriotic official named Lin Zexu tried to resist by destroying opium and arresting the traders but was thwarted by a combination of superior British military power and the corrupt Manchu government. An ignoble compromise was reached. Treaties were signed by traitors to the Chinese race. Hong Kong was given away, and the imperialists ravaged China.

Sex and politics are invariably linked in such tales of national humiliation: a pure and beautiful Chinese girl is sacrificed by Manchu officials to a loathsome, hairy barbarian, who rapes her in the night. Her screams express the agony of the Chinese race. The message is made explicit at the end of the movie: Only a powerful, unified nation under the leadership of the Communist Party will wipe out China's shame.

What is remarkable is not the message but the sense of wounded cultural, as well as racial, pride. An extraordinary gesture by one of the barbarians was needed to help restore it. In a scene set in the House of Commons, a British member of Parliament compares British efforts to force their way into China to the destruction of a priceless Ming-dynasty vase. The same man then extolls to his astonished barbarian audience the five thousand years of glorious Chinese civilization. He points out that Chinese philosophy is so profound that it would take several generations of the greatest European thinkers to realize just how profound it is.

This is odd propaganda to come from a Communist government, which not long ago did its best to smash all vestiges of traditional Chinese civilization in the name of scientific-socialist progress and the thoughts of Mao Zedong. During the Cultural Revolution, simply owning a Ming vase was enough to get one into very serious trouble.

And yet the romance of a glorious history, of ancient philosophers "far more profound than Aristotle," of a national family united in shared memories of greatness, was all that an oppressive and ideologically bankrupt Chinese government had to offer the citizens of a territory that was richer and freer than China. A sense of patriotism built on enlightened political institutions would have been an absurdity. Racial pride, based on a sense of past grievances, was all that was left.

The Opium War had some success in China but was a flop in Hong Kong, as were other celebrations of official "Chineseness." The propaganda was crude, confusing, and insulting. That Chinese girl in the movie, sacrificed after the Opium War to the hairy barbarian, stood for Hong Kong. The awkward thing is that Hong Kong thrived as a result. Without the Opium War, Hong Kong would not have existed in its present form but remained a modest Cantonese town, spared the indignity of colonial rule but not the ravages of civil war and dictatorship. As a result of the Opium War, countless refugees from various catastrophes in China achieved prosperity and a high degree of freedom in Hong Kong. The insult to Hong Kong, born of ignorance and ideology, as much as from northern prejudice against the Cantonese, is that only the prosperity is acknowledged. Official celebrations in Beijing always include the "minorities," dancing and singing, dressed in exotic costumes, and beaming with pleasure at the privilege of being a happy part of the Chinese empire. On the night of June 30, 1997, the people of Hong Kong were represented, too, by dancers jumping up and down to the beat of patriotic pop songs. They were dressed up as dollar signs and credit cards.

In the end, however, not long after the stroke of midnight on July 1, it was the defenders of political institutions who staged the most passionate and moving demonstration of where their loyalties lay. It was still hot and humid, but the rain had changed from a torrent to a steady drizzle. The fireworks had fizzled out in the low, wet clouds. The last governor, Chris Patten, had shed his tears and pulled out of the harbor with the Prince of Wales, who retired for the night to watch British comedy films. Martin Lee and his fellow democrats had asked for permission to wish their voters well from the balcony of the LegCo building. Permission had been refused. They defied the ban and sneaked in anyway—Lee, Szeto Wah, and the others. They came out on the balcony to face a crowd of several thousand people.

It was a sentimental moment; the ex-legislators, a mixture of lawyers, activists, and trade union leaders, held hands, cried, and made the V sign. Lee pointed out that the same building had been used once by the Japanese to torture "our people who refused to surrender." In the same spirit, he said, the Hong Kong people would refuse to surrender their freedoms. "We know," he went on in his typical fashion, "that without a democratically constituted legislature, there is no way for our people to be assured that good laws will be passed to protect our freedom." The elected legislators would come back the following year, he promised, and retake their seats after an election.

Was this just an Anglicized laywer speaking wishfully, making a last stand for a system of government that would end because it was not suited to the Chinese? Was it the rhetoric of a regime, set up by a British governor in a fit of last-minute imperial guilt, a regime, moreover, that had lasted only a few years and was already over? Was Lee an alien body in the celebration of "Chineseness," as his opponents would say? In fact, other demonstrations were taking place elsewhere in Hong Kong. Emily Lau had marched with members of her Frontier Party and vowed to fight for democracy. And there, outside the new Convention Center, where the final ceremony of the handover was taking place, where Li Peng and Jiang Zemin were shaking hands with Prince Charles, was the April 5 Action Group.

I saw a photograph of their demonstration in the *South China Morning Post* the next day. One man was holding up a picture of a dead student in

Beijing covered in blood. The text said, in English: "Who killed this guy in 1989? Li Peng. I am a Chinese dissident. I think Li Peng is a murderer." And next to that man was the unmistakable figure of Lau San-ching, his face a picture of rage, his glasses askew, a megaphone in his hand. He was being pushed away by a burly policeman. And his shouts against the Chinese government were being drowned out by police loudspeakers, which had been strategically placed for just such an event and which, in a final piece of Hong Kong irony, were blaring Beethoven's great ode to freedom, the Ninth Symphony.

—

The first LegCo election in the Special Administrative Region (SAR) of Hong Kong, held in May 1998, came at an interesting time. General Suharto had just been forced to step down as the strongman of Indonesia. Student demonstrations against corruption and lack of civil liberties—the very things that had galvanized the students in Beijing a decade before—had finally cracked the dictatorship.

I happened to be in China on the day it happened, on Hainan, an island in the South China Sea. The Chinese newspapers had given a very one-sided version of the news from Jakarta; they barely mentioned the students but played up every instance of violence and disorder, especially when the victims were of Chinese descent, as was often the case. Suharto's resignation speech, broadcast live on CNN, was suddenly cut off in China, even though the only people who were able to watch it were guests at international hotels. But most Chinese know how to read between the lines, and people understood perfectly well what had happened.

"This is very important news for all Asian people," said the keen young reporter for a local newspaper in Hainan. He was greatly excited, unusual in China when it comes to foreign news. We were sitting at the editorial office of a literary magazine. Most of the editors were there, as were some of the main writers. A young secretary passed around paper plates containing bananas and grapes. I was asked for my "foreign" view.

I could only repeat what I had read in the papers in Hong Kong. I said the Indonesian students had been inspired by the example of Tiananmen. This was received with nervous looks and polite laughter. One or two people scraped the floor with their feet. What did I think of the possibility of democratic change in China? It was not a question I relished, for I did not like to hold forth, in my imperfect Chinese, to people who knew the problems of their country better than I ever would. Still, I had to say something. So I said I saw no reason why Chinese could not handle a democracy if the Koreans, the Filipinos, the Taiwanese, the Japanese, and now, one hoped, the Indonesians could.

The usual discussion—usual among Chinese intellectuals, that is—about the peculiarities of Chinese culture ensued. It would take a long time for democracy to develop in China. China was too big. China was too poor. China was too complicated. Chinese history was too long. Chinese people needed to be more educated. They had little idea of democratic rights. If democracy came too suddenly, there might be chaos. And so on. The keen young reporter then asked me whether I could comment on a particularly "sensitive topic." What about June 4, 1989, the Beijing Massacre? But one of the editors, the most senior person in the room, swiftly intervened, pointing out that I was a "distinguished foreign guest," who had traveled far, so perhaps I could offer them some insights into the wider world outside China.

Later that same day, I went out on my own for a snack. Opposite my hotel was a half-finished concrete shell of a building. Much of Haikou, the main city on Hainan, was like that. The building boom of the early 1990s had come to a sudden halt, victim of the Asian financial crisis. Parts of Haikou looked as though they had been bombed. A kitchen had been improvised in one of the rooms of the half-finished building. Next door a jerry-built "beauty parlor" was a front for a brothel. A young man, his shirtless back shiny with sweat, was tossing noodles about in a large pot. After some diffidence, he wiped his hands on his trousers and came over for a chat. We were joined by two of his friends and a girl in a filmy evening gown, who worked at another "beauty parlor." They stared at me and said nothing.

The cook had come down from a village in Sichuan with his sister, who was helping him run the food stall. But he was in debt to the businessman who paid his wages. That was the trouble with the economic reforms, he said: The rich bosses now controlled everything. I nodded, and slowly ate my noodles with garlic and squid. The chef then shifted in his seat and emptied his nose, by first blocking one nostril and snorting in a short, sharp burst, then repeating the procedure with the other nostril. His manners were far from elegant. But he was no fool. "You know," he suddenly said, "in your country the individual has the right to control his own life. Not here in China. Everything is controlled from above. The Communist Party has complete power. That is why we have no rights here."

The intellectuals at the literary magazine might well have shared the cook's view. In fact, some almost certainly did. But one of the oddities in contemporary China is that it often takes a lack of education to be able to express things clearly. Or, to put it differently, it is those who live near the bottom of society who feel the lack of individual rights most keenly. That is why they generally get to the point more quickly.

Few people had high hopes for the legislative elections in Hong Kong. The weather was terrible and the election rules were rigged. Of sixty seats, only twenty would go to people being directly elected. This made it impossible for directly elected candidates to gain a majority in LegCo. The rest of the seats, mostly occupied by patriotic businessmen, would be given by appointment or would go to people chosen by their professional peers. In other words, even if every democrat was elected, they could neither initiate nor block any laws. Hong Kong in 1998, with its highly educated population and a higher per capita income than Britain's, was less democratic than India before independence. And yet Tung Chee-hwa, the chief executive, still spoke of the need for a lengthy process of political education, and warned of the grave risk of instability and chaos if people should have too much political freedom too soon.

In the week of the election, I ran into Lau San-ching at a meeting for overseas Chinese dissidents in Macau. This was the occasion when his former jailmate Wang Xizhe stood up and proposed a cheer for the students in Jakarta. Lau said he was in favor of boycotting the coming elections. To take part in a rigged exercise was to support a humiliating charade. Yet that was not the prevailing sentiment among the overseas dissidents who had gathered at the Diocesan Catholic Center for Youth in Macau. There was much optimistic talk that day of Hong Kong "liberating" China. Democracy would come from the south, said one of the speakers. After all,

Sun Yat-sen had started his republican revolution in the south. The same kind of thing would happen again. Yan Jiaqi, the bespectacled former adviser to Communist Party secretary-general Zhao Ziyang, said that Hong Kong's freedoms would serve as an example to China. Unfortunately, Yan was unable to express this view in Hong Kong, where he was refused an entry permit. That is why we were in Macau, at the time still a Portuguese colony.

Rigged or not, the LegCo election was an important test for the proposition that people in Hong Kong were not interested in politics. It would surely take considerable interest to brave the foul weather and vote for a minority of seats.

Emily Lau's constituency is in the New Territories, where sprawling housing complexes rise like monstrous cliffs from land that was green and rural only a decade or so ago. Laundry flutters from bamboo poles that poke out of the windows. At street level amid cheap fast-food restaurants, old men play Chinese chess on concrete tables in the small spaces left between the housing blocks.

Residents of the New Territories came to see Emily to discuss their problems at her tiny campaign office on the ground floor of one of the housing complexes. In the afternoon, local housewives offered to help distribute leaflets and do other odd jobs. Almost none of the people who came to Emily's office spoke English. A few spoke Mandarin. These were not westernized students of Adam Smith or John Stuart Mill. I spoke to a nurse, who worried that the poor were not represented in government. "The politicians are mostly rich men who have no idea how we live," she said. A housewife was worried about the cost of public housing: "Our lives in Hong Kong are controlled by property tycoons." A man, who had done business in China, was concerned about the effects of "patriotic" propaganda being introduced in Hong Kong schools by people "with connections in Beijing." Emily Lau, he said, spoke about individual freedom and human rights, and that is why he wanted her to have a voice in the legislature.

But the most interesting person I spoke to was Emily's driver. I had seen him before, a slim, quiet, smiling figure dressed in neatly pressed brown corduroy trousers. He said little but tried to be helpful in various ways.

Someone told me he was a retired policeman. Yes, he confirmed, when I asked him, that was true, he had been in the Hong Kong police force for thirty years. His name was Cheng. I asked him how he had become Emily Lau's driver. Let me tell you a story, he said.

One day, several years ago, when Cheng was still a policeman, his uncle, an elderly man, had gone for his daily cup of tea in a teahouse in Kowloon. The man was minding his own business when, suddenly, policemen rushed into the teahouse and arrested him as a suspected drug dealer. The charge was absurd, of course. But he was beaten at the police station. When the old man was pushed back into the street, he could barely walk. Cheng immediately realized what had happened. The police needed to make a certain number of arrests. To fill their quota, anybody would do. "That is why we need representation," said Cheng. "To protect us from brute force."

I made an appointment to see Cheng again the next day. He waited for me at a small office in another housing development. We sat down on plastic chairs. Children played outside. The gray and blue high-rise buildings blocked our view of the sky.

Cheng had been interested in politics before his uncle's arrest. Born in China, he had moved to Hong Kong with his family in 1948, the year before the Communist takeover. When I used the conventional mainland phrase "liberation," Mr. Cheng shook his head: "What do you mean, 'liberation'? Nobody was liberated. The government never represented the people."

Cheng had tried to keep in touch with his relatives in China. They would tell him how bad things were. You couldn't criticize the government; indeed, you couldn't tell the truth about anything. That is how the Cultural Revolution could happen, said Mr. Cheng. "The Chinese government in the 1960s was out of control because nobody had the right to correct it."

Still, I said, Chinese were now able to voice their opinions more freely, weren't they?

"Yes," said Mr. Cheng, "but people's opinions don't count for much if they lack the right to vote. Without the right to vote, no government will listen to people's opinions."

Hong Kong, he continued, was free but not democratic. If you were rich, you could influence the government. But if you had no money, anything could happen to you. You could be arrested, like his uncle. "The police," he said, "had connections with criminal bosses. They had far too much power. That is the problem in Hong Kong. Without democracy, a government can do anything it wants."

Such views would not have gone down well with his former colleagues in the police force. Cheng was clear about that: "Policemen didn't support democracy. They believed that the police should have absolute power, for otherwise Hong Kong would descend into chaos." So Cheng joined a discussion group in the 1980s. Among friends, he was able to speak his mind. But it was only in 1989, with Tiananmen, that he decided to become more active. He saw the killings on television and heard Emily Lau speak about the need to protect free speech, to protect Hong Kong. He was nearing retirement age. So he supported Emily's campaign in 1991, and drove her around for several weeks without pay in 1998. Rich people, he said, should not be allowed to monopolize power. He was afraid that the people in charge of Hong Kong would turn the place into something like Singapore, and then "we will be defenseless against arbitrary power."

I was touched by the policeman's words, but not because they were original. Like the noodle chef in Haikou, Cheng was stating the obvious. But the obvious is too often drowned in propaganda. Anyone who believes that Chinese people in Hong Kong (or indeed in Taiwan or China) have no interest in politics and do not really want democratic rights has to ignore Cheng and many others like him.

On May 25, 1998, 1.49 million people—more than half the voting population—turned out to vote, despite the driving rain, the mudslides, and the flooded roads. The democrats got 60 percent of the vote, enough for them to have formed a government if Hong Kong had been a democracy. Martin Lee, Szeto Wah, and Emily Lau all won back their seats. Though they would continue to dominate the legislature, the pro-Beijing businessmen and their allies won only a handful of seats through direct election.

This made the celebrations inside the Convention Center, where the vote counting took place, a colorful but also melancholy spectacle. Everything was scrupulously fair, more so perhaps than in any other election in Asia, or in much of the West for that matter. The ballot counters, wearing pink armbands, were surrounded by policemen in dark blue uniforms. Cheers went up as the results were announced. The democrats were delighted: Frontier Party members, in yellow shirts, gave three cheers to Emily Lau. Democratic Party members, in green shirts, surged forward as Szeto Wah and Martin Lee, dressed in a sober dark suit, entered the hall. It was all very civilized, without any of the sentimental raucousness of Taiwan or the childish pizzazz of America, more like a jolly cocktail party than an election-night celebration. A cynical journalist for one of the local financial dailies—a man who had often described himself to me as a "self-hating Chinaman," a Hong Kong patriot who never wanted to set foot in China—told me how deeply moved he was by the election.

And yet a deep insult lay behind this happy occasion. In desperation, just before his downfall, Suharto had offered the Indonesians a system of indirect elections much like the one in Hong Kong but more generous. The Indonesians turned it down. They wanted more. But the people of Hong Kong had to make do with less. One of the legislators, who won his seat through a small appointed electoral committee, found the words to drive the insult home. Democracy, he said, was "like a fine wine. It needs many years to mature." True, perhaps, as a general statement, but singularly inappropriate to the situation in Hong Kong. In politics, the people of Hong Kong were being treated like children, as colonial subjects always are. As well as their victory, the democrats were celebrating their own humiliation.

—

It used to be the case, until only a few years ago, that you could spot a mainlander in any Hong Kong crowd. The men wore ill-fitting suits and crude, pudding-bowl haircuts and the women wore dowdy skirts and flesh-colored stockings. You would see them walking around Central or Wanchai, gaping at the tall buildings, their brown country faces pictures of sheer wonder. Such mainlanders are few these days. Young people in Shanghai, Beijing, or Guangzhou follow the same fashion rules as their peers in Hong Kong. Mainlanders have their own big buildings at home. They now blend into the crowd.

In fact, many mainlanders are more or less hidden in Hong Kong. PLA soldiers in grass-green uniforms are kept in their barracks, like chained dogs, lest they upset the citizens of Hong Kong. Mainland prostitutes and bar girls come out at night but have their own reasons for discretion. The legal status of mainlanders in Hong Kong is often precarious, and popular sentiment is so prejudiced against them that Tung Chee-hwa, the chief executive, scored political points by trying to stop children in China from joining their parents who are legal residents of Hong Kong. This hasty move was overturned by the Hong Kong Court of Final Appeal, which ruled that the policy did not accord with Hong Kong's constitution, the Basic Law. Tung then asked the National People's Congress in Beijing to decide. The NPC overruled the Hong Kong court's decision, whereupon the court reversed is earlier ruling; one more chip off Hong Kong's promised autonomy. Martin Lee warned about undermining judicial independence. But there were few protests. The prospect of thousands of mainlanders coming in, even if they were only children, was more terrifying.

One reason that Hong Kong, though still relatively free, is not a bastion of mainlander dissidence is that not enough mainland dissidents can get in. And the few that do get in tend to be ignored. Jin Guantao, one of the writers of the mainland television series *River Elegy,* the polemical documentary that was blamed for inspiring the students' revolt in 1989, is now a resident scholar at the Chinese University in Hong Kong. Together with his wife, Liu Qingfeng, he edits an excellent literary journal, *21st Century.* I asked them one day why they preferred to be in Hong Kong rather than, say, the United States, with most of their old colleagues. Well, Jin said, the obvious advantage was the proximity of China. It was easier to stay in touch. Telephone calls were cheaper. You could almost look into China from his office window.

But then he began to complain in a stream of words, as if he had been starved of conversation. Hong Kong intellectuals, he said, really don't understand mainland China. Liu Qingfeng chimed in: "After 1997, we assumed people here would be interested, but they have no idea." And Jin said: "Even our colleagues at the university don't understand China. They don't know the history . . ." Liu again: "They know more about Japan. Especially young people. They like Japan. You know, people's thinking here is still in the Qing dynasty. They have kept traditions alive. But they know nothing about modern China."

They exaggerate. But Hong Kong, to be sure, is unlike Shanghai in the 1920s or Guangzhou in the 1910s. Revolution is not in the air. There are, nonetheless, two mainland dissidents who have somehow managed to slip through the net. One is Lu Siqing, a wiry Hunanese who operates out of one room in Kowloon, from where he tracks human-rights abuses in China and makes sure the world knows about them, via news services, human-rights organizations, and the Internet. The other is Han Dong-fang, the man who tried to set up China's first independent workers' federation, in a small tent, in May 1989 in Tiananmen Square.

Han was a brave man. The Communist government fears rebellious workers far more than students or intellectuals. If the workers turned against the Party, whom could the Party still claim to represent? The students could still be described, sometimes, as innocent idealists led astray by bad elements, but the workers in Tiananmen were denounced as counterrevolutionary "hooligans." None of the students was executed, but many workers were, with a shot in the neck, publicly, in football stadiums. When Han turned himself in at a police station in Beijing—not to confess to his "crimes" but to "clarify" his position—he was treated more brutally than any of the students.

He was thrown into a dark cell and kept in solitary confinement for months, refused medical treatment when he became seriously ill, had plastic tubes rammed down his nose when he went on a hunger strike, was locked up with murderers, and, worse, crammed into a small, damp, verminous cell for four months together with seventeen men suffering from contagious diseases and coughing their lungs out. When Han came out of prison, for medical treatment, after almost two years of torture and neglect, he was emaciated, barely conscious, and delirious with fever. He was coughing up what doctors call "green oysters." The diagnosis was easy: tuberculosis. Han was hardly able to talk. But before his parole, he still managed to scrawl a few words on a piece of paper: "I refuse to co-operate."

As soon as he was able to get up from his bed, Han rode his bicycle to the National People's Congress, to hand in a petition for workers' rights.

Like Lau San-ching or Wei Jingsheng, his commitment to his cause was total. Principle, as he saw it, was absolute. He would never give up.

And now he was sitting opposite me at a French café in Hong Kong, minus one lung but neatly groomed in casual Hong Kong fashion. He took care of his good looks. Only his height and his hazelnut eyes, set in a long, handsome face, gave him away as a northerner. He spoke mostly in English, which he had learned in Hong Kong after 1993. His residence in Hong Kong was really a matter of chance. For fear of bad publicity should a famous activist die in custody, the Chinese had sent Han to the United States for medical treatment in 1992. But when he tried to return, he was stopped at the border. Memories of 1989 were still fresh. Chris Patten, the last governor, was sympathetic to democrats and granted Han asylum in Hong Kong, something that is no longer possible today. Han is now a Hong Kong citizen.

He keeps in touch with people in China through a talk show, broadcast three times a week on Radio Free Asia. Hong Kong, after all, still has press freedom. Listeners phone in from anywhere in China where RFA is not blocked. They ask him for advice on work-related problems: workers laid off without pay; bosses who pocket their workers' wages; injuries resulting from faulty equipment or dangerous working conditions; workers who are sent to prison for complaining. Han, in short, deals with the dark side of capitalism with "Chinese characteristics," the explosion of problems caused by economic reforms unsupported by political reforms.

But even Han does not violate the deal made with Hong Kong: He refuses to be drawn into revolutionary politics. All he can do is advise workers on how they might best solve practical problems. He cannot tell them to overthrow the Communist Party, even though some of his desperate listeners might welcome such radical advice.

Though Han spoke softly, in a polite monotone, like Lau San-ching and others who had suffered for their absolute principles, the frequent tightening of his lips showed a barely suppressed anger. I noticed it especially when he talked about his relations with intellectuals and students. The students in Tiananmen Square, he said, did not want workers to join them. This was *their* movement, they had said; rougher elements might disrupt things, provoke violence, give the government an excuse to crack down. Han went and talked to them, trying to forge an alliance. But they kept him waiting or fobbed him off like a noisome supplicant. He tried to convince them that labor would be the biggest issue in China for years to come. They didn't care.

Later, when Han visited some of the prominent dissidents in New York and again stressed the importance of labor problems in China, they said that workers were "troublemakers" and "shouldn't be involved in political reforms."

"You know," said Han, very quietly, "Chinese intellectuals despise workers. Either they want nothing to do with us or they talk about workers as political tools to bring down the Communist Party. People say China is doing well. But the workers are not. We are the losers, and we have no freedom to speak out. It's no good relying on the intellectuals. The Communist Party was set up by intellectuals. We helped them come to power and look what happened. We are oppressed. No, we must organize ourselves."

Listening to Han's precise English and looking at his refined features and soft hands, I could understand why workers sometimes suspected him in 1989 of being an intellectual impostor posing as a working-class hero. Yet Han Dongfang *was* a worker, born in a dirt-poor village, in Shaanxi, one of the poorest provinces. His father had been a farmer and his mother a construction worker in Beijing. Han barely finished high school in Beijing, and worked as a prison guard and later as an electrician at a depot for old locomotives. But he did have a curious mind and a rebellious streak. During a six-month job in a university library, he read everything from Greek myths to Hemingway. And in the militia, he caused outrage by protesting that the officers were feasting on their soldiers' rations while the men went hungry.

This much about Han's life I knew already, from newspaper profiles and a book, *Black Hands of Beijing,* by Robin Munro and George Black. But I wanted to have a better understanding of the source of his rebellion, apart from generalities about labor problems in China. What was it that hardened his resolve to the extent that he was prepared to die in misery rather than give in? Where did his absolute dedication come from?

We took the ferry to Lamma Island, where Han lived with his wife and two sons, Nathan and Jonathan. At night the skyscrapers of Hong Kong Island are lit up like giant Christmas trees on one side of the bay. On the other side is Kowloon, with gleaming ocean liners moored at the quay, and ahead, toward the outlying islands, as far as the eye can see, are ships of all sizes, like stars in a velvety sky. On a very clear night, you might even see a few lights on the horizon blinking all the way from China.

"I was always bullied at school," Han said while staring into the distance. It was difficult to imagine this powerful man as a schoolyard victim. Then he told me how his parents got divorced and how he resented his father and felt uncomfortable when other children talked about their fathers. The children would bully him because he was poor. Even the teachers abused him at school. They said he was only fit to collect garbage. "Nobody liked us, because we were poor and from the provinces." When he was beaten up by other children, the teachers blamed him. If you're afraid of your teachers, he said, you're afraid of everything. His lips tightened, and he said, still in that soft voice: "I still loathe teachers."

Finally, he said, he could stand the abuse no longer, his patience snapped, and he wrestled the worst bully to the ground, kicking him and beating him until his face was bloody. He wouldn't let go until the boy promised never to hit him again. From then on, Han says, he had always stood up for himself and others in need. He repeated this story on several occasions. It was, as it were, his foundation myth. And yet he still didn't feel safe. Teachers, and by extension all figures in authority, were still a constant menace.

Six months later, in the summer of 1999, I saw Han again. We had breakfast near the waterfront in Central Hong Kong. Men and women in business suits rushed in and out of the Stock Exchange next door. Han ordered an espresso and a croissant. There was one more thing I wanted to know, something I had not asked him before, though I had been told it was important. During his short time in America, Han had become a fundamentalist Christian. I asked him why.

He hesitated, made as though to speak, stopped himself, nodded, and said: "Basically, it all comes down to trust."

When I didn't get his drift, he explained. Han was too young to have vivid memories of the Cultural Revolution—he was born in 1963, only three years before it began. But he does look back on a childhood packed with lies. His parents were ardent Maoists. His own name, Dongfang, meaning East, alludes to a popular song celebrating Mao rising, like the sun, in the east. Teachers would tell stories about proletarian heroes, like Lei Feng, the legendary soldier, selfless, ever ready to serve Mao, the people, and the Chinese revolution, the man who said that he would be "a bolt in whatever part of the state machinery the party wants to screw me," the martyr who was done in by a falling telegraph pole. Schoolchildren all over China, and adults too, had to sing the praises of Lei Feng's "screw spirit." Han wanted to be another Lei Feng. But he saw how teachers hated boys like himself, because they were poor. And he saw how officers abused their men. White began to look more and more like black. He came to realize that nobody in China could be trusted. Nobody at all.

"Nobody, not even your mother?"

"That is hard to say. Even my mother, yes even my mother. I cannot say I trust her. She would say: Criticize me if I'm wrong. But when I did, she would beat me. You see, I have a bad character, like a bull, I have three horns. But when the only person you feel safe with, when she betrays her own principles, you feel . . . confused."

For a long time he thought that communism was good, that the Party might contain some bad people but still stood for its principles. "The dream I grew up with was so beautiful, promising equality, a government serving the people. And yet reality looked so different." In the winter of 1986, when the astrophysicist Fang Lizhi was actively promoting democracy in his lectures, students demonstrated in Tiananmen Square for democratic reform. Han was not yet an activist. Fang Lizhi meant nothing to him. But his tiny courtyard dwelling was near the Square, and he happened to see the students being arrested. A militiaman kicked one in the face. Another was thrown into a jeep, like a pig. It was then, he says, that his communist dream was over.

It was then, also, that he began to turn to alternative beliefs. He spent time at a Buddhist temple. But he didn't know what to pray for anymore—a better life, a good future, or what? It was like "living in hell—losing your dreams." And the monks just mouthed platitudes about loving the Party, the people, and the motherland. Han tried to communicate directly to the Buddha. That gave him some relief, but not enough and not for long.

I felt what I had felt before when talking to brave men who craved an absolute faith: admiration mixed with the sense that here was an area I could never enter. It put us in different worlds.

"Religion," said Han, "is very important. Even believing in Mao makes you feel stronger, makes you feel that you are a human being, living more than a material, physical life. Any religion is better than no religion. If young people have no faith, no dream language, they are living in hell. That is what China is like now. If it goes on, it will fall apart."

Han was restating the position of many religious converts. It is not Christianity per se that leads to activism but the other way around. To be an activist with total dedication to the cause, it helps to have absolute faith. The need to believe in something, a dream, a God, a "principle," is largely what drives Han. It is how he survived torture and isolation. And it is why he was receptive to the blandishments of a Taiwanese priest who translated for him when he was being restored to health in the United States. Priests, he was told, were the only people you could trust.

Han's eyes lit up as he spoke: "I could not believe it at first. I thought it had to be for show. But people in the church trust one another. The church makes you feel strong."

"Like Maoism?"

"Yes, like Maoism, but communist heroes hate. The church is based on love, and on true equality. Jesus was a carpenter, the lowest of the low."

In the church, then, Han and others like him rediscovered a version of their Maoist dream. But Han, like everybody else involved in politics, however indirectly, faced a moral dilemma. How can trust be absolute if you have to make practical compromises? It was a problem that haunted him. He gave me a concrete example. Three men, working as long-distance bus drivers, called into his radio show one day to say they had not been paid by their company for three years. Meanwhile, their bosses had spent the equivalent of forty thousand U.S. dollars on nightclub entertainment, girls, gambling, airfare for private holidays, and fixing up their own houses. What should they do?

What should they do? "I don't want to be an irresponsible person and say the country is hopeless and incite bloody rebellion. Blood is valuable, and only the poor will be sacrificed. Rich people need only an airplane ticket to get out, and their children probably have green cards anyway. So I tell them to do everything openly, be responsible, and address their problems directly to the central government. And that is precisely what those three men did. They wrote an open letter to Jiang Zemin. But their bosses had good connections with Party officials. And as soon as they found out what had happened, the three workers were arrested for 'plotting to overthrow the government.' They could face jail sentences of more than ten years. And God know what will happen to them inside."

What could Han do? What can anybody do in China? Han feels guilty, to the point of despair, about advising people to take risks while he sits safely in his radio studio in Hong Kong. Han believes that slow, evolutionary change would be better, though much harder, than revolution. The price of violence is too high. And yet he fears an explosion. It is all very well to tell workers to complain to the central government, but there are no proper channels. All desperate people can really do is go into the streets and protest in ever-larger numbers. Many of Han's listeners are waiting for that day when things explode. "They don't like my advice," Han says. "They say my advice just gets people thrown in prison."

Han's anguish is all the more painful for the fact that in his heart he knows they are right.

Part III

The Motherland

Chapter 1

Frontier Zones

To cross the border into Shenzhen from Hong Kong at Lowu station is no longer the dramatic transition it once was. On the China side of the stinking canal, lined with fortified fences and watchtowers, are billboards for dot-com companies, massage parlors, fancy hotels, and houses in urban developments with names like Golden Villas and Dragon Park. The first thing you see as you step into the steaming streets of Shenzhen is the Marlboro Man facing the railway station. Beggars with livid stumps where once there were legs kneel on the railway bridge, whining with outstretched arms, a plastic bowl clutched in one hand. Country girls in high-heeled shoes whisper invitations. The contrast with Hong Kong is not so much between capitalism and communism as between the relative order of modern capitalism and a cruder, more lawless version. Shenzhen is where the rest of China is heading. The other difference is also immediately apparent. The moment you cross the border, you leave behind the liberties of Hong Kong, a free press, freedom of speech, freedom to openly criticize the government.

Shenzhen is best seen after midnight. The fetid air cools down. And the ugliness of a sprawling city built on the site of a minor agricultural town in Guangdong province is transformed into something almost glamorous. Hastily erected high-rise buildings, monuments of anxious post-Maoist grandiosity meant to impress through their sheer size, become great beacons of twinkling lights after dark. Some of the streets in the shabbier part of town, the part that is older than the fifteen years it took to build the rest of the city, are taken over by outdoor bars and restaurants. These are filled with crowds of largely young men and women from all over China: traders, computer salesmen, company managers, secretaries, bar hostesses, copywriters, prostitutes, graphic designers, disc jockeys, government officials, Hong Kong businessmen, and gangsters of one kind or another. The atmosphere is young and brash. A raw, even primitive, vitality—life reduced to food, sex, and money—flows through these new streets like a muddy river.

Shenzhen is not officially a city but a Special Economic Zone, a product of the Open Door policy, devised in the early 1980s by Deng Xiaoping. Like the old treaty ports, the SEZs are enclaves in the Chinese empire in which controls on commerce with the outside world are relaxed. Designed as a rival to Hong Kong, as well as a kind of Chinese Communist–style copy of it, Shenzhen was built by government fiat, as a monument to the Open Door. There, foreign goods and influences can be imported and, so far as possible, contained. A Chinese citizen needs special permission to live near the Open Door. The borders around the Zones are almost as formidable as the one sealing the rest of China off from Hong Kong.

The buildings are close approximations, and sometimes even direct copies, of buildings in Tokyo, Taipei, Singapore, and Hong Kong. But the political model, the kind of place Shenzhen, and in the long term perhaps the whole of China, is supposed to resemble, is not Hong Kong, let alone Taipei, but Singapore, where economic liberties are matched with political authoritarianism. Capitalism in the southern Chinese periphery is not supposed to evolve into democracy. Individual freedoms are subordinate to the patriotic demands of the state. That, at least, is the idea. Hence the other billboard at Lowu station, between ads for dot-com companies and massage parlors, which reads LOVE THE MOTHERLAND, LOVE CHINA.

China in this instance is like the Cosa Nostra: The main beneficiaries of capitalist enterprise are the local bosses who represent the state, the Party dons, and their minions. It is a world where official connections count for more than private initiative. To a lesser degree, and certainly in a less crude fashion, the same is true of Hong Kong and Singapore.

Another difference from Hong Kong is that Shenzhen, although located firmly in the Cantonese region, is not Cantonese. You can hardly hear Cantonese spoken in the streets. People come from all over, in the way that American pioneers headed west a hundred-odd years ago. Shenzhen is what Shanghai was in the early twentieth century, a city of immigrants, from such places as Hunan, Sichuan, Anhui, Beijing, or the industrial northeast. In the late 1970s there were about seventy thousand Cantonese living there. In 2000 there were almost 3 million people from everywhere else. The average age is about thirty. And the beggars are either old or very young.

People come to Shenzhen for all kinds of reasons, mostly to do with money. Village girls from Sichuan or Hunan come to work in the factories, dreaming of independence from the drudgery of rural life but also from fathers, brothers, or even husbands. If they are unlucky, their permits will be confiscated by the bosses, salaries reduced to a pittance, and their dreams of freedom turned into nightmares of virtual slavery. The prettier ones might escape the sweatshops and find work in bars, massage parlors, barbershops, discos, or brothels. Some will be taken up by businessmen from Hong Kong as "second wives." Certain areas in the zones have so many second wives living in pleasantly appointed apartment blocks that they have become like dormitory towns for mistresses. The female body is a basic commodity in Shenzhen.

Shenzhen, with its vast underground of illegal and exploited labor, is also a place of refuge for shadier characters. There, I once met a man who told me he was a military intelligence officer on the run. We sat in a bar called Chicago, in a haze of stale cigarette smoke.

He had the wild-eyed look of a young patriot in a Chinese propaganda poster: ablaze with sincerity. He spoke in a staccato of Chinese and broken English. Based in a provincial city in central China, so he said, his unit had been told to crack down on a demonstration of workers who had lost their jobs without pay. The PLA soldiers, including the intelligence officers, were sent in to do their job disguised in uniforms of the People's Armed Militia. The demonstrators were mostly old people. Shots were fired. The young officer protested and was reprimanded for "incorrect thinking." When he still wouldn't shut up, he was jailed. He felt his patriotism had been betrayed; trained to protect China against foreign enemies, he was not prepared to fire on unarmed Chinese. Now he would have his revenge. He would blow up banks; he would spy against the communists. He loved his country, but China was too corrupt. Did I know any intelligence people in the U.S.? His was one story in many. I do not even know whether it was true. But I wished him good luck before he disappeared into the seedy underworld of gangsters and "snakeheads," who smuggle people across the border for a fee.

Many young people with a higher education come to Shenzhen to learn English and to work for foreign companies. The Pearl River delta has been a source of emigrants for centuries, but the new type of emigrant is different from the Cantonese peasants who used to flee hunger and violence. In a sense, moving to Shenzhen allows you to get away from "China," with its oppressive central government, its patriotic dogmas, and its rigid family hierarchies, while still living in China. Shenzhen, people like to say, is a "cultural desert," a place "with no tradition," a zone "without history." The Chinese tradition is represented in large theme parks on the edge of town: a Chinese Folk Village, with mountains made of concrete, and Splendid China, where you ride in a golf cart past the Forbidden City of Beijing, along the Great Wall, and from there past the great Buddha of Leshan and the Wild Goose Pagoda of Xian, to the Dalai Lama's old palace in Lhasa. As the past is being obliterated everywhere in China, it is being reconstructed here.

Shenzhen, then, is "nowhere." But for many young Chinese that is precisely its attraction. To be relieved of the burdens of home, history, and tradition is a form of liberation. Opportunities await at the frontiers of the wild south—opportunities to make money, but also to carve out a modicum of personal freedom.

———

I was standing on a balcony of the seventeenth floor of a gigantic high-rise housing complex. It was built eight years ago, for relatively rich people. In the Zones, only the poor live near the ground. But the building already had a shabby, weatherworn look, with obscene graffiti in the elevators. I was standing there with Yang Yong, an artist from Sichuan, who came to Shenzhen with his wife, Yu Dongyu, a native of Beijing. We gazed at the urban skyline shimmering in the brownish, humid haze. On the far side was the soccer stadium, which is rarely used for sports but comes alive at night when the bars and discos clustered inside the stadium open up. Farther along were the green hills of the Hong Kong Special Administrative Region, out-of-bounds to Yang, and to most people living here. Between the stadium and those hills was downtown Shenzhen, its skyscrapers gleaming in the distance, and all around us was a sea of similar high-rise apartments, with barbershops, restaurants, supermarkets, and massage parlors on the ground floors.

Yang is a small, pudgy man in his early twenties, with bushy eyebrows and quick, inquisitive eyes. "All this," he said, making a sweeping gesture with his right arm, as though gathering the city in his arms, "didn't exist until about ten years ago. It was just countryside." I had heard almost the exact same words only the night before, from a publisher who came to Shenzhen from Yunnan in the early 1990s. We were having a drink in the bar on the top floor of a grand hotel, where a Filipino band was softly playing "Guantanamera." He had pointed out the window and down to the streaks of red and white lights from traffic rushing along a wide boulevard flanked by office buildings. "Nothing existed there before." Nothing at all, until Deng Xiaoping decided that a city should be built. And Deng came down from Beijing in 1992 and said it was good.

Yang likes Shenzhen—indeed loves it, "because everything is new." He could have gone to Beijing, the center of contemporary arts, but "politics is too complicated," and in Shanghai, he said, there was too much nostalgia. Shenzhen is simpler, and life, in Yang's phrase, is more "straightforward."

He had been a painter but now takes photographs, mostly intimate pictures of women sleeping, washing, eating, sitting on the toilet, brushing their teeth, lolling about in coffee shops and department stores. Some are self-consciously arty, "urban youth" posing with sunglasses, cigarettes, plastic guns; one girl injects herself with a needle—or pretends to. Some of the women are prostitutes. One is only fifteen. Yang has seen the work of American and Japanese photographers engaged in similar projects. But there is a freshness, a lightheartedness about the best of his pictures, a lack of cynicism, a reveling in a kind of freedom, that is remarkable. These urban youths, even the young prostitutes, don't look disaffected. Yang calls them lovable—*keai*. *Keai* is his favorite word of approval. Shenzhen people are *keai*. Hong Kong, in his view, is the opposite of *keai*: frenetic, grasping, hard-bitten. *Keai* is probably not the word most Chinese would use for Shenzhen. But compared to the rather metallic sophistication of Hong Kong, it is possible to see what he means.

We took the elevator to another apartment in the same block, where a friend of Yang's ran a small television production company. Yang wanted to borrow a video monitor to show me a film he had made. It was, like some of his photographs, a self-consciously arty film, based on one idea, which went on too long: Yang had superimposed an American porno film onto footage of a political demonstration in Shenzhen. The film was of three blond women licking and sucking each other on a large bed, making appropriate noises of pornographic lust. The demonstration was an officially orchestrated protest in 1999 against the NATO bombing of the Chinese embassy in Belgrade. The grunts and squeals of the women contrasted weirdly with the aggressive chanting of the crowd.

I had been in China during the summer after the bombing, and recalled the emotional intensity of those demonstrations, when the press was full of denunciations of U.S. "imperialist" aggression, recalling folk memories of older Chinese humiliations at the hands of alien powers. In Chengdu, the capital city of Sichuan, I saw an exhibition of news photographs taken at the bombing site, with gory pictures of the Chinese "martyrs"—a number of journalists rumored to have been intelligence agents. A youngish man poked me in the ribs and silently pointed at a sheet tacked onto the wall. It was filled with scribbled comments by the irate "people" of Chengdu. He was especially anxious that I read two sentences, in English, which he tapped hard with his forefinger, still without saying a word: "Fucking NATO! Clinton is number-one war criminal!"

And here we were watching a film that ridiculed these angry patriots. "Surely," I said to Yang, "this cannot be shown publicly in China." He chuckled and asked me why not. For political reasons, I said. Oh, but he wasn't interested in politics. This wasn't meant to be a political film, he said. It was about sex, about fucking, about coming to a climax. The frenzied demonstrators were no different from the porno actresses.

The film reminded me of "underground" movies I had seen in Japan during the 1970s, when many former political radicals had turned to pornography as a desperate antidote to the disappointments of failed activism in the 1960s. Japan was becoming ever more prosperous, and there was less and less room for political alternatives: Dissent had become irrelevant; the students no longer cared. Nihilism filled the vacuum of exhausted idealism. Only raw sex still had some vaguely subversive meaning.

———

China in 2000 was not Japan in the 1970s. But the mood of Yang's short film—and indeed his photographs—reflected a certain aspect of life in Shenzhen. There is something skewed, even unhinged, about a society that encourages raw commercial enterprise but stifles any kind of thinking, any personal initiative, or any organized expression that departs from government dogma. Privately people can think and even say more or less what they want. Compared to Maoist times, this is progress. But in the public sphere, you have Party propaganda, with its periodic campaigns promoting the "theories" of the current leaders, and you have the semi-liberated marketplace. But there is no official forum for debate, no public expression of private views, except in Internet chat rooms.

The marketplace is a wild and lawless place, fueled by corruption and sharp practices. Every time I came to Shenzhen, there were new revelations of scams in high places. In the summer of 2000, the Land Bureau of the Special Economic Zone government had virtually ceased to function, because too many officials, including vice-mayors, were being taken in for questioning. Vast bribes had been paid for building contracts. Government funds were used for stock-market speculation, making a few people enormously rich if it worked—and if it didn't, well, the money just leaked away unnoticed. Huge state loans were pocketed by friends and relatives of Party bosses. The Hong Kong press was full of other stories too, of a more violent nature: workers who had been maimed by faulty machines fired without compensation; prostitutes, or their clients, found dead in shabby hotel rooms; "connected" businessmen having rivals arrested on trumped-up charges.

The unintended consequence of a quasi–market economy is that some of these stories have appeared in the mainland press and on the Internet. Newspapers and magazines that do not rely on Party funds have to attract readers. Scandal is a universal lure, and there are few other checks on official abuse. Once in a while, if only for a limited time, a truly critical voice will slip through the net that normally shields government from public scrutiny.

He Qinglian came south in 1988 to work as a journalist for the *Shenzhen Legal Daily.* Ten years later she was famous. That *Pitfalls of Modernization,* her bestselling critique of the new China, appeared at all was more a function of official patronage than of the marketplace. After having been turned down by nine Chinese publishers, the book was rescued by Liu Ji, one of President Jiang Zemin's chief advisers and one of the authors of his political "theories." Communism is a bookish creed, so every Communist leader has to have his theory, usually published in heavy tomes and forced down the public throat in the form of tedious slogans. Jiang's main theory is the "Three Representations," meaning that the Party must be "represented"—that is, play a dominant role in the development of technology, culture, and economic progress. But Liu was more than a hack theorist. As vice-president of the Chinese Academy of Social Sciences, he made a cautious case for political reform. He Qinglian's ideas fitted Jiang's agenda. If she toned down some of her language and refrained from criticizing Party leaders directly, the book might strenghten Liu's case at Jiang's court. So with Liu's backing, the book was published. The first printing of 100,000 copies sold out quickly, an astonishing number for a heavy essay on economics, full of graphs and statistics. But criticism, especially good criticism, is almost as sexy as scandal in a country starved of intellectual debate. After the official publication, more than 300,000 copies were sold in five pirated editions.

He Qinglian's book confirms, in academic prose, what the scandal papers can only hint at—that China's capitalism is a dangerous hybrid of politics and criminality. She argues that power is the main commodity to be bought and sold. A small elite of bureaucrats and Party bosses use their positions to make vast amounts of money, mostly illegally, by squeezing a "simulated market," which is only quasi-free, since political power "determines the allocation of resources but has no need to see to their efficient use." She describes, among other things, how state officials buy natural resources at fixed government prices and sell them for huge profits on the private market and how they "privatize" a state industry by dismissing workers without pay and picking the enterprise clean of its assets. The result is a mafia economy, where the difference between political bosses and criminal dons is blurred, an economy where military officers profit from gambling and prostitution and gangsters lean on citizens to pay their taxes to local officials.

This sounds like a leftist attack on capitalism. But He is not against economic reforms, or capitalism per se. She simply points out that without democratic institutions, a quasi–free market becomes a tool for institutionalized crime and oppression. This is close to what the students were saying in 1989. But He, in fact, comes from an earlier generation. Her first mentors were the former Red Guards who attacked "bureaucratism" in the 1970s. Her book is in some ways an updated version of the famous Li Yi Zhe wall poster put up in Guangzhou in 1974 by Wang Xizhe and Chen Yiyang, among others.

He Qinglian writes about her debt to the former Red Guards, who learned their political lessons the hard way. She was a schoolgirl in Hunan when the Cultural Revolution raged and corpses of alleged class enemies came floating down the local river. While the brutality was shocking, she was excited by the idealism of young people going out to the countryside to build socialism with the peasants. After the worst violence was over, she was put to work on a rural railroad. A solitary girl of seventeen, she had little in common with the others on the construction site. She preferred to be alone with any books she could find. But reading was dangerous. When she picked up an anthology of Song- and Tang-dynasty literature, she was denounced for being a "feudal capitalist revisionist." Desperate for some kind of intellectual rapport, she made friends among former Red Guards who were a few years older. She remembers these encounters with the intensity of a religious revelation. Her new friends talked through the night about the future of China, and discussed Diderot, Voltaire, and obscure nineteenth-century Russian social critics with giddy enthusiasm. It was from them, He recalls, that she learned the meaning of humanism. Most of them disappeared into obscurity. They were the "lost generation." And the idealism of those terrible years faded with them. He's book about the corruption of post-Mao China was, she says, an attempt to recapture some of the intensity she had felt in those early days, and to revive the idealistic spirit of her lost comrades. Like them, she felt a patriotic duty to help China.

He Qinglian had learned another lesson from the past. Chinese intellectuals had too often become servants of the state, and in most cases its victims. By the late 1970s, when she entered Fudan University in Shanghai to study economics, Deng Xiaoping had begun his economic reforms and the Soviet-style economics taught by He's professors was hopelessly out of date. These professors were lost men, who had never had the freedom to think for themselves. But for a short while in the early 1970s, when everything was topsy-turvy, a certain kind of independence had been forged by a few young people as a result of the Cultural Revolution's violent anarchy. City girls would go into the country filled with socialist idealism and end up being raped by brutalized peasants. Boys, who believed the Maoist slogans about fighting class enemies, found that Party bosses were the worst offenders against the common people. Disillusion, chaos, and a residue of idealism had made them question all dogmas and certainties. It is that spirit of independence, as well as the humanism, that He sees as her most precious inheritance from the lost generation.

He's voice, like that of other independent thinkers, could not be tolerated for long. When I arrived in Shenzhen in the summer of 2000, she had become the latest "liberal" to be silenced. Earlier in the year, President Jiang Zemin announced that "bourgeois liberals" and other thinkers who failed to heed "Party discipline" were to be purged. The editor of a liberal magazine was ousted, other magazines and websites were closed down, and several prominent members of the Chinese Academy of Social Sciences lost their jobs after publishing articles advocating political reforms and human rights. One of them was He's mentor, Liu Ji. The Internet was seen as a particular threat to Party dogma, so operators of several websites that posted unwelcome arguments or information were arrested. None of this was accompanied by violence. Times had changed to that extent. Repression was more subtle now.

So it was with He Qinglian. She published a long article in a Hunan literary journal restating the arguments of her book, bluntly this time. Corruption was not just a matter of individual malfeasance, she said, but had become systemic. In a one-party state, the political elite cared only about its own interests. Corruption had become a "source of political capital." And any attempt by those outside the Party elite to defend their interests through political parties, independent organizations, or public criticism was crushed. The result, she argued, was catastrophic for China. The environment was being systematically wrecked, national resources were plundered, and masses of people were turned into beggars or slaves. Without democratic reforms, there was no way to stop the country from being ruined by official mafiosi, who had already taken the precaution of sending their own children abroad.

He's article appeared in March 2000. This was the last time her voice would slip through the official net. Returning from a trip to America in June, she was told by her editor at the *Shenzhen Legal Daily* that she would no longer have her old position. She was demoted with a hefty salary cut, and her writing would no longer be published. The editor was embarrassed, but what could he do? It was all done very quietly. He Qinglian was famous. To arrest her would cause more trouble than it was worth. But a few words of intimidation slipped like poison into the ear of her boss were enough to snuff out one more critical voice in China.

He Qinglian lives with her husband and child in a housing complex not far from the center of Shenzhen. I could not immediately find the right apartment, but saw an open door on her floor, leading into a virtually bare room. Three men were lolling about in their undershirts in a haze of cigarette smoke. I noticed the peculiar odor of cheap scent. I asked them if they knew where apartment 15G was. They looked me up and down, and one of the men lazily waved his hand at a door without saying a word.

He, dressed in a Chinese-style shirt buttoned at the neck, asked me to come in, and offered a cup of delicious green tea. The sound of soupy Chinese folk melodies played on some kind of electronic organ came rather too loudly from the bedroom. He pointed at the wall separating her apartment from the men next door. "I don't want them to hear what we are saying," she said.

I asked her who they were. She shrugged. *"Man haowan,"* she said, in a Hunanese accent—"great fun." It was a favorite expression. She proudly showed me a message on the Internet praising her article. That too was "great fun." The fact that her writing was going to be published in a British journal, the *New Left Review,* was also great fun. And so were the men next door. But she didn't smile. She hummed nervously instead. Usually, when I asked her a question, she jumped up from her chair, saying, "I wrote about that very clearly," and reached for a book or magazine article she had written. A dark, smallish woman with rather severe eyes peering through a pair of steel-framed glasses, He might seem arrogant. Perhaps she put a little bit too much stress on how often she was being interviewed these days by this famous foreign newspaper or that. There was a framed article on the wall, from an English-language news magazine, that featured her as one of the "rising stars" in Asia. She was proud of her reputation.

It is always tempting to overrate the importance of intellectuals. They are the people most journalists and academics talk to in a country like China. And intellectuals have a keen sense of their own importance, fed, perversely, by the close attention paid to them by their authoritarian governments. Whatever her own sense of self-worth, He Qinglian writes very well about the role of intellectuals in China, whom she places among the losers after Deng's reforms. They are not so much needed anymore as official scribes and ideologues now that ideology, largely bankrupt anyway, is no longer the main point. In the world of the quasi-marketplace, intellectuals count for less.

He Qinglian still makes a strong case, however, for the importance of independent thinkers. What impressed her most during her visit to the United States was the freedom of people to criticize their government. I asked her what she thought of the dissidents abroad. Was Wei Jingsheng still a force? Did people read émigré writings, on the Internet perhaps? She said their influence on China was quite small. They had gained a kind of independence but had lost their public. Could she see herself living abroad? She said she would rather not. "Our voices in China are already so few. If I leave, that would mean one critic less." She poured me another cup of green tea, humming under her breath. Then she glanced at the wall, with the framed article praising her as a "star," the wall that separated her from the men who were watching her day and night, and said: "But then it isn't only up to me, is it?" We exchanged e-mail addresses. "Great fun," she said with sadness in her eyes as she showed me out the door.

Almost exactly one year later, He escaped to the U.S., after security agents had broken into her apartment and taken away documents, her cell phone, and even photographs of He with foreign friends.

———

He Qinglian, like Martin Lee, thinks the rule of law is impossible in a society without democratic institutions. Laws protect citizens from the arbitrary power of the state, and the best way to make sure that law functions in that way is to have a judiciary that is independent of the state and lawmakers who are accountable to the citizens who elect them. This is not the way things were traditionally done in China—or, indeed, until not so long ago, anywhere else. The Chinese ideal was rule by virtuous men, not by law. The law was an instrument for officials to control the people, which is why some argue that benevolent authoritarianism is more natural to China than democracy, that Jiang Zemin is more "Chinese" than "bourgeois liberals" such as He and Lee.

In fact, however, Chinese thinkers reflected on the rule of law and how to limit the power of rulers long before bourgeois liberalism or communism were even thought of. Huang Zongxi, a seventeenth-century scholar, wrote a famous treatise, entitled *Waiting for the Dawn: A Plan for the Prince,* that somewhat resembles Machiavelli, even in its title. But more to the point, Huang was wrestling with some of the very same issues that exercise liberals in China today. Once, he says, princes were unselfish guardians of the empire's well-being, but that was long ago. Now, once a ruler had attained absolute power, "he clubbed and flayed the bones and marrow of the empire, and he scattered the sons and daughters of the empire, in order to provide for his own sensual pleasure. He deemed it natural, and said that this was the profit from his own business."

And here is Huang's solution: "Should it be said that 'there is only governance by men, not governance by law,' my reply is that only if there is governance by law can there be governance by men. Since unlawful laws fetter men hand and foot, even a man capable of governing cannot overcome inhibiting restraints and suspicions."

By unlawful laws, Huang meant dynastic laws, which only served the interests of the imperial family. Rulers, in his view, should be subject to higher laws, devised by the ancient sages Confucius and Mencius and administered by learned mandarins. That Huang, a Han Chinese, resented being ruled by a dynasty of Manchus no doubt had something to do with this opinion, as did his desire to strengthen the position of scholar-officials like himself. But still, his ideas, which were to have a profound influence on the republican revolutionaries less than three hundred years later, illustrate that Chinese also understood how law could be the most effective tool to limit the inevitable excesses of absolute power.

Lawyers who attempt to use the law in that way are often heroes, and, like many critics of Chinese despots in the past, often end up as martyrs.

In 1998, a young lawyer in Nanjing was asked to defend a rural official who had been accused of taking bribes. It appeared to be a straightforward case. The lawyer did his best, and he found people willing to testify to his client's innocence. But local authorities had decided to find the official guilty—probably because he had gotten in some higher official's way. The defense witnesses failed to turn up in court. And the lawyer himself was jailed for "illegally obtaining evidence."

In Shaanxi, farmers protesting that they were being forced to pay too much tax had been tortured by village officials. The lawyer who agreed to petition the central government in Beijing on their behalf was promptly arrested, then sentenced to five years in prison for "disturbing social order."

One day I chanced upon an article about yet another lawyer, Zhou Litai. It was a short report from the Agence France-Presse: An eighteen-year-old named Fu Xulin had his right hand ripped off by a molding machine in a factory in Shenzhen, where he had been making Christmas toys for U.S. $40 a month. The factory owner, from Hong Kong, refused to pay for surgery that would have restored Fu's hand, but offered to send him away with a modest sum. When Fu refused the offer, he was locked up in a room at the factory. In the end, Fu might well have ended up on the streets clutching a plastic begging bowl in his left hand. But he was rescued by the lawyer Zhou Litai, who gave him shelter and took up his case for nothing.

Fu Xulin was extraordinarily lucky. About twenty thousand men and women in the Shenzhen area suffer disabling accidents every year. The old and badly maintained machines are operated by poorly trained workers for ten or more hours a day. Factory owners, often from Hong Kong or Taiwan, know that the supply of workers is endless. Local officials, wined, dined, and often bribed by the factory owners, care only about profits. And although workers are supposed to be covered by state insurance, in case of accidents, the money rarely comes their way. Zhou Litai is the only lawyer in the Shenzhen area prepared to take up some of their cases.

To visit Zhou I took a taxi from Shenzhen to Longgang, an industrial town on the other side of the border that divides the Special Economic Zone of Shenzhen from the rest of China. Cars rush through from the Shenzhen side. Cars coming from the opposite direction stand idle, in long queues, their drivers honking in a blue carbon-monoxide haze. Longgang is a grubby town with a wide road running through raw-concrete housing blocks. There are many new hotels, however, with Hong Kong and foreign businessmen hanging around the air-conditioned lobbies. And there are the usual seedy-looking karaoke bars, discos, and massage parlors decorated with fairy lights and white-plaster statues of Venus. Around the town is a strip of factories, belching yellow smoke into the rank, humid air.

Zhou rents an apartment in a housing complex. It was hard to get hold of him, for his telephone was usually out of order. I was shown the way by a young man dressed in jeans and a cotton shirt, with one short sleeve flapping, armless, in the wind. He was from Hunan and his arm had been mangled in a plastics factory. The street outside the apartment block was unpaved and filled with discarded plastic bags and broken bottles. We climbed the concrete stairs, which were still slimy from a burst waterpipe. I noticed a smell of blocked drains in the hall.

Zhou greeted me from a sofa in his main room. A stocky man in his forties, with a wide, crooked mouth and a bad haircut, he was dressed only in shorts and plastic sandals. Around him were a few men, all of whom were lacking something, a limb or a hand. One man had no arms. Zhou offered to show me around the place. He opened a few doors to small, stuffy rooms filled with old mattresses. People, some barely out of their teens, were sleeping snugly together, like puppies in basket. They too were handicapped in various ways. Altogether, Zhou had taken seventeen workers into his apartment. A blackboard in the main room listed various household duties and the dates of court appearances.

We sat down in a tiny room, which functioned as Zhou's office. Zhou's naked stomach bulged, like a small melon, over his shorts. On the floor was a sleeping figure with hideous burns on his back and legs. Occasionally he would stir, moaning. I asked Zhou how he managed to finance his law practice. How could he make these cases pay? Instead of giving a direct answer, he gave me a summary of his life, occasionally interrupted by loud screams from another room, whereupon he would leave the room to see what was going on. I heard more shouting, followed by a whining sound. Then Zhou would return to resume where he had left off.

Zhou Litai was born in 1956 in a small village in Sichuan. His parents were poor farmers. Two and a half years in the village school were all the formal education he had. But at least he had learned to read. Like He Qinglian, he read anything he could lay his hands on, mostly stories of Communist heroes, such as Lei Feng, the self-sacrificing martyr who wanted to be a "rustless" screw in the Maoist machine. In 1974, Zhou joined the army, inspired perhaps by the heroic stories. It was also the quickest escape from village life. He was sent to Tibet, where discipline was harsh, but again Zhou escaped into the heroic world of Communist literature: uplifting stories about patriotic soldiers in the Korean War or self-sacrificing workers in steel foundries.

There was not much Zhou could do with a mere two and a half years of formal schooling. After leaving the army in 1978, he worked in a brick factory in Hunan. And there his idealism, shaped by official fantasies of heroism, turned into anger. The workers were treated like slaves, bullied, humiliated, and driven to the limits of their endurance. When they were injured, they were simply replaced by others. That is when Zhou realized that people had to stand up for their rights. It was the only way to stop the bosses from getting away with capricious brutality.

Zhou left the factory for a menial job in a prosecutor's office near his old hometown. He dedicated the next few years to teaching himself the law, sitting up nights studying, copying, reading. In 1986, at last, he was able to take the national exams and qualify as a lawyer. After setting up an office in Chongqing, he came down to Shenzhen to specialize in workers' rights.

Factory bosses hate him, the social security bureaucrats wish him dead, and there have been threats—and violence. Some of his clients, who finally got paid thanks to his efforts, ran off without giving him a cent in legal fees. He has to rely on charity, some of it from Hong Kong, on loans from friends, and on the odd commercial case. Yet, in the way of the self-sacrificing heroes of his youth, Zhou carries on, because, as he puts it, "Seas change into mulberry fields, and mulberry fields into seas"—that is to say, everything changes over time.

Zhou spoke to me softly, in a heavy Sichuan accent. It was clear he had rehearsed the story many times before. His life has been reported in the Chinese press, as a tale of heroism and self-sacrifice. It had the pattern of traditional Chinese tales of virtue: the heroic industriousness of the poor scholar beating all the odds, the willingness to give up everything to serve others. It was a Confucian pattern, often adapted by the Communists. Perhaps that is why Zhou became too well known to disappear easily into a prison. What is extraordinary, however, about his version of the traditional narrative is that he turned it into a story about the rule of law. Here was a stubborn, intelligent man, who could not be called westernized in any meaningful way. In terms of social background, political culture, or education, Zhou Litai could not be further removed from Martin Lee, and yet he had reached a similar conclusion: Only under the rule of law can people be safe from official bullies.

But can the rule of law exist without democratic institutions? Zhou is not a political activist. Nor is he a revolutionary, who aims to save China. He does not talk about China in abstract terms. Zhou believes in rights, in legality, in a more "positive social environment, where the rule of law prevails." If one believes, as do He Qinglian, Martin Lee, and Wei Jingsheng, that such an environment can come about only after a systemic change, which would constitute a revolution, then Zhou's mulberry fields will never change into seas. He will do good, force factory bosses to concede here and there, perhaps even bring about some changes in the law. But the rule of law will remain elusive. And Zhou, like others scattered across the Chinese empire, will be a lonely hero, sacrificing, fighting against all the odds, but limited in the end to putting bandages on the wounds of a fatally flawed system.

—

According to He Qinglian, 60 percent of China's wealth is owned by 1 percent of the population. Yet this is still nominally a socialist society, ruled by a Communist party. "To Get Rich Is Glorious," the slogan coined by Deng Xiaoping to justify his economic reforms, is fine as far as it goes. Enough young people still hope to get rich, and enjoy the new freedoms of life in the large coastal cities and economic zones. But what will happen when the gold rush ends, when millions fall behind, when the promise of riches turns out to be hollow? What then? How can the Communist Party justify its monopoly on power when the quasi–free market goes bust? People will not have the satisfaction of voting their rulers out of power. They cannot even criticize them for their mistakes. But what will the rulers have left?

The Pearl River delta, stretching between Shenzhen and Guangzhou, is a frontier zone of new cities, destroyed landscapes, and cultural poverty, despised by northerners as a crude, cultural desert. Yet the area is soaked in history. Guangzhou is where the Chinese revolution of 1911 began. The first republican prime minister of China, Dr. Sun Yat-sen, was born in the delta, in a place that now bears his name. You can visit his old house, a comfortable two-story gray-brick building in a bamboo grove, a short walk from a kind of religious theme park featuring huge golden Buddhas and Indian-style temples. But the grandest, newest, flashiest historical museum in the region is about an hour's drive from Shenzhen, on the site of China's greatest official humiliation.

The Naval Warfare Museum is rather like a large American convention center, with an enormous parking lot. It looks out onto the muddy

Pearl River, spanned by a brand-new suspension bridge near the town of Humen. Under the bridge, next to the museum, are the old gun batteries, built in the 1830s, that were supposed to have stopped the opium-pushing barbarians from reaching Guangzhou. These fixed cannon were the finest made in China. A folk rhyme about Humen, or Boca Tigris as it was then called, went: "Hard to enter, even harder to get out." And yet when the barbarians forced open China's door to sell drugs, and anything else the Chinese might wish to buy, the guns hardly did any good at all. In 1834, two British frigates sailed past them. In 1840, a larger fleet simply ignored them. And a year later, they were destroyed.

It might seem a little odd to erect a huge museum to commemorate such a humiliating defeat. In fact, there is a second, only slightly older, museum in the town of Humen itself, which is now a veritable Lourdes for wounded patriots. On the spot where, in 1839, the imperial commissioner Lin Zexu had 3 million pounds of raw opium dissolved in pits filled with water, salt, and lime, you can visit the Opium War Museum and the Lin Zexu Memorial.

Commissioner Lin was not a xenophobe but a brave and honest man, who ordered a translation of Vattel's *Law of Nations* and wrote a famous letter to Queen Victoria protesting the opium trade: "Suppose there were people from another country who carried opium to England and seduced your people into buying and smoking it; certainly [you] would deeply hate it and be bitterly aroused. . . ." After China's defeat in the first Opium War, poor Lin was sent away in disgrace.

Outside the Opium War Museum is a small, dark shrine where Lin, the "patriotic hero," is worshipped together with other deified heroes, whose statues are placed next to those of the God of War and the Yellow Emperor. The museum is earmarked as a "National Educational Model Base of Patriotism," to which schoolchildren, company employees, and soldiers are bused in for patriotic propaganda.

The shrine reminded me of a similar monument in Taiwan, where the legendary loyalist to the Ming dynasty, Cheng Ch'eng-kung (Koxinga), is remembered. Koxinga had to retreat to Taiwan to escape the Manchu invaders of the Qing. There, in 1662 he expelled the Dutch from their trading post. He, too, fought against foreign domination, but at least he was never defeated, and even enjoyed a victory of sorts. In Nationalist patriotic education, Koxinga's heroic retreat was the model for the KMT's last stand against the Communist regime—an enemy that was of Chinese blood but enslaved to an alien creed. I visited the Koxinga temple in Tainan after the KMT had lost its dominance on Taiwan. It was a sad, dilapidated place. The few visitors were mostly old.

Not many people were around when I visited the Lin Zexu Memorial, either. Two young men lay fast asleep where the opium had been dissolved. I read the words engraved in rather clumsy calligraphy on the stone wall: THIS IS WHERE LIN ZEXU HAD THE OPIUM DESTROYED. This banal statement was written by Premier Li Peng, the man most people hold responsible for the Tiananmen killings. Opposite the shrine for Lin and the Yellow Emperor was a wall with a painting of nineteenth-century British warships. For a small fee, visitors were invited to shoot rubber bullets at them. The ships had begun to fade, as though shrouded in gunsmoke, where countless bullets had hit home.

Once more the Communists have updated an earlier myth of patriotic resistance against foreign imperialists. A text on the wall of the Naval Warfare Museum explains, in Chinese and English, inside a large tableau of furious Chinese people, eyes bulging with rage, like revolutionary workers in a socialist-realist Soviet poster: "Facing the invaders with sharp weapons, the Chinese people were not afraid, but bravely resisted. As the Qing government was corrupted and the ruler pursued a compromise policy, the resistance finally failed. However, the sublime national integrity and great patriotic spirit of Chinese people displayed during the anti-invading struggle had cast a national statue that would never disappear. And it has been encouraging one Chinese generation after another to make a sustained effort for the prosperity of the nation."

"Prosperity of the nation," the Party's post-Maoist goal, dates the text accurately. It suggests that the nineteenth-century heroes were forerunners of Deng Xiaoping's economic reforms. The facts are more complicated. Opium was an unfortunate product with which to inaugurate trade with China, but demand in China was high, and foreign and Chinese merchants, the latter often in league with criminals and corrupt officials, were making huge profits in the opium trade. In a way, the barbarians who came to China's shores in the 1830s were the pioneers of the Open Door policy. They wanted freedom to trade and legal protection.

The last imperial government was poorly placed to grant such favors, for it had an attitude as well as a currency problem. Imports and domestic taxes had to be paid in silver, while other domestic transactions were done in copper. People were hard-pressed to pay their taxes, while the opium trade was draining the country of precious silver. A further complication was the imperial court's refusal to accept foreigners as equals. China was late in adjusting to the practices of the modern world. Foreigners were supposed to bear tribute, not trade. The resulting clash between traditional imperial ideas and modern trade practices cost China dearly. And yet officials who persisted in hopeless resistance are still worshipped as patriotic heroes, whereas those who advocated compromise and more freedom to trade are remembered as traitors to the Chinese race.

The wording of the patriotic myth is telling, if a little disingenuous. The hopeless fight against superior British forces is equated with the "sustained effort for the prosperity of the nation." And the "integrity of the nation" for which the brave Chinese people fought is modern code for national reunification with Tibet, Hong Kong, and Taiwan. But the most important message is that the "patriotic spirit" of the "anti-invading struggle" was a question not only of national but of ethnic pride. Indeed, the Chinese "nation" becomes—or became in the nineteenth century—an ethnic idea: the Han Chinese against the barbarians, but also against the corrupt Manchus. This idea of China, born in humiliation, is meant to include all those of Han Chinese blood. In fact, it has little resonance in Taiwan or in cosmopolitan Hong Kong, which have their own foundation myths, though overseas Chinese in Europe and the United States are more susceptible to this last refuge of a bankrupt Communist government.

I was surprised at first to see Li Peng's calligraphy carved into the Lin Zexu Memorial's wall, for it seemed rather late to be putting so much effort into the history of the Opium War. But in fact it makes sense. After the debacle of 1989, the government needed every shred of legitimacy it could find. Economic growth through mafia capitalism is not enough. And throwing the door open to foreign trade, however beneficial in the long run, is a risky enterprise. Some Chinese will end up richer; many will not.

So the more China's door widens and the wilder things get in the wild southern Zones, the more people must be reminded of earlier humiliations. By claiming to be heirs of the "patriotic heroes" and not of the collaborators of foreign traders, the government can blame the ill effects of its own policies on wicked barbarians. Only the Chinese Communist Party can protect the Chinese people from another bout of racial impotence. This is the only claim it has left.

Chapter 2

Roads to Bethlehem

A recorded voice over the public address system on the train to Guangzhou pointed out, rather too loudly, the historic beauty spots of the region while I looked out the window at the landscape flashing by: sad stumps of dynamited hills, orange-brown, like dried blood; uniform rows of numbered concrete housing blocks; high-rise buildings with colonial-style finishes; factories belching plumes of pus-colored smoke; bulldozers, cranes, open pipelines, a half-finished overpass broken off in mid-air; and here and there, a duck pond, rice paddy, or polluted canal to show what this part of the country had looked like as recently as fifteen years ago.

I was heading to meet Grace Liu, a friend from America. Grace had left her native Guangzhou for the United States in the 1980s, when she was still a schoolgirl. She had become a sassy, well-dressed New Yorker, with high ambitions and a brassy voice, which, if you disregarded the American accent, sounded rather like that of the Cantonese announcer on the train. I had noticed in the U.S. that she used the word "we" a lot: "We Americans," "We conservatives," and, on occasion, "We Chinese."

Grace was staying with her aunt. From the great height of her aunt's apartment, on the twenty-fifth floor, the urban chaos of Guangzhou looked like a cheap mishmash of Tokyo, Taipei, Hong Kong, and Singapore, a jumbled conglomeration of highways, overpasses, high-rise office buildings, apartment blocks, shops, discotheques, and hotels, all built at great speed and with minimum taste. Guangzhou lacks the style of Tokyo or even Taipei and has none of the cosmopolitanism of Shenzhen. And apart from the odd colonial-style villa or tarted-up Buddhist temple, there was not much evidence of the city's rich history.

It was hot and only just past lunchtime. We drank iced Coca-Cola from tall green glasses. Grace's aunt was married to a successful businessman, one of the beneficiaries of the Open Door. So she no longer needed to work. Dressed in a frilly purple satin housedress, she padded around the apartment, which was furnished with a shiny brown sofa, covered in plastic, facing a gigantic black television with a video player. A crystal waterfall cascaded from the ceiling, and the mantelpiece was adorned by a large gold clock, which every so often broke into a tune.

I was rather relieved when Grace suggested a visit to a Buddhist temple. In the taxi, she told me of her plans. She wanted to help build a "civil society" in China and restore Chinese "spiritual values." This time she spoke of "we Chinese."

Civil society?

Yes, Grace said, for China was lacking in spiritual values. What was badly needed was religion, to hold the country together in preparation for democracy, which was the ultimate aim. But you couldn't have democracy overnight. That would plunge the country into chaos. The first thing was to revive religious faith.

Grace herself was a Buddhist. Not, she said, that she was like those "granola kids," looking for their roots in the exotic East. She despised them. No, with her it was something deeper, more a matter of common ancestral feeling. We arrived at the temple, a crude concrete building plus pagoda, elaborately decorated in the Qing-dynasty style. The site was old, but the temple had been destroyed during the Cultural Revolution and then rebuilt in the 1980s. Grace asked me whether I would like to burn some incense, to "share" the experience, as it were, though this was not an expression she would have used; that was more for the granola kids. She got on her knees before a coarsely made, brightly shining golden Buddha and folded her hands in prayer.

I asked her why she thought a religious revival was so important for China's democratic prospects. Well, she said, "we Chinese share common values. Buddhism is deeply ingrained in us."

Talk of common values shared by an entire race always makes me edgy. I said something dismissive, which put Grace on the defensive. We were racing along in a taxi from the Buddhist temple to the Academy of Social Sciences, where I had made an appointment with Chen Yiyang, co-author with Wang Xizhe and others of the 1974 Li Yi Zhe manifesto, with which the pro-democracy movement in China began. He was also the former boyfriend of my friend in Washington D.C., Gong Xiaoxia, who had joined his group of activist friends in the 1970s. Grace repeated her assertion, raising her voice a fraction: "We Chinese have a common feeling about China, you know, like, we love China and want to make China strong again."

Chen Yiyang came out to meet us at the elevator on the top floor of the academy building. He was in charge of the classical Chinese library. There was nobody else around, only Chen, a slim man in sandals, with long, thin hands and the fine, bony face of a monk. He looked older than his fifty-odd years. It was hard to imagine that this scholarly figure had once led tens of thousands of Red Guards in ferocious street battles. He placed two cups of hot water—what Chinese call white tea—on a long wooden table and poured none for himself.

Chen was on his own in the library, he explained, because no one was interested in classical Chinese literature anymore. Hardly anybody came up to his floor these days, not even to destroy the old books. Young people found it hard to read anything published before 1949, let alone 1900. The characters were too complicated, the style too abstruse. It suited him fine, Chen said, to be on his own. I looked at the dusty stacks of hand-stitched classical tomes, mostly from the nineteenth century, some older. It suited him, he said, because it gave him time to think.

Chen was one of the pioneers of the dissident movement in Communist China, but his radicalism had long ago faded into resignation. Perhaps he never had the temperament of the absolute believer, dedicated totally to a cause. Like Wang Xizhe, Chen had done hard labor in the countryside, and I knew from Gong Xiaoxia that he had suffered terribly from his two years in jail as a "counterrevolutionary" in the late 1970s. But he was not made to be a martyr. And now he seemed to have pulled back from the world, away from danger. Questions about his past met with short answers and an embarrassed smile.

The nature of his embarrassment was not easy to fathom. Was it guilt about the violence in which he had been caught up, and had perhaps instigated, in the 1960s? Guilt for having beaten up innocent people? His teachers, or perhaps even his parents? Remorse is not something I had often found among former Red Guards. Su Xiaokang, the writer of *River Elegy* who now lives in Princeton, was an exception. "We all feel deep guilt," he had said. "All of us who went through the Cultural Revolution feel guilty." If Chen felt the same, he never said so. I don't think Chinese culture offers much of a clue for this common reticence. It is more likely that suffering often cancels out feelings of personal guilt. Almost no one who lived under Mao was entirely a victim or a perpetrator. Most people were both. This is part of the wickedness of Maoism: Almost every urban Chinese was an accomplice at one time or another.

On later occasions, in the same library, Chen told me about his mother, who had been very ill while he was in jail. She was literally worried sick. He had not wanted to give her more grief. In his fine handwriting, Chen wrote down four Chinese characters on a piece of paper: "Live in peace, work in joy." That is what most Chinese want, he said: Everyone is terrified of more upheavals. So he lived a quiet life now, with his wife, child, and mother. "A small paradise" was the phrase he used, and his gaunt face creased in a look that was both rueful and, apparently, contented.

Chen was no longer actively concerned with contemporary politics. A few years ago he had tried to write something about the importance of civil liberties but couldn't get it published. Democracy would in any case be a slow process. It was no good just believing in slogans, "as we used to do." First people had to learn to think freely. Chen showed us two books he had written, one on Buddhism and one on Taoism. "Religion is very important," he said. Although he himself was not a believer, he often visited temples and shrines, for "Chinese forms and traditions must be pre-served."

I could see Grace's face light up when she heard this. She was nodding vigorously, perhaps a bit for my benefit, too. But Chen's interest in religion was not the same as hers. His was less emotional and more intellectual. Whereas Grace had spoken about the need to "bond" as a people, through "shared values," Chen criticized the Chinese for their lack of self-scrutiny. Too much in China, he believed, goes unexamined. "People talk about the Chinese as though they were one people," he said, "but the very idea of China goes unexamined. After all, what is China? Taiwan, Hong Kong, the People's Republic? The great weakness of Chinese civilization is the lack of analysis, of logical criticism." Grace had stopped nodding and wore a puz-zled frown.

What, I asked, did the lack of analysis have to do with religion?

His answer should not have surprised me, for I had heard it before, from Li Lu, the former student leader, and Fang Lizhi, the astrophysicist, among others. Like them, Chen believed that Christianity had laid the foundation for Western inquiry and science. Belief in a universal God had raised philosophical questions about the nature of the universe, whereas to the Chinese, faith had always been a pragmatic affair, a set of rules to gain power and wealth. That is why Europe had science while China had only "technique." Europeans explored the truth, whereas Chinese had learning and dogmas. They were not interested in the truth.

Each time I met Chen on subsequent occasions, surrounded by his Qing-dynasty books, we argued about this rose-tinted take on Christian-ity and Western civilization. What about the Greek tradition? Wasn't logi-cal analysis far more rooted in that? And wasn't the Christian religion responsible for a great deal of obscurantism and intolerance? Well yes, of course, there was that too, but the belief in God . . . And so it went, neither of us able to convince the other.

In their different ways, both Grace Liu and Chen Yiyang were emi-grants of a kind. Grace had literally emigrated with her family. Having left, she had developed a romantic view of "China." Kneeling to the golden Buddha was her way of sharing ancestral feelings. Later that summer, she visited other Buddhist temples in the hope of rekindling more of those feelings. Tibet was to be the final destination. But she gave up halfway. The hotels were too shabby and the toilets too dirty. In the chaos of the real China, her feeling of "we Americans" gained the upper hand over "we Chinese." Yet she romanticized "we Americans," too, and complicated matters with a third "we": "we conservatives." Like others of her generation, Grace had rebelled against her professors, who had come of age in the 1960s. She hated "political correctness."

"We conservatives" had different "shared values," such as "order, stability, religion, and a certain suspicion of democracy." She tried to explain all this in a famous restaurant that specialized in dog stew. People at other tables shouted, red-faced, over their steaming hotpots and looked happy in the heat and the noise. "Foreigners," Grace said, were "irritating." I wasn't immediately sure whom she meant. But then: People who don't speak English with an American accent were "annoying." Grace was happy when she saw an American flag.

This was partly her way of getting a rise out of me, a European who grew up in the 1960s. I decided to challenge her nonetheless. What exactly was that "bond" of which she spoke, the one "shared" by "us Americans"?

She hesitated, reaching for the right words: "Ah, greatness, uniqueness . . ."

Unique in what respect?

Again, hesitation. "Freedom, openness to immigrants, um . . ."

Grace combined the ethnic patriotism of Chinese propaganda with the conservative American patriotism of the first-generation immigrant. Groping for community, she had tried to reconstruct the collectivism of her early childhood in China in the now more familiar surroundings of the New World. Bonding was important to her. She could take personal freedom for granted, but not national belonging.

Chen's emigration was of a very different kind, more akin to what German intellectuals in the Third Reich called "inner emigration." He escaped from China by withdrawing into himself. His preoccupation with spirituality and the distant past was a refuge, "a small paradise." There is a great deal of inner—as well as outer—emigration in China. There always was. The mountain hermit, the sage in his rustic teahouse, the retired scholar, these are all familiar images in Chinese art and poetry. Inner emigration is the traditional way out. It is why some former activists turn to religion, in the way others turn to sex—a quest for individual freedom, as well as a sign of quiet desperation.

—

One month after my first meeting with Chen Yiyang, the issue of religion exploded all over China. On April 25, 1999, ten thousand members of the religious group named Falun Gong, also known as Falun Dafa, suddenly appeared in front of Zhongnanhai. Most of them were middle-aged or elderly; they insisted on their right to carry out their religious practices in public. Like all believers, they did not like being criticized. So when they were attacked by a professor in a small literary magazine, there had been a noisy demonstration denouncing the critic. Some members were arrested. And that is why they had come to protest the arrests, by train, by bus, sometimes even on foot. They gathered silently in the center of Beijing, sat down in disciplined rows, meditated for a whole day, and left in the same ghostly manner in which they had come.

Falun Gong was just one of many Chinese cults, based on a mixture of Buddhism, Taoism, and various folk beliefs. Like the others, it promised good health, enlightenment, spiritual salvation, and release from wordly desires through meditation, breathing exercises, and a particular guru's wisdom. But no other sect had shown such organization or claimed a membership of 100 million people: more than the Chinese Communist Party itself. The police had had no idea. The government leaders were shocked. So on July 22 the group was banned as an "evil cult" that "corrupted people's minds" and "sabotaged national stability." Falun Gong was considered the biggest threat to Chinese society since the student rebellion in 1989.

Within seventy-two hours, twenty-six thousand people were arrested. Ten thousand more were jailed in the next four months. Official denunciations—on television and radio, in newspapers, magazines, and public meetings—went on relentlessly. The curious charge of "disseminating state secrets" was added to the others. More than twenty believers were said to have died of ill-treatment in jail, a number that was to grow to more than a hundred. Many members were not always in the best of health. One woman choked to death when a food tube, shoved down her throat, punctured her lung. Others jumped out of detention-center windows. And yet despite all this (or perhaps because of it), many believers kept turning up in Tiananmen Square, sometimes several hundred a week, always quietly, to be promptly taken off by policemen on the lookout for meditators. Many claimed to be ready to die for their faith. Most gave themselves up.

Then, one wintry day in 2001, the drama escalated: Seven people set themselves on fire by drinking gasoline from Sprite bottles. One was a girl of twelve, who was told that fire could not hurt her. The police arrived with fire extinguishers. One of the believers cried: "Let me go to heaven!" The girl survived. Her mother died in the flames.

It has happened many times in Chinese history, when the rulers, corrupted by too many years in power, are in danger of losing their grip. Peasant messiahs appear, millenarian cults form, and, crazed by illusions of immortality, masses of people embark on violent rebellions. In the second century A.D. the Yellow Turbans staged a revolt that helped to bring the government down. After the Opium Wars, in the mid-nineteenth century, Hong Xiuquan, the man who claimed to be Christ's younger brother, named his sect Taiping, Great Peace, in homage to the Yellow Turbans. His rebellion cost millions of lives but hastened the downfall of the Qing dynasty. Barely fifty years later, the Boxers revolted.

History and its uses are always a complicated business. The Boxers are officially regarded by the Communists as "anti-imperialist" heroes. And the Taiping rebellion, too, is often described as an anti-imperialist revolt, even though some of the imperialists initially helped their supposedly fellow Christians and the revolt was aimed mainly at the Qing court. The Communist government, at any rate, was surely conscious of history when it decided to crack down on Falun Gong. There was about the cult the usual air of fraudulence and internal politicking, to be sure, with disgruntled gurus fighting each other for the spoils of others' gullibility. There were fights on the Internet between the founder, a former martial arts master named Li Hongzhi, and a woman from the south named Belinda Peng Shanshan, who claimed that she was the true leader. But there could be no doubt that Falun Gong was an organized challenge to the

Communist Party's right to rule. Once again self-appointed men of superior virtue had come to save China from godlessness and corruption.

But there was no sign that this particular sect was about to erupt in violent rebellion. On the contrary, most Falun Gong believers saw their faith as a private affair, a form of inner emigration. Falun Gong is in fact an offshoot of a faith-healing technique, based on breathing exercises, called Qigong, which became wildly popular, not least among Communist Party cadres, in the 1980s. Many claims were made for it: Cancer patients who gathered in a public park in Beijing to practice Qigong thought it would cure their illness (proof is yet to be conclusive). In 1992, Li Hongzhi, a young Qigong enthusiast from the industrial northeast of China, decided to found his own school. His tract, entitled *Zhuan Falun*, a mixture of science and religion, promised to lift those who "cultivate" themselves in Falun Gong to a higher moral and spiritual plane, as well as cure them of ill health. The contents range from the zany to the banal. "Master Li" preaches the virtues of compassion, forbearance, and truth. Alcohol and drugs are banned. And cultivators are told to withdraw from politics and other worldly affairs so they can elevate themselves from base human nature toward "higher dimensions."

Master Li, who left the grime of China's northeast for a reclusive existence in New Jersey, doesn't seem remarkable. You might mistake him for a pharmacist or an accountant. But his public relations skills are impressive, and much boosted by modern technology. He changed his birthdate to that of the Buddha, something he claims is a coincidence, but every little thing helps. Videos of the Master levitating in yellow silk robes and accompanied by mystical New Age music added to his appeal. The Internet spreads Li's message not just in China but all over the world, and it was the main reason ten thousand people could be mobilized to demonstrate in Beijing.

I should have known that bigger trouble was brewing. Later in 1999, in the summer, I was introduced to a follower of Falun Gong in Beijing, a university professor whom I shall call Wang. We met at a bar named Frank's Place. Bored waitresses in miniskirts listened impassively to an Eric Clapton tape. Wang, a tall, lanky man in his forties, dressed in jeans and a plaid flannel shirt, laughed a great deal, and not always in the appropriate places, which gave the impression of nervousness rather than mirth. Though he was a scientist by profession, Wang was interested in history, especially Chinese history of the nineteenth century.

The great thing about the late Qing period, he said, was that everyone believed in another world then, an invisible world, no matter what it was—ghosts, or spirits, or gods. And the biggest problem with China now, Wang continued, was the lack of faith in anything. Wang used to be like that himself, an unbeliever. The invisible world did not exist for him until he was sent to the countryside after the Cultural Revolution. There, he heard stories about ghosts and other supernatural happenings. The villagers had retained their beliefs, but Wang was still a listener, not a believer, except perhaps, back then, in "scientific socialism." Gradually, his interest took a more serious turn. In the 1970s, when others were beginning to question Maoist dogmas and the Democracy Wall kindled faint hopes of more political freedom, Wang spent his time studying Buddhism, as well as Christianity. He was deeply moved by the Bible.

Wang had had an unhappy family life. There was violence at home, which he wouldn't specify. His father drank heavily; his mother was depressed. Wang hinted at suicide attempts, but did not wish to go into detail—the memory still distressed him. But he did mention that his parents' unhappiness was linked to a deep but unexpressed feeling of betrayed idealism. Both his parents had been army officers and good Communists. But the Party dealt carelessly with people who were no longer useful. In retirement, Wang's parents were left with nothing. After all the sacrifices and violence of the Maoist years, they saw everything they had stood for turn to dust in the new age of "To Get Rich Is Glorious." I asked Wang whether his parents still had faith in communism. He giggled, as though it were a joke. "I don't really know," he replied. "I'm fairly sure my mother doesn't. Probably my father doesn't anymore, either. You know, nobody in China really believes in communism."

People like Wang's parents, elderly, disillusioned former Communists, often poor and without proper medical insurance, fitted the mold of typical Falun Gong followers. After years of Marxist indoctrination, a new faith shows a way back to a more familiar, more Chinese world. In this case, however, it was not the parents but the son who took that route. As is true of so many religious conversions, Wang's came after a depression, which lasted for two years. The failure of the student movement in 1989 had left him in despair. He had lost all hope for China. All that was left now was to cultivate oneself and find one's own little paradise. But the way to go about this was revealed to him only later, when a friend introduced him to Master Li's teachings. Wang began to read the *Zhuan Falun* every day, and felt his depression lift. He gave up drinking. He meditated in the prescribed fashion, a kind of mixture of yoga and Zen, and at last he felt that his mind was at peace. Because the Master says you must not be involved or even interested in politics, he tried to be detached from public affairs. This, he admitted, was not easy.

We left Frank's Place together, and Wang politely walked me to the taxi stand. He was trying to say something, but I had trouble hearing what it was, for there was a clamor of rock music and building construction going on across the road. I asked him to repeat. He came closer. "Things are very tense now," he half whispered. "The government is frightened of us, because Falun Gong is so big and so many members are Party cadres and army officers. They fear the numbers and the organization. In fact, there is hardly any organization. It's all very informal, really. You just turn up in the park and do exercises together, that is all." I suspected there was a bit more to it than that, but didn't challenge him.

I said I would call again. Wang said that would be fine as long as I didn't mention Falun Gong on the phone, for "anything might happen now." He laughed, then shrugged: "Politics is hopeless in China anyway. China is too big, too complicated." I left with a sense of sadness, but not because I could have known that tens of thousands of people like Wang would be thrown into jail just one month later, in July. I couldn't have. I later heard Wang had gone underground. What filled me with melancholy was the sense of waste, the desiccation of energy and talent. For here was yet one more intelligent Chinese who had been forced to withdraw, with a nervous giggle, into his own private garden.

Neither a history of peasant messiahs nor the scale and efficiency of the Falun Gong organization entirely explains the panicked reaction of the Chinese government in 1999. It is something more like the paranoia of seventeenth-century Japanese shoguns, or that of the current Chinese government, for that matter, about Christianity. What people think or say in private is one thing, but religious or political organizations are forbidden. Falun Gong and Christianity are seen as particular threats, not just because they offer alternative dogmas and moral codes, as well as spiritual leaders. Their potent appeal is in some ways similar to that of communism. They too come at a time of rampant corruption, when a few are making dishonest fortunes while many feel left behind.

Much is made in Falun Gong and Christianity of egalitarianism. Master Li, like the Catholic popes, may be revered as a superior human being, but he preaches that with sufficient "cultivation" we all have an equal chance of salvation. We are all sinners, but as one Chinese testified in English on a Falun Gong website, "Falun Gong possesses such magic powers. It can correct people's heart. I cannot face up to [the Falun Gong believers] anymore. Their heart is so decent and noble while mine is so dirty in comparison. . . . What we have been doing is irrational, full of sin, unforgivable and against the wishes of the people."

The person who ostensibly (one can never be sure on the Internet) posted this message was a policeman in the Public Security Bureau, a benighted servant of state oppression. His testimony was a moral confession with political overtones: ". . . the wishes of the people." He was worried about the crime rate and the lack of trust among Chinese citizens and the fact that the law does not rule, for "laws cannot bind people's heart." It is precisely because the official Party dogma no longer binds people's hearts that a large number of disillusioned Communists seek refuge in Falun Gong, or in the arms of Christ. And because the Party knows this, it feels the need to stamp out those alternatives. Sadly, however, those alternatives are as unlikely as communism to put China firmly on the road to Mr. Democracy.

It is telling that Falun Gong shares with communism a touching faith in Mr. Science, but it is a science of a peculiar sort—alternative. Master Li challenges "empirical science," and speaks vaguely of invisible energies and dimensions. We must "break through" our "energy levels" to touch "other dimensions." Here is a testimony—in English—on a Falun Gong website from a Chinese scientist working in the United States: "Though the purpose of Falun Dafa is not for the development of the science of mankind, it will in effect enable man's science to take a great leap forward, because it is the science at a much higher level. If the scientific community can appreciate that Falun Dafa is the most profound and supernormal science of all, the science in the future will be able to study the universe from a different angle."

I like the "great leap forward," a probably wholly unconscious echo of another scientific experiment, one carried out by Mao more than forty years ago. Mao, like Master Li, believed that the human spirit could, through collective willpower, overcome mere material obstacles; inspired by crackpot scientific theories of the Stalin era, he ordered all the people in China to melt down iron pots in their backyards and plant crops where they couldn't grow, and "overtake" the British economy in ten years. Mao had behaved like a pseudoscientific peasant messiah, and caused more than 30 million deaths.

The reaction of Mao's successors to those who believe that Master Li holds the key to their good health revealed a peculiar dilemma. Falun Gong was attacked not only for being an "evil cult" but also for being a "sham science," spread by alien conspirators (since the Master lives abroad) to "confuse the minds of the Chinese people." And the official antidote to this latest manifestation of a Chinese folk tradition? People were ordered to redouble their efforts to study scientific socialism, atheism, and dialectical materialism. Some science. Some alien conspiracy.

———

In Shenzhen, there are as many cults and religious groups as there are discos. They range from the purely private—lone seekers of some sacred way or other—to official, state-sponsored churches. Predictable explanations are given for the religious boom: the "spiritual vacuum" in the wake of Maoism, search for meaning in a materialist world, and so forth. And with increased economic and social freedoms comes a greater sense of individualism. In Shenzhen and the rest of China, personal belief is an escape from the group-think imposed by official dogma. Folkish cults such as Falun Gong, with Buddhist or Taoist trappings, hark back to older traditions; they make people feel more "Chinese." Religion, along with good food, was the first thing to revive from the Maoist demolition of Chinese civilization.

In the autumn of 1999, a few months after the July crackdown on Falun

Gong followers, I was in Shenzhen to see a friend, who was studying religions in China. She told me to meet her at a Buddhist restaurant. There
was some confusion, since the place had been obliged to change its name.
Formerly, it had included *Dafa,* an ancient Buddhist term, meaning Great
Law, that was also adopted by the Falun Gong—which was enough to attract unwelcome attention from agents of the Public Security Bureau, who
are no experts in Buddhist terminology. My friend was waiting, together
with a young woman dressed in elegant charcoal-gray designer jeans. The
young woman, whom I shall call Zhang, had graduated from the University of Science and Technology in Hefei and was now in the business of ex-
porting artificial Christmas trees to the United States. She was also a
Buddhist, and her guru was in jail on suspicion of being connected to
Falun Gong. His organization, the Life Science Institute in Beijing, had
been closed down. In fact, according to Ms. Zhang, it was all a gross slander. Her "Master" had nothing to do with Falun Gong. But he *was* a remarkable figure. Ms. Zhang, who spoke in a slightly hectoring manner, at
great length, as though to a crowd, and always with a tolerant smile for the
unenlightened, recounted some of his miracles. For one thing, he could
fly. And he performed more useful feats, too. One day in Shenzhen, she
was robbed of her wallet. So she called the Master in Beijing. The wallet
was returned to her the next day. Then she lost her registration card, without which you cannot move in China. This time, despite his physical absence, the Master managed to conjure it up from a glass of water. I said
nothing but must have registered some skepticism. She beamed at me in
silence, through clenched teeth.

It was, however, Ms. Zhang's attitude to religious persecution that surprised me. You would have thought that she might have had some sympathy with Falun Gong followers, especially since her own Master had been
arrested. But no, she approved of the crackdown. It was a good thing. This
time I must have looked dismayed. Still beaming, she said: "You see, this Li
fellow teaches superstition. He is very bad. I saw it myself on television.
His followers are dying because they believe in miracle cures. They must
be stopped."

I asked her whether she believed in the principle of religious freedom.
She looked around the table, and we became a crowd again. She repeated

the evils attributed to Falun Gong. I tried her a few more times on the principle of freedom but never got a satisfactory answer. I recalled stories I had read about the 1950s and 1960s, when writers commonly denounced each other even though they all had been victims of official purges.

—

It is hard to say how many Christians there are in China, since most of them do not belong to officially registered "patriotic" churches. People all over the country gather in private homes, or "house churches," to pray and preach and generally share in various hybrid forms of folk Christianity. Like Falun Gong, these are often classified as "evil cults" by the government, and believers are regularly arrested. A friend from Beijing once told me that clandestine Christians were the toughest dissidents, because of their willingness to die for their faith. I wanted to meet some of them, but this was not simple to arrange. It was easier to see the official "patriotic" believers first.

The patriotic Catholic church in Nantou, a small typically Cantonese town north of Shenzhen, is housed in an old, rather dilapidated orphanage, a gray-brick building about a century old. Outside is a Chinese-style rock garden, with tiny Chinese temples set in the miniature landscape. A stone Virgin Mary peeps out daintily from a rocky grotto. Mass is celebrated in the old school hall. Illustrated biblical scenes, cut from an old children's book, hang on the peeling, white walls. Although the church is nominally Catholic, it cannot defer to the spiritual leadership of Rome, for the spiritual leadership of all Chinese is supposed to be in Beijing.

The priest was a young man from Hebei, with gapped teeth and a prominent jaw, which gave the impression less of manly strength than of a mild deformity. My first question immediately caused a mutual misunderstanding. He had been explaining that the most sensitive topics in China were religion and the ethnic problem. Perhaps it was his Hebei accent, perhaps I had misheard the tones, but I thought he had referred to the democratic problem. So I asked his opinion about something I had often heard, namely that China needed Christianity as a step toward democracy.

He said it was impossible to be a Christian as well as a member of the Communist Party. Since atheism was the basic doctrine of the Communist Party, a Christian had to choose Christianity or communism. You couldn't be both, for in fact atheism, and indeed communism, were also religions. Yes, I thought, that made sense. But then he said something that puzzled me deeply. "It is different for the Muslims, since they are an ethnic minority. They can be Communists as well as Muslims." The logic of this escaped me at first, but then I realized the nature of our misunderstanding. *Minju* and *minzhu*, the words for "democracy" and "ethnic group," sound almost the same, especially in a regional accent. It was, in any case, still a peculiar thing to say. Not all Muslims belonged to ethnic minorities, and, surely if one monotheistic religion was incompatible with communism, then so was another.

So what about the Falun Gong?

"Oh," he said. "The government is quite right to crack down on *them*. They treat their leader as God. And that is of course absurd, for there is only one God and He cannot be human. So Falun Gong is a cult, and cults are dangerous in China, for they cause great disorder. Just remember the Taiping rebellion in the nineteenth century. No, the government is quite right to preserve order."

Yes, but what about religious freedom?

"Falun Gong is not a religion but an evil cult."

I was not really surprised to hear this. Many Catholics in China don't belong to the official patriotic Church. But the Catholic Church always knew how to take care of itself by staying on the right side of authority, and this is particularly true of the patriotic Church in China. As I walked out the front gate, my eye fell on a sign posted outside the old orphanage. It read, in large red Chinese characters: LOVE GOD. LOVE OUR MOTHERLAND. There were almost the same words that I had seen at the Hong Kong border, amid the commercials for dot-com companies and massage parlors.

—

It was high time to talk to Chinese who were neither urban intellectuals nor official patriots. My chance to meet "house Christians" came through a lucky introduction. A friend of a friend had a Christian mother who lived in a remote village in Sichuan and had recently been taken in for questioning by the police. I was told to give the friend of the friend a call. Her name was Ping, but she liked to be called Cindy. She asked me to meet her in the lobby of a certain hotel in Shenzhen. After that, she said, we might go to the beach for a swim. At night? Yes, she said. Everyone went to the beach at night. I could buy some swimming trunks on the way.

Cindy had been described to me as small, thin, with short hair. I waited. She was late. But finally there she was, just as she had been described, except that she wore unusually heavy makeup. I introduced myself, she smiled, we walked out of the hotel, and I suggested we buy a pair of swimming trunks. She looked at me, shrugged, and said something like, "Well, whatever you fancy." Then she asked me what my name was and which hotel I was staying at. Suddenly I realized my mistake. It had been a typically Shenzhen encounter, which I decided to abort. She took it well, offered me a stick of chewing gum, and returned to the hotel to find another customer.

The real Cindy was not a prostitute but was, at first, a bit coy about the precise nature of her living arrangements. Her comfortable apartment in the center of town was far more expensive than what most women of her age could afford. In the apartment was a large computer, which Cindy used to send e-mails and to log on to various English-language chat rooms. Learning English was her passion. Like many young people in Shenzhen, Cindy dreamed of going abroad. She had a vague plan to go to Israel, where she had a contact, another friend of a friend.

I heard the story of Cindy's life bit by bit: a drunken father, who beat his wife and died young after a severe depression; an elder brother, who beat Cindy before moving to Guangzhou, where he worked in a restaurant; an uncle back in Sichuan, who demanded a regular cut from Cindy's earnings and got testy when transfers were late. In fact, one of the few men whom Cindy didn't curse was the wealthy Hong Kong businessman who kept her as a mistress in Shenzhen. She referred to him sometimes as her boyfriend and sometimes as her uncle. Although he seemed not to be excessively demanding, sex with him was no pleasure. But at least Cindy was spared from having to work in a factory for pitiful wages. The "uncle" in Hong

Kong was her potential ticket out of China. She had not done badly for a village girl whose formal education had ended after four years of primary school.

A plan was made. Cindy had some business with her uncle in Sichuan, who as the current head of the family had to help her get permission from the local authorities to apply for an exit visa, without which she could not go to Israel. Her mother's village was not far from the county town where the uncle lived. So we would fly to Chongqing, the wartime capital of China, to see her cousin, who was studying there, then go on by train to a small provincial town and from there, by bus, to her mother's home, where we would stay for a day or two.

Despite her experience of urban life, Cindy still had the village girl's habit of transforming every public place into a rubbish dump: Within fifteen minutes on the plane, and later on the train, our seats were soaked with spilled water and covered in poppy seeds, bits of used tissue paper, and so on. What she did to our seats, other people were doing to China's streets, rivers, and lakes. And what individuals do, factories do on a much grander scale.

Sprawling along the banks of the Yangtze, surrounded by mountains, Chongqing in June sits beneath a permanent layer of hot, damp industrial air and gives one the sense of being smothered under a blanket. High-rise buildings in the nouveau-riche Communist style have sprouted in the old city center, high above the riverbanks. But the closer you get to the river, the shabbier the housing: brick shantytowns with prewar factories, stinking public latrines, and outdoor eateries offering delicious stews of frogs, fish, and pigs' brains simmering in red-hot chilies. Small, dark brown men from the villages carry heavy loads up and down the hills on bamboo poles. And the mighty Yangtze itself is like a slow-moving sewer.

I shared a room in a newish hotel in the town center with Cindy's cousin, the student. He was a serious young man, with only vague childhood memories of 1989. Students today, he said, were different. They were more practical, more realistic, and would not be used by people who wanted to bring down the government. In any case, he added, the campus was now under very tight control. His dream was to go to the United States.

Before turning in, we watched television for a bit. Young women in green People's Liberation Army uniforms and sexy black boots sang patriotic songs about being "ordinary women" today but prepared to "kill for the motherland tomorrow." Their eyes blazed with patriotic fervor, rather like those Maoist heroines in revolutionary operas of the 1960s or like the "spy" I had met in Shenzhen. I thought of Mel Brooks and "Springtime for Hitler," in his film *The Producers.* We switched the television off but could not get to sleep for some time, since the phone kept ringing with inquiries: Did we want a "special massage"?

Daquan, where we got off the train from Chongqing, is a provincial dump: wide, barely paved streets lead to the large new railway station, in front of which shady young men in sunglasses hang about with nothing much to do. The arrival of a foreigner provides a temporary diversion, but soon everything settles down again in a late afternoon torpor, like the dust on a country road after a car has gone by. Cindy warned me several times to hold tight to all my belongings. "You cannot trust anyone here." When I showed insufficient fear, she said: "You foreigners just don't understand. Chinese people are bad, very bad."

Still, Daquan has a sleazy charm, not unlike what one imagines Mississippi gambling towns must have been like when Mark Twain was alive. The streets are filthy, and the local river is filled with plastic bottles and other rubbish that people casually toss away while having their meals on the rusty boats moored to a jetty not far from the town center, with its massage parlors, seedy hotels, and cheap restaurants. The men tend to dress like Latino gangsters, in their shades, garish shirts, and loud suits, and most women dress like nightclub hostesses, even if they are not, tottering around in impossibly high heels, diaphanous evening dresses, or skimpy velvet shorts. There is much vitality in these towns, but it is a rustic, earthy vitality, that of people who are not yet used to urban living but who enjoy some of the freedoms it brings.

Daquan was a metropolis compared to the county town where Cindy's uncle lives. We arrived in K. at dusk. It had rained that afternoon and the main street, lined with small shops, was a muddy strip. Bicycle-rickshaw riders strained every muscle in their wiry bodies to negotiate the puddles, which sat like little ponds in the road, while a rickety bus splashed us with sheets of muddy water. A man was hacking the head off a chicken. There was a dance hall with pink neon lights and a painted picture outside of a blond woman in a ball gown. There were two barbershops offering various kinds of massages. Women in flesh-colored stockings squatted outside, skirts hitched up almost to their waists, while men sat around in small groups, fanning themselves and drinking tea. The younger men nudged one another and sniggered as Cindy and I walked by. The women tittered, and the older people stared openmouthed.

Uncle and Aunt lived on one of the side streets, which was, like the town itself, littered with rubbish. The house was a three-story concrete building, with one barred window. From the outside it looked like a garage, or a jail. Cindy shouted. Her aunt, a chubby, smiling woman in her late forties, let us in. She wore plastic sandals and a filmy brown dress, which clung to her thick hips.

Downstairs was a dark room with a wooden table, some chairs, a sink, and no further decoration. It was where Uncle and Aunt had dinner. The living room and two bedrooms were on the second floor. There was a plastic-covered sofa in the living room, an enormous television set, a karaoke machine, a calendar on the wall with a picture of Guanyin, the Goddess of Mercy, and a kind of bunk, upon which Uncle was sitting, dressed in a pair of black boxer shorts and a white undershirt. Uncle, too, had a short, flabby figure, with a potbelly that bulged under his shirt. He was reading a paper, and made short grunting noises. Uncle was a school inspector. His small eyes, set in a round, sallow face, were bloodshot and shrewd.

After he had finished with his paper, Uncle sidled up to me and asked me whether foreigners in my country took drugs and had sex with prostitutes. I tried to answer his questions as best I could. He nodded and said: "In China, prostitution is strictly forbidden."

When I put it to him that prostitution seemed to be rather common in China nonetheless, he shrugged and told me that the police were in cahoots with the brothel owners. He had a friend who owned a massage parlor. Business was good, because the owner had been a classmate of the police chief. "The main problem in China today," he said, as though launching into a speech, "is corruption." Uncle planted his hands on his thighs, making dents in the soft flesh. "Even the Party bosses," he went on, "pocket public money, or give it to their friends to do business."

It was not entirely clear how much Uncle disapproved of all this, for he was proud to know one or two of those Party bosses himself. Indeed, he said, his relations with the local authorities were excellent. And with a stagey whisper, so the women couldn't hear, he asked me whether I would like to visit the massage parlor with him. Since the owner was his personal friend, he said, the service would be "first class."

Uncle, it turned out, was not officially a Party member but had been told to join one of the official "democratic" parties, sanctioned and effectively controlled by the Communist Party to give China a wholly false image of political pluralism.

I had hoped to be able to set off with Cindy to her mother's village the following morning, but things did not turn out to be so simple. I was told the village was a very long way from the town. Also, since it had been raining, the roads would be flooded. Besides, there was nothing of interest in the village. And the facilities were very primitive, no good at all for a foreign guest. The food wouldn't agree with me, and conditions were most unhygienic. No, it would be much better for me to stay in town. Cindy nodded her agreement. She still needed Uncle's help to apply for permission to leave China.

Staying in town actually meant staying in the house. Whenever I said I would like to go out for a walk, Uncle and Aunt, and Cindy too, waved away this ignorant notion. It was much too hot to walk around, and too dangerous for a foreign guest to go out alone. There might be trouble. That would not do at all. Why didn't I just sit down and relax. They would switch on the karaoke machine and play some music videos for me.

Of course these were all excuses. To "take care" of someone, whether a foreigner or a subordinate, is to control him. Authoritarianism in East Asia—my Japanese experiences came to mind while I traveled in China—is often wrapped in a warm maternal cloak. Don't do anything on your own, it is too dangerous, we will take care of everything. And soon one is reduced to the state of a helpless child.

And so I sat and sat while Uncle played his music videos, cranking up the volume, and took turns with his wife singing syrupy pop songs through a loud and weirdly echoing microphone. The videos were of girls in long white dresses and young men in tuxedos running in slow motion through clouds of dry ice, or romping through the tourist sites of Taiwan, Hong Kong, or Paris.

Aunt actually had a fine singing voice, which she used to good effect when she sang Chinese folk songs while doing the laundry. Unlike Cindy, Aunt still had some knowledge of an older, rural culture, before it was stamped on in the Mao years, but she seemed barely conscious of the effortless grace of her singing. No one in the house, except myself, appeared to be listening to her. It was just the hum of her physical labor, the rhythm of her daily life.

I must have looked glum when, on the second evening, Uncle and Aunt spent three solid hours warbling their Hong Kong and Taiwanese pop songs through the karaoke machine. At one point Uncle repeated the same wretched song four times, until he felt he had got it right. The sound of his voice, echoing from the concrete walls of the small living room, sounded like that of a wounded animal howling in pain. But Uncle and Aunt were trying to be solicitous hosts and wondered whether I might not prefer something more familiar to my ears. There followed thirty minutes of video footage of Abba and then of some French Muzak. When this didn't make me seem any happier, they simply turned up the volume, with encouraging smiles. When I looked even glummer, I was asked what was wrong. Didn't I like music? So I said an unforgivable thing. I said I preferred Aunt's natural singing voice when she did the laundry. I said I liked the old folk songs.

Aunt's face went through several emotions in quick succession. First there was bafflement. Then there was hurt. Here I was, an honored foreign guest, and I was making fun of their backwardness. Or at least I was not sufficiently appreciative of the fact that they were modern, educated people, who had left village life behind them. I was implying that Uncle and Aunt still belonged to the world of old folk songs, to the world, that is, of Cindy's mother, the world they didn't really want me to see.

When he wasn't on the karaoke machine, Uncle was proud to show off his official credentials as an educated man, as a demonstration of his *zige*. One morning, after having once again ignored my request to head off for the village, Uncle told me to sit down and ordered his wife to produce "the box" for my inspection. The box was covered in red felt and had the PRC flag embossed on it. While Uncle gave me a sidelong glance, grinning in anticipation, Aunt took out a brown envelope that contained a newspaper article, something about the evils of "feudalism," written by Uncle. He explained that he used to teach history at a middle school. There was also a document testifying to his later appointment as a school inspector.

Though I dreaded being cooped up in the house, I soon realized that our twice-daily outings, once for tea in the morning, once for dinner in the evening, offered only limited relief. Uncle insisted that we walk together, ahead of the women, and would proceed to hold forth about China. China was an old country, he said, with five thousand years of history. China was a very complicated country, too, which foreign friends could never truly comprehend. China had fifty-six minorities. And all Chinese people loved China. For example, when the U.S. and NATO bombed the Chinese embassy in Belgrade, all the Chinese people were furious. Uncle pulled an angry face.

Partly out of boredom, partly out of a desire to needle him, I asked Uncle who the Chinese people were. Did they include the Tibetans or the Uighurs in the Muslim western areas? Was there any difference between the Han Chinese and the minorities? Did they perhaps have different views on certain matters? I knew he wouldn't give me an honest, or even an interesting, answer but it was something to do. "China," he solemnly intoned, "has fifty-six minorities. All citizens of the PRC are Chinese. And we all love our motherland."

I did not like Uncle, and began to feel he did not much like me, either. When I voiced my dissatisfaction to Cindy about being trapped in the house, she looked concerned and said she understood my feelings but there was still plenty of time to go to the village. Why didn't I relax and talk to Uncle. He was an educated man and could tell me many interesting things. But of course the main thing was that she still needed to sort out her visa problems, and Uncle was not to be rushed.

I decided to sulk, a demeaning but effective way in China to get your feelings across. And finally, on the fourth day, it was decided that we might proceed to the village. Aunt would come with us. As soon as we left the town behind us, bumping along in a small bus, my mood lifted. Rain had turned the landscape, with its gentle hills, bamboo groves, and watery rice paddies, into a beautiful emerald green. A water buffalo stood in a distant field, like an ink dot on a Chinese scroll, and a plume of smoke curled up from a gray-brick farmhouse with a pretty tiled roof. At last I felt I had truly arrived in China, or should I say "China," for it was a notion, a romantic idea, a fiction that I carried with me which was no more concrete than any other idea of the country or culture or history or people that we call by that name.

Picking their way through the rice fields, past the village school and the duck pond, my two companions, Aunt in a semi-diaphanous dress with bits of silver glitter, Cindy in a miniskirt and high heels, were giggling like village girls returning home from the big city.

The family farm consisted of three houses built at the foot of a green hill. In the middle was a newish, two-story house with modern white tiles pasted onto the front wall. Two older farmhouses, quaint, but dark and cramped inside, and slowly crumbling, stood on either side of the main house. Cindy's grandmother lived in one of the old houses. The other was occupied by Cindy's uncle, the only man left on the farm and, from what I gathered from Cindy, the black sheep of the family; he was always drunk. Cindy's mother lived in the main house. In front was a large yard, where Grandmother fed the ducks and grabbed one by the neck when it was needed for dinner.

Meals were taken on the ground floor of the new house. The second floor looked unused, almost as if it were a showroom of some kind. A new television set and a karaoke machine, bought in Guangzhou by Cindy's brother, still stood there, wrapped in Styrofoam. Various parts of a pig, slaughtered some time ago and already turned reddish brown, hung out to dry on a clothesline strung across the room. Occasionally I noticed a large, black rat scurrying toward the kitchen, which was next to a narrow courtyard where we washed ourselves at night with pails of boiled water.

There was a mystery about the pigs that I didn't immediately grasp. While drinking tea with Grandmother soon after we arrived, I heard grunting. Later I spotted a large pink ear spilling out from under the door of one of the rooms. But when I asked how many pigs there were, I got shifty looks and evasive answers. No pigs. Sometimes pigs, but not now. There used to be pigs. And so forth. I realized that I was not dreaming only when I was told later that farmers had to pay tax according to the number of pigs they kept. It was the crude but only way for local tax collectors—often petty gangsters paid by Party officials—to have a rough idea how much money people had.

Cindy's mother was a small, thin, dark-skinned woman, who managed to carry enormous loads despite her lean frame. She showed me where she received her congregation of Christians once a week, on Monday nights. It was a room to the side of the place where we ate, containing a blackboard and a few wooden benches. She had written the words of a Chinese hymn on the blackboard, asking the Lord Yehova to come to China and relieve people of their troubles. I asked her whether she was a Protestant. Of course, she said, for Catholics are different: "They worship the mother of Jesus."

What about her recent problems with the police? She smiled, and said it was no problem. They had taken her in for questioning and had wanted to know who her leader was. She answered that she had only one leader, and his name was Jesus. The police insisted that she was a member of a subversive organization and ordered her again to reveal the leader's name. When she refused to name anyone but Jesus, they eventually let her go, but said they could come back for her anytime. "Stupid idiots!" she said. "As though there was any other boss but Jesus!"

Mother was firmly convinced that Christians went to heaven while sinners roasted in hell. Her conversion had taken place two years before, after her husband died of a diseased liver and Cindy and her brother left for the south. Perhaps she had felt depressed and lonely. But it was not immediately clear how she was converted. There was some talk about "a man in the village." But it was impossible to get her to say whether this man was an itinerant evangelist or a local "underground" Christian. Some areas of Sichuan have a long history of peasant Christianity, which reemerges as soon as the repression is relaxed.

One thing was clear: Neither Cindy nor Aunt approved of it. Cindy called her mother's faith "evil." She used the word *xie,* which can mean "heresy" or "fallacy," as well as "evil." It is the official government term used for Falun Gong and other banned religious groups. Cindy told Aunt stories about Christian baptism. People took off all their clothes, she said, and danced around naked. Both erupted in derisive laughter. Aunt hitched up her dress and slapped her plump thighs. It was the funniest thing she had ever heard.

Later the conversation took a nastier turn. Mother had prepared a freshly killed duck, which we ate in the Sichuan style, with hot chili peppers. Grandmother was there, and so was the uncle's family, including his twenty-three-year-old daughter, Cindy's cousin. A shy young woman, she spoke the clearest standard Chinese and was better educated than the others. I often saw her sitting alone with a book. After a stint as a factory worker in Guangzhou, she had come home to study for the entrance exam to a medical college, but even if she passed the test, she still might not make it, for a college education was expensive, and nobody was prepared to pay for her, a mere girl.

Cindy then lectured her mother. She was just being used by other people, she said, to bring the government down. Aunt added that this "superstition" had caused trouble for the rest of the family, what with the police coming and all. Mother listened in silence but then shouted back that if Christianity was just superstition, then how come all the rich countries in the West believed in Jesus? In fact, she continued, they were rich because of their faith. That is why Chinese, too, needed Jesus. First Cindy put her hands to her ears and then she cried, in English, "Stop!" Aunt began to sing a popular Maoist song, about the Chairman rising like the sun. Whereupon Mother, Grandmother, and the bad uncle's wife, who were all converts, sang a hymn to Yehova. And that was the moment the bad uncle chose to make his unsteady appearance.

He took one look at me and grinned. Although he could never have been described as handsome, there was a mischievousness about him that was not unattractive. Like most village people of his generation, he was small and wiry. He sat down and smoked a thick tobacco leaf, like a crude cigar. I asked him what life was like for farmers these days. He answered in Sichuanese, which his daughter, the aspiring medical student, translated into standard Chinese. I felt that this embarrassed her. She apologized several times for her father's lack of education. I shouldn't take him too seriously, she said.

Things were bad now, he said. It was different under Mao. At least then all people were treated the same. Educated people couldn't lord it over the peasants, not if they knew what was good for them. But now things were different. The peasants were either ignored or they were harassed by the authorities. His daughter smiled apologetically and said that her father knew little about the world. I asked him about the Great Leap Forward. Surely Mao had not been so good for the peasants then. True enough, replied the uncle. People were dying of hunger all over the place. Mao had his bad side. People realized that.

Mother listened with a benevolent smile. Cindy and Aunt were huddled together in a separate conversation. Grandmother said nothing and stared at the wall. Cindy's cousin looked pained.

"Mao was sometimes bad," the uncle continued, "but the current leaders are all rotten." This elicited nervous titters around the table, as though a naughty child had once again spoken out of turn.

"You know," said the uncle, "we had a saying during the war against the Japanese: There were two kinds of officials, corrupt officials and murderous officials. Now we have mostly corrupt officials. They make us pay for this and that, whether we want it or not. . . ." His daughter looked positively ill. "He doesn't understand taxes," she said. Her father went on: "They make us pay for roads and all kinds of stuff we never asked for. Why don't they pay themselves?"

It was the age-old problem: unwilling peasants being squeezed for money by officials who in turn are pressed by a remote, unelected, authoritarian central government. It was unfair to blame the local officials, who were squeezed for funds by other officials, higher up than they were. Yet I felt sympathy for the uncle, too. Who wants to pay for a non-representative government that uses gangsters to collect its dues? I knew from many newspaper reports that such dissatisfaction often turned into violent anger. Thousands of farmers would suddenly appear in county towns and smash government buildings and assault officials in protest. Sometimes it took the armed police days to put these riots down.

The uncle said he had a question, too. Did I think Jesus Christ was in favor of democracy? At first I was baffled. I said the concept probably would not have occurred to Jesus, but there was no reason to assume he would have been against it. The uncle nodded and said that Jesus was a simple man, a worker, and, like Mao, he treated everyone equally. In other words, Jesus was a democrat. And after that, much to the relief of his daughter, the uncle said good-bye and made his way back to his room. He's drinking, said Aunt with a look of disgust. No, said Cindy's mother. He stopped drinking since he was saved by Jesus.

I do not know how much the uncle drank, but he had a certain dignity. More dignity, at any rate, than Uncle and Aunt back in town. After we had gotten back there from the village, Cindy and Aunt entertained Uncle with stories of Cindy's mother and her beliefs. The three of them were shrieking with laughter. Cindy mimicked her mother's voice and imitated her Christian pieties. Tears of mirth moistened Uncle's small, red eyes. I asked him why his sister-in-law shouldn't believe in Jesus if it made her feel happy. Still chortling at the stupidity of his rural relations, he slapped a damp hand on my leg and explained that "Marxism is based on a materialist philosophy and all religion is mere superstition."

I was aware of the danger of feeling superior to the half-educated ways of Uncle and Aunt, and yet could not help detesting them. There was so much anxiety and shame in their ridicule of the village life they had barely left behind. Hearing their laughter, I could understand the powerful attraction of egalitarian beliefs to people who felt the contempt of the educated classes, and it hardly mattered whether the peasant messiah was called Jesus Christ or Mao Zedong.

Uncle's faith in political dogma made him feel superior to his village relatives, not only because mastering some of the Marxist jargon marked him as an educated man, just as reciting Confucian texts had for previous generations, but because it sounded scientific and modern, like his giant karaoke machine; and to be "scientific" was to be out of the village, with its age-old superstitions. Perhaps the increasing popularity of many faiths in China is a kind of revenge, against the oppressive dogmas of a morally and politically bankrupt state, but also against the little mandarins who are paid to impose them. It is a case of village China hitting back.

Chapter 3

The View from Lhasa

The first time I visited Tibet, in the fall of 1982, scars of the Maoist years were still plain to see: Buddhist wall paintings in temples and monasteries were scratched out or daubed with revolutionary slogans. Han Chinese from China proper (the "inner land") were already there, though not in large numbers, almost all of them in military uniform. But the early 1980s was a time of relatively liberal policies. There was little sign of current terror. And the towns still looked entirely Tibetan. Chinese influence was confined mainly to the barracks. Hotels hardly existed, restaurants were few and mostly bad. Even in the main cities of Lhasa, Gyangtse, and Shigatse there was hardly any evidence of a modern economy.

Things have changed greatly since then. Modernization has replaced class struggle as the official aim of the Chinese government. The Maoist graffiti that disfigured religious places has mostly disappeared, to be replaced by new slogans displayed in Chinese characters on almost every public building, slogans that promise prosperity, education, and the warm embrace of the motherland. Modernization is how many colonial powers before the Chinese justified their imperial rule in Asia. And it is to a large extent how the Communist Party of China justifies its grip on the "outer lands" today. A huge amount of government money is being poured into the "Tibet Autonomous Region," and Chinese fortune hunters are flocking there in ever larger numbers. Stories I had been hearing, from travelers and reporters, were disturbing and often seemed a little fantastic: gambling casinos, gigantic discotheques, four-story brothels. These are not uncommon establishments in the wild frontier towns of Chinese-style capitalism, but it took some imagination to picture them in front of the Potala palace or the Tashilhunpo monastery.

The night before I flew into Lhasa from Chengdu, the capital of Sichuan, I had a drink with two young Chinese who were off to Tibet for a holiday. Both worked for a bank. One of them, Su, was also studying to get into an American university, where he hoped to get a degree in business administration. They were intelligent, well educated, in their twenties, products of the Deng Xiaoping era, with only hazy memories of 1989. Their English was excellent, though neither of them had ever been outside China.

Tibet was like "a foreign country" to them. The word they used several times was "mysterious." What made Tibet seem mysterious and attractive was the religion. They said that Tibetans had retained something profound that the Han Chinese had lost. For the Chinese people, they believed, were very practical, very clever, very good at making money, but had no feeling for religion.

I did not wish to argue with them. The evening was balmy, the beer cool. Chengdu can no longer be called a beautiful city, but it still has a lazy southern charm; not all the teahouses are gone, even though the professional storytellers have made way for video and karaoke sets. Su, who was more assertive than his friend, suddenly remarked that the trouble with China was politics. A one-party state was no good. What was needed in politics, just as in business, was competition. Since I could not disagree, I said nothing much. But then Su made another point, which, though familiar, still took me aback. He said: "The most important thing for China is unification." He was referring, of course, to the inclusion of Taiwan and Tibet. His friend, a thin man named Li, nodded his agreement. I asked why national unification was of such great importance to them personally. Wasn't freedom of speech, say, a matter of greater concern? Yes, yes, they said, that was important too. But unification was even more important, "because we are all Chinese."

What did he mean, all Chinese? What did Chinese in Vancouver or Taipei have in common with people in Lhasa or Chengdu? Li, less hearty, more pensive than Su, mulled this over, shook his head slowly once or twice, and said: "Children of the dragon. We are all children of the dragon."

I didn't really know how to respond to this, and in the event, I didn't have to, for Su brought up the "Taiwan problem." I said there wasn't a Taiwan problem, only a mainland problem. No, said Li, it was a problem for all Chinese, for if Taiwan were torn from China, it would hurt the feelings of all Chinese, including Chinese in Taiwan. My argument that most people in Taiwan felt they were Taiwanese and saw no advantage in reunification was dismissed as ignorance. No, no, the Taiwanese only wanted to be independent for materialist reasons, because they were more developed. But their emotions were different. I should understand that all Chinese were like one family. Indeed, he said, all Asians felt that way about their countries. In Asia, he said with great conviction, your own people are like your blood relations.

All right, I said, so what were those feelings shared by all Chinese? Ah, Li said, it was "the Chinese spirit." I see. And what was that spirit, exactly? Well, the spirit of hard work, and wanting "to make China great after two hundred years of humiliation." Su added gravely that Chinese civilization had lasted for five thousand years.

It was depressing to hear these textbook clichés from people who were otherwise so intelligent, reasonable, and well educated. Perhaps they said these things because I was a foreigner, though Chinese returning from overseas tend to run into the same slogans. It is also possible that these "Chinese feelings" are actually the products of higher education. Romantic nationalism is an intellectual affliction, which comes more readily to educated minds than it does to people preoccupied with daily survival. In any case, as long as the humiliation of two hundred years lingers, the borders of the old Qing empire, which included Tibet and Taiwan, will not be negotiated away. Chinese colonization of Tibet cannot be separated from the colonial practices of European powers in nineteenth-century China. Lhasa in this sense is a late victim of the Opium War.

And yet neither Li nor Su could pretend that Tibetans were part of the Chinese family. Tibet, after all, felt like a foreign country. So in China's neocolonial rhetoric, Li's argument about Taiwan has to be turned upside down. If the Taiwanese want to be independent for materialist reasons, Tibet has to be part of China for materialist reasons—because Tibet needs to be modernized, developed, enriched.

—

I did not see a gambling casino in front of the Potala palace, but the road into Lhasa *was* lined with shabby little bordellos masquerading as karaoke bars. That same road passes by a large, hideous sculpture of two golden yaks, which stands where the old West Gate of the city used to be until it was smashed by Red Guards in the 1960s. The golden yaks were a gift from the Chinese government to celebrate the fortieth anniversary of "peaceful liberation."

Much of the dilapidated charm of the old Tibetan city I had seen in 1982 has gone. Lhasa looks more like the market towns one finds around the borders of Thailand or in southern China, the East Asian versions of Dodge City in the Wild West, teeming with Chinese carpetbaggers, hucksters, hookers, gamblers, hoodlums, corrupt officials, and other desperadoes lusting after quick cash. At the same time, as though from another planet, there are the Tibetan pilgrims, fingering their beads, spinning their prayer wheels, and moving their lips to endless mantras, and the nomads, carrying silver daggers and with their long hair tied up in red silk, and the countrywomen in long skirts and striped aprons, and the monks dressed in saffron and red. There is the constant din of Chinese and Hindi pop songs, market salesmen pitching their wares, and rattling machine-gun fire from the video arcades (a group of young monks stared in rapture at Tom Hanks stopping a tank in *Saving Private Ryan*). Weaving their way through all this hurly-burly with an air of imperial swagger are riot police in green uniforms and regular police in white, country boys with almost unlimited power, speeding along in jeeps or cruising very slowly in unmarked Chinese-built Volkswagens.

One quickly gets a sketchy idea of the general divisions of labor. The shops, restaurants, and most other forms of commercial enterprise are in the hands of Han Chinese—mostly from Sichuan, to judge from their accents and the preponderance of Sichuanese food. Petty traders, market salesmen, money changers, and so on are often Muslims from the poor western provinces, such as Qinghai. They wear white caps and you see them hanging around the central market, huddled in small groups, offering you this or that. Tibetans tend to fall into two categories, country folk in traditional dress, who have come to the city to visit the holy places, and middle-ranking government employees, who sit around the Chinese fast-food restaurants wolfing down plates of rice or noodles. Like many colonial people dependent on government jobs, they tend to run to fat.

The pilgrims, nomads, and country people walked the same streets as the Chinese hustlers and traders, but they might as well have been in another country. They were also in a minority. More than half the people in Lhasa are Chinese, even though few of them stay there for very long and almost none speak Tibetan. This coming and going of fortune hunters is what gives Lhasa the impermanent, feverish atmosphere of a typical cowboy town. What makes it look more and more Chinese, apart from the people, is the new architecture, much of it gimcrack, most of it ugly, but all of the same type you see all over the modern Chinese empire: squat white-tiled buildings with blue-tinted windows, topped here and there with kitsch Chinese-style roofs. In Shigatse, the second city of Tibet, I saw a huge billboard in the center of town featuring a picture of Zhuhai, the new seaside town in the Pearl River delta that faces the gambling casinos of Macau. It had palm trees, "international hotels," discos, a golf course, and wide boulevards. This, the display seemed to say, was the glorious future.

The old Tibetan economy, before "liberation," had been, like so much else in Tibet, an integral part of religious life, for the monasteries were more than spiritual institutions: They managed real estate, acted as brokers and moneylenders, and ran schools and other public services. These functions have been taken over by government institutions. There was once a Tibetan merchant class, too, trading mostly with India and Nepal, but I was told it had pretty much disappeared. Trade with India has been blocked by the Sino-Indian border problems and by the government's successful policy of making Tibet dependent on China. Merchant families either fled abroad or found jobs in the government.

In one of the Tibetan restaurants near the seventh-century Jokhang temple, where pilgrims and tourists mingle with hawkers of incense, jewelry, and religious objects ("hello, look look, cheap cheap!"), I met two Tibetan men, both in their twenties, like Su and Li. Also like my Chengdu acquaintances, they worked for Chinese financial institutions. They spoke Tibetan the way well-educated Indians speak Hindi or Hong Kong Chinese speak Cantonese—larding their native language with words, or even entire sentences, from the language of the colonial power. Chinese is the language of their education, their workplace, and some of their social life. Both were doing well. One rode a fine Japanese motorcycle. They said it was people like themselves who benefited most from Chinese education, for it had opened up a wider world—of technology, economics, politics, and even Western ideas. Tibetans in the countryside, they said, still led traditional lives, getting by on very little, and deriving no benefit at all from China.

One of the men ordered a pizza; the other had Chinese noodles. Then, what had begun as a quiet conversation about the economy turned into an argument, in which I was merely a bystander. Perhaps for my sake, out of courtesy, they spoke Chinese, but with more and more Tibetan words thrown in. They disagreed about religion. The more studious of the two friends believed that religion was important. Without it, he said, the human spirit withers. He explained that without religion, most Tibetans would never have survived the harsh conditions of life in arid, icy highlands, with little more to eat than dried yak meat and clumps of flattened barley. But affluence, he said, creates a thirst for religion too; you cannot live on materialism alone. I thought of Richard Gere and the other Hollywood Buddhists. But then his friend took the opposite, more conventional Chinese Communist line: Religion was out-of-date; contemporary problems could be solved only by science. Science, in his view, had replaced religion.

There was more to this argument than a straightforward clash between a man of faith and an atheist. The "atheist" was from a Muslim family. His grandfather on his mother's side had come from India. His father was Tibetan. Although he didn't believe in religion himself, he still stuck to many of his family traditions. He did not eat pork, and said he would marry a Muslim girl, if only to please his parents. He even said he might go on a pilgrimage to Mecca one day, as his parents had done. But although he felt entirely Tibetan, religion to him did not carry the same meaning it did for his Buddhist friend. He told me that Muslims had sometimes been persecuted in the past by Tibetans who wanted to keep Tibet "pure," that is, purely Buddhist. Buddhism, to a Tibetan, cannot be separated from nationalism—to be Tibetan is to be Buddhist—which is why the Chinese government wishes to control it and why those from religious minorities view it with a sense of unease.

Later that evening, the Buddhist and I repaired to a Tibetan nightclub. These are good places to talk. They are noisy, and there are few Han Chinese around. The decor looked vaguely Tibetan, with white curtains lined with blue, green, and red stripes, and the singers, some in traditional dress, sang Tibetan as well as Chinese songs. There are rules about this: The number of Tibetan songs and their content are strictly controlled, so as not to provoke unwelcome outbursts of nationalism. Video screens showed clips from Hollywood movies. I saw bits of *Titanic* and the burning of Atlanta in *Gone With the Wind,* as well as stock images of Tibet, copied perhaps from videos promoting tourism: the Potala, country dances, yaks grazing, monks blowing horns, and horse fairs. A reproduction of the *Mona Lisa* hung on the wall next to the plastic head of a bodhisattva.

I asked my friend what went through his mind when he saw the representations of Tibetan folklore at official celebrations in Beijing, those pumped-up occasions for endless parades past Tiananmen Square, where, between the tanks and the missile launchers and the adoring schoolchildren, the fifty-six official minorities dance in colorful costumes for the Chinese leaders who wave from their platform in front of Chairman Mao's portrait. He said it was both ridiculous, because many details were wrong, and outrageous, because it was so patronizing.

Despite the noise from the stage, where a woman in a red ball gown was singing a Chinese song in praise of the Tibetan mountains, my friend lowered his voice and studied his knees. The trouble, he murmured, was that it had become almost impossible to study Tibetan culture seriously, especially religious culture. And without the latter, you could not possibly understand Tibet. To take a serious interest in religion invited suspicion of political subversion. You might be denounced as a "splittist," a promoter of Tibetan independence, splitting the country from the "motherland." And the monasteries were no good anyway, because the monks were government employees who knew little about religion. Yet my friend wanted to know about his own culture and be more literate in Tibetan as well. He spoke of his shame at not mastering his mother tongue. The fact that he was compelled, through his own education, to read about Tibetan Buddhism in Chinese made his situation even more galling. The Tibetan-language textbooks he had read at school were all about the glories of Chinese communism, and the few books he had studied about Tibet were written by Chinese. I glanced at the video monitor with its tourist images of yaks, horse fairs, and white mountains, and wondered whether in the end Tibetan culture would be reduced to this: the commercial equivalent of the folk dancers in Tiananmen Square.

On another night, at a similar nightclub in Lhasa, this one with a small dance floor lit by a revolving ball splashing the dancers with specks of blue light, I had another discussion about the Tibetan identity. There were video screens showing the same stock images of Tibet that had been shown at the other place. A rather fey young man, dressed as a Tibetan herdsman, sang a folk song, prompting a female admirer to wrap a silk scarf around his neck in the traditional Tibetan manner of showing respect. After his act, he came up to me and told me in English that he was an art student. He sat down, and I asked him what kind of art. Any kind, he said—oil painting, Western art, any kind. What about Tibetan art? He hesitated. Yes, he finally said, Tibetan art too. But he wanted to go to the United States, to work with computers. What about his art? I asked. He shrugged and said he couldn't express himself in art. I asked him why not. He drew closer and whispered in my ear: "Politics." He wanted to do Tibetan painting but was not allowed to study religious art, and without that, Tibetan painting made no sense.

After the singer had gone back to the stage, to do a comedy routine in Tibetan, which failed to provoke much laughter, I sat awhile nursing my glass of beer. Couples were dancing under the revolving ball, men with women, women with women, men with men, some of them going through the well-practiced moves of Western ballroom dancing. I felt a tap on my shoulder. "Where you from?" asked a neatly dressed man of about thirty. He looked Han Chinese, which was indeed what he turned out to be. He had been living in Lhasa for three years and was almost due to go home. He wanted to know what I thought of the Tibetan situation. Not knowing who he was, I made a banal remark about every place having its problems. He nodded gravely. Then he asked what I thought of human rights in China. Again, I erred on the safe side. And what about democracy? Well, living in a democracy myself, I had to say I was rather in favor of it. He nodded, and said the one-party state was no good. There was too much corruption and abuse of power. China needed more political parties.

I was surprised to hear this, especially when he told me he was a Communist Party member and had been sent to Tibet by the government. But nothing had prepared me for the next question. Did I think Tibet was like Kosovo? I gulped, took a long sip of beer, recalled the nationalist fervor in China after the bombing in Belgrade, and asked him whether he meant China was like Serbia. He looked me in the eye and nodded quickly. Living in Lhasa had opened his eyes to many problems, he said, problems of nationality and human rights. "In the West," he said, "people are allowed to choose their own governments. Here in Tibet, the government chooses its people."

A thin, dark-skinned man, sitting on my other side, was straining to hear what was being said. He turned out to be a Tibetan friend of the Chinese cadre. Now it was his turn to talk. He cupped his hands around my ear and said in perfect Chinese that he was working for a Tibetan company. What did I think of human rights in Tibet? Once more, I played it safe: Human rights were important everywhere, in the rest of China as much as in Tibet. "No, no," he said. "We have a special problem in Tibet. We are losing our language, our religion is controlled, our culture is disappearing. You see, the forces of economic modernization are directly opposed to our own traditions." Still trying to be as bland as I could, I mumbled something about national traditions having survived modern-

ization in other countries. This agitated him. Surely all foreigners understood, he said, that Tibet was special: "As long as we are part of China, we
cannot survive. We are like a man who is thrown into a lake but can't
swim. We are drowning. You foreigners must help us."

There was nothing much I could say. All three of us drank in silence.
Perhaps they were government agents. I thought not, but I could not be
sure. The Chinese cadre had told me that others in the Party shared his
views, but they lacked the power to act on them, or even to mention them
in public. His friend merely repeated that I should let the world know
about Tibet. The world should come to the rescue. And I knew that the
world would do no such thing.

The impression I got from these limited conversations in Lhasa was
that the Tibetans who suffered most from Chinese cultural imperialism
were the most educated, the ones who benefited from economic modernization. The better you were able to function in Chinese, the more successful you were bound to be. Without Chinese, you were cut off from the
urban economy. The man in the nightclub was right: Chinese-style modernization, with its eradication of the past, its official atheism, its consequent intolerance toward organized religion, and its emphasis, politically,
philosophically, and economically, on materialism, is opposed to the Tibetan tradition. This does not mean that the Chinese-educated Tibetans
all yearn for the revival of a Buddhist theocracy. Few, if any, want that. But
to survive in the Chinese economy, Tibetans are forced to blot out their
own cultural identity, and that leaves a sense of deep colonial humiliation.

The only Tibetan I spoke to who did not seem to care about the grad-
ual replacement of the Tibetan language by Chinese or the new dominance in urban areas of Chinese low life and pop culture was the Muslim.
He spoke like a true modernist. It was inevitable, he said, that traditions
were hollowed out by modern life. It happened everywhere, in Europe and
Japan as much as in Tibet. And if Chinese was more practical than Tibetan, why then people would speak Chinese or English or whatever. It
was surely a waste of time to regret the past. After all, things were much
better now; there were banks and hospitals and more schools. But it was
easier for him to praise these developments than for his Buddhist friends,
for the monasteries that used to perform some of these functions were not

part of his spiritual tradition. The crude new cosmopolitanism of Lhasa was, on the contrary, part of his emancipation.

The last time I saw my Muslim friend was in an outdoor café on the lake behind the Potala. It was a beautiful, clear Saturday afternoon. Policemen with red country faces and green uniforms were splashing about in crimson pleasure boats, making a lot of noise. We were joined by a friend of the Muslim, a scholarly young man in a frayed brown jacket and gold-rimmed glasses. He was introduced to me as a computer scientist. But he spoke little and, when he did, very softly. He was from a Buddhist family in Qinghai, where life was better than in Lhasa, for Tibetans lived among themselves, in a "purer community," not "mixed like Lhasa." He said he was studying English, to get into a university in the United States. Things were very bad in Tibet. I saw the Muslim shift uncomfortably in his seat. He didn't like it when conversations took this turn. And what, I asked, would the scientist study in America? The man looked pensively at the splashing policemen on the lake. The only way he could get a place in an American university was to apply as a computer scientist, he murmured. But once he was there, he would switch to Tibetan language and literature. After a short pause, he said: "The Tibetan department of the university here in Lhasa was closed in 1999."

———

Leaving Lhasa is in a sense to leave China, not officially, of course, but culturally. Little or no Chinese is spoken in the villages, let alone among the nomads who roam the vast, empty highlands, which to most Han Chinese are as strange and intimidating as the surface of the moon. Where the outside world does happen to glance off Tibetan village life, economic transactions of the crudest kind take place.

There is only one road from Lhasa to Gyangtse, the town passed by in 1904 by a British expedition led by Sir Francis Younghusband on his way to Lhasa. Before reaching Gyangtse, he had mowed down some seven hundred unruly Tibetans with a Maxim gun, an event that is still remembered in Tibet. A rocky, unpaved road winds along some terrifying mountain passes with straight drops down to a glorious, deep blue lake. Jeeps and minibuses hired by tourists always stop at the same scenic spots, marked by Tibetan prayer flags fluttering from ceremonial piles of stones, or outside villages with whitewashed-stone houses, inhabited by people in richly embroidered boots and coarse brown robes slung across their shoulders. The villagers are well aware of their photogenic appeal, and as soon as a tourist vehicle is sighted, women and children, the smallest of whom is dressed in his finest silk jacket, take up their positions together with a yak, whose long black hair contrasts prettily with red ribbons tied around its horns. The tourists are surrounded by children in states of remarkable squalor, with long, matted hair, like old rope, green mucus clotted around their noses and mouths, various kinds of milky eye infections, and layers of hard, black grime on every inch of exposed skin. "Hello," cry the children, while rubbing their thumbs along the palms of their hands. "How are you, money, money!" An old man in dark rags, with a black face, sticks out his pink tongue in the old-fashioned Tibetan gesture of obeisance to social superiors. The child in the fine silk jacket is placed on top of the yak, and the mother holds up five fingers: five Chinese yuan for a photograph. The only way these villagers know how to make money from the tourist economy is by posing as themselves.

Few villages are on the tourist beat, however. Most villagers don't even have the occasion to pose or beg. I visited a village several hours away from Lhasa. It was actually less a village than a cluster of small, gray-stone huts in a beautiful green valley. The inhabitants herded yak and sheep. The richest person had several hundred yaks, the poorest just a few. Only the village head, elected by the villagers, understood some Chinese. I was taken to the village by a man who had been born there. He had not had any formal education; he called himself "a man without culture." But he had managed to leave the village and make a life in Lhasa by serving for a few years in the People's Liberation Army. It had not been a pleasant experience; the few Tibetan soldiers were harshly treated. But at least he had made some money and learned to speak Chinese. He was an intelligent, humorous man in his forties with the wrinkled, reddish-brown face of someone much older.

Most of the people in the village looked poorer than the ones I had encountered on the road to Gyangtse. But there was a new school nearby, and a few of the younger people could read and write. I was politely offered cup after cup of yak-butter tea, which tastes like greasy soup but keeps one's lips from cracking in the bone-dry air. One of the herdsmen reached inside his filthy shirt, tore off a chunk of dried raw meat, and kindly handed it to me. The meat was a year old. His hands were encrusted with dirt. My friend explained that most people suffered from intestinal diseases. The hard, raw meat tasted sweet, a bit like horse meat.

The poorest house consisted of one dark room, home to a family of six, but the richest was more sturdily built; it had a gate, decorated with yak horns, and whitewashed walls. It was pleasantly furnished with painted wooden chests and sofas covered in carpets. On the wall were four religious paintings, one of which looked old and was finely drawn. The wooden ceiling beams were painted bright blue, apple-green, and pink. Both the rich and the poor displayed pictures of the current Dalai Lama, for which a person in Lhasa would be arrested. I also noticed a photograph of the Karmapa, the young head of the Kagyu sect, who had escaped to India in 1999. Since he was officially recognized by the Chinese government as well as by his followers, his flight was extremely embarrassing to the rulers in Beijing.

I asked my friend, the driver, whether there was any risk in displaying these pictures. He made a dismissive gesture and said that Party officials hardly bothered to come to the villages. "They wouldn't be welcome here," he said. I asked, naïvely, whether the villagers knew about the Karmapa's escape to India. "Of course," he snorted. "They knew before the government in Lhasa did. Every night before going to sleep, they listen to the Voice of America."

It was clear from his account that the links between Tibet, even in the villages, and India had not been cut. People knew where the Dalai Lama was and what he had been saying on his trips around the world. Young people still make their way to Dharamsala, despite border patrols and the risk of arrest. "They can't control what is in our heads," my friend said. It was not the first time I had heard that phrase in Tibet. He said: "They can make us say we love the Communist Party, but they can never make us hate the Dalai Lama."

Later, while we picnicked at the side of the river, my friend showed the first sign of despair. He had told me before that he had thought many times of going to India but had never had the opportunity. "It's all over for me now," he said. I kept silent. Then: "But maybe not for my son." He asked me where I was from. I said that I lived in England, in London. "Ah yes," he replied. "You English . . . you English came here with guns and killed many Tibetans. . . . When was it again?" I said it was in 1904. He smiled as though it were a fond memory and said: "If only you English would come here again, with many guns. Then we Tibetans would dress up in our finest clothes and give you a warm welcome."

It was only a passing fancy, of course. He went on to talk of the hard times in the past, of the killings during the Cultural Revolution and the destruction of temples and monasteries, often carried out by Tibetan Red Guards. They were the worst, he said. The Tibetan cadres were the most fanatical. "Long Live Chairman Mao," I said facetiously. He looked at me, and casually tossed an empty beer can into the clear blue river: "Bullshit!" he said. "Long live us, the people!" We could both drink to that.

—

Religion is the glory and the tragedy of Tibet. In China, religions and cults challenge the official Marxist dogma and test the limits of spiritual freedom. Religion, whether Buddhist, Confucian, Taoist, or some mixture of all three, can make Chinese feel anchored in their tradition; it can make them feel more Chinese. But no matter how much successive Chinese governments and their scribes try to make it so, China is not defined by a single faith. Tibet is.

Tibet is not a state defined by borders. More Tibetans in China live outside the Tibetan Autonomous Region than inside—in Qinghai, Sichuan, Gansu, and Yunnan. The government led by the Dalai Lama is in India. But what almost all Tibetans have in common, apart from variations of the same language, is their worship of this religious figure as the highest representative of their faith, and thus of their nation. Without Tibetan Buddhism, most Tibetans would have no conception of Tibet. To keep their faith, then, is not just a matter of individual liberty but of national survival.

The Chinese Communists know this, which is why they tried for a time to destroy its monuments. Most of the damage was done in the 1960s. Few of the thousands of temples and monasteries that once dotted the Tibetan landscape remain. Before the storm of Maoism there were about twenty-five hundred functioning monasteries. By 1972 there were ten. Now, however, a more subtle strategy prevails. When Chinese tourists arrive in Lhasa, tour guides tell them that the Tibetans are a religious people and that their faith must be respected. Booklets in Chinese are richly illustrated with pictures of the main religious landmarks, or what is left of them, the Potala, the Jokhang, and the Tashilhunpo in Shigatse, where the Panchen Lama, whose spiritual status is equal to the Dalai Lama's political status, traditionally resides. And during their customary week in Tibet, the Han Chinese tourists are photographed with their friends against the exotic backdrop of praying monks and gorgeous pagodas; and they sigh at the mystery of it all.

What the tour guides fail to mention is that much of this is a façade, a kind of theater of religious freedom, orchestrated by the Chinese authorities. My banker friend in Lhasa exaggerated when he said that all monks were government stooges. Some only pay lip service to official propaganda. Some are "unofficial" monks, who slip through the net of state control. Many monks and nuns spend many years in prison. And even the official monks, if the time were ripe for open rebellion, might well prove to be unreliable government employees. Still, the government's aim is to control every aspect of Tibetan Buddhism and make it as colorful and lifeless as those official jamborees of minority peoples dancing in unison in Tiananmen Square.

This macabre theater often verges on the absurd. When the popular tenth Panchen Lama died in 1989, the reincarnation of his soul had to be found in the body of a child. There are set ways of going about this. High Lamas scan a sacred lake for signs of the reincarnated soul. They blow on conch shells, pray to the embalmed body of the late Panchen Lama. Little boys are vetted and presented with possessions of the late Lama, to provoke signs of recognition. And once the incarnated Lama has been found, the Dalai Lama must endorse him. But since the Chinese authorities refused to recognize the authority of the Dalai Lama, they decided that they themselves would be the final arbiters of divine rebirth and cut the Dalai Lama out altogether. So the abbot of Tashilhunpo was told to find a suitable reincarnation. This he set out to do. Prayers were said, omens scrutinized, and names collected, but in the end the abbot's loyalty to the Dalai Lama proved to be stronger than his political reliability to the Chinese.

A plan was made for the abbot to pass on a name to the Dalai Lama, who would then endorse him in secret, after which the candidate would be revealed to the Chinese authorities. Then the Dalai Lama could claim to his people that the Chinese candidate had in fact been his choice to begin with. This way, Beijing would be happy and the Dalai Lama's authority would be intact. It was a clever ruse. But things went wrong. Messages between the Dalai Lama and the abbot failed to get through, and the Dalai Lama announced the name of his candidate before the Chinese had a chance to do so. The Chinese were furious. The abbot was arrested for his treachery. The young boy, blessed by the Dalai Lama, was kidnapped. Monks at Tashilhunpo were thrown into jail. And the Communist authorities, quite absurdly, accused the Dalai Lama of acting "contrary to the dignified and deeply felt religious rituals of Buddhism."

It was a most remarkable situation. Marxist-Leninists from Beijing posed as defenders of the Tibetan faith, and names of the official, Chinese-backed candidates were wrapped in silk and put in a sacred urn. Then handpicked Tibetan monks ceremoniously divined the Panchen Lama's incarnation, who happened to be the son of two loyal Communist Party members. His photograph was distributed for display all over the Tibetan areas. Yet few Tibetans believe in him. They might pray to his image, but as one Tibetan told me: "They can make us show any picture they want. The real thing is inside our heads."

The tragedy is that politics in Tibet has come to this: religious charades played out in a battle for sovereignty and authority. The almost purely religious definition of the Tibetan nation precludes more secular ways to establish a freer, more open society, so Tibetans have to choose between Chinese-style modernization, as brutal communism or brutal capitalism, and government by high priests. Of course, many priests, including the Dalai Lama, claim that they want democracy. But when the highest temporal authority is also the center of metaphysical truth, freedom is impossible.

Some Tibetan aristocrats, who had been educated in India and were aware of this problem even before the Chinese revolution, sometimes backed the Chinese Communists to free their country from what they saw as a corrupt theocracy. I met a Tibetan poet in Lhasa, whose father was a nobleman educated at a British school in Darjeeling. When he came home in the 1930s, he was appalled by the corruption and backwardness he found and became one of the first Tibetans to join the Communist Party. Not that it helped him during the Maoist storms. He was arrested, tortured in front of his family, and sent to do hard labor in a remote area of China. Soon after that, his heart gave out. His son, the poet, makes a living translating Tibetan poems into Chinese.

—

Late one afternoon, when the sun was about to set, a chill wind began to blow around the Tashilhunpo. I was told by a young monk that there would be some "activity" at six o'clock. So I waited, with Tibetan pilgrims, covered in dust and grime, and tourists, armed with cameras. Soon the sounds of long horns and clashing cymbals echoed from the whitewashed walls. An elderly monk with a huge yellow hat, like a great cockscomb, appeared at the head of about twenty monks. They went up to a bundle of straw outside the main gate tied together with rope, rather like a stake for a public execution. After more banging, a young monk was handed a bow and arrow. He shot several arrows into the straw. The old monk handed him a torch. It was lit and the straw went up in flames, leaving a black smudge on the street after it had burned out.

"What was all that about?" a plump German woman asked her husband, who had been recording the event on his video camera. "Something symbolic," he answered with great authority.

He was right. It was a symbolic driving out of evil demons. But who were the demons?

Chapter 4

A Deer Is a Deer

In the late summer of 2000, a poet named Bei Ling was arrested in Beijing. Bei Ling, a genial figure in round glasses and a ponytail, was on a visit from Boston, Massachusetts, where he edits *Tendency*, a highbrow literary journal with a refreshing cosmopolitan perspective. It features interviews with international writers and poets and articles by and about dissidents in the former Soviet empire, such as Václav Havel, as well as works by Chinese authors, some of whom are banned in the People's Republic of China.

Although his sympathies are with the dissidents in China, Bei Ling is not really a political activist. His crime was decribed as "illegal commercial activities," that is to say, he had printed the latest issue of his journal in Beijing, because it was cheaper there, and distributed a thousand-odd free copies. The contents of this issue were not particularly provocative, except perhaps for a photograph of Wang Dan, the student leader in 1989. Bei Ling was to have attended a party in Beijing, but failed to turn up. The police got to him first.

Luckily for Bei Ling, his friends and contacts in the West were able to make a fuss. Famous authors wrote angry pieces in *The New York Times*. Keeping him in jail was more trouble to the Chinese authorities than it was worth. Li Peng was about to visit New York. So after a week in detention, Bei Ling was released and sent back to the United States. His family was told to pay the police a considerable fee to clinch the deal. This was business as usual.

In the grander scale of things, it was an event of small importance. Yet it raised an interesting question: Why should a powerful regime, protected by a huge network of secret police and security agencies, a regime that had successfully crushed all attempts at organized opposition, be afraid of a minor poet and editor of an obscure émigré literary journal?

The answer lies in the Communist Party's paranoia about critical writers but also in the nature of what Václav Havel once called the post-totalitarian system. Such a system is different, in his view, from a classic dictatorship, which rules mainly through brute force. The post-totalitarian system will use violence if necessary, but prefers to cloak its coercive power in a quasi-religious ideology, a tissue of falsehoods, which offer an answer and an explanation for everything. These answers, however, are usually the opposite of the truth. In Havel's words, "Government by bureaucracy is called popular government . . . the arbitrary use of power is called observing the legal code . . . the expansion of imperial power is presented as support for the oppressed; the lack of free expression becomes the highest form of freedom; banning independent thought becomes the most scientific of world views . . ."

This is of course also how a totalitarian or Stalinist system operates, and the distinctive quality of "post-totalitarianism" is not always clear. Perhaps Havel means that post-totalitarian subjects have internalized the official lies so effectively that force is no longer necessary. In that sense, China is not yet a post-totalitarian society; violence is still used extensively, especially in such areas as Tibet or against members of unofficial religious groups. But China is post-totalitarian in another sense. The Communist government no longer tries to control every aspect of people's lives. There is a certain amount of freedom now to choose a job or a marriage partner or even, in larger cities, a "lifestyle." Young urban people enjoy a sexual freedom that was unheard of only a decade or so ago. It is almost as if energies that might be turned toward politics are deliberately channeled toward a giddy hedonism—the age-old formula of bread and circuses.

And yet much of what Havel says applies to China, too. His point about the center of power being the center of truth is as true today as it was in many periods before the Communists came to power. When the president of the People's Republic of China says that censorship is essential because otherwise the press (or the Internet) will disseminate falsehoods and "confuse people's minds," he speaks like a typical exponent of Confucian authoritarianism. Perhaps he even believes it. But communism added a perverse twist to this kind of thinking. Havel again: "Because the regime is captive to its own lies, it must falsify everything. It falsifies the past. It falsifies the present, and it falsifies the future. It falsifies statistics. It pretends not to possess an omnipotent and unprincipled police apparatus. It pretends to respect human rights. It pretends to persecute no one. It pretends to fear nothing. It pretends to pretend nothing."

People need not believe these lies. In private they may even say so. But in public they must behave as though they do. They must, in Havel's phrase, "live within a lie." Those who refuse to conform to this apparently simple, even comforting, but actually most cruel form of human degradation, who choose, in other words, to "live in truth," are ostracized, bullied, deprived, and spit out of the system. This is essential for the system to survive, for once the lies are publicly exposed and the emperor is naked for all to see, only brute force remains as a method of control. And no force, however brutal, can be up to the task, in the long run, of controlling 1.3 billion Chinese.

The problem with China is that the old lies no longer work. They are simply too absurd. When the government's answer to the corruption produced by its own economic policies is to order people to redouble their study of Marxism-Leninism, even the most trusted cadres are hard-pressed to stay within the lies. And that is why the authorities appear so panic-stricken in their attempts to stop anyone from living in truth, even a rather innocuous poet who behaves as though he were in Boston instead of Beijing. He must be punished to discourage others who might do the same.

—

I arrived in Beijing in the summer of 1999, the tenth anniversary of the Tiananmen demonstrations. It seemed a good time to be reaching the final destination of my journeys. The truth about June 4 was still a smoldering political issue that could yet explode. I found that people were ready to talk about the past in private conversation. But the government was nervous about public displays of grief or anger. The capital was more heavily policed than usual. On the anniversary of the June 4 massacre, Tiananmen Square itself was sealed off from the public with police barricades.

Beijing is the most public city in China, public not in a democratic but in an official sense—a city given to massive, mostly state-driven occasions. It is a political city, with its monumental government buildings, Mao's mausoleum, its high-rises with phony Chinese-style roofs, its Forbidden City, and, of course, at "the heart of China," Tiananmen, "the largest square in the world," center of the new Chinese empire and the place of power worship and occasional protest. Beijing is all that, and at the same time it is a city of dark and intricate intimacy, a city of walled compounds, narrow lanes, and whispered conversations.

I have come across many Chinese who expressed a dislike of Beijing because it is "too political." Power, not commerce, is the business of Beijing. Just as Shenzhen was built as a monument to commerce, Beijing was planned as a monument to imperial power. Few capital cities make such a show of official authority. The thick red walls of the Forbidden City still project the majesty of the Ming and Qing emperors. Scanning the vast expanse of Tiananmen Square, all 444,000 square meters of it, the Stalinist-fascist Great Hall of the People at the west, the Museum of History and Revolution at the east, and the Mao Zedong Memorial Hall at the south, one gets the impression of a regime of provincial upstarts, trying not just to live up to the splendor of its imperial predecessors but to outdo it, by building on an even larger, more grandiose scale.

Official Beijing is a monument to its lies. The Great Hall of the People belongs no more to the people than the Forbidden City did in the past. The quasi-religious cult of Chairman Mao is encrusted in official myths.

The cheesy corpse of the late chairman, lying in its embalmed state in the middle of Tiananmen Square, may not even be the body of the great dictator but a wax effigy.

The greatest lie of all is something that cannot be spoken. A taboo lies at the center of Beijing. What happened around Tiananmen Square on June 4, 1989, is officially dismissed as an "incident." As soon as the killings were done, tank tracks were covered in asphalt, bloodstains scrubbed off the streets, and bullet-scarred walls whitewashed. Not a trace remains. Ten years later, Prime Minister Zhu Rongji told foreign reporters that he had forgotten all about June 4. Nobody knows how many victims there were. Nobody is allowed to know. Their names were never released. Their relatives have to suffer in silence, as though they were criminals, or outcasts, with a shameful secret. And the mere publication of a photograph in a literary journal of one of the student leaders gets you arrested.

To live in this lie is humiliating. One day, during my 1999 visit, I had tea in the apartment of a literary critic, a friend of a friend. His study was a murky grotto piled with books, papers, and literary journals, some banned, some from Hong Kong or Taiwan. Zhou, as I shall call him, had the cultivated bohemian look of many Chinese (or Japanese) intellectuals, vaguely redolent of Paris in the 1920s: long, greasy hair, nicotine-stained teeth, sandals, and a drinker's paunch. He told me about his daughter, who at twelve, was too young to remember the Beijing Massacre.

She knew nothing about what had happened ten years before. How could she? The events of June 4 were never mentioned at school. Some of her teachers had participated in the demonstrations and might have lost friends in the killings, but they have to remain silent. Instead, they teach the children lies: that the Party is always good, that the army loves the people, and that American imperialists must be resisted, because foreigners want China to stay weak. The most agonizing thing is that parents, who know better, are not able to discuss June 4 with their children either, or not in any way that might land them in trouble at school.

Zhou lit up a cigarette, shrugged, and said: "In any case, the children aren't interested. Chinese kids quickly acquire a sharp sense of what might get them in trouble. They develop fine antennae for unmentionable subjects. They know that being interested in sensitive historical topics is not good for them, so they don't ask questions. And that means the parents don't have to answer them."

It was one of the saddest things I heard in Beijing. The worst humiliation of having to live in a lie is that it forces people to share their oppressors' cover-up. It makes them accomplices, for, as Václav Havel puts it, by living in the lie, "individuals confirm the system, fulfill the system, make the system, *are* the system."

I was in Shanghai a week or so before I met Zhou in Beijing. A young woman, who was highly educated and had taken part in the student demonstrations of 1989, took me to an Internet café. It was a well-lit place, decorated with plastic flowers and movie posters. Rows of young people sat at long tables, working the computers and drinking coffee under the gaze of Madonna and Brad Pitt. There was no sound except for the whirring and screeching noises of machines going on-line. We surfed the Net together, my friend and I. Out of careless curiosity, which I later regretted, I logged on to an English-language website—often blocked—called China News Digest, which featured a BBC story on the Beijing Massacre, with pictures of dying students, PLA soldiers firing, and portraits of Wang Dan, Chai Ling, and others. My friend stiffened, perhaps in apprehension, and then said: "You foreigners always want to find bad things to say about China." In the presence of an outsider, the government's shame had become her shame, too.

It is always a moving experience to come across people who refuse to live in the lie. It can happen at the most unexpected moments. I took a taxi to the Beijing Art Museum one morning. The driver was a large man in his forties, with a sad, horsy face. We passed a low nineteenth-century, gray-brick, Chinese-style building. I asked him what it was. This question unleashed an extraordinary tirade.

It had belonged, he said, to one of Sun Yat-sen's ministers, a deeply corrupt man. But not as corrupt as the bunch in power today. The driver banged the dashboard of his Volkswagen and said: "Things are much worse now than during the late Qing dynasty. Fuck your mother! China is like a huge prison. There is no progress here, because of our history of dictatorships, one after the other, one after the other!"

I asked him whether he remembered June 4. A stupid question. "Of course," he barked. "Everyone in Beijing remembers." He himself had driven wounded students to the hospital in his taxi. "How can we forget? The government feels so guilty that every year on June 4, the city is swarming with police. If they didn't feel guilty, would they still need to protect themselves like that from the people?"

We were nearing the museum. The driver negotiated his way through the traffic at murderous speed as though by instinct, looking at me as he spoke. "The problem," he said, "is that anyone who resists the Communists gets shot. And because the people can't criticize the government, the government makes big mistakes. It's not like in your country. We live in a prison here. Everything you hear is lies. All those years of communism, and we still have nothing." The taxi came to a halt. He took my hand and said: "You foreigners must help us Chinese people. We all want to be free, like you."

———

One of the speakers in Hong Kong on the tenth anniversary of June 4 was a retired philosophy professor named Ding Zilin. A white-haired motherly woman, she was not permitted to use her phone, so she spoke by a videotape, recorded in Beijing, which was projected on a large screen in Victoria Park in front of the seventy thousand people gathered there. Ding didn't have to say much about herself, for everyone knew who she was. Her presence was fitting in the quasi-religious atmosphere of candlelight and tears.

In 1991, just before Qing Ming, the festival when Chinese sweep the graves of their loved ones, Professor Ding decided to break the silence in Beijing. Together with another woman, she began to talk openly to Hong Kong and American reporters about how they had lost their children on the night of June 3. Ding's son was a seventeen-year-old high school student when he was shot in the back while running for cover. The two mothers demanded an investigation into what had really happened, not just to their children but to others who died in obscurity. And so the Tiananmen Mothers were born. They wanted to live within the truth, like the Argentinian mothers who gathered every week on the Plaza de Mayo in Buenos Aires, dressed in black, the names of their "disappeared" children on white headbands.

A year before she decided to speak out in public, Ding was handed a note found in a cemetery in Beijing. It was from a woman who had lost her husband on June 4. She wanted to contact others so they could break the silence together. Ding, with her husband and a few friends, set themselves the task of finding as many relatives of victims as possible so that the deaths could be recorded, the names remembered, the truth established. She traveled all over China, often acting on the slightest information—a name, a half-remembered address, a grave inscription. The police harassed her constantly, tapping her phone, stopping her from leaving her apartment, barring guests, once even preventing her from buying offerings for her son's grave. She was threatened with arrest and called a "traitor to the nation," by policemen, but also by anonymous callers, who would phone her late at night.

In 1994, on the fifth anniversary of June 4, Ding published a book with private funds, listing the names and circumstances of ninety-six victims' deaths. The list has grown since then to more than 155, while the official obstruction, the threats, and the intimidations continue. Sometimes it is possible to see her, sometimes not. Lois Snow, the widow of Edgar Snow, the American journalist who did more than any other Westerner to promote the Maoist revolution, was not permitted to see her. Snow's grave in Beijing is marked with the words FRIEND OF CHINA. But his widow's friendship with the Communists finally soured on June 4, 1989. When she came to Beijing with her son in March 2000 to offer solidarity to the Tiananmen Mothers, plainclothes policemen kept Ding Zilin away from her. Lois Snow then threatened to take her husband's ashes back to America. She still was unable to see Ding.

Ding reckons that during the fifty years of communism, 80 million people died of unnatural causes. In the light of this catastrophe, 155 dead may not seem much. And yet, she wrote, "I have come to realize that even if I had documented only one of these names, I would still consider my life to have some sort of significance. If our fellow countrymen had squarely faced the successive onslaughts of death that occurred in China's past, perhaps we could have prevented this most recent tragedy."

I was unable to see Ding Zilin, although I spoke to her on her cell phone. But a friend in Beijing passed on the telephone number of another Tiananmen Mother, close to Ding, who was also actively trying to live in the truth. She is Su Bingxian. Her son was twenty-one when he caught three bullets in the chest, somewhere on Chang'an Avenue, not far from the Square. She had warned him not to go out that night. Already on the afternoon of June 3, the streets were filled with menace. But Su Zhaolong wanted to be "a witness to history," he said. When the shooting started later that night, his mother thought of firecrackers on New Year's Eve.

It wasn't easy to find Mrs. Su's apartment in a block of redbrick flats in Beijing's university area surrounded by other blocks, for I had been given the wrong number. Officious-looking women with armbands guarded the gates. A man in a green uniform smirked and nudged his friends as I walked by, anxiously trying to find my bearings. I finally got there after an elderly lady guessed whom I was looking for and told me where to go.

The two-bedroom apartment was sparsely furnished, like most Chinese homes. We sat at a simple wooden table drinking green tea. Two large black-and-white photographs hung on the walls, like ancestral portraits. One was of a thin, scholarly old gentlemen dressed in a Mao jacket. The other was of Su Zhaolong, a handsome boy with thick hair and a pensive expression. His father, Su's husband, was in the countryside. I sensed a degree of tension when Su spoke about him. A retired naval officer, like Su herself, he was, she said, "disillusioned."

Su, a round-faced woman with frizzy hair, noticed that I was looking at the portrait of the old man on the wall and told me it was her father, a famous poet, Su Jinsan, who "suffered from all the Chinese troubles of the twentieth century." She spoke in the clear Mandarin of a highly educated person. The story she told of her family would fill a book of tragedies. It was, in many ways, the story of China's modern fate.

When Su Jinsan graduated from Beijing University, he was full of literary ambition and patriotic idealism. The two were linked in his mind. He wanted to be a writer and save China. Like many early Communists, including Mao, Su had joined the KMT for three years in the late 1920s. Those were murky times, full of infiltrations, short-term alliances, and betrayals. Suspected, rightly, of being a Communist, Su was arrested during a purge of the left and managed to escape from prison, and almost certain death, only through the help of a sympathizer in the KMT. He joined Mao in the caves of Yan'an, for Su loved the Communist revolution, which saved China from the "black gang" of the KMT. He loved it, but not blindly. He still had half a mind to live in the truth.

This was not easy, for even in those early days, writers and poets with minds of their own were persecuted for deviating from Mao's strict guidelines. Mao demanded absolute loyalty, especially from writers and intellectuals, whom, as a class, he never trusted. Perhaps he felt inferior, a provincial lacking in style. He always suspected treachery.

After 1949, Mao needed a literary scapegoat to whip all intellectuals into line. He picked on a gifted poet named Hu Feng, an ardent Communist, who, like Su, still retained his critical faculties. Hu particularly resented Mao's rigid, dogmatic rules on style as well as content. He was too good a writer to have to conform to Mao's literary regulations. So Mao unleashed a public assault on Hu Feng and his "clique" for being "bourgeois reactionaries."

Su Jinsan not only defended Hu Feng but followed Mao's orders in the 1950s to be critical of the Party's mistakes. For this he was arrested, tortured, and robbed of his rights. To be branded an "extreme rightist" in the 1950s was to be an outcast, a non-person, who could be bullied by anyone at will. Su Jinsan was still able to find refuge in a lowly job at a library. But ten years later, during the Cultural Revolution, he was terrorized once again, not just for being a "rightist" this time, but for having been a member of the KMT in the 1920s. The distinguished poet was taken from his home, beaten, and made to kneel in front of young thugs, some still in their teens, who made him "confess" his "crimes" while yanking his arms back behind his neck in the "airplane" position. His wife, who had been sent to a labor camp in 1957 as an "extreme rightist," was forced to publicly denounce him, which didn't save her from being sent again to work in the countryside, where she almost starved to death. And yet, despite every horror that came his way, Su never lost his loyalty to the Party. He died as a firm believer in the faith that had wrecked his life.

At this point in her story, Su Bingxian paused to wipe the tears from her eyes. She had loved her father, and his treatment shook her own faith in the Party, but she had to keep her doubts to herself. She could not talk to her husband, for "he didn't understand a lot of things." It was only in the 1980s, after Mao's death and Deng's reforms, that she and her husband began to question the dogmas they grew up with. But she never told her son what had happened to his grandparents. It was too dangerous, and too painful. He grew up ignorant of his family history.

"You know," she said, "my husband and I were of the Mao generation. We had closed minds. And people of my father's age had to be interested in politics, because politics was interested in them." But Zhaolong, her son, had no interest in politics or literature, including his grandfather's poems. "My son's generation," Su said, "had no use for reading. They like to go shopping, have fun."

Zhaolong also liked to play his guitar. But he was evidently a bright boy who wanted to go to university. In the spring of 1989, Zhaolong was working in a clothes market, hoping to earn enough for his tuition fees. Many of his former schoolmates were sleeping in Tiananmen Square, and Zhaolong would bring them food and water. It was the first time he felt any interest in the wider world. He joined the protest marches. Suddenly there was hope and excitement. Politics was no longer dull propaganda. The heady air of freedom touched him too. His mother saw a big change in him. She realized that he "had learned to think critically." For the first time he reminded her of her father.

It took three days to track down Zhaolong, three days of going from hospital to hospital, mortuary to mortuary. His face was twisted out of shape when they found him, but the bloody yellow T-shirt, the blue jeans, and the Nike shoes were clearly his. He was buried in a cemetery opposite the grave of his grandfather. Three years later, the police came to Su Bingxian's apartment. They told her to remove her son's ashes from the cemetery. Otherwise they would be disposed of. Too many graves marked with the same date would not do. People might start asking questions. Silence had to reign even among the dead.

—

Few Chinese, whether on the mainland or Taiwan, compare June 4 (6-4) with that other bloody date on the Chinese historical calendar, February 28, 1947 (2-28), when thousands of Taiwanese were killed in the "white terror" of the KMT. There are huge differences, of course. June 4 lacks the component of quasi-ethnic resentment. Whatever else Deng Xiaoping and Li Peng might have been, they were not regarded as foreigners. The idea of national independence isn't part of 6-4 as it is of 2-28. But in political significance, they are comparable. This was pointed out by Bao Tong, right-hand man in the 1980s to Zhao Ziyang, the reformist Party secretary-general who was fired for being too sympathetic to the students.

Bao Tong is a loyal Communist in the Dubček or Gorbachev mold, a reformist who believed that the Party could become democratic without abolishing itself, or even losing power. He was at the heart of reformism, as deputy director of the State Commission for Economic Reform and, later, as director of the Office of Political Reform of the Party's Central Committee. But his cause, too, was smashed on the night of June 4. Or perhaps two weeks earlier, on May 19, when Zhao Ziyang told the students in Tiananmen Square that it was "too late," that he had lost his capacity to influence his government. Or, maybe, even earlier than that. Bao Tong now regrets that economic reforms weren't matched with political reforms in the early 1980s. When corruption and abuses of power drove the country into a crisis in 1989, it was too late; there was no other public forum for people to express their discontents than the streets.

Zhao Ziyang was put under house arrest in June 1989, for "supporting turmoil and splitting the Party," but he was still allowed to play golf, though not on courses open to foreigners. Bao Tong, accused of leaking plans of the crackdown to the students, was purged from the Party and jailed for seven years. The Party elders had never liked the look of Bao Tong anyway. Li Xiannian, the former state president who advocated force in 1989, is reported to have disapproved of Bao's style as much as his politics: "I know the man. He's over fifty but follows fashions like a youngster. He wears gaudy jackets and blue jeans inside Zhongnanhai—what kind of Party official is that?" Bao is still under permanent surveillance; his phones are tapped. Whenever he leaves his house, men with walkie-talkies follow him in unmarked white Mercedeses. Things get particularly tense on the anniversaries of June 4. In the spring of 2000, he was shoved into a police car in the center of Beijing, and his wife, who was almost seventy, was wrestled to the ground. When Bao demanded to see a legal document, the policeman sneered: "Don't talk to us about the law."

Bao's writings cannot be published in China. Yet his words get out, on the Internet, through magazines and publishers in Hong Kong. He has sent open letters to President Jiang Zemin, criticizing the government for its poor human-rights record and demanding a reversal of the official verdict on June 4. It was in one of those open letters, in 1999, that he compared 6-4 to 2-28. He wrote: "You cannot really believe that these ten years of covering up have succeeded. The history of bloodshed remains in people's hearts; they will not forget. No one can ever successfully cover up such an event. Remember that after 50 years of attempted cover-up, the truth about the February 28 incident in Taiwan was revived."

Bao Tong is a courageous man. But perhaps even he still lives in a half-truth. For he still believes that reversing the verdict on Tiananmen will save the Communist Party. Those who reverse the June 4 decision, he writes, "will win the hearts and minds of the Chinese people. . . . If such a legacy were to fall into the hands of non-Party members, it would be a tragedy for the Party."

Bao joined the Communist Party fifty years ago, because he believed it would set the Chinese people free. He saw Mao as a democrat. Later, when Mao's "mistakes" could be publicly acknowledged, Bao believed his boss Zhao Ziyang when the latter talked about solving China's problems in "the framework of democracy and law." And now Bao believes that once the problem of June 4 "is solved . . . the common people will be extremely happy. Everybody would raise all kinds of suggestions. Everybody's political activism would immediately increase. Their sense of political responsibility would also increase."

The Party and the people, then, will be reconciled, and Zhao Ziyang's ideals will win the day. Bao believes that the media will become the true "voice of the people." And corruption will be defeated. After all, he says, "Marxism is a work-in-progress, and the Communist Party ought to change with the times. . . . There is a scholar named Tsou Tang. He said that China should move from 'totalitarianism' to 'totalism.' And then move from 'totalism' to democracy. I think that if we can successfully make this transition, then the whole world will see that the Chinese Com-

munist Party is at the forefront of all other communist parties in democratic development. What's wrong with that? I can't see what's wrong with
that."

There is nothing wrong, except that it is yesterday's dream, reflecting
the hope of a believer to redeem the faith of a lifetime. It is too late for
that. Most other Communist parties have already died. And the Chinese
Communist Party has learned its lesson from Gorbachev. It knows that
suicide lies at the end of that reformist road. So even good Communists
like Bao Tong must be silenced. And if Communist reformers are treated
that way, what hope is there for real democrats?

The suggestion that I meet Bao Tong in Beijing came from Dai Qing,
the independent scholar and journalist, who was home again when I
returned to China in the spring of 2000. She was in a feisty mood, and
recalled some recent confrontations with officialdom with cackles of sardonic laughter. The only time her lips would purse and her voice sharpen
is when the subject of June 4 came up. For her hopes, too, had been
smashed on that occasion. Like Bao Tong, she had invested too much in
the reformist dreams.

We arranged to meet at a tea shop near her house. The idea was to
record a discussion about the problems of speaking the truth in China,
which we might publish in an American journal.

Yes, she said as she sat down. She understood exactly what I wanted to
talk to her about. She asked for my pen and scribbled some Chinese characters in my notebook. She had written: "From 'calling a deer a horse' to
'speaking the truth.' " It was of course Confucius's phrase, from his story
about the despot who tested the loyalty of his subjects by pointing to a
deer and calling it a horse. And Dai spoke about her discovery of the truth
about her real father, a Communist executed by the Japanese, and about
the poet Wang Shiwei, persecuted to his death and only rehabilitated in
1991. She had written a book about him. She spoke of her own, and subsequently her readers', discovery of having been "cheated of the truth" by
the Party. And finally, with a sense of melancholy resignation, she spoke of
being attacked, mostly by dissidents abroad, for her take on June 4, which
she still regards as a reckless "Great Leap Forward" by student extremists
and not as a democratic rebellion.

Democracy can only come slowly, she said. The Party must keep some kind of control. Chaos has to be avoided at all costs. For the cause of reform must not suffer another setback, as it did in 1989. So what could be done to make it go forward? She thought about that for a while, and said: "To break through the lies. To tell the truth. To tell stories, like mine about Wang Shiwei. To give a different view from the orthodoxy."

That night Dai called me at my hotel. Would I like to meet Bao Tong? But if I did, she warned, I would have to be prepared for trouble with the authorities; I might not get a visa again. I said that would be a risk worth taking. Good, she said, and told me to be at a certain subway station at seven o'clock the next morning. He would be there to take his grandchild to school. She would give him a copy of his book of essays, banned in China and just published in Hong Kong, and then we would board the same train.

It was a typical Beijing spring day. The sky was a deep blue, before the sandstorms began to blow from the Gobi Desert to turn the sky yellow. I waited at the entrance of the subway station opposite the bright new McDonald's, from which the sound of Muzak filled the crisp morning air. There was a constant flow of people on the subway stairs. I saw one or two shifty-looking men, but then, on these occasions, everyone begins to look sinister. I tried to be inconspicuous, a difficult task when you are the only white person standing still in a crowd of Chinese. There was a man leading a small child quickly through the turnstiles. I did not have a chance to look at them carefully. They were in too much of a hurry. It may not have been them. The appointed time came and passed. I left after an hour.

Around lunchtime the phone in my hotel room rang. It was Dai Qing, cackling as usual. The police had swooped down on her the moment she stepped out of her apartment building. They told her they knew exactly where she was going, pushed her into an unmarked car, and sped to the police station, where they lectured her for four hours on the need for stability and order and civil obedience.

Perhaps I had glimpsed Bao Tong after all, rushing through the turnstiles; he didn't know he was meeting a foreigner: Dai Qing, wisely, had not told him that. But I couldn't be sure. I couldn't be sure of anything anymore. And in any event, it was too late.

I often wondered why many Chinese intellectuals were so skeptical about the possibility of democracy in China and why China's intellectual class had produced more Dubčeks than Havels. History must have something to do with it. Czechs and Poles had a model to fall back on. Their countries had experienced democracy before being swallowed by the Soviet empire. China, instead, has a history of violent rebellions. And during periods of calm, rulers buy potential dissidents off by offering rich rewards for their collaboration. Perhaps the Taiwanese broke the mold, because ethnic tensions prevented most dissidents from being co-opted by the KMT. Then there is the brutal fact that most Chinese democrats are either broken in jail or pushed abroad to languish in dreary exile. But in truth there are not so many Chinese Václav Havels in exile, either.

Fear is another factor, fear of violence and disorder, fear of public hysteria, or what Li Lu, talking about his experience as a student on Tiananmen Square, called "raw emotions": fear of the uneducated, common people, who are prone to run amok. Given the history of violent rebellion in China, this fear is understandable. It is why Dai Qing, and others, talk about the slow process of "educating the people," of learning the art of compromise.

Again, one sees what she means, but the analysis is flawed. For the people responsible for persecuting intellectuals, from the early days of the Communist movement in the caves of Yan'an all the way to the present time, are not uneducated peasants or ignorant workers but Party leaders, often assisted in their inquisitorial work by fellow intellectuals. And political liberties are unlikely to result in people running amok. On the contrary, the raw emotions, the latent hysteria, the pent-up aggressions seething under the surface of Chinese life are the result of living in a lie. As long as people cannot speak freely, nothing can be exposed to the light of reason, and raw emotions will take over. But to acquire the right to free speech, there will have to be a change of system, and it is hard to see how that can happen unless the Communist Party is forced out of power. What makes the future so hard to read is that the raw emotions are as much of a help to the government as a threat. Sometimes these emotional storms change direction, as when students protesting foreign imperialism suddenly turn on their own government.

Two months after the NATO bombing of the Chinese embassy in Belgrade, when anti-Western sentiments were still fresh, I went to see a play at a theater in Beijing, *Fields of Life and Death*. The story, written in 1935 by a famous novelist and poet, Xiao Hong, is set in a village in the northeast of China. The poor villagers are oppressed on all sides, by their landlord and by the Japanese army, which comes rampaging through on a spree of rape and murder. Used to adapting to the violence of new masters, the villagers don't resist at first but hope that the storm will blow over, as they always do, until the next time, and the next. They have little idea of the world outside the village. They barely have an idea of "China," or of what it means to be Chinese. Nor do they much care. But then, toward the end of the play, one bright young villager goes off to join the anti-Japanese war. And when he returns, full of fire, he makes a great patriotic speech, telling the villagers to rise up for China, avenge past humiliations, and resist the foreign invaders. Patriotism has reached village China at last.

Xiao Hong was quite a complicated writer, a leftist with sardonic views of both village life and Chinese patriotism. She even dared to make fun of the anti-Japanese war. And her play was directed as much against the Chinese government as it was against the Japanese. She died in Hong Kong under Japanese occupation, at thirty-one.

None of this complexity came out in the production I saw, which had all the lurid imagery of a Communist propaganda poster: the landlords and Japanese were cartoons of evil, the people blazed with righteous patriotic virtue, and in defeat, the wicked fascists cringed, like worms, while the victors, bathing in the blue spotlights, struck the heroic poses of revolutionary monuments. It might have been one of Jiang Qing's model revolutionary operas of the 1960s.

But the production didn't surprise me so much as the reaction of the mostly young audience. During the slow, creaky scenes, there was a great deal of shifting in seats, chattering, and trips to and from the toilets. But as the climax built, I could feel the tension rise, until in the final scene, when the villagers decide to fight, crying, "We are the Chinese people! We are the Chinese people! The Chinese people are united against the foreign enemy!" the audience rose too, shouting and hooting and clapping. It was like the high point in a revivalist church, a religious crescendo, a kind of orgasmic release.

At first I thought there was irony intended here, a sly dig at the government's attempt to stir up patriotic fervor in the aftermath of the Belgrade bombing. But my companion, a professor of Chinese history, soon disabused me. "No, no," he said. "We all feel like this in our hearts."

Walking out of the theater into the throng of shoppers on Wangfujing, with its fashion boutiques, department stores, and the largest McDonald's in China, Professor Mao Haijian told me about the legacy in China of social Darwinism—the idea, that is, of a struggle for survival among nations. A small, neatly dressed academic, with a pink nose and a diffident manner, he spoke softly and picked his words with fastidious precision: "All Chinese intellectuals, including myself, are social Darwinists. We are all sensitive to Western superiority, and boast about the Chinese race because in our hearts we feel inferior. We realize this is irrational, dangerous, even wrong, but still we feel it."

I was fascinated to hear this from Professor Mao, for he was a man who had chosen, to some degree and at a personal cost, at least in his professional career, to live in the truth. Mao had challenged one of the most cherished national myths by writing a version of the Opium War that diverged sharply from the official history. What is more, he based many of his conclusions on his careful reading of Western sources. In the professor's version, the Qing officials who argued for a compromise with the British, and who were subsequently denounced in Chinese history books as traitors, were right, and the patriotic martyrs, whose monuments I had visited in southern China, the men who wanted to fight the Western imperialists to the death, were deluded. China should have done what Japan did in the 1850s, when the Americans arrived in their "black ships": surrender to the barbarians and learn from them to strengthen the nation. His book was published, but his career at the Academy of Social Sciences did not flourish.

Professor Mao was not a political activist. In fact, he abhors zeal of any kind. Wei Jingsheng, he explained, got into trouble because he didn't understand what was possible in China. It wasn't that Wei's views were wrong. Indeed, most people knew they were right. But there was no point in stating those views, because that just led to confrontation. The smartest intellectuals in China, Mao said, knew the truth but remained silent.

Surely, I said, with all the easy conviction of an outsider, that cannot be right. Without open debate, there can't be any advance in knowledge. How can we find the truth without discussing it? He looked at me calmly. Nothing I said was new or especially surprising to him. They were, after all, commonplaces repeated in hundreds of articles published in Chinese intellectual journals or on Internet websites. To state the obvious in the abstract is simple. "Well," he said, politely putting me in my place, "that is the difference between China and the West. It is not a good thing, but it is the way it is."

I asked him whether he feared the Chinese masses. Again he spoke with a kind of verbal shrug of resignation. Yes, he said. "There is a fear that the uneducated people will violently resist the right of others to speak out. The rule of the majority would be a tyranny. It took Europeans many years to realize that minorities had rights, too. In China it would be every man for himself. I am a historian. Never in history have sudden transitions been a good thing."

That is what most intellectuals in China believe, and perhaps they speak from superior wisdom, as well as fear. Mob violence, so quick to surface in China, is a fearful thing, and many intellectuals over fifty were the victims as well as perpetrators, depending on the time and place. Their present-day moderation may be one way of doing penance, of dealing with the guilt, as well as the terror, that few express but some at least must feel. But this does not mean that their analysis is right. Political liberties may come slowly, in an orderly process, initiated by liberal-minded leaders in the Party, but it is unlikely. Dictatorships fall in many ways, often sparked by unexpected events, which serve as catalysts for protest and resistance. Dictators, having been so sure of their power before, can suddenly lose their nerve, and their subjects, so used to being cowed and passive, can suddenly lose their fears. It happened in Bucharest in 1989. It almost happened in Beijing. It could happen again. But one ingredient that is essential in any struggle for freedom was missing in Tiananmen Square: All those who oppose the dictatorship, whether reformers, liberals, radicals, religious believers, activists, philosophers, leftists, or conservatives, must make common cause. For if they do not, the regime will exploit their differences, and stay in power. In China, however, intellectuals are so frightened of disorder that they are prone to shun the common cause, and opt instead for stability.

Again, one understands why. But it is a phantom stability; there are great cracks showing in the Communist order, and the longer this system continues, with its increasingly desperate attempts to hide the truth of its moral and political bankruptcy, the greater the chaos is likely to be when Chinese explode once more in an orgy of raw emotion. It is happening already, in small towns, where farmers vent their rage at arbitrary taxes by destroying public buildings. It is happening in the rust-belt cities of the northeast, where thousands, tens of thousands, perhaps millions, suddenly find themselves jobless when factories close and the loot is divided among the Party *nomenklatura*.

Nationalism will be the only thing the Chinese rulers have left to deflect rebellious energy from themselves onto the outside world. But to deflect these energies outward, against Taiwan, say, or the United States, they would have to tap the same well of resentment and humiliation that nurtured rebellions in the past. It would take a brave, or desperate, government to arouse these passions.

Dai Qing and others are right to fear another round of mass violence. For an outsider to dismiss their fear and advocate revolution is irresponsible; the Western observer, or indeed the Chinese exile, does not have to face the consequences of such advocacy. I am aware of this, yet cannot shake off my doubts about the way many reformists discuss change. Is the emphasis on ethics, on moral education of the common people, really the best way to break the infernal cycle of tyranny and violent rebellion? Or is it the same kind of thinking which keeps that cycle in motion? Moral reformists, Confucianists, Chinese Communists, and religious zealots seem to share the assumption that good government depends more on human virtue than on democratic institutions. Wei Jingsheng may be lacking in many virtues, but I believe his Fifth Modernization, pinned to the Democracy Wall in 1979, still contains a profound truth: "Anyone seeking the unconditional trust of the people is a person of unbridled ambition. . . . We can trust only those representatives who are supervised by us and responsible to us. Such representatives should be chosen by us and not thrust upon us."

Whether one thinks this applies to China as much as anywhere else really depends on whether one believes that democratic institutions can work in a country that has had no history—or, if you prefer, culture—of democracy. The examples of Taiwan and South Korea, Japan, Thailand, India, or indeed any other democratic country in the world would seem to show that democracy is relatively indifferent to culture. It functions better in some places than others, for all kinds of reasons, but it can be attempted anywhere with some chance of success. Culture is too often used by rulers as an excuse for perpetuating their monopoly on power. That is what the "Asian values" propaganda in Singapore is all about. But Chinese culture is not some monolithic barrier to building democratic institutions. This also means that, contrary to the beliefs of the more fanatical "westernizers" of May 4, 1919, or indeed their Communist heirs, there is no need to smash everything old to change the form of government. Chinese do not have to become Americans or Europeans to be free.

Wei Jingsheng is not naïve about the costs of a transition from a one-party dictatorship to a democratic system. He has told me many times that it will be a messy, probably violent process. But he is convinced, and I fear he may be right, that the longer that process is delayed, the greater the violence will be.

This is the Chinese dilemma. To force a sudden transition by bringing the government down after a rebellion, which could be sparked by any number of things—religious zeal, intolerable corruption, or mass unemployment—could result in a period of frightful chaos. But the risk of hanging on to a bankrupt system in the hope of prolonging an illusion of stability could be worse. Conservatives like Dai Qing and Professor Mao argue, as David Hume did two hundred years ago, that history should be our guide and that a bad established order is still better than unpredictable change. Christians zealots like Yuan Zhiming, who wrote parts of the television series *River Elegy*, are convinced that a spiritual transformation is necessary before a democracy can take hold. Then there are those for whom, in the May Fourth spirit, Mr. Science holds the key to solving all our human problems.

But democracy is not the result of spiritual transformations, moral crusades, or blind faith in science. For unlike in the ancient Chinese system of government, or in its Communist incarnation, the center of power in a democracy cannot be the center of truth. To try and replace one center of truth with another is not the way to freedom. This is the cycle that has to end. Dai Qing's advocacy of critical argument and compromise is just a beginning. Political argument must be institutionalized, not behind the closed doors of one party or among a tiny intellectual elite, but in various parties contending for people's support through the powers of persuasion. As long as only one party rules, talk of the "rule of law" or of carefully controlled village elections or of conferences about "social democracy" is just window dressing to confer an air of respectability upon a desperate regime.

Traveling in China, one easily picks up the rank smell of political decay. I left Beijing more convinced than ever that Communist Party rule would end, but without any better sense of how this might happen. The peaceful revolutions in Taiwan, South Korea, and Eastern Europe give no firm clues. Circumstances are not the same. I do not share the optimism of those who cling to the hope that the Chinese, in their infinite subtlety, will find a slow, gentle road to the Fifth Modernization, shepherded by the Communist Party. The KMT did it in Taiwan, but the Chinese Communist Party is not the KMT. Whatever it is that brings this rotting regime to an end, one can only hope it will be peaceful. But hope is not the same as expectation. The Chinese verb *qidai* can mean both "to expect" and "to look forward to." It was the word used by Chai Ling when she gave that rambling interview to an American reporter days before the massacre of June 4. It is at the heart of the *Rashomon* story of Tiananmen. Did she mean to say she looked forward to the bloodshed that would at last unite the Chinese people in opposition? Or did she simply expect it? To hope for such a thing would be a terrible thing. But she was not wrong to expect it, not then and not in the future—not until that old cycle of Chinese tyranny and violence is broken.

———

Before leaving Beijing in the spring of 2000, I decided to have one more look at Tiananmen Square, so I rented a bicycle and set off together with an Italian friend. We had been advised against cycling that day, for the sand was expected to blow fiercely from the Gobi Desert. I had read an article in the *China Daily* that warned that the desert was creeping several meters closer to Beijing every year.

We stopped to take some pictures in front of Tiananmen, the Gate of Heavenly Peace, where Chairman Mao declared in 1949, in his oddly high-pitched Hunanese voice, that the Chinese people had risen. His face still gazes permanently across the Square, like a rosy moon over the Forbidden City. In 1989, at the height of the student demonstrations, three young workers from Mao's province of Hunan flung a pot of black paint in the Chairman's face. The students, afraid that the raw emotions of the people might get out of control, dutifully handed the three men over to the police. They were in prison for years. One is supposed to have gone mad.

I noticed patches of green lawn on one side of the Square, laid out for the fiftieth anniversary of the Chinese revolution. More alterations were in store. In the bid for the 2008 Olympic Games, plans were made to turn the Square into a giant venue for beach-volleyball games. Great sandpits would be built for the swimsuited athletes to play ball in front of Mao.

Policemen in olive-green uniforms were guarding every corner of the Square, where Falun Gong supporters still arrived every day, in defiance of government orders, to do their breathing exercises, until they were grabbed and carted off to jail. Sometimes there were a dozen or so arrests, sometimes more. But the believers kept coming. And the police kept watching for the telltale signs. When there were no signs, they would ask people if they belonged to the Falun Gong. Those who answered yes were arrested.

I stood in front of the towering Monument to the People's Heroes, with its white-stone reliefs of former rebellions: the Taiping "Christians," who wanted to establish God's kingdom in China; the Boxers, who besieged the foreign legations; the republican revolutionaries under Sun Yat-sen; the students of May Fourth; and of course the People's Liberation Army marching to power. It was there, at the feet of the stone heroes, that the students in 1989 had established their headquarters, made their patriotic speeches, sang "Descendants of the Dragon," and went on hunger strikes. So much martyrdom, so much raw emotion.

When we mounted our bikes to ride away from the Square, toward the

Xidan intersection on Chang'an Avenue, the cloudless sky turned a milky gray. The desert sand was blowing in. Furry white pollen was falling like warm snow, clogging our noses and throats. Chang'an Avenue, where the tanks rolled and much of the killing took place, was smooth as glass. Once I felt a little bump. Tank tracks, I thought; a little bit of the road that they had forgotten to pave over. But when I stopped to satisfy my morbid curiosity, it turned out to be nothing but a patch of dried vomit.

Along the avenue were the brash monuments to the new China, huge buildings, like concrete monsters, expressing raw bureaucratic power. Every ten blocks or so, the monotony of gray concrete and black granite was broken by the yellow and red of a McDonald's.

Xidan is where the Democracy Wall once stood, where Wei Jingsheng drew the crowds with his manifestos, crowds that were hungry for a fresh voice, hungry to hear something other than Party propaganda. The wall, like those tank tracks, has disappeared. Now there is a vast new plaza, called Culture Square, and where the wall once stood is a Bank of China. It was near here that Su Bingxian's twenty-one-year-old son was killed. A gust of wind almost threw us off our bikes, and the sharp sand blew in our faces. Women drew filmy scarves around their head in protection, giving them the mottled look of lepers.

We pushed on past the Palace of the Minorities, toward Muxidi, another address bathed in the blood of June 4 victims. Not far from there, on the right side of the avenue, looming up in the fog of yellow sand, was a gigantic new building, designed in the style of 1930s Japanese fascism, with brutal classical pillars and a Chinese roof. It was one of the most grandiose buildings I had seen in Beijing. A white-granite stele added a further Oriental touch, and a star over the main gate cast a pale red light in the afternoon gloom. The gate was guarded by two young soldiers, one of whom looked fairly relaxed, while the other stood rigidly to attention, like a wax doll.

I asked the relaxed one what this building was. "Guest house," he barked. And what is it called?

"Classified information. We cannot divulge."

We stopped at the Army Museum. It was built long enough ago, in the Stalinist style, to have taken on a period quaintness. The inside too, with its bombastic display of missiles and rocket launchers and anti-tank weapons, its collection of machine guns, bayonets, and revolvers, its uniforms, and its tableaux of bygone heroics, such as the seventeenth-century hero Koxinga upholding "the integrity of Chinese territory and sovereignty" by battling the Dutch in Taiwan, has a distinct nineteenth-century feel. The entrance hall is decorated with large portraits of Stalin, Lenin, Marx, and Engels. And in a side hall are "gifts to the People's Republic of China." There is a tawdriness about them, an air of stuffy bad taste, that is less quaint than depressing. Ceauşescu, president of Romania, gave the Chinese people a clock in the form of a peasant's face, with little wires sticking to its chin, like whiskers. And the gifts from the German Democratic Republic were several identical plastic tanks, handed from one dreary bureaucrat to another, year after year.

On the second floor, we entered a room filled with bronze busts. Here were the heroes of the Chinese revolution, from Chairman Mao to President Jiang Zemin. The "Ten Marshals," including Ye Jianying, Dai Qing's stepfather, were there. So were Zhou Enlai, Deng Xiaoping, and General Zhu De. As a fraternal gesture, the North Korean "Great Leader" Kim Il Sung was smiling benevolently from his pedestal. And there, perhaps as a salute to another authoritarian Chinese leader, was a scowling Lee Kuan Yew, scourge of the Singaporean Communist movement, standing among the Communist rulers of China. It all looked extraordinarily old-fashioned yet still menacing, all these bronze balls of power.

I heard laughter. It was my Italian friend. "Listen to this," he said as he knocked his hand against Deng Xiaoping's head. A hollow sound echoed through the room. I tried it too, and started knocking Lee Kuan Yew, then Kim Il Sung, then Mao himself. We went about the room like children who had discovered a new game, knocking one great leader after another. And all of them sounded hollow, for they were made to look like bronze but in fact were made of plastic.

The sky outside had turned from pearly gray to yellowish brown. The wind was blowing fiercely, filling even our ears with sand. I could just make out another monstrosity not far from the Army Museum. It looked new, which indeed it was: a kind of ziggurat with a large spike sticking out from the top, like a missile. There was a sign on the front. I tried to read what it said. Something about the millennium, a millennium monument. And then I could just make out the year 2000, except that the figure 2 had already broken in half. The storm was getting so bad that we had to hide inside the museum. I looked back once more at the capital of China, but by now the yellow cloud obliterated everything. Even the year 2000 had disappeared from view.

Acknowledgments

I cannot, alas, mention everyone who helped me with this book. Most people in the People's Republic of China will have to remain anonymous until times change for the better.

Without the help of Dimon Liu, Perry Link, and Gong Xiaoxia, I would hardly have known where to begin. Jason Epstein was there from start to finish, as a friend, and as the finest editor I could have hoped for. Richard Nations offered his thoughts, companionship, and hospitality in Hong Kong. Robin Munro did the same in London and Hong Kong. In Beijing and Washington, D.C., Dai Qing was a most generous guide, interlocutor, interviewee, colleague, and friend.

Wang Juntao, Hu Ping, David Welcker, Tong Yi, Margaret Scott, David Rieff, Carma Hinton, Richard Gordon, Xiao Qiang, Merle Goldman, Christopher Hitchens, Carol Blue, Barbara Epstein, Roderick MacFarquhar, Susan Sontag, Li Hong-kuan, Yan Yunxiang, Ge Yang, Smarlo Ma, Judy Chen, Andrew Nathan, Richard Wich, Lyman Miller, Ramon Myers, Bei Ling, Cheng Xiaonong, Reuel Gerecht, Diane Zeleny, Nancy Hearst, and Leon Wieseltier all helped me in various ways during my stay in the U.S.

A scholarship from the invaluable Woodrow Wilson International Center for Scholars enabled me to do my research in the perfect environment. I owe special thanks to Warren Cohen, Robert Hathaway, and Mary-Lea Cox. The Alistair Horne Fellowship at St. Antony's College, Oxford, provided precious time and space in Britain.

Mary Lee and Gopal Baratham were enormously helpful in Singapore. Gopal was also kind enough to read parts of my manuscript. Others who made my trip to Singapore a stimulating pleasure include Philip Jeyaretnam, David Martin-Jones, Lena Lim, Wang Gungwu, and Kwong Yuen-chung.

In Taiwan I would like to thank Antonio Chiang, Chen Tsai-tung, Julian Baum, Kathy Wei, Richard Vuylstek, Dirk Bennett, Matei Mihalca, Hu Ching-fang, Yang Ze, Hsu Lu, H. C. Chen, Stephen Lee, Su Tzen-ping, Chang Fu-mei, and Sisy Chen.

Liu Kinming was invariably generous with his help in Hong Kong, as were Christine Loh, Emily Lau, Jimmy Lai, Johnson Chang, John Minford, Harvey Stockwin, Frank Lu, and Sophia Woodman.

Others who smoothed my passage on the road were Geremie Barmé, Mia Turner, Fang Lizhu, Leonardo Griglie, Ying Ma, Kate Saunders, Jonathan Napack, Koh Siew-eng, and Li Feifei. And it is hard to imagine how I could have finished my book without the inspiring company of Yang Lian, You You, Huang Bao-lian, Tsering Shakya, Jonathan Mirsky, Tong Yi, and Wang Chaohua, who were unfailingly helpful and generous with their time.

With Andrew Wylie, Jin Auh, Rose Billington, and Sarah Chalfant of the Wylie Agency I always knew I was in the friendliest of professional hands. I am grateful to Robert Silvers of *The New York Review of Books* for being the most encouraging and stimulating editor in the English-speaking world. Commissions from him, as well as from David Remnick of *The New Yorker,* Kyle Crighton of *The New York Times Magazine,* and Sheila Glaser of *Travel and Leisure,* enabled me to travel and produce some of the material that appears in a revised form in this book. Finally, a special thanks to Jason Epstein's efficient assistant, Judy Sternlight, and the fine copy editor Veronica Windholz.

Glossary of Names

THE STUDENTS OF 1989

Wang Dan: Student at Beijing University, and leader of the Autonomous Federation of Students (AFS) in 1989. After seven years in prison, he was allowed to go to the U.S. on medical parole. Currently studying at Harvard University.

Chai Ling: Graduate student at Beijing Normal University in 1989. Chief commander in Tiananmen Square. She escaped to Hong Kong, became an M.A. student at Princeton University, then an M.B.A. graduate at Harvard. She is now a businesswoman.

Wu'er Kaixi: Student at Beijing Normal University, and one of the leaders of the AFS in 1989. He escaped after June 4 and spent time in Paris and the U.S. He lives in Taiwan, where he is the host of a radio show.

Li Lu: Student from Nanjing University. In 1989 he was Chai Ling's deputy, and chief commander of the non-Beijing students in Tiananmen Square. He fled to the U.S., where he studied law and business administration at Columbia University. He runs an investment business in New York.

Wang Chaohua: Graduate student at Beijing University in 1989. She was a leading activist in the Autonomous Association of Beijing College Students, and escaped to the U.S. after June 4. She is a Ph.D. student of modern Chinese literature at UCLA.

INTELLECTUALS AND ACTIVISTS IN EXILE

Liu Binyan: Former journalist for the *People's Daily* in Beijing. He specialized in corruption stories. Expelled from the Party in 1987 for supporting student demonstrations, he has lived in the U.S. since 1988.

WEI JINGSHENG: Dissident and author of "Democracy: The Fifth Modernization," which was put up on "Democracy Wall" in 1978. Sentenced twice to
prison, to a total of twenty-nine years he was told to leave for the U.S. on
medical grounds in 1997.

WANG XIZHE: Activist in the 1970s in Guangzhou, co-author of the Li Yi Zhe
manifesto, promoting democratic socialism in 1974. He lives in the U.S., as
an active supporter of the China Democracy Party.

WANG BINGZHANG: Co-founder in the U.S. of the China Democracy Party. Like
Wang Xizhe, and unlike Wei Jingsheng, he believes in organizing an underground political party in China.

GONG XIAOXIA: Program director for Radio Free Asia in Washington, D.C. She
joined Wang Xizhe's group of activists in Guangzhou in 1974, was jailed for
several years, studied at Beijing University, and went to the U.S. in the
1980s.

FANG LIZHI: Astrophysicist. Academic promoter of democracy and free speech in
China during the 1980s. After taking refuge in the American embassy in
Beijing for one year, he went to the U.S. in 1991. He is now a professor at the
University of Arizona.

SU XIAOKANG: Author of the 1988 television series *River Elegy* and strong supporter of the student demonstrations in 1989. After June 4, he fled to the
West, and now lives in Princeton, New Jersey.

YUAN ZHIMING: Co-author of *River Elegy*, Yuan supported the students in 1989,
and later fled to the U.S. where he was converted to Christianity. He hopes
to convert his native country to the Christian faith.

XIE XUANJUN: Co-author of *River Elegy*, he lives in the U.S., where he is a devout
Christian.

XIAO QIANG: A former student of Fang Lizhi in China, Xiao runs the Human
Rights in China organization in New York City.

LIU QING: A prominent activist, together with Wei Jingsheng, during the Democracy Wall period in 1978 and 1979. He published the court transcripts of
Wei's first trial in 1979. After many years in prison, he went to the U.S.,
where he works for Human Rights in China.

YAN JIAQI: A reformist intellectual who advised Party general-secretary Zhao
Ziyang, Yan became the first director of the Institute of Political Science in
1985. In 1989, he became a radical supporter of the student demonstrations, and was forced to flee after June 4. He lives in New York City.

HARRY WU: After spending nineteen years in forced-labor camps for being a
"rightist," Wu went to the U.S., where he is actively trying to expose the conditions in the Chinese gulag.

RICHARD LI: Former science teacher in China, now a cyberspace activist who puts together a dissident website from Washington, D.C.

YANG LIAN: Member of the "Misty Poets" group in Beijing during the early 1980s, he left China before 1989 and now lives in London.

DAI QING: Journalist and historian. Though not living in exile, she spends much time abroad. While critical of the Communist government, she is also known for her harsh line on the "radical" student leaders in 1989.

POLITICIANS

DENG XIAOPING: Paramount leader of China from 1978 until he died in 1997. A liberal reformer in economics, he took a harder political line. Deng decided to crack down on the 1989 student movement.

ZHAO ZIYANG: Party general-secretary in 1989, he was ousted from his post and put under house arrest for being too sympathetic to the students. Zhao was never a democrat, but he played a major role in liberalizing the economy. Unlike his boss, he was in favor of talking to the student activists to reach what he called a "democratic" solution.

HU YAOBANG: A reformist Party general-secretary before Zhao, he was removed from his leadership role in 1987 for not opposing "bourgeois liberalism" with enough vigor. His death in 1989 sparked the student demonstrations.

LI PENG: Prime minister in 1989, blamed by many for the killings. A conservative Communist apparatchik, he persuaded Deng to crush the Tiananmen demonstrations with force.

JIANG ZEMIN: He was promoted just before June 4 from Party secretary in Shanghai to Party general-secretary. Not as hard-line as Li Peng, he was nevertheless regarded by Party conservatives as a safe pair of hands.

SINGAPORE

LEE KUAN YEW: Former prime minister, now senior minister of Singapore.

CHIA THYE POH: Former Socialist member of Parliament. He was a political prisoner, accused of being a Communist, from 1963 till 1989. He now lives a quiet life as a researcher of developmental economics.

CHEE SOON JUAN: Leader of the Singapore Democratic Party. He sacrificed his career as a neuropsychologist to engage in politics.

TEO SOH LUNG: A lawyer, accused in 1987 of being involved in a "Marxist conspiracy to overthrow the government."

PATRICK SEONG: Lawyer who took up the cases of Catholic social workers in 1987, accused of being part of the "Marxist conspiracy." He was detained along with them.

J. B. JEYARETNAM: Leader of the Workers' Party. In 1981, he was the first opposition politician to win a parliamentary election since 1965. He has been hounded by the PAP government ever since.

TAIWAN

YU TENG-FA: Political patriarch in Kaohsiung County. Sided with the opposition to the KMT in the 1970s. He died under mysterious circumstances in 1989.

YU CHEN YUEH-YING: Yu Teng-fa's daughter-in-law, who became the leading non-KMT boss in Kaohsiung County in the 1980s and early 1990s.

YU JENG-DAO: Successful candidate in Kaohsiung County for the DPP. Son of Yu Chen Yueh-ying.

CHEN SHUI-BIAN: Longtime opposition activist, elected first as DPP mayor of Taipei, then, in 2000, president.

"BEN" WEI RUI-MING: Activist, who returned from exile in the U.S. in 1994 to help Peng Ming-min in the first free presidential elections in 1996.

KATHY WEI: Ben Wei's daughter.

CHIANG KAI-SHEK: Loser of the civil war in China. After 1949, the first president of the Republic of China on Taiwan.

CHIANG CHING-KUO: Chiang Kai-shek's son, former security chief, premier of the ROC from 1972 to 1978 and president from 1978 until his death in 1988.

"MARK" CHEN TAN-SUN: Independence activist, returned from exile in the U.S. in 1994, and elected mayor of Tainan County.

"PETER" HUANG WEN-HSIUNG: The man who tried to assassinate Chiang Ching-kuo in 1970. He is now the director of the Taiwan Association for Human Rights in Taipei.

BO YANG: Writer, born in mainland China in 1920, moved to Taiwan in the late 1940s. He was arrested in 1967 for "defaming the leadership." His most famous book is *The Ugly Chinaman*.

SHIH MING-TEH: The main organizer of the Kaohsiung Incident in 1978. A political prisoner between 1962 and 1977, he is now a DPP senator in Taipei.

"ANNETTE" LU HSIU-LIEN: Famous feminist and political activist. Jailed after the Kaohsiung Incident. Elected vice-president in 2000.

HONG KONG

MARTIN LEE: Barrister and legislator. Leader of the Democratic Party.

SZETO WAH: Leader of the Democratic Party. Founder in 1989 of the Hong Kong Alliance in Support of the Patriotic Democratic Movement in China.

TUNG CHEE-HWA: Shipping tycoon who became chief executive in 1997.

EMILY LAU: Former journalist, democratic activist, and legislator for the Frontier Party. She is the most popular politician in Hong Kong.

LAU SAN-CHING: Trotskyite who tried to help Wang Xizhe and other activists in China build "real socialism" during the 1970s. Arrested in 1981, he spent ten years in prison. He is now a Democratic Party candidate for the Hong Kong legislature.

HAN DONGFANG: Founder in 1989 of the first independent workers' federation on Tiananmen Square, he was jailed until 1992, when he was released on medical grounds. He became a Christian in the U.S. A citizen of Hong Kong, he now hosts a call-in radio show for Radio Free Asia, aimed at workers in China.

THE PEOPLE'S REPUBLIC OF CHINA

HE QINGLIAN: Journalist of the *Shenzhen Legal Daily* and author of the bestselling *Pitfalls of Modernization,* she was forbidden to publish anymore in 2000.

ZHOU LITAI: Lawyer in Shenzhen, specializing in cases of victims of industrial accidents.

CHEN YIYANG: One of the authors of the 1974 Li Yi Zhe manifesto, calling for democratic socialism in China. Gong Xiaoxia's first boyfriend; currently working as a librarian in Guangzhou.

LI HONGZHI: Founder of the Falun Gong, now living in the U.S.

DING ZILIN: Professor at Beijing University who started a movement to record the names of victims of the 1989 Beijing Massacre.

SU BINGXIAN: The mother of Su Zhaolong, one of the victims of the Beijing Massacre in 1989.

BAO TONG: Secretary of Zhao Ziyang and leading economic reformer. Accused of leaking plans of the government crackdown to the students in May 1989, he was sentenced to seven years in prison. He is still under house arrest in Beijing.

Notes

INTRODUCTION: CHINESE WHISPERS

XVI. **walled kingdom in the middle of the world:** See Arthur Waldron's *The Great Wall of China: From History to Myth* (Cambridge: Cambridge University Press, 1990).

XVI. **author from Hong Kong once wrote:** Sun Longji, quoted in *Seeds of Fire: Chinese Voices of Conscience,* edited by Geremie Barmé and John Minford (New York: Hill and Wang, 1988).

XIX. **Deng said:** Quoted in *The Tiananmen Papers,* edited by Andrew J. Nathan and Perry Link (New York: Little, Brown, 2001).

PART I: THE EXILES

4. **crushing the plot:** Quoted in *Black Hands of Beijing,* by George Black and Robin Munro (New York: John Wiley, 1993).

8. **with tears in their eyes:** Quoted in *"Wild Lily," Prairie Fire,* edited by Gregor Benton and Alan Hunter (Princeton: Princeton University Press, 1995).

12. **Chai accused the filmmakers:** Quoted in Geremie Barmé's *In the Red: On Contemporary Chinese Culture* (New York: Columbia University Press, 1999).

20. **people who protested were tortured and killed:** Liu Binyan's *A Higher Kind of Loyalty,* translated by Zhu Hong (New York: Pantheon, 1990).

24. **degeneracy of Chinese culture:** Bo Yang's remarks are quoted in *Seeds of Fire,* edited by Geremie Barmé and John Minford (New York: Hill and Wang, 1988).

35. **as Dai Qing once said:** See Perry Link's *Evening Chats in Beijing: Probing China's Predicament* (New York: W. W. Norton, 1992).

35. **her year in prison:** Quoted in Dai Qing's *My Imprisonment,* translated by Geremie Barmé. *Index on Censorship,* 8/1992.

38. **through political reforms:** Quoted in *New Ghosts, Old Dreams: Chinese Rebel Voices,* edited by Geremie Barmé and Linda Jaivin (New York: Times Books, 1992).

43. **"Where there is God, there is freedom":** For Yuan Zhiming's religious quest, see his *Shiliao Dadi, Deliao Tiankong* (Petaluma, California: CCM Publishers, 1994).

45. **clubbed to death with heavy poles:** See Jonathan D. Spence's *God's Chinese Son: The Taiping Heavenly Kingdom of Hong Xiuquan* (New York: W. W. Norton, 1996).

46. **gathering of dissident forces:** See Jonathan Spence's *The Search for Modern China* (New York: W. W. Norton, 1990).

47. **histrionic and didactic at the same time:** Quoted in Craig Calhoun's *Neither Gods nor Emperors* (Berkeley: University of California Press, 1994).

47. **Intellectuals, they claimed, had found it hard:** Quoted in *New Ghosts, Old Dreams.*

48. **coined the phrase "Mr. Science and Mr. Democracy":** See *East Asia: The Modern Transformation,* by John K. Fairbank, Edwin O. Reischauer, Albert M. Craig (Boston: Houghton Mifflin, 1965).

49. **in Jin's words:** Quoted in *From Youthful Manuscripts to River Elegy,* by Jin Guantao and Chen Fong-ching. (Hong Kong: The Chinese University Press, 1997).

60. **Fang ended his piece:** The article was reprinted in Fang Lizhi's *Bringing Down the Great Wall: Writings on Science, Culture, and Democracy in China,* translated by James H. Williams (New York: Knopf, 1991).

62. **read it over and over again:** See Orville Schell's introduction to *Bringing Down the Great Wall.*

62. **In Fang's words:** From *Bringing Down the Great Wall.*

64. **need for intellectual and academic freedom:** Ibid.

65. **addressing the Wizard of Oz:** See Andrew J. Nathan's *China's Transition* (New York: Columbia University Press, 1997).

67. **delivered in Shanghai:** reprinted in *Bringing Down the Great Wall.*

70. **Fang admires:** From *Bringing Down the Great Wall.*

71. **leave his friends and colleagues behind:** Ibid.

77. **As he observed:** Quoted in Gordon Craig's "The End of the Golden Age," *The New York Review of Books,* November 4, 1999.

85. **Li Yi Zhe manifesto:** Quoted in *"Wild Lily," Prairie Fire.*

87: **the arrest of Wei was defensible:** *"Wild Lily," Prairie Fire.*

94. **The point, writes Wei:** See Wei Jingsheng's *The Courage to Stand Alone* (New York: Viking, 1997).

94. **the stubborn rural conservatism of the survivors:** Ibid.

98. **almost fatal, conclusion:** Interview with China News Digest, October 16, 1999.

101. **One of the things Wei said was:** From *The Courage to Stand Alone.*

104. **After being robbed by village ruffians:.** Lu Xun: *Selected Works, Volume One,* translated by Yang Xianyi and Gladys Yang (Beijing: Foreign Languages Press, 1956).

110. **Chineseness, he said:** Published in *Index on Censorship,* 3/1997.

PART II: GREATER CHINA

126. **as he put it in his memoirs:** Lee Kuan Yew's *Singapore Story: Memoirs of Lee Kuan Yew* (New York: HarperCollins, 1999).

132. **"can only confuse the English-educated world":** See T.J.S. George's *Lee Kuan Yew's Singapore* (Singapore: Eastern Universities Press, 1984).

140. **he was told (by a young financial consultant):** Reuters report, January 6, 1998.

146. **group of young people were being arrested for organizing:** See Francis Seow's *To Catch a Tartar: A Dissident in Lee Kuan Yew's Prison* (New Haven: Yale University Southeast Asian Studies, 1994).

147. **attendant nuns:** Quoted in Lee Kuan Yew's *Singapore Story.*

153. **most decent men and women:** D. J. Enright's *Memoirs of a Mendicant Professor* (London: Chatto and Windus, 1969).

199. **"You can read it all in here":** Annette Lu's book about the days of revolt is entitled *Chongshen Meilidao* (Taipei: Qianwei Chubanshe, 1997).

214. **inspired by nobler sentiments:** Reported in *The South China Morning Post,* June 6, 1999.

217: **where she described the British legislators:** See Jan Morris's *Hong Kong* (New York: Random House, 1985).

219. **Lee used a gardening metaphor:** Quoted in *Asiaweek,* June 2, 1995.

221. **able to piece his extraordinary story together:** See Kate Saunders's *Eighteen Layers of Hell* (London: Cassell, 1996).

PART III: THE MOTHERLAND

256. **Ten years later she was famous:** He Qinglian's book in Chinese is entitled *Xiandaihuade Xianjing* (Beijing: Jinri Zhongguo Chubanshe, 1997).

257. **only quasi-free, since political power:** See "The Great Leap Backward," by

Perry Link and Liu Binyan, in *The New York Review of Books,* October 8, 1998.

261. **wrote a famous treatise:** See Wm. Theodore de Bary's *Asian Values and Human Rights: A Confucian Communitarian Perspective* (Cambridge: Harvard University Press, 1998).

261. **once a ruler had attained absolute power:** Quoted in Joseph R. Levenson's *Confucian China and Its Modern Fate, Book 1* (Berkeley: University of California Press, 1958).

262. **here is Huang's solution:** Ibid.

267. **protesting the opium trade:** Quoted in *East Asia: The Modern Transformation.*

314. **"religious rituals of Buddhism":** For a more detailed description, see Isabel Hilton's *The Search for the Panchen Lama* (London: Viking, 1999).

317. **These answers, however, are usually the opposite of the truth:** All quotes from Václav Havel on the following pages are taken from his *Václav Havel or Living in Truth* (London: Faber and Faber, 1987).

323. **155 dead may not seem much:** Quoted in *June Fourth Massacre: Testimonies of the Wounded and the Families of the Dead* (New York: Human Rights in China, 1999).

327. **house arrest in June 1989:** see *The Tiananmen Papers,* edited by Andrew J. Nathan and Perry Link (New York: Little, Brown, 2001).

327. **Bao's style as much as his politics:** Ibid.

328. **in one of those open letters** and **reverse the June 4 decision:** Bao Tong's letter was reprinted in the periodical *China Rights Forum,* Summer 1999.

328. **Bao believed his boss:** See Rebecca MacKinnon's interview with Bao Tong for CNN, June 2, 1999.

328. **After all, he says:** Ibid.

333. **learn from them to strengthen the nation:** Mao Haijian's book is entitled *Tianchaode Bengkui* (Beijing: Sanlian Shudian, 1995).

Index

Ian Buruma studied Chinese in the Netherlands and cinema in Japan. He has spent many years in Asia, which he has written about in *God's Dust, Behind the Mask,* and *The Missionary and the Libertine.* He has also written *Playing the Game, The Wages of Guilt,* and *Anglomania.* Buruma lives in London and writes for *The New York Review of Books* and *The New York Times Magazine,* as well as other publications.

ABOUT THE TYPE

This book was set in Minion, a 1990 Adobe Originals typeface by Robert Slimbach. Minion is inspired by classical, old-style typefaces of the late Renaissance, a period of elegant, beautiful, and highly readable type designs. Created primarily for text setting, Minion combines the aesthetic and functional qualities that make text type highly readable with the versatility of digital technology.